THE CAMBRIDGE COMPANION TO

HOBBES

Each volume of this series of companions to major philosophers contains specially commissioned essays by an international team of scholars, together with a substantial bibliography, and will serve as a reference work for students and
nonspecialists. One aim of the series is to dispel the intimi-
dation such readers often feel when faced with the work of a
difficult and challenging thinker.

It was as a political thinker that Thomas Hobbes first
came to prominence, initially through the publication of a
brief book about good citizenship, *De cive,* and ultimately
through *Leviathan.* And it is as a political theorist that he is
most studied today. Yet the range of his writings extends
well beyond morals and politics. Hobbes had distinctive
views in metaphysics and epistemology, and wrote about
such subjects as history, law and religion. He also produced
full-scale treatises in physics, optics, and geometry. All of
these areas are covered in this Companion, most in considerable detail. The view of Hobbes and his intellectual preoccupations that emerges is, thus, much broader than is presented in most studies of the philosopher. The volume also
reflects the multidisciplinary nature of current Hobbes scholarship by drawing together perspectives on Hobbes that are
now being developed in parallel by philosophers, historians
of science and mathematics, intellectual historians, political
scientists, and literary theorists.

New readers and nonspecialists will find this the most
convenient, accessible guide to Hobbes available. Advanced
students and specialists will find a conspectus of recent de-
velopments on the interpretation of Hobbes's philosophy.

D1354532

OTHER VOLUMES IN THE SERIES OF CAMBRIDGE
COMPANIONS:

AQUINAS *Edited by* NORMAN KRETZMANN *and*
ELEANORE STUMP *(published)*
ARISTOTLE *Edited by* JONATHAN BARNES *(published)*
BACON *Edited by* MARKKU PELTONEN
BERKELEY *Edited by* KENNETH WINKLER
DESCARTES *Edited by* JOHN COTTINGHAM
(published)
EARLY GREEK PHILOSOPHY *Edited by* A.A. LONG
FICHTE *Edited by* GUENTER ZOELLER
FOUCAULT *Edited by* GARY GUTTING *(published)*
FREGE *Edited by* TOM RICKETTS
FREUD *Edited by* JEROME NEU *(published)*
GALILEO *Edited by* PETER MCCHAMER
HABERMAS *Edited by* STEPHEN K. WHITE *(published)*
HEGEL *Edited by* FREDERICK BEISER *(published)*
HEIDEGGER *Edited by* CHARLES GUIGNON
(published)
HUME *Edited by* DAVIS FATE NORTON *(published)*
HUSSERL *Edited by* BARRY SMITH *and*
DAVID WOODRUFF SMITH *(published)*
WILLIAM JAMES *Edited by* RUTH ANNE PUTNAM
KANT *Edited by* PAUL GUYER *(published)*
KIERKEGAARD *Edited by* ALASTAIR HANNAY *and*
GORDON MARINO
LEIBNIZ *Edited by* NICHOLAS JOLLEY *(published)*
LOCKE *Edited by* VERE CHAPPELL *(published)*
MARX *Edited by* TERRELL CARVER *(published)*
MILL *Edited by* JOHN SKORUPSKI
NIETZSCHE *Edited by* BERND MAGNUS *and*
KATHLEEN HIGGINS
OCKHAM *Edited by* PAUL VINCENT SPADE
PEIRCE *Edited by* CHRISTOPHER HOOKWAY
PLATO *Edited by* RICHARD KRAUT *(published)*
PLOTINUS *Edited by* LLOYD P. GERSON
SARTRE *Edited by* CHRISTINA HOWELLS *(published)*
SPINOZA *Edited by* DON GARRETT *(published)*
WITTGENSTEIN *Edited by* HANS SLUGA *and*
DAVID STERN

The Cambridge Companion to
HOBBES

Edited by Tom Sorell
University of Essex

CAMBRIDGE
UNIVERSITY PRESS

PUBLISHED BY THE PRESS SYNDICATE OF THE UNIVERSITY OF CAMBRIDGE
The Pitt Building, Trumpington Street, Cambridge, United Kingdom

CAMBRIDGE UNIVERSITY PRESS
The Edinburgh Building, Cambridge CB2 2RU, UK   www.cup.cam.ac.uk
40 West 20th Street, New York, NY 10011-4211, USA   www.cup.org
10 Stamford Road, Oakleigh, Melbourne 3166, Australia
Ruiz de Alarcón 13, 28014 Madrid, Spain

© Cambridge University Press 1996

First published 1996
Reprinted 1996, 1999

Printed in the United States of America

Typeset in Trump Mediaeval

A catalog record for this book is available from the British Library

Library of Congress Cataloging in Publication Data is available

ISBN 0 521 41019 3 hardback
ISBN 0 521 42244 2 paperback

CONTENTS

List of contributors   *page* vii

Method of citation   xi

Introduction
TOM SORELL   I

1 A summary biography of Hobbes
   NOEL MALCOLM   13

2 Hobbes's scheme of the sciences
   TOM SORELL   45

3 First philosophy and the foundations of
   knowledge
   YVES CHARLES ZARKA   62

4 Hobbes and the method of natural science
   DOUGLAS JESSEPH   86

5 Hobbes and mathematics
   HARDY GRANT   108

6 Hobbes on light and vision
   JAN PRINS   129

7 Hobbes's psychology
   BERNARD GERT   157

8 Hobbes's moral philosophy
   RICHARD TUCK   175

9 Hobbes's political philosophy
   ALAN RYAN   208

v

vi   Contents

10 Lofty science and local politics
    JOHANN SOMMERVILLE   246

11 Hobbes on law
    M. M. GOLDSMITH   274

12 History in Hobbes's thought
    LUC BOROT   305

13 Hobbes on rhetoric
    VICTORIA SILVER   329

14 Hobbes on religion
    PATRICIA SPRINGBORG   346

    Bibliography   381

    Index   399

CONTRIBUTORS

LUC BOROT is Professor of British Civilisation at Université Paul-Valéry in Montpellier, France. He is translator of *Behemoth* in the Vrin edition (1990) and is the author of several articles on English political ideas in the English civil war period.

BERNARD GERT is Eunice and Julian Cohen Professor for the Study of Ethics and Human Values at Dartmouth College and Adjunct Professor of Psychiatry at Dartmouth Medical School. His books include *Morality: A New Justification of the Rules* (Oxford University Press, 1988) and *Man and Citizen* (Hackett, 1991), an edition of Hobbes containing the English version of *De cive* and an English translation of chapters X–XV of *De Homine*.

M. M. GOLDSMITH is a Senior Lecturer in Philosophy at Victoria University, Wellington, New Zealand, and former Professor of Political Theory at the University of Exeter. His publications include *Private Vices, Public Benefits: Bernard Mandeville's Social and Political Thought* (Cambridge University Press, 1985) and *Hobbes's Science of Politics* (Columbia University Press, 1966) as well as a number of articles on contemporary political philosophy and on seventeenth- and eighteenth-century political thought. He is currently working on rights.

HARDY GRANT recently retired from the Department of Mathematics and Statistics, York University, Toronto. He is the author of a number of articles on the influence of mathematics in cultural history, including the role of mathematics in the thought of such figures as Galen and Leibniz, in addition to Hobbes.

vii

DOUGLAS JESSEPH is Assistant Professor of Philosophy at North Carolina State University. He is the author of *Berkeley's Philosophy of Mathematics* (University of Chicago Press, 1993) and articles on philosophy, mathematics, and methodology in the seventeenth and eighteenth centuries. He is currently writing a book on the controversy between Hobbes and John Wallis.

NOEL MALCOLM is a General Editor of the Clarendon edition of Hobbes's works. A Fellow of Gonville and Caius College, Cambridge, from 1981 to 1988, he later became Foreign Editor of the *Spectator* and a political columnist of the *Daily Telegraph.* He has published an edition of Hobbes's correspondence (2 vols, Oxford 1994), and is also editing *Leviathan* and a volume of Hobbes's autobiographical works for the Clarendon edition. His shorter studies of Hobbes include the chapter on Hobbes and Spinoza in the *Cambridge History of Political Thought, 1450–1700* (Cambridge University Press, 1991).

JAN PRINS studied philosophy and psychology at the University of Utrecht in the Netherlands. His special interest is in the relationship between renaissance philosophy and the rise of mechanicism in the seventeenth century. He has written articles on the origins of Hobbes's ideas about the nature of science and method as well as on the sources of his optical theories.

ALAN RYAN is Professor of Politics at Princeton University and former Fellow of New College, Oxford. He is most recently the author of *Bertrand Russell: A Political Life,* and his study of John Dewey's liberalism is due to appear in 1995. He is editor (with G. A. J. Rogers) of *Perspectives on Thomas Hobbes* (The Clarendon Press, 1988).

VICTORIA SILVER teaches English at University of California, Irvine. She has completed a book on Milton, *The Predicament of Milton's Irony,* and is at work on another about the relationship between Cicero's philosophy and rhetoric – especially as it pertains to the state – and seventeenth-century literature. She has published essays and articles on Browne, Hobbes, Johnson, and Milton, as well as a response on Hobbes for *Critical Quarterly.*

JOHANN SOMMERVILLE is Professor of History at the University of Wisconsin, Madison. His writings include *Politics and Ideology in*

England 1603–1640 (Longman, 1986) and *Thomas Hobbes: Political Ideas in Historical Context* (Macmillan and St. Martin's Press, 1992). He has edited *Sir Robert Filmer: Political Writings* (Cambridge, 1991) for the series of Cambridge Texts in the History of Political Thought.

TOM SORELL is Professor of Philosophy at the University of Essex. He is the author of *Hobbes* (Routledge, 1986) and the Past Masters volume on *Descartes* (Oxford University Press, 1987), and he has edited *The Rise of Modern Philosophy* (The Clarendon Press, 1993). He has published many articles on Hobbes, on Descartes, and on aspects of the historiography of early modern philosophy. He is working on a book about the reaction against Cartesian ideas in twentieth-century philosophy.

PATRICIA SPRINGBORG is Reader in Government at the University of Sydney. She is the author of *The Problem of Human Needs and the Critique of Civilisation* (George Allen & Unwin, 1981) and *Royal Persons* (Polity, 1992), and is at present completing an edition of the political writings of Mary Astell (1666–1731) for Cambridge University Press.

RICHARD TUCK is a Lecturer in History at Cambridge University and a Fellow of Jesus College. He is the author of *Natural Rights Theories* (Cambridge University Press, 1979) and the Past Masters volume on Hobbes (Oxford University Press, 1989), and is editor of Hobbes's *Leviathan* in the Cambridge Texts in the History of Political Thought. He is preparing *The Elements of Law* for the Clarendon edition of Hobbes.

YVES CHARLES ZARKA is Professor and Director of a Research Group of the Centre National de la Recherche Scientifique in Paris on the moral and political philosophy of the seventeenth century. He now teaches at the Ecole des Hautes Etudes en Sciences Sociales. He is the author of a large number of studies in the history of political thought, notably *La décision métaphysique de Hobbes – Conditions de la politique* (Vrin, 1987) and the forthcoming *Hobbes et la pensée politique moderne* (Vrin). He has recently edited *Raison et déraison d'Etat. Théoriciens et théories de la raison d'Etat au XVIe et XVIIe siècles* (Presses Universitaires de France, 1994).

METHOD OF CITATION

The most widely used edition of Hobbes's works is Sir William Molesworth's. It consists of an eleven-volume *English Works* (1839) and a five-volume *Opera Latina* (1845). References are to '*EW*' or '*OL*', followed by the relevant volume number and page number. Molesworth's edition is incomplete, and its presentation of the texts is now widely regarded as inadequate; accordingly, many of the contributors to this book have avoided it. Unfortunately, there is nothing else of comparable scope in English. The Clarendon Press in Oxford has an edition in preparation, but it will not be complete for a long time. References to volumes of the Clarendon edition that have already appeared contain the abbreviation '*HW*'. When references are without *EW* and *OL* numbers, notes to the individual articles should be consulted for the exact editions and translations of works by Hobbes being referred to. The following is a list, in alphabetical order, of the short titles used to refer to works.

AT: Descartes, Oeuvres (ed. C. Adam and P. Tannery)
Aub: Aubrey's Briefe Lives
AW: Anti-White (1642/3)
B: Behemoth (1668)
*Cons Rep.: Considerations on the Reputation . . . of Thomas
    Hobbes* (1662)
Corr: The Correspondence of Thomas Hobbes (1622–79) (ed. N.
    Malcolm [*HW, vols. vi and vii*].)
CSM: The Philosophical Writings of Descartes (eds. J.
    Cottingham, R. Stoothoff, and D. Murdoch)
De Cive: Elementorum philosophiae sectio tertia de cive (1642).
    Where citations refer to *EW, vol* II, it is the English-language

version of *De cive, Philosophical Rudiments concerning Government and Society* (1651).

De Corp.: Elementorum philosophiae sectio prima de corpore (1655). Where citations refer to *EW*, vol. I, it is the English translation of *De corpore, The Elements of Philosophy, the First Section concerning Body.*

D.H.: Elementorum philosophiae sectio secunda de homine (1658)

DP: Decameron Physiologicum (1678)

DPRG: De principiis et ratiocinatione geometrarum (1666)

Dial: Dialogue between a Philosopher and a Student of the Common Laws of England (1681)

DiPh.: Dialogus Physicus (1661)

EL: The Elements of Law (1640)

Lev.: Leviathan (1651)

L&N: Liberty and Necessity (1654)

LNC: The Questions Concerning Liberty, Necessity and Chance (1656)

M&C: Man and Citizen (ed. Gert.)

MDO: A Minute or First Draft of the Optiques (1646)

Prob. Phys.: Problemata physica (1662)

SL: Six Lessons to the Professors of Mathematics . . . in the University of Oxford (1656)

SPP: Seven Philosophical Problems (1662)

ST: Short Tract on First Principles (ed. F. Tonnies) (1630?)

T: Hobbes' Thucydides (ed. R Schlatter) (1628)

TO I: Tractatus Opticus I (1640)

TO II: Tractatus Opticus II (1644) (ed. F. Alessio)

OTHER ABBREVIATIONS

BL: British Library

Harl.: Harleian

HMC: Historical Manuscripts Commission

MS: Manuscript

Ep. Ded.: Epistle Dedicatory

Introduction

Hobbes made his name as the author of a brief book about citizenly duty published in 1642. In its various editions, *De cive* brought his ideas about the need for undivided sovereignty to a wide, and mostly admiring, Continental audience. Similar ideas in an earlier, unpublished, but well-circulated treatise of Hobbes's came to the notice of men of political influence in England in 1640, so that he was known, in parliamentary circles at least, as a political thinker some years before any of his work had gone into print. It is as a political theorist that he is still studied today. Hobbes's *Leviathan* has eclipsed *De cive* as the official statement of his theory, but it has much in common with the book he published in 1642 and the manuscript that he circulated in 1640. It is Hobbes's political doctrine that continues to get attention, and new editions of *Leviathan* are still being issued.

His writings, however, range far beyond morals and politics. They present distinctive views in metaphysics and epistemology, and they go beyond philosophy in the narrow modern sense altogether, to include full-scale treatises in physics, optics, and geometry. Hobbes's thought extends to history and historiography, to law, biblical interpretation, and something like rational theology. All of these subjects are represented in the essays that follow, most in considerable detail. One aim of the volume is to offer a much broader view of Hobbes's intellectual preoccupations than is usually available to the English-speaking general reader. Another is to bring together the different perspectives on Hobbes that are now being developed in parallel by philosophers, historians of mathematics and science, historians of early modern England, political scientists, and writers on literary studies: current scholarship on Hobbes is more than ever a multidisciplinary enterprise. It is also international, involving people in most

English-speaking countries and beyond. French, Italian, German, and Dutch scholars have long been at the leading edge of Hobbes studies, and some of them are contributors to this book.

Hobbes's interests were formed and pursued through intellectual networks to which he gained entry as a member of the household of important English aristocrats. He worked for more than one generation and more than one branch of the Cavendish family, and their connections became his. The influences of the different circles in which he moved are brought out in the opening biographical essay, which presents much new research conducted by Noel Malcolm on Hobbes's life. At least four different networks emerge from Malcolm's account as influences upon Hobbes's principal writings, those he composed in the 1640s and '50s. The first network centered upon the second earl of Devonshire, whom Hobbes was hired, straight out of Oxford, to serve as page. While in the service of the second earl, Hobbes came into contact with Francis Bacon, and also, on the earl's Continental travels, with Venetian writers who opposed papal claims to have authority over the rulers of Christian kingdoms. The Venetians were interested in Bacon's writings, and after 1615 Hobbes participated in dealings between them, Bacon, and his master. Antipapal ideas are prominent in Hobbes's political writings; so also, on some readings, are Baconian ideas in his nonpolitical writings. Two other networks involved Hobbes in the 1630s. One was the so-called Great Tew circle, named for the Oxfordshire home of its focal point, Lucius Cary, Viscount Falkland. This group influenced Hobbes's thinking on religion. The other was centered on Sir Charles Cavendish, a relation of the earls of Devonshire, and was carried on partly by correspondence with scientists in England and on the Continent. It brought Hobbes into contact with the chemical experimenter Robert Payne and the optical theorist Walter Warner, and it stimulated Hobbes's already developing ideas on the workings of light and vision.

The fourth network, to which Sir Charles Cavendish may have helped to introduce Hobbes, was made up of the scientists and theologians grouped round Marin Mersenne in Paris from the 1620s to the 1640s. It is hard to overstate the importance of Mersenne and Mersenne's circle to Hobbes's intellectual development. He probably first made contact with Mersenne while accompanying the third earl of Devonshire on the Grand Tour of the Continent in 1634. He became a regular and active member of Mersenne's circle when he fled England for Paris in 1640, in the days leading to the English Civil War. It was Mersenne who arranged for the publication of *De cive*. It was Mersenne, too, who approached Hobbes for one of the sets of Objections to Descartes's *Meditations*. Mersenne acted as intermediary in a correspondence between Hobbes and Descartes on optics and physics. He encouraged Hobbes to write the commentary on Thomas White's *De mundo* that is now a main source for Hobbes's metaphysical ideas. Intellectuals in Mersenne's orbit also played their part in the development of his scientific ideas. The mathematicians Gilles Roberval and Claude Mydorge and the philosopher Pierre Gassendi were notable figures among them.

Intellectual exchanges on so broad a front over several decades might have produced a miscellany of theories, but in Hobbes an interest in the problems of mathematics, physics, optics, and politics combines with a predilection for system and synthesis. He was concerned to impose order and coherence on his own ideas and discoveries; but he was also concerned with order and coherence in the body of the new science in general – not only his own contributions but those of other mathematicians, optical theorists, astronomers, and physiologists, mainly Continental ones, who presented the explanation of effects in proper deductive form and found mechanical causes for phenomena. These two ambitions, of systematizing his own science and of systematizing contemporary deductive science in general, are sometimes confused together in his writings, as I argue in the essay on Hobbes's scheme of the sciences. His trilogy of *De corpore, De homine,* and *De cive* present the "elements" of science in general, but science in general contains two sciences that Hobbes thought he had invented himself, optics and civil science. In Hobbes's scheme, different natural sciences are sciences of different kinds of motion; and politics comes after the natural sciences in the order of teaching. But it is far from clear whether politics is a science of motion, or whether Hobbes is only claiming that it can be understood in the light of the sciences of motion. Again, his understanding of the elements of science in general may produce an inadequate and incomplete account of the scope of science, and a worse such account than Bacon's, to which Hobbes's was up to a point indebted.

Science as a whole was supposed to start with "first philosophy," a set of definitions, distinctions, and arguments required to make intelligible the explanatory concepts of the mechanical philosophy. Yves Charles Zarka shows how Hobbes's first philosophy was simultaneously a radical revision of the concepts of Aristotle's physics and metaphysics, a conscious departure from Descartes, *and*, paradoxically, a doctrine founded on a theology of voluntarism. Hobbes revamps Aristotle's doctrine of causation, and he purports to derive the fundamental concepts of science – those of body and motion, for instance – from traces of sense-experience in the corporeal human subject, not the innate ideas of an immaterial Cartesian soul. So far Hobbes's first philosophy has contents that are firmly rooted in a temporal and material reality: is there any need for theology? Making extensive use of the the *Anti-White*, Zarka argues that God and God's omnipotence, which the categories of the first philosophy are supposed to exclude from the foundations of science, are actually presupposed by those foundations. In particular, God is needed to unify what are otherwise entirely separate causal chains in the world, and to make intelligible the distinctive Hobbesian notion of an "entire" cause. Just how well Hobbes's first philosophy grounds the natural sciences is unclear, according to Zarka. It works well for the pure sciences of motion – geometry and mechanics – but it may not provide adequate materials for the explanation of sensible appearance.

Douglas Jesseph's essay takes up Hobbes's conception of the method of discovery and demonstration in natural science. The way in which this method is modeled on the method of geometry is discussed and illustrated. Jesseph focuses on Hobbes's identification of science with knowledge of causes, and his identification of knowledge of causes with knowledge of motions. Geometry has a highly intelligible subject matter, according to Hobbes, because we have a maker's knowledge of it. We know the properties of the figures from the motions we use to construct them. Accordingly, in teaching geometry to someone else it is crucial to get over the relevant motions from the beginning. The very definitions of the figures must mention them. Natural science in general is less certain and demonstrable than geometry, because a maker's knowledge of its subject matter – bodies independent and external to us – is available only to God. To understand the properties of natural bodies, we have to make hypotheses about the motions that might have caused them. The reliance of his method of physical explanation on hypotheses about motions put Hobbes at odds with English scientists, and his methodology of natural science in general was attacked by members of the Royal Society in the period after he returned to England from Paris. Hobbes is not consistent in linking science or natural science to knowledge of motions; he sometimes claims that science has its starting point in semantic information, and that the meanings of terms are no more than human stipulations. This is the context from which Hobbes's nominalism is sometimes improperly abstracted. Jesseph keeps the connections between Hobbes's theory of science and his theory of names, operations on names and concatenations of names, quite intact.

In Hobbes's scheme of the sciences, geometry is the most basic science of motion, and the first science after first philosophy to be acquired if science as a whole is being learnt from the elements. Hardy Grant suggests that Hobbes's valuable – and correct – insight about the importance of geometry to the rest of natural science is largely independent of his idiosyncratic, mechanistic philosophy of mathematics, and independent again of his failed ventures in circle-squaring. Grant explains what was at stake in these ventures, and makes intelligible to the general reader the mathematical point of the long series of exchanges between the Oxford mathematician John Wallis and Hobbes on the squaring of the circle. He also explains for the mathematically more able what goes wrong in some of Hobbes's "proofs" in this area. Grant then turns to what he thinks was valuable in Hobbes's mathematics. He takes the requirement that motions be specified in geometrical definitions and shows how it made sense in its time. He notes that Hobbes's standards of definition left their mark on no less a mathematician than Leibniz. Grant also explains clearly how, despite the difficulties in Hobbes's own criticisms of algebra, one could be respectably skeptical of the value of algebra.

Hobbes claimed that he laid the foundations of the science of optics, and optical material dominates *De homine*, the second section of his account of the elements of science. Prins's essay shows how in his practice as a writer on optics, Hobbes combined geometry and mechanics in the way that his methodological writings required them to be combined. Probably optics was the prototype of a Hobbesian natural science, and the requirements for natural science in general were drawn from Hobbes's understanding of how this subject worked. There is some controversy among scholars – discernible if one compares Noel Malcolm's text with the notes to Yves Charles Zarka's essay – about whether all of the optical writings that have traditionally been attributed to Hobbes are in fact Hobbes's work. Most commentators say that the *Short Tract* is by Hobbes; others, including Malcolm and Richard Tuck, conjecture that Robert Payne, a member of the Cavendish circle, composed it. Prins includes the *Short Tract* in the long series of treatises in which Hobbes was concerned with the explanation of light, vision, and sensible qualities, especially in the 1630s and 1640s. Prins argues that Hobbes's own good opinion of his achievement in optics has some foundation, and that he was certainly a sophisticated and well-informed writer on the subject.

Bernard Gert turns in his essay to what Hobbes regarded as the after-effects of sense, especially visual sensation: namely imagination, memory, passion, and action. Gert emphasises the point that Hobbes's understanding of many of these phenomena is eked out from the meagre resources of the concepts of matter and motion. Hobbes's determinism is considered, and Gert ends by considering the way in which passion and reason can interact to produce the behavior called for by Hobbes's moral philosophy. Although self-interest is crucial to the rational control of the passions, Gert denies that for Hobbes it provides the sole motivation for doing anything. Hobbes, he says, is no psychological egoist. Certain passages in *Leviathan* and elsewhere may make it seem as if Hobbes was supposing that there was only one kind of motivation in human beings, and as if it were always selfish; but, Gert says, Hobbes's theory of human nature is never about all, only about many, human beings, and plenty of room is left for variety of motivation not only between human beings but within human beings over time. The picture of the typical Hobbesian agent as a selfish being ruthlessly propelling himself by the shortest path to his gratification is probably closer to the picture Hobbes gives of the human child than of the human.

Richard Tuck's essay starts out with a discussion of the distinctive subject matter that Hobbes allocates to moral philosophy – human passions and patterns of behavior – and tries to explain why Hobbes chooses to link that subject matter with the subject matter of optics in *De homine*. The two subject matters belong together, on Tuck's interpretation, because optics and moral philosophy both acknowledge and correct different types of error and illusion. Optics explains the difference between the thing as it appears to the senses and the thing, and moral philosophy specifies the different sources – principally linguistic – of illusions about the good and conflict between human beings. Moral philosophy then hits upon a good that is likely to be universally acknowledged as such – self-preservation – and tries to present certain behaviors – the ones traditionally regarded as virtuous – as means to self-preservation or peace. These are the behaviors prescribed by what Hobbes calls the "laws of nature." Tuck is struck throughout by the way that Hobbes can have it both ways in his moral philosophy – being subjectivist about valuations, but objectivist about the moral laws. Moral laws can be objective in the sense of commanding universal assent and leading to a condition (peace) that everyone will find subjectively preferable to its absence (war), without there being an independently existing rightness that they conform to. As Tuck reads him, then, Hobbes can therefore concede something to skepticism about the objectivity of values, and yet not conclude that, morally speaking, anything goes. For related reasons Hobbes's doctrine can actually have an effect on the valuations it criticizes. By showing how the all-out drive for short-term advantage leaves everyone worse off when all or most participate in that drive, Hobbes gives people a motivation for revaluing short-term gain, and indeed all other apparent goods whose pursuit might involve war. As an effectual or productive science, Hobbes's moral philosophy has more in common with the branch of learning traditionally known as rhetoric than has often been acknowledged.

Alan Ryan's essay on Hobbes's political philosophy overlaps significantly with Tuck's and with the sequence of essays that completes this volume. The sequence concerns the relation of Hobbes's political philosophy to Hobbes's time, its status as a branch of learning in comparison to history and rhetoric, and its bearing on Hobbes's writings about law and religion. Some of these connections are indicated in Ryan's general essay. It presents Hobbes's theory of the institution of sovereignty as an answer to the question of who has the right to declare what is law. Hobbes's theory suggests that the sovereign is the source of the law and that therefore the sovereign is the authoritative pronouncer of what it requires of the many who submit to the sovereign. As for the many, they are the source of the institution of the sovereign. They agree with one another to abide by the laws that some designated individual or assembly declares for the purpose of securing their safety. They may not like the laws, but they cannot justly refuse to obey them: that would be to break an agreement, the very essense of injustice. A host of problems attend Hobbes's account of how an agreement can be made in a pre-political setting, and also his assumptions about the power of agreement-making to explain political obligation. Few people con-sciously become parties to a social contract or perform acts that indisputably make them parties to one. And even on Hobbes's as-sumptions, which come close to requiring subjects of a sovereign to abstain altogether from making judgments about their own safety, the many need not put up with just anything the sovereign declares legal. Clear and present danger to one's life, or the appearance of such danger, restores the right of private judgment. Hobbes evi-dently believed that the conditions for the resumption of private judgment were very far from being met in England when subjects of Charles I resisted his edicts, but Hobbes was alive to the ease with which people could be convinced that life under a sovereign power was intolerable. Worse, because he sometimes insists that the public safety the sovereign secures goes far beyond mere protection of life and limb, there is uncomfortably extensive scope for the judgment that life under the sovereign is unsafe. Ryan discusses further diffi-culties that arise from the detail of Hobbes's theory of punishment. Along the way he contrasts Hobbes's treatment of a number of these matters with those of Harrington, Filmer, and Rousseau.

Hobbes's politics was supposed to be a science. It was supposed to offer sure principles of submission and sovereignty that might be applied universally. It was not a plan for government drawn from the example of civilizations of the past; and officially, at least, it was supposed to solve a perennial problem: that of how to keep states from dissolving. On the other hand, Hobbes's discovery and state-ment of this science was supposed to be timely. Why had *De cive*, which was planned as the third of the three-part *Elementorum philosophiae*, appeared in print long before the first two volumes were close to completion? Because, Hobbes said, the disorders in his country – the English Civil War – had wrested the book from him. Was the political theory in fact commentary on current events mas-querading as science, or was it science being made available just when it was needed? Johann Sommerville's essay shows that the truth lies somewhere in between. Hobbes's picture of the causes of dissolution of commonwealths in general is suspiciously close to his description of the causes of the Civil War in England, which suggests that he was working from historical example rather than deriving his account of the sources of instability in states from the operations of certain passions present in different groups of human beings. Sommerville shows that Hobbes's absolutism, as evidenced in his theories of the rights of sovereigns, evolved during the Civil War period, so that the doctrine of *Leviathan* is recognizably different from that of the *Elements of Law* and *De cive*. Hobbes always made clerical powers subject to the sovereign's authority, and held that the sovereign could autonomously determine property rights; but in *Leviathan*, Sommerville argues, he took the opportunity of making his account of the rights of sovereigns reflect his disagreements with some moderate royalists, notably in respect of the division of powers between sovereign and assembly.

In Maurice Goldsmith's essay, Hobbes's doctrine about law, so central to the political philosophy, is clearly explained, related to positions in twentieth-century jurisprudence, and, finally, considered in the context of Hobbes's disagreement with Sir Edward Coke and the attack on Hobbes by Sir Matthew Hale. At the center of the discussion is Hobbes's theory of sovereignty and his view that, as Goldsmith puts it, "the sovereign is above, not beneath the law." In comparison to Coke, Hobbes thinks little of common law, except where "common law" is redefined as his own laws of nature. Its accumulation of precedents smacks too much of experience and too little of reason. In practice it waters down sovereignty, giving lesser officials too much of a free hand in the interpretation and application of the law. He prefers statute law, written, highly general, straight from the legislator. The reservations that might be felt about handling legal and political matters by a neat rule book were expressed by Hale, whose criticism of Hobbes was an indirect defense of Coke.

There is an account of the English Civil War between the lines of Hobbes's treatises on morals and politics, but there is also an explicit account of it in *Behemoth*. This is a work of history on the Civil War, rather than a scientific treatise on government, and Hobbes's understanding of the difference between these genres – between a history and a work of science – is one of the topics of Luc Borot's essay. The distinction between history and science is continuous in Hobbes's thought with the distinctions between prudence and sapience and between experience and reason. Science, sapience, and reason are the favored sides of the distinctions, and Borot explains why. Part of the explanation is that they draw on different cognitive faculties, and that the faculty engaged by history, namely memory, is more limited than the faculty of reasoning engaged by science. Memory stores truths only for a time, and only particular truths. Reasoning affords both generality and depth. It can reach conclusions that are universally valid, and can penetrate to the grounds of truths that are witnessed and remembered. A written history makes what is remembered last, but, without the help of science, it cannot achieve generality and depth; it cannot be genuinely explanatory. Another way of putting the point is by saying that for Hobbes, history cannot teach, in the sense of demonstrating things. On the other hand, Hobbes thinks that history *can* be politically instructive, that it is more accessible than science, and that it needs to inform civil science. So it is not valueless, and indeed is better suited to instructing a wide audience than science. Both *Behemoth* and his very first published work, a translation of Thucydides' *History of the Peloponnesian War*, were supposed to be politically instructive, Thucydides through its sub-text, and *Behemoth* through its surface meaning. The bulk of Borot's essay concerns the relation of history to different forms of public instruction.

Victoria Silver's essay on rhetoric also dwells on Hobbes's translation of Thucydides, and on Hobbes way of marrying the goal of instruction – of teaching the truth – with the instrument of vivid, persuasive speech, whether in the form of history, or, despite its pretensions to do without all of these adornments, in the form of philosophy. She locates Hobbes's views on the relation between rhetoric and philosophy within a long tradition of seeing the relation as one of antagonism. Up to a point Hobbes gets beyond that, struggling to reconcile eloquence and reason.

Hobbes's views on religion, touched on by so many other contributors to this volume, are impressively disentangled by Patricia Springborg in the concluding essay. An important distinction for undertanding Hobbes in this connection is that between what goes on invisibly and privately and sometimes involuntarily in one's head – the formation of belief – and what is done in public with consequences for other people. The inner sphere is outside the sovereign's control, and not one he can effectively legislate for. This is the sphere fundamentally engaged by religion, and it is belief that matters to salvation. Visible action, including public speech and public religious observance, is another matter. This is well within the domain of legislation, and it is for the sovereign alone, not a church or its leaders, to make the relevant rules. Hobbes has much to say in his writings about the source of religious belief both in the passions and scripture, and about the main points of Christian doctrine. Springborg covers all of this and more.

In a book that touches on so many aspects of Hobbes's thought, the parts are likely to be more conspicuous than the whole. Is there a way of unifying some of the elements? There is more than one way. An important connecting link between some of the elements is Hobbes's understanding of the nature and variety of motion. His allegiance to mechanical explanation influences his distinction between science and non-science, the content of his first philosophy, his methodology for natural science, and his organization of geometry, optics, physics, and psychology. But though Hobbes was a mechanical philosopher of nature, natural philosophy was not the only kind of philosophy he recognized, and he ventured into fields that he never regarded as philosophical – history, to name an important one. The relevance of motion and matter to these fields is uncertain.

A way of connecting Hobbes's work in natural science with his work in the rest of what he took to be science and beyond, is by considering his modernity – his modernity as a philosopher, as a historian, and as an intellectual in general. Although he was a keen student of antiquity and especially of classical literature, he was a participant in, and a propagandist for, a decidedly new or modern science. Whatever else natural and civil philosophy had in common in Hobbes's view, they were both largely developed in what for him was the recent past. Except in geometry, the new science was not indebted to antiquity, and anyway, the content of geometry was not identifiably of one era or another: it could speak to the reason of the Athenian intellectual just as powerfully as the seventeenth-century visitor to a gentleman's library in Geneva. Natural philosophy, he wrote in the 1650s, was "but young," and civil philosophy even younger. What made the modern or new sciences better than their ancient counterparts was, among other things, their absorption of, and generalization of, the geometer's method of identifying the elements, defining clearly and inferring transparently. Outside philosophy there was also a "modern" tinge to his thought. His writing on law applies the values of or an admirer of science to jurisprudence. Borot's essay shows that what Hobbes required and praised in the writing of history was not always traditional.

Caution is required in taking modernity as a unifying theme of Hobbes's thought. Sometimes what Hobbes presents as new, or what is conventionally regarded as original in his work, is a reworking of something one can find in Greek philosophy and in the rhetorical tradition stretching back to Rome and Athens. Modernity needs to include reworked antiquity. In any case, there are signs of Hobbes's modernity in virtually all of the essays that follow, and that is because in one way or another virtually all of the essays touch on his concept of science. His project of teaching science from the elements, his claim to have put moral and civil philosophy on a scientific footing, his claim to have been the inventor of a science of optics, his interest even before the 1640s in a science of human nature, his fascination with astronomy in his early years in Oxford, his application of the techniques of reason to religion and law, and his interest in history as a lesser counterpart of civil science all convey Hobbes's sense of participating in at least one revolution – a revolution of ideas – that was uncharacteristically beneficial to human beings.

1   A summary biography of Hobbes

Both Hobbes and Locke came from families of West Country clothiers, and Bacon was the grandson of a sheep-reeve (a chief shepherd).
All three family stories tell us something not only about the importance of wool in the English economy but also about the role of
education in stimulating social mobility during the sixteenth and
seventeenth centuries. Bacon's father, thanks to his studies at Cambridge, was able to become a prominent lawyer and marry into the
aristocracy. Locke's father was also trained as a lawyer, although he
remained a humble country attorney; thanks to his own education
at Oxford, Locke was able to pursue a career that included diplo-
matic work, secretarial assistance to a rich politician and, eventually, a well-paid government administrative post. Of the careers of
these three philosophers, Hobbes's was certainly the least adventur-
ous. But it too would not have been possible without his education
at Oxford, which gave him his entrée to the Cavendish family, with
whom he was to spend most of his life. The expense of educating a
son up to university level may have been a threshold over which the
poorest in society could not cross; yet the threshold was set rela-
tively low, and once it had been passed a wide range of possible
careers opened up.

One career that did not exist during this period was that of a
professional philosopher. Not only was philosophy not defined or
demarcated as a discipline in the way that it is today (the term was
used to include the whole range of physical sciences as well), but
there was no professionalization of the subject. Some of those who
wrote about philosophical matters, such as Henry More or Ralph
Cudworth, may have been employed as academics. By publishing
philosophical works, however, they were not exhibiting academic

"research" so much as entering a republic of letters that was inhabited equally by churchmen, physicians, noblemen, officers of state, schoolmasters, and even, in the case of Hobbes's friend Sir Kenelm Digby, a one-time amateur pirate. With the proliferation of printing houses in seventeenth-century England, it was not difficult to get published. The modern system of royalties did not exist, but the code of patronage ensured that a well-chosen dedication might be handsomely rewarded. Books were expensive to buy, however; for example, *Leviathan*, when it was first published, cost eight shillings, which was more than most ordinary laborers earned in a week. Any writer who wanted to keep up with what was being published on philosophical subjects needed one of four things: a private income, a well-paid job, membership of a circle of book-lending friends, or access to a well-funded library. Hobbes's career as tutor and secretary to the Cavendish family gave him the last of these four in full; over the years he enjoyed the other three in smaller measure. He was content to remain the employee or retainer of a great noble household – a somewhat old-fashioned career pattern that gave him access to a higher social world without making him a member of it, and which kept him for months at a time in physical seclusion from the metropolitan intellectual scene. But it also gave him security, time to write a large quantity of works on a huge range of subjects, and powerful political protection against the public hostility to some of those works during the last three decades of his life.

I

Hobbes was born on April 15, 1588, in Westport, a parish on the northwestern side of the small town of Malmesbury, in north Wiltshire. His father, an ill-educated country clergyman, was curate of the small neighboring parish of Brokenborough, which was one of the poorest livings in the area.[1] Some members of the family had grown prosperous in the cloth-making business. These included Edmund Hobbes (probably Hobbes's great-uncle), who became Alderman, i.e. Mayor, of Malmesbury in 1600; an even richer cousin, William Hobbes, who was a "great clothier"; and Francis, the elder brother of Hobbes's father, who was a prosperous glover and became Alderman of Malmesbury in 1625.[2] Other Hobbeses in and around Malmesbury included some less prominent clothiers and two alehouse-keepers, Edmund and Robert Hobbes of Westport, whose exact relationship to Thomas Hobbes cannot be established.[3] It seems likely that Hobbes's father spent more time in the Westport alehouse than he did in his church at Brokenborough; during the archdeacon's visitation of the deanery of Malmesbury in October 1602 he failed to appear before the visitors, and two months later he was hauled up before the archdeacon's court "for want of quarter sermons and for not cathechisinge the younge."[4]

Worse trouble was to follow. In October 1603 Hobbes's father was accused in the episcopal court of slandering Richard Jeane, the vicar of Foxley (a nearby parish), whom he had described as "a knave and an arrant knave and a drunken knave." Required to make a public act of penitence in Foxley church, Hobbes's father failed to turn up for the occasion; fined 33s 3d, he failed to pay and was threatened (and eventually punished) with excommunication. In February 1604 he chanced on Jeane in the churchyard at Malmesbury, whereupon, in the words of a witness, he "followed the said m[r] Jeaine revyling him and calling him knave and coming neare vnto him strooke him the saide M[r] Jeaine wth his fiste vnder the eare or about the head."[5] Any act of violence in a church or churchyard was an excommunicable offense, but laying violent hands on a clergyman was an even more serious crime in ecclesiastical law, for which corporal punishment was possible; and any excommunicated person who failed to seek absolution from the church could be arrested and imprisoned by the civil authorities after forty days.[6] Hobbes's father "was forcd to fly for it" and died "in obscurity beyound London."[7]

By the time these dramatic events occurred, Hobbes was already at Oxford; whether he ever saw his father again is not known. It is possible that he had been sent to university because, like his father, he was a younger son who was expected to go into the church. (His elder brother, Edmund, was to pursue the family trade as a clothier.) If so, we may suspect that these events strengthened whatever anticlerical tendencies were already present in Hobbes's character. Hobbes owed his Oxford education to two people: his uncle Francis, who paid for it, and a young clergyman, Robert Latimer, who had taught Hobbes Latin and Greek to a high standard at a little school in Westport. Latimer was evidently a keen classicist and an inspiring teacher who may have become an intellectual and moral father-figure for Hobbes; as it happened, it was Latimer who replaced Hobbes's father as curate of Brokenborough.[8] Latimer had been an undergraduate at Magdalen Hall in Oxford, and it was there that Hobbes was sent to study at the age of thirteen or fourteen.[9]

Magdalen Hall was one of the poorer foundations at Oxford, having developed out of a grammar school attached to Magdalen College. Both the College and the Hall had been regarded as centers of Puritanism since the 1560s and 1570s; Magdalen Hall's reputation for Puritanism was strengthened under a principal, John Wilkinson, who was appointed in 1605. The Hall, unlike the College, had no chapel, and since its daily services of morning and evening prayer were said in an unconsecrated building (the dining hall), it was possible to add Puritan "exercises" to the forms of prayer contained in the Prayer Book.[10] The sympathy for some of Calvin's teachings that Hobbes displayed in later life may date from his time at Magdalen Hall. On the other hand, Calvinism was not the same as Puritanism, and his later hostility towards Presbyterians in particular and religious "enthusiasts" in general is well known. In his autobiographical writings, Hobbes passes no comment on the religious climate of his undergraduate years. He tells us little about his studies either, except to dismiss the Aristotelian logic and physics that he was taught. Instead of such useless stuff, he says, he preferred to read about explorations of new-found lands and to study maps of the earth and the stars.[11] Astronomy thus emerges as his earliest scientific interest – an interest he evidently kept up, since we know that he observed the appearance of a comet in 1618.[12] In retrospect, Hobbes evidently regretted that he had not been taught the key to the exact sciences, mathematics. He complained in *Leviathan* that until very recently geometry had "had no place at all" in the universities, and his advice on education was that a boy should be "entered into geometry when he understands Latin [because] it is the best way of teaching logic."[13]

It is hard to judge the fairness of Hobbes's criticisms of Oxford. The official curriculum laid down in the statutes of 1564–5 was indeed conservative and dominated by works of Aristotle (although it did include some standard astronomical and geometrical works, including Euclid, which Hobbes would have had to study if he had wanted to proceed MA). Hobbes's complaint that the philosophy taught at the universities was "Aristotelity" had some truth to it.

There had been a definite revival of Aristotelianism in England in the latter part of the sixteenth century, and extra decrees were issued in Oxford in 1586 to exclude the use of authors who disagreed with the "ancient and true philosophy" of Aristotle.[14] But, on the other hand, there is a mass of evidence that academics in the early seventeenth century had intellectual interests, especially in the sciences, which went far beyond the official curriculum, and that these interests were often reflected in their teaching.[15] Nor should we assume that Hobbes's hostility to scholastic logic would have found no sympathetic echo in the Oxford of his day. The humanist criticism of scholasticism lingered on at the university. One fiercely antischolastic oration delivered in Magdalen Hall two or three years before Hobbes's arrival attacked the "clumsy and barbarous words, 'entities', 'formal essences', and 'quiddities'," and asked rhetorically: "How are ethics improved by the knowledge of propositions or the manufacture of syllogisms?"[16]

II

For someone who did not intend to pursue a career in the church or the university, there was little point in staying on for the further degree of MA. Fortunately, Hobbes was offered employment immediately after completing his BA. On the recommendation of John Wilkinson he was taken on as a tutor by William Cavendish, a rich Derbyshire landowner who had been created a baron in 1605 and was to become first earl of Devonshire in 1618. Hobbes's pupil, the future second earl (also named William Cavendish), was only a few years younger than Hobbes himself. He had been entered briefly at St. John's College, Cambridge; Hobbes joined him there in the summer of 1608 and accompanied him from Cambridge to Derbyshire in November.[17] Thereafter Hobbes's relation to his charge seems to have been less that of a tutor than that of a servant, a secretary, or a friend. In Aubrey's words, "He was his lordship's page, and rode a hunting and hawking with him, and kept his privy purse."[18]

The young William Cavendish was not without intellectual and literary interests. In 1611 he published (anonymously) a short but elegant work, *A Discourse against Flatterie*, the essayistic style of which suggests the influence of Bacon.[19] Three years later Hobbes and Cavendish went on a tour of France and Italy. During their stay in Venice in the winter of 1614–15 they both learned Italian, and Cavendish's exercises in the language included preparing a translation into Italian of Bacon's *Essayes*. Back in England, Cavendish was in personal contact with Bacon by 1616, and Bacon himself helped to revise the Italian translation of the *Essayes* before it was published in 1618.[20] We know from Aubrey and another source that Hobbes became acquainted with Bacon and did some secretarial work for him, taking down dictation "in his delicate groves where he did meditate," and helping to translate some of his *Essayes* into Latin.[21] This contact has traditionally been assumed to have taken place during the final years before Bacon's death in 1626 (and it was from Hobbes that Aubrey learned the story of how Bacon died from a chill caught when experimentally stuffing a chicken with snow); however, Hobbes's personal acquaintance with Bacon probably dates from the work on the Italian translation of the *Essayes* in 1617–18. From the first earl of Devonshire's account book it is clear that Hobbes also visited the Lord Chancellor on his employer's legal business in May 1619, and another entry records the disbursement of the sum of two shillings "to Mr Hobbs wch he gaue away at ye Lo: Chanc." in May 1620.[22]

Despite all these personal contacts, it is hard to find any evidence of a strong or direct Baconian influence on the substance of Hobbes's later philosophy. Some elements of Bacon's thinking may find an echo in Hobbes's works: the tendency toward naturalism or physicalism (as shown by Bacon's interest in ancient atomism or modern writers such as Telesio), for example, or the attack on false entities generated by language (the idols of the marketplace). The general project of replacing scholasticism with a new but equally all-encompassing system of knowledge was also common to both writers. But none of these tendencies or projects had been peculiar to Bacon. It is clear, on the other hand, that Hobbes rejected Bacon's obscure but largely traditional metaphysics of "forms," and that the so-called inductive method propounded by Bacon had little influence on Hobbes compared with his later discovery of the Euclidean method of definition and deduction.

The influence of Bacon's *Essayes* on the young William Cavendish, however, was evidently powerful. In 1620 an original collection of essays was published anonymously under the title *Horae subsecivae*. It included a version of the *Discourse against Flatterie* and a group of other essays in the Baconian style that can definitely be attributed to Cavendish; a fair copy of these essays, in Hobbes's hand, survives at Chatsworth.[23] In addition to the *Discourse against Flatterie* and the essays in the Chatsworth MS, the published text of *Horae subsecivae* also included three new discourses. One was a description of Rome, obviously the fruit of Hobbes's and Cavendish's visit there in October 1614; the others were "A Discourse upon the Beginning of Tacitus" and "A Discourse of Lawes." A recent statistical analysis of the prose characteristics of *Horae subsecivae* suggests that while the rest of the work was not composed by Hobbes, these three discourses may have been.[24] This is a little surprising in the case of the description of Rome, since writing such accounts when on a tour of Europe was a traditional exercise performed by pupils, not their tutors.[25] But in the case of the other two discourses, it is possible to see resemblances between the arguments of these writings and Hobbes's later thinking. The discourse on Tacitus, for example, coolly assumes the importance of deception and self-interest in political affairs, and both discourses stress the unique evil of anarchy or civil war. On the other hand, the claims made in the "Discourse of Lawes" about the relationship between law and reason and about the independent status of common law as something grounded in "the Iudgement of the people" are in conflict with Hobbes's later position.[26] Even if these discourses were by Cavendish and not by Hobbes, they give us an important insight into the thinking of the man who was intellectually and personally closest to him at this time.

Hobbes's introduction to political life and contemporary political thinking came largely through Cavendish's activities. Cavendish was never a prominent politician, but he was a member of the 1614 and 1621 parliaments, and Hobbes would no doubt have followed those debates that Cavendish attended.[27] On his return from Italy in 1615, Cavendish kept up a correspondence with the Venetian friar Fulgenzio Micanzio, who was the friend and personal assistant of Paolo Sarpi; Micanzio's letters were translated by Hobbes for further circulation.[28] In this way Hobbes must have gained a special interest in the writings and political actions of Sarpi, who had defended Venice against the Papal interdict of 1606 and developed a strongly anti-Papal theory of church and state in which the temporal ruler alone "is the source from whom all jurisdictions flow and to whom they all return."[29] And through Cavendish and the connection with Micanzio, Hobbes must also have come into contact with the Croatian-Venetian churchman and writer Marc'Antonio de Dominis, who came to England in 1616, assisted in the project of translating Bacon into Italian, supervised the publication of Sarpi's *Historia del concilio tridentino*, and published a large and influential anti-Papal treatise of his own, *De republica ecclesiastica*.[30] Also thanks to Cavendish, Hobbes became a member of two trading and colonizing companies in which Cavendish had an interest: the Virginia Company and the Somer Islands Company (which organized the settlement of the Bermudas). Hobbes was granted a share in the former by Cavendish in June 1622; the date of his formal involvement in the latter is not known, but his role as assistant to Cavendish would certainly have involved him in the affairs of both companies before he became a shareholder himself. At the thirty-seven separate meetings of the Virginia Company's governing body that Hobbes attended in 1622–4, he came into contact with prominent politicians and writers such as Sir Edwin Sandys (who criticized royal policy on taxation and foreign affairs in the parliament of 1621) and the lawyer John Selden (whose friend Hobbes later became).[31]

William Cavendish succeeded his father as second earl of Devonshire in 1626, but he died only two years later, at the age of forty-three. At the time of his death, Hobbes was finishing work on a translation of Thucydides, which was published, with a dedication to Cavendish's elder son (the third earl), in the following year. This was an important work of scholarship; it was the first translation of the work into English directly from the Greek, and it also included a detailed map of ancient Greece compiled from many sources and drawn by Hobbes himself. Although Thucydides' work is famous for its speech by Pericles in defense of Athenian democracy, its publication by Hobbes may nevertheless have been an implicitly pro-royalist political statement, since the main theme of the book is the gradual subversion of the Athenian state by ambitious demagogic politicians. In his verse autobiography Hobbes emphasizes this aspect of Thucydides' work, saying that Thucydides was Hobbes's favorite historian because "he shows how incompetent democracy is."[32]

After the death of the second earl, Hobbes left the service of the Cavendishes for two years. He was again employed as a tutor for the son of a rich landowner, Sir Gervase Clifton, and in 1629–30 he traveled with the young Gervase Clifton to France and Switzerland.[33] From later accounts by Hobbes and Aubrey we learn that it was during his stay in Geneva in April–June 1630 that Hobbes began to read Euclid's *Elements* in "a gentleman's library" and fell in love with its deductive method. It is unlikely, given his known earlier interest in astronomy, that this was Hobbes's first encounter with geometry; nor need we assume that he had never encountered Euclid's work before. What he stresses in his own account of the incident is that the work delighted him "not so much because of the theorems, as because of the method of reasoning."[34] This strongly suggests that Hobbes's mind was already preoccupied with some philosophical problems to which Euclidean method seemed to supply the solution. Of the nature of those problems, however, there is no direct evidence from this period itself.

After his return to England, Hobbes was taken back into the service of the widowed countess of Devonshire in early 1631 as a tutor to her son, the third earl. Possibly Hobbes was already spending much of his time reading about mathematics and other scientific subjects; in a legal document written in 1639 he explained that he had accepted this tutorship "amongst other causes chiefly for this, that ye same did not much diuert him from his studies."[35] The boy was only thirteen, and Hobbes now had to teach at a more elementary level than he had done before. One of the methods he used was to go through a Latin translation of Aristotle's *Rhetoric*, making a "digest" of it with his pupil. A version of this digest was later published in English by Hobbes. It is a largely faithful summary of Aristotle's analysis of how people can be swayed by appeals to their passions and interests.[36]

III

The 1630s were crucial years in Hobbes's intellectual development. They saw not only the growth of his interest in science (especially optics) but also the formation of the main outlines of his political philosophy, which appeared as *The Elements of Law* at the end of the decade. Although we know more about his intellectual and personal life in this decade than in the previous ones, there is much that remains obscure. Recent studies have tended to locate Hobbes in two particular intellectual groups during this period. One was the

"Welbeck academy" of scientists connected with the earl of Newcastle (so called after one of his family seats, Welbeck Abbey in north Nottinghamshire). They included Newcastle's brother, Sir Charles Cavendish, a talented mathematician who corresponded with mathematicians and scientists on the Continent; Newcastle's chaplain, Robert Payne, who conducted chemical experiments with Newcastle; and Walter Warner, who had been one of a number of scientists and free-thinkers (including Thomas Hariot) patronized by the earl of Northumberland in the 1590s and 1600s.[37] Hobbes was especially close to the Cavendish brothers in the late 1630s. He corresponded with Payne, who became one of his closest friends, and he also took an interest (although not an unskeptical one) in Warner's work on optics. We know that he was in contact with Warner, sending him suggestions of his own about the angle of refraction, as early as 1634.[38]

The other grouping was the so-called Great Tew circle that gathered round Lucius Cary, Viscount Falkland (whose house, Great Tew, was near Oxford). Its members included theologians such as William Chillingworth, Oxford divines such as George Morley and Gilbert Sheldon, London lawyers such as Edward Hyde (the future earl of Clarendon), and poets such as Edmund Waller.[39] At the heart of the Great Tew circle lay the collaboration between Falkland and Chillingworth in an attempt to formulate a moderate and rational Anglicanism as a defense against Roman Catholicism. This defense of "rational religion" was characterized as "Socinianism" (an anti-Trinitarian heresy) by hostile critics, especially the more extreme Protestant ones; and the Great Tew writers' rejection of traditional ideas of spiritual authority in the church, with their tendency to judge questions of church government in terms of mere convenience or conduciveness to temporal peace, set them apart from Laudians as well as Catholics. These characteristics would also be found in Hobbes's later writings, and attacked in even stronger terms. Hobbes certainly owed some of his ideas about religion to members of the Great Tew circle, even though his defense of rational religion was not based, as theirs generally was, on assumptions about the essential reasonableness of God.

Although Hobbes's connections with various members of these two intellectual groupings are not in doubt, the idea of him belonging to two "circles" located at Welbeck and Great Tew is misleadingly schematic. The phrase "Welbeck academy" is just a metaphor for a group of people connected with the Cavendish brothers and does not refer to physical gatherings, either formal or informal; there is no evidence, for example, that Walter Warner ever set foot in Welbeck Abbey. As for Great Tew, while it is clear that there were physical gatherings there, it is unlikely that Hobbes was more than a very occasional visitor to Falkland's house. One possible opportunity for a visit came in 1634, when Hobbes may have stayed for a while in Oxford, using that town also as a base for a visit to his old friends in north Wiltshire.[40] Otherwise Hobbes is most likely to have encountered members of Falkland's circle in London. Outside its inner core of Oxford men, this circle had a more peripheral membership of London-based intellectuals, court wits, and poets, and it is among these that most of Hobbes's personal friendships with Great Tew writers are to be found – men such as the poet Edmund Waller and the lawyer Edward Hyde. Yet the intellectual and social world of early seventeenth-century England was so closely knit that one has only to begin pursuing possible connections to see any neat pattern of separate "circles" break up before one's eyes. Thus, for example, Hobbes's intellectual contacts with the liberal Oxford theologians are likely to have come in the first place from Robert Payne, an Oxford man who was a friend of Sheldon, Morley, and Hammond; many of the poets and wits attached to Falkland's circle were also friends and admirers of Ben Jonson, whom Hobbes had known in 1628, before the Great Tew circle came into being; Jonson was himself a protégé of Newcastle and a friend of Payne; and Hyde was also connected with Walter Warner, whose patron during this period was Hyde's father-in-law, Sir Thomas Aylesbury.

In 1634 Hobbes embarked on another Continental tour with his pupil, the third earl of Devonshire. They spent nearly a year in Paris, setting off for Italy at the end of August 1635; they were in Rome in December of that year, in Florence in April 1636, and back in Paris in early June, whence they returned to England four months later.[41] Even before he set out on this tour, Hobbes's mind had been filled, thanks partly to the stimulus of the earl of Newcastle and his mathematician brother, Sir Charles Cavendish, with thoughts about optics, physics, and psychology. In early 1634 he had been commissioned by the earl of Newcastle to find a copy of Galileo's *Dialogo*, and his earliest surviving letter sent from Paris during this tour

answers a query from an unnamed correspondent about the functioning of vision and memory.[42] The two prolonged stays in Paris that
this Continental trip allowed him were clearly of great importance
to Hobbes's intellectual life. From the earl of Newcastle and Sir
Charles he had introductions to French scientists and mathematicians such as Claude Mydorge, a writer on geometry and optics who
was a close friend of Descartes.[43] It was probably through Sir
Charles's good offices, either directly or indirectly, that he was introduced to the learned, pious, and charming friar Marin Mersenne,
who was also a friend of Descartes, and who was already functioning
as the center of a huge network of scientific and philosophical correspondents. Hobbes later recorded in his autobiography that he had
investigated "the principles of natural science" in Paris at this time
(principles that "he knew . . . were contained in the nature and variety of motions"), and that he had communicated his ideas on this
subject to Mersenne on a daily basis.[44] We know that he observed
experiments carried out by William Davisson, a famous Scottish
chemist who taught at Paris, and during his final months in the
French capital he was discussing philosophical matters with the
maverick Catholic intellectual Sir Kenelm Digby.[45]

By the time Hobbes returned to England in October 1636 he was
devoting as much of his time as possible to philosophical work: "the
extreame pleasure I take in study," he wrote, "ouercomes in me all
other appetites."[46] His pupil came of age in the following year, and
although Hobbes remained in his service, his time was now largely
his own; much of it was probably spent with the earl of Newcastle
and his brother at Welbeck. In a letter to the earl from Paris in 1635,
Hobbes had expressed an ambition to be the first person to give
"good reasons for ye facultyes & passions of ye soule, such as may be
expressed in playne English"; and from a later letter from Sir
Kenelm Digby it appears that Hobbes had been planning, during his
final months in Paris, a work on "Logike" that would begin, in
Euclidean fashion, with the definitions of primary terms.[47] Whether
these writings on logic and psychology or epistemology were conceived from the outset as a single, systematic project cannot be said
with certainty, but all the evidence of Hobbes's later work indicates
that the urge to systematize was located deep in his intellectual
character. It is unfortunate that any manuscript drafts of this project
that Hobbes may have written during this crucial period of his intel-

lectual formation, 1636–9, have apparently not survived. One manuscript traditionally attributed to Hobbes (and dated by some authors to this period, although by others to the beginning of the 1630s), the so-called Short Tract, is in the handwriting of Robert Payne and can more plausibly be attributed to him.[48] Another manuscript on metaphysics and epistemology, which definitely does contain material written by Hobbes and which has previously been dated to the period 1637–40, can more probably be dated to some time after July 1643.[49]

The earliest surviving scientific-philosophical work by Hobbes is a manuscript treatise on optics, the so-called "Latin Optical MS", which must have been completed by 1640.[50] This important work evidently formed part of a larger body of writing; it refers back to a previous *sectio* (section) in which basic principles of physics had been discussed, such as the rule that "all action is local motion in the thing which acts."[51] Since Hobbes was later to use the term "section" for each of the three works that made up his tripartite "Elements of philosophy" (*De corpore, De homine,* and *De cive*), and since Hobbes put his main discussion of optics in *De homine,* it is possible that this optical treatise was a version of what later became *De homine,* and that the earlier "section" to which it refers was a body of work corresponding to what was eventually published as *De corpore.*[52] How roughly the missing "section" corresponded to that work can only be guessed at, but Hobbes's slow and hesitant drafting and redrafting of *De corpore* during the 1640s suggests that whatever existed before 1640 was probably more like a set of notes than a polished text. (This would fit the account of Hobbes's working methods given by Aubrey and by Hobbes himself.)[53]

The striking thing about the Latin Optical MS, which probably set it apart from the previous "section," was the fact that so much of it took the form of a running critique of Descartes's "Dioptrique." This was the short treatise on optics (in particular, refraction) that had been published as one of the essays accompanying Descartes's *Discours de la méthode* in 1637 (Hobbes had been sent a copy of the book by Sir Kenelm Digby soon after its publication). Descartes's work had an unsettling effect on Hobbes, for two reasons. First, Descartes's mechanistic physics, and his assumption that perception is caused by physical motions or pressures that have no intrinsic similarity to the qualities (redness, heat, etc.) that are perceived, corresponded very closely to Hobbes's own theories. Although neither Descartes nor Hobbes was the first to have such ideas (they had been preceded by Isaac Beeckman and Galileo), this was still very much the frontier of modern thinking, and it must have been galling for Hobbes to see some of his own research preempted in print. In 1640–1 an exchange of letters between Hobbes and Descartes on optics and physics turned (at Descartes's prompting) into an acrimonious dispute about who had preempted – or even plagiarized – whom.[54]

The second reason for Hobbes's troubled reaction to Descartes was that the metaphysics of the French philosopher seemed to be radically out of step with the proper assumptions of his physics. That Hobbes had already possessed distinctive ideas of his own on metaphysics before he read Descartes's book is indicated by the shrewd comment Digby made when he originally sent the *Discours de la méthode* to Hobbes: "I doubt not but you will say that if he were as accurate in his metaphysicall part as he is in his experience [i.e., his account of physical phenomena], he had carryed the palme from all men liuing."[55] In the Latin Optical MS, Hobbes attacked the dualism at the heart of Descartes's theory, challenging the idea that the mind could be affected by the motion of objects without itself being a physical object. "Since vision is formally and really nothing other than motion, it follows that that which sees is also formally and strictly speaking nothing other than that which is moved; for nothing other than a body . . . can be moved."[56] And in a set of "Objections" to Descartes's *Meditationes*, commissioned and published by Mersenne in 1641, Hobbes broadened his attack on Cartesian metaphysics, suggesting that Descartes had failed to extricate his thinking from the assumptions of scholastic philosophy, with its hypostatized qualities, its degrees of reality of being, and its blurring of the distinction between existent beings (*entia*) and essences.[57] In general, therefore, Descartes's philosophy was more an irritant than a stimulant to Hobbes. The idea that transcending Cartesian skepticism became a major aim of Hobbes's philosophical work cannot be supported by anything in Hobbes's writings; his belief in the causal dependence of all ideas (including qualities and "essences") on the physical properties of existing objects was part of the primary assumptions of his metaphysics, by which radical skepticism was simply precluded.

Hobbes's work on science and metaphysics was interrupted at the end of the 1630s by politics. A number of issues were prompting discussion of the "absoluteness" of sovereign power during the final years of King Charles I's personal rule. Of these, the most famous was the Ship Money case of 1637, which raised the question of whether any limits could be set to the power of the king, given that his normal powers could be exceeded in exceptional circumstances, and that the king might judge which circumstances were exceptional.[58] The Short Parliament of April 1640 (to which the earl of Devonshire unsuccessfully tried to get Hobbes elected as MP for Derby) voiced its concerns on these issues before it was abruptly dissolved. As one speaker put it, "if the Kinge be judge of the necessitye, we have nothing and are but Tennants at will."[59] Four days after the dissolution of that parliament, Hobbes signed the dedicatory epistle of a treatise, *The Elements of Law*, in which he aimed to settle all such questions by working out the nature and extent of sovereign power from first principles. The dedication was to his patron, the royalist earl of Newcastle; the principles contained in the work, Hobbes explained, "are those which I have heretofore acquainted your Lordship withal in private discourse, and which by your command I have here put into method."[60]

That this was a polemically pro-royalist work was obvious; as Hobbes plainly stated in one of its final chapters, the idea that subjects could maintain rights of private property against the sovereign was a claim that he had "confuted, by proving the absoluteness of the sovereignty."[61] But *The Elements of Law* was no mere polemical pamphlet. In it Hobbes had attempted to base his political principles on an account of human psychology that was compatible with (although not necessarily dependent on) his mechanistic physics. The reduction of "reason" to instrumental reasoning was an important part of this psychological picture. Reason, on this view of things, did not intuit values, but found the means to ends that were posited by desire; desires might be various, but reason could also discover general truths about how to achieve the conditions (above all, the absence of anarchic violence) in which desires were least liable to be frustrated. By defining that which is "not against reason" as "right," Hobbes also made the transition to a different type of general truths: definitional truths about rights and obligations, which would make the claims of the anti-royalist politicians as necessarily false as those of incompetent geometers. For sovereignty to exist at all,

Hobbes argued, it was necessary for all the rights of the subjects to be yielded to it; what he tried to show was that the reasons that made sovereignty necessary also made it absolute. This was a work of extraordinary assurance, an almost fully fledged statement of Hobbes's entire political philosophy. His two later published versions of his theory, *De cive* and *Leviathan*, would develop further some of the points of detail, but the essential lineaments would remain the same.

The *Elements of Law* circulated in many manuscript copies, which, Hobbes later recalled, "occasioned much talk of the Author; and had not His Majesty dissolved the Parliament, it had brought him into danger of his life."[62] Possibly Hobbes was already thinking, during the summer of 1640, about going to live in Paris, for reasons of political safety and intellectual stimulus. Apart from the scientists he had met through Mersenne, an old friend of the Cavendish family was there, the French courtier Charles du Bosc, whom Hobbes had known in the 1620s, and who may have extended a general invitation to Hobbes when he visited England in 1638.[63] In September 1640 Hobbes recovered £100 which he had asked the steward of Chatsworth to invest for him; he also had £400 banked with the Cavendish family (at 6 percent interest), so if he withdrew all his money on deposit he must have felt financially independent enough to embark on a long period of residence abroad.[64] What finally prompted him to leave England was a debate on November 7 in the newly convened Long Parliament, in which John Pym and other anti-royalists attacked "Preaching for absolute monarchy that the king may do what he list."[65] Fearing that he might be called to account for *The Elements of Law*, Hobbes fled to Paris.

IV

Thanks to his connection with Mersenne, Hobbes was quickly absorbed into the intellectual life of the capital. Mersenne had acted as intermediary for the correspondence between Hobbes and Descartes, and it was Mersenne who (as mentioned above) commissioned Hobbes's "Objections" to the *Meditationes*, which were published, in 1641, with five other sets of objections and Descartes's replies. Mersenne also arranged the publication of *De cive* in 1642, over the initials "T. H." This book, a remodeled version of the arguments of

The Elements of Law, was much admired for the cogency and conci-
sion of its arguments about the nature of the state, but the reductive
treatment of Christian theology in the final section of the work
caused many eyebrows to be raised.[66] It was De cive that really
established Hobbes as a political writer of European repute when it
was reissued (in two further editions, with additional explanatory
notes by Hobbes) by the Dutch printer Elzevir in 1647. Meanwhile
Mersenne had also published some small samples of Hobbes's work
on physics and optics in two volumes of scientific compilations that
he edited in 1644, Cogitata physico-mathematica and Universae
geometriae synopsis.[67] And through Mersenne Hobbes became acquainted, in the early 1640s, with a number of French philosophers
and scientists, including the anti-Aristotelian Pierre Gassendi, the
mathematician and anti-Cartesian Gilles Personne de Roberval, the
Huguenot physician Abraham du Prat, and two other younger Hu-
guenots with scientific interests, Samuel Sorbière and Thomas de
Martel.[68]

For most of the 1640s Hobbes was preoccupied with physics, metaphysics, and theology rather than political philosophy. In 1642–3 he
wrote (probably at Mersenne's request) a huge blow-by-blow refutation of a scientific and theological work by the Catholic Aristotelian
philosopher Thomas White. Mersenne studied this refutation in
manuscript and may well have encouraged Hobbes to have it
printed, but it was to remain unpublished until 1973. The Anti-
White (as it is now generally called) is a strange work, written obviously in a great outpouring of ideas but having recourse to a mass of
earlier notes and drafts. It is not surprising that Hobbes, who had set
himself the task of arranging all such material methodically in his
tri-partite "Elements of philosophy," should have been reluctant to
publish it in this haphazard and repetitive form. And it is clear,
within the text of the Anti-White itself, that one of the topics that
was giving him the most difficulty was the nature of scientific
method itself. Two different models of scientific knowledge jostle
for position: the knowledge of causes, and the knowledge of definitional meanings.[69] Hobbes made some unsatisfactory attempts to
reconcile or unite these two models; possibly his own dissatisfac-
tion with this aspect of his work was one reason for the slowness
with which he drafted and redrafted his major work on logic, metaphysics, and physics, De corpore, throughout the 1640s.

Several fragmentary early drafts of this work (which was not published until 1655) survive, the most puzzling of which is a rough copy in another hand of a text that mixes English and Latin phrases. The traditional assumption that this was a semi-translation of Hobbes's Latin text by somebody else is probably false, since one whole section of the English reappears in a later English work by Hobbes. This draft was probably written in the years 1643–4; the material it contains was later used in chapters 7, 8, 11, and 12 of *De corpore*, but in this draft the material forms the opening chapters of the entire work.[70] The exposition begins here with Hobbes's "annihilatory hypothesis," which asks the reader to consider the nature of ideas after the annihilation of the world that those ideas described. This was not a skeptical device, but a way of severing the connection between real being and "essences" (which in Hobbes's view were nothing other than descriptions of existing things, with no ontological status of their own). Later drafts (an undated manuscript by Hobbes, and a closely related set of notes taken by Sir Charles Cavendish in 1645–6) inserted, before this material, a more traditional account of logic, explaining the functioning of terms, propositions, and syllogisms.[71] Through Sir Charles's letters to the mathematician John Pell, we get a sense of the trouble Hobbes had with this work. "Mr Hobbes puts me in hope of his philosophie which he writes he is nowe putting in order," wrote Sir Charles in December 1644, "but I feare that will take a long time." And again, in May 1645: "I doubt [i.e., suspect] it will be long ere Mr Hobbes publish anything . . . he proceeds every day some what, but he hath a great deal to do."[72]

There were many interruptions to Hobbes's progress, and the arrival in Paris of Sir Charles and his brother in April 1645 was the cause of several of them. In the summer of that year Hobbes was encouraged by the marquess (formerly earl) of Newcastle to engage in a disputation with an exiled Anglican cleric, John Bramhall, over the nature of free will. The short treatise that Hobbes wrote was eventually published (without his authorization) as *Of Libertie and Necessitie* in 1654, and caused a long-running controversy with Bramhall on a range of theological matters. In late 1645 Hobbes composed, at the marquess's request, a treatise on optics in English, half of which would eventually form part of *De homine* (published in 1658).[73] And in the summer of 1646, just when Hobbes was planning to leave Paris to work intensively on *De corpore*, he was asked to be the mathematical tutor to the young Prince Charles, who had arrived in July. The marquess of Newcastle, who had been in charge of the prince's education in 1638, probably had a hand in this offer of employment. Hobbes did not need the job for financial reasons (two years later he was actually lending money to Newcastle), but it was not an offer he could refuse.[74] It brought him into closer contact with the politicians, courtiers, and churchmen who gathered at the Louvre and S. Germain: men such as John Cosin, the future bishop of Durham, and Henry Bennet, the future secretary of state Lord Arlington.

Given such contacts with royalist exiles, Hobbes's thoughts would naturally have turned more often in the later 1640s to the political situation in England. He maintained his friendship with the poet Edmund Waller, who was in exile in France after 1644; he became well acquainted with the poet Sir William Davenant (for whom he wrote a long commendatory letter, published in 1650, on his poem *Gondibert*), and he also kept in contact with Edward Hyde. Hobbes kept up some correspondence with the earl of Devonshire in England, and he also wrote regularly to his old friend Robert Payne, who was ejected from his Oxford college in 1648 but remained in England.[75] In May 1650 Robert Payne learned about *Leviathan* for the first time, when Hobbes told him that he had completed thirty-seven chapters out of a projected total of fifty.[76] Clearly, Hobbes's work on this new book had been rather secretive and very rapid; he probably did not begin it until the autumn of 1649 (he told Sorbière in June of that year that he was working on *De corpore*, which he hoped to finish by the end of the summer), and he seems not to have mentioned it to Hyde when the latter saw him in Paris in August and September of that year.[77] By the time Hyde returned to Paris in April 1651, Hobbes was able to inform him that "his Book (which he would call *Leviathan*) was then Printing in England, and that he receiv'd every week a Sheet to correct . . . and thought it would be finished within little more than a moneth."[78]

That Hobbes went to the trouble of arranging the printing of the work in London confirms the essential validity of the joking remark he made to Hyde when the latter asked why he wanted it published: "The truth is, I have a mind to go home."[79] As recently as May 1648, when Hobbes had discussed the possibility of returning to England in a letter to earl of Devonshire, he had written: "When I consider how dangerous a time there is like to be for peaceable men, I am apter to wish you on this side, then my selfe on that side the sea." But he had qualified this reluctance even then: "I haue no inclinations to the place where there is so little security, but I haue such inclinations to your Lo[rdshi]p as I will come to any place (if I may haue a passe) where your Lo[rdshi]p shall be."[80] Thereafter things had changed in England, with the execution of King Charles I in January 1649. Things had changed too for Hobbes in Paris. The death of Mersenne in September 1648 and the departure soon afterward of Gassendi to the south of France meant that he was deprived of his two dearest philosophical friends.

It would, however, be too limited an explanation to say that Hobbes wrote *Leviathan* merely to ease his passage to England. Certainly he was keen – and entitled – to point out that his theory of political authority based on necessary consent (and necessary consent based on a rational understanding of ultimate self-interest) was not inherently pro-royalist (as the trappings of the argument in *The Elements of Law* and *De cive* might have made it appear to be). His argument, as *Leviathan* makes clear, was about sovereignty per se, which might be exercised by a king or an assembly; the shift in a subject's obligation from one holder of sovereignty to another would occur "when the means of his life is within the Guards and Garrisons of the Enemy" – it then being rational to consent to obey the conqueror.[81] Such calculations of interest had been a living issue for people such as the earl of Devonshire, who had had to compound with the parliamentary authorities for his estates. Sir Charles Cavendish had done the same in absentia for his estates in 1649, and would be persuaded by his brother and by Sir Edward Hyde to return to England in 1651 to renegotiate for them. A decade later, Hobbes would explain that he had written *Leviathan* on behalf of "those many and faithful Servants and Subjects of His Majesty" who had been forced to compound for their lands. "They that had done their utmost endeavour to perform their obligation to the King, had done all that they could be obliged unto; and were consequently at liberty to seek the safety of their lives and livelihood wheresoever, and without Treachery."[82]

It was reasonable of Hobbes to assume that this element of his argument would not cause intolerable offense among the courtiers of the young Charles II in Paris. Another aspect of the book that might reasonably be brought to the new king's attention was its attempt to analyze the nature of the false beliefs and harmful political practices – above all, those of organized religion – that Hobbes believed to have caused the destruction of Charles's father's kingdom. So it is not surprising that Hobbes actually presented a manuscript fair copy of the work to Charles II when the latter returned to Paris after his defeat at the Battle of Worcester in September 1651. Nor is it surprising that the theological arguments of the work, especially its ferocious attack on the Catholic Church, caused grave offense to some of the English courtiers in exile, notably those who were close to the Catholic Queen Mother, Henrietta Maria. Hobbes was barred from the court; and not long afterward, according to the recollections of both Hobbes and Hyde, the French Catholic clergy made an attempt to have him arrested.[83] He fled from Paris in mid-December 1651 and soon thereafter crossed the Channel to England.[84]

V

Hobbes settled in London, where he was able to make contact again with Sir Charles Cavendish, who had arrived there a couple of months earlier.[85] Soon he was back in the employment of the earl of Devonshire and had reverted to the old rhythm of life of a noble household, spending the summer months in Derbyshire and much of the rest of the year in London. His work for the earl probably amounted to little more than some light secretarial duties and general intellectual companionship; otherwise his time was his own. He spent some of it in the stimulating company of the lawyers John Selden and John Vaughan, and the physicians William Harvey and Charles Scarborough. Scarborough, a mathematician as well as a medical man, held gatherings of scientists at his London house which Hobbes sometimes attended. Hobbes was also moving in the more unorthodox and free-thinking circles of Thomas White (the Catholic philosopher whose *De mundo* he had refuted), John Davies (who published Hobbes's *Of Libertie and Necessitie* in 1654 with a bitterly anticlerical preface), and John Hall of Durham (the educational reformer and apologist for Cromwell).[86] It was probably in Davies's circle that Hobbes met Henry Stubbe, a young Oxford scholar and radical anticlericalist who began work – which he never completed – on a Latin translation of *Leviathan*.[87]

The notoriety that *Leviathan* obtained for Hobbes was slow in coming. Early readers of the book were understandably startled by some of its theological contents, but there was no immediate outcry. A typical judgment was that of the moderate Anglican bishop of Salisbury, Brian Duppa, who wrote to a friend in July 1651: "as in the man, so there are strange mixtures in the book; many things said so well that I could embrace him for it, and many things so wildly and unchristianly, that I can scarce have so much charity for him, as to think he was ever Christian."[88] That some of the theological arguments in *Leviathan* were phrased in such a way as to make them sound highly unorthodox is undeniable; Hobbes himself seems to have recognized this when he pruned some of them (notably the passage in which he appeared to make Moses a member of the Trinity) from his later Latin translation of the work. It is also true that his application of historical method – and caustic common sense – to biblical criticism had yielded some results, such as the denial of Moses' authorship of the Pentateuch, which were unacceptable to ordinary belief. But Hobbes was probably correct in thinking that his work would not have received the vast amount of subsequent denunciation had it not been seen as threatening by a number of special-interest groups. Of these the most important were "ecclesiastics" of various sorts – Catholic, Anglican, and Presbyterian – who saw that the basis of priestly or ministerial authority was undermined by Hobbes's arguments.

One particular interest group that Hobbes managed to offend was the universities. His attack on these institutions in *Leviathan* became suddenly topical when a proposal was made in the Barebones Parliament in 1653 to abolish them altogether.[89] Two of the leading scientists at Oxford, Seth Ward and John Wilkins, published a defense of the universities in 1654 that included a frosty reply to Hobbes; Ward (who had previously been an admirer of Hobbes, regarding him as a fellow exponent of the mechanistic new science) also published a full-length attack on Hobbes's philosophy and theology.[90] The publication of Hobbes's *De corpore*, which contained a number of incompetent attempts at geometrical proofs, made Hobbes an easy target for another Oxford scientist, the mathematician John Wallis. Hobbes became embroiled in a sequence of polemical exchanges on mathematical subjects with Wallis that would last for nearly twenty years. The real animus behind this feud was, however, their disagreement over church politics, with Hobbes regarding Wallis as the chief representative of the Presbyterians.

Since Hobbes had, by the late 1650s, acquired the enmity of three leading scientists, it is not surprising that there was some reluctance to enlist him in the Royal Society (as it later became) when it first met in 1660. But the basic reason for his exclusion was probably not just personal animosities; he had more personal friends than enemies among its membership, and there was no provision for blackballing in its elections of new Fellows. Nor was he less of a scientist than many of the active members of that body. Although his mathematical work was sometimes incompetent, his major works on physics and optics, De corpore (1655) and De homine (1658), were comparable to similar work by other scientific writers who did become Fellows of the Royal Society, and he continued to publish works on the explanation of natural phenomena, such as his Problemata physica (1662) and Decameron physiologicum (1678). The underlying problem seems to have been that the aura of religious notoriety clinging to Hobbes meant that any public association with him would be a source of embarrassment to the active members of the Royal Society, given that his basic assumptions about a mechanistic physical universe were quite similar to their own. Many traditionalists still regarded such a world-view as leading inevitably to atheism; several key members of the Royal Society were highly sensitive to such criticism, and reacted in a preemptive and diversionary way by directing fierce criticisms of their own against Hobbes.[91]

Throughout the 1660s and 1670s Hobbes was frequently attacked, in print and from the pulpit, for his supposed atheism, denial of objective moral values, promotion of debauchery, and so on.[92] At its crudest, this sort of criticism depended on a popular notion of "Hobbism" that had little to do with Hobbes's philosophical arguments and instead constituted a veiled attack on the libertinism of the Restoration court. Occasionally, however, there were more serious threats to investigate Hobbes's writings. In the early 1660s there was rumor that some Anglican bishops were planning to have Hobbes tried for heresy, and in 1666 a House of Commons committee was empowered to "receive Informacion toucheing such bookes as tend to Atheisme Blasphemy or Prophanenesse or against the

Essence or Attributes of God. And in perticular . . . the booke of Mr Hobbs called the Leuiathan."[93] Hobbes responded to the first of these threats by composing a treatise on the law of heresy (demonstrating that people should not be burned for that offense); on one or other of these occasions he was sufficiently worried to consign many of his own manuscripts to the flames.[94] In a number of writings during these final decades, Hobbes publicly defended himself against the criticisms of his conduct and beliefs. These defenses include a short autobiographical work, *Mr Hobbes Considered* (1662); the dedicatory epistle to *Problemata physica* (also 1662); an important appendix to the Latin translation of *Leviathan* (1668), in which he defended the work from charge of heresy; an angry public letter of complaint about libelous remarks inserted by the Oxford academic John Fell into a short biography of him published in 1674; an autobiography in Latin verse (1679); and, among his posthumously published works, a further defense of *Leviathan* against Bishop Bramhall (1682) and a polemical church history in Latin verse, *Historia ecclesiastica* (1688), which ends with a Hobbesian credo in praise of simple Christian virtues.[95]

These various publications (plus a number of other works on mathematics and complete translations into workaday English verse of Homer's *Iliad* and *Odyssey*) testify to the extraordinary vigor of Hobbes's old age. He was, after all, sixty-three when *Leviathan* was published, and he continued writing until his final year (aged 91). This productivity is all the more impressive when one remembers that the "shaking palsy" (probably Parkinson's disease) from which he suffered was so severe that he was forced to dictate his writings to an amanuensis from late 1656 onward.[96] Hobbes continued to live with the third earl of Devonshire, alternating between his London residence and his country houses, Chatsworth and Hardwick. The earl's patronage gave him protection and security. He benefitted too from a resumption of friendly personal relations with his old pupil, Charles II, to whom Aubrey cleverly arranged a re-introduction in London soon after the Restoration. The king gave him – for a while – a generous pension of more than £100 per annum and ordered that Hobbes should have "free access to his majestie." Hobbes was able to use this privilege in 1674 to get permission to print his public letter of complaint against John Fell, after approaching the king in person "in the Pall-mall in St James's parke."[97] But there

were limits to the king's indulgence of his old tutor. Hobbes's request for permission to print his dialogue-history of the Civil War,
Behemoth, was turned down; attempts to reprint *Leviathan* in 1670
were abruptly suppressed by the Stationers' Company.[98]

While Hobbes was generally vilified in print, he retained some
loyal personal friends and admirers, such as the lawyer John
Vaughan and the scientist and antiquary John Aubrey. But he must
have felt that he was a prophet without honor in his own country
when he compared his reputation in England with the glowing
praise of his philosophical achievements that came from his many
foreign correspondents. The circle of French scientists and writers
who, after Mersenne's death, had clustered round Gassendi in Paris
in the early 1650s (men such as Samuel Sorbière, Thomas de
Martel, and Abraham du Prat) regarded Hobbes, after Gassendi's
death in 1655, as the greatest living philosopher, and told him in
their letters that they eagerly read every new work of his that they
could obtain.[99] Even more adulatory was François du Verdus in
Bordeaux, who learned English in order to translate *Leviathan* into
French (a project that never saw the light of day, although Hobbes
seems at first to have encouraged it).[100] Samuel Sorbière was not
only a talented self-publicist but also an energetic publicizer of
Hobbes's works; and it was through Sorbière's efforts that a collection of Hobbes's Latin writings, including a Latin translation of
Leviathan made specially for it by Hobbes, was finally published by
the Dutch printer Blaeu in 1668.[101] This edition, together with
frequent reprintings of *De cive* on the Continent, helped to trans-
mit Hobbes's ideas to a wide range of readers, including Spinoza
and Leibniz. The latter, indeed, was more influenced by Hobbes
than by any other writer during his period of philosophical awaken-
ing late in the 1660s and early in the 1670s, and wrote to Hobbes to
say so: "I shall, God willing, always publicly declare that I know of
no other writer who has philosophized as precisely, as clearly, and
as elegantly as you have – no, not excepting Descartes with his
superhuman intellect."[102]

Hobbes died on December 4, 1679. He had been seriously ill since
October and apparently suffered a severe stroke one week before his
death. As the earl of Devonshire's secretary wrote to the Oxford
historian Anthony Wood, this prevented Hobbes from taking holy
communion: "but as I am informed by my Lords Chaplaine (a wor-

thy Gent) he has severall times lately received the Sacrament of him . . . And I did once see him receive it and received it my selfe with him, and then he tooke it with seemeing devotion, and in humble, and reverent posture."[103] Hobbes was buried at the parish church of Hault Hucknall, near Hardwick Hall, under a tombstone with a modest inscription, apparently written by Hobbes himself: "He was a virtuous man, and for his reputation for learning he was well known at home and abroad."[104] Rumor had it that he had also considered a different inscription, one that would have reminded those who knew him of one of his personal qualities which is too seldom mentioned, but which no reader of his works can fail to discover: his splendid sense of humor. The proposed inscription was "This is the true philosopher's stone."

NOTES

1 John Aubrey mistakenly claims that Hobbes's father was vicar of Westport (*Brief Lives*, vol. i, p. 323). Ecclesiastical records for 1602–3 describe him as curate of Brokenborough (Wiltshire Record Office, Trowbridge: Archdeaconry of Wiltshire, Act Books [Office], vol. 1 [formerly vol. 40], fos. 107ʳ, 132ᵛ, 177ʳ). The church at Brokenborough had been one of the most poorly equipped in 1553 (Nightingale, *Church Plate of Wiltshire*, p. 195), and in 1649 its tithes yielded an income of just £20 per annum (Bodington, "Church Survey of Wiltshire," p. 6).
2 Aubrey, *Wiltshire*, p. 235n. (where "1660" is a misprint for 1600); Aubrey, *Brief Lives*, vol. i, pp. 323–4, 387; Luce, "Malmesbury Minute Book," pp. 322, 325; Ramsay, ed., *Two Taxation Lists*, p. 48.
3 Edmund received a license to keep an alehouse in 1600 (Wiltshire Record Office, Trowbridge, Quarter Sessions, Criminal Business, 1598–1603, p. 20). Robert, possibly Edmund's son, is listed as an alehouse-keeper in 1620 (Williams, ed., *Tradesmen in Early-Stuart Wiltshire*, p. 30).
4 Wiltshire Record Office, Trowbridge: Archdeaconry of Wiltshire, Act Books (Office), vol. 1 (formerly vol. 40), fos. 107ʳ, 132ᵛ.
5 Wiltshire Record Office, Trowbridge, Episcopal Deposition Book (Instance), vol. 22b (1603–1603/4), fos. 19–20ʳ (first quotation), 48ᵛ (second quotation); Episcopal Act Book (Instance), vol. 33a, fos. 56a (inserted loose sheet), 73ʳ, 80ᵛ, 108ᵛ. See also Rogow, *Thomas Hobbes*, pp. 25–9.
6 Coote, H.C. *Practice of Ecclesiastical Courts* (London, 1847), p. 111; Cosins, *Apologie for Sundry Proceedings*, pp. 58–60; Consett, *Practice of Spiritual Courts*, pp. 41–2.
7 Aubrey, *Brief Lives*, vol. i, p. 387.

8 Ibid., vol. i, pp. 35, 324, 328–9, 332, 393 (where Aubrey calls Latimer "a good Graecian"); Wiltshire Record Office, Trowbridge: Bishops' Transcripts, Brokenborough, bundle 1, and Westport, bundle 1 (which includes elegant Latin tributes by Latimer to two dead parishioners).

9 Foster, *Alumni oxonienses*, entries in vols. ii, iii. The exact date of Hobbes's matriculation is not known; his autobiography states that it was during his fourteenth year (*Thomae Hobbes angli vita*, p. 1; *OL* vol. i, p. xiii), i.e., between April 1601 and April 1602. He adds, however, that he stayed at Oxford for five years (ibid.), and we know that he was admitted BA in February 1608. Aubrey says he entered Oxford "at fourteen yeares of age," and dates his arrival there, plausibly, to the beginning of 1603 (*Brief Lives*, vol. i, pp. 328, 330).

10 Hamilton, *Hertford College*, pp. 100–11; Curtis, *Oxford and Cambridge in Transition*, pp. 191–2. On the general differences between a hall and a college, see Fitzherbert, *Oxoniensis academiae descriptio*, p. 28.

11 Hobbes, *Thomae Hobbes angli vita*, p. 1 (*OL* I, xiii); *Thomae Hobbesii malmesburiensis vita*, p. 3 (*OL* I, lxxxvi–lxxxvii).

12 Hobbes, *AW*, p. 151.

13 L (1651 ed.), 370; *Aubrey on Education*, p. 61.

14 Gibson, ed., *Statuta universitatis oxoniensis*, pp. 389–90 (1564–5), 437 (1586). On the Aristotelian revival, see Kearney, *Scholars and Gentlemen*, pp. 81–3; Schmitt, "Philosophy and Science in Sixteenth-Century Universities"; Schmitt, *John Case*, pp. 13–76.

15 See Feingold, *Mathematicians' Apprenticeship*.

16 BL MS Harl. 6460, fos. 1ᵛ, 2ʳ. This oration, an attack on logic, seems also implicitly anti-Ramist; but the Ramist movement (which divided logic from rhetoric and asserted the primacy of the former) was also hostile to scholastic logic.

17 Cavendish proceeded MA (a privilege of nobility) in the summer of 1608, and Hobbes also incorporated at St. John's (which he was entitled to do as an Oxford BA): Foster, *Alumni oxonienses*. Payment for the November journey is recorded in Chatsworth, MS Hardwick 29, p. 38.

18 *Brief Lives*, vol. i, pp. 330–1.

19 The work is dedicated to Cavendish's brother-in-law Lord Bruce and can be confidently attributed to Cavendish both because of the wording of that dedication and in view of its later inclusion in *Horae subsecivae* (see below).

20 Malcolm, *De Dominis*, pp. 47–54.

21 Aubrey, *Brief Lives*, vol. i, pp. 70, 331; *HW* vol. vii, Letter 168.

22 Chatsworth, MS Hardwick 29, pp. 605, 633.

23 From the nature of the corrections in this MS, which are in another hand, it can be demonstrated that Hobbes was not the author of these

essays, as has sometimes been claimed: Hobbes was evidently transcribing from a rough draft that he sometimes misread. Although published anonymously, *Horae Subsecivae* is attributed to Cavendish in an early (c. 1657) library catalogue at Chatsworth, and the copy of the book in that library (pressmark 31 H) is inscribed "written by Candysh" ("Candish" was the seventeenth-century pronunciation of "Cavendish"). For other evidence confirming this attribution, see Bush, "Hobbes, Cavendish and 'Essayes'."

24 I am grateful to Noel Reynolds for allowing me to see details of a forthcoming study of this evidence by him and John Hilton.

25 See, for example, Brennan, ed., *Travel Diary*, p. 1.

26 Cavendish, *Horae subsecivae*, pp. 239, 267, 516–17 (civil war); 531 (law and reason); 541–2 (common law).

27 Richard Tuck, misled by the traditional but false belief that Hobbes and Cavendish began their European tour in 1610 (on which see Malcolm, *De Dominis*, p. 120, n. 280), has mistakenly identified the William Cavendish who was an MP for Derbyshire in 1614 as Cavendish's cousin, the future earl of Newcastle (*Philosophy and Government*, p. 281). Both Cavendishes were elected to this parliament: see Jansson, *Proceedings in Parliament, 1614*, pp. 447, 451. For the 1621 parliament, see Notestein, Relf, and Simpson, eds., *Commons Debates*, vol. ii, pp. 467, 482.

28 Gabrieli, "Bacone, la riforma e Roma."

29 This quotation is from a *consulto* (statement of advice to the Venetian government) of 1609: see Francescon, *Chiesa e stato nei consulti di Sarpi*, p. 121n. On Sarpi's theories of church and state, see also Ulianich, "Considerazioni per una ecclesiologia di Sarpi."

30 See Malcolm, *De Dominis*.

31 See Malcolm, "Hobbes, Sandys, and the Virginia Company."

32 *Thomae Hobbesii malmesburiensis vita*, p. 4 (*OL* I, p. lxxxviii). For a valuable discussion of Hobbes's translation of Thucydides, see Reik, *Golden Lands of Hobbes*, pp. 36–52.

33 See *HW* vol. vi, Letters 3–8.

34 Hobbes, *Thomae Hobbes angli vita*, p. 4 (*OL* I, xiv); Aubrey, *Brief Lives*, vol. i, p. 332 (where Aubrey's manuscript gives the name of the city as " . . . . . a").

35 Chatsworth, MS Hobbes D. 6, fo. 2^r.

36 See Harwood, ed., *Rhetorics of Hobbes and Lamy*; Strauss, *Political Philosophy of Hobbes*, pp. 35–42.

37 On Newcastle, Sir Charles Cavendish, and Robert Payne, see *HW* vol. vii, Biographical Register. On Warner, see ibid., vol. vi, Letter 16, n. 3. On the Welbeck circle and its connection with Warner and Hariot, see Kargon, *Atomism in England*, pp. 6–42.

38 A proposition about the angle of refraction, in Hobbes's hand but entitled "Mʳ Hobbes analogy" in Warner's hand, is in BL MS Add. 4395, fos. 131, 133.

39 On Great Tew, see especially Wormald, *Clarendon*; Trevor-Roper, *Catholics, Anglicans and Puritans*, pp. 166–230; and Hayward, "The *Mores* of Great Tew."

40 See *HW* vol. vi, Letter 11, n. 2.

41 Ibid., vol. vi, Letters 12–21.

42 Ibid., vol. vi, Letters 10, 12.

43 Ibid., vol. vi, Letter 18.

44 *Thomae Hobbes angli vita*, pp. 4–5 (*OL* I, xiv). For a brief reference to the contents of one such discussion, see *HW* vol. vi, Letter 34.

45 *HW* vol. vi, Letter 19, n. 4; Letters 20, 25.

46 Ibid., vol. vi, Letter 21.

47 Ibid., vol. vi, Letters 16, 25.

48 For a modern edition of this MS (BL MS Harl. 6796, fos. 297–308), see "Hobbes," *Court Traité des premiers principes*. For the attribution to Payne, see Tuck, "Hobbes and Descartes," pp. 16–18, and *HW* vol. vii, Biographical Register, "Payne."

49 For a modern edition of this MS (National Library of Wales, MS 5297), see Hobbes, *AW*, pp. 449–60. For previous datings, see Rossi, *Alle fonti del deismo*, pp. 120–3, and Pacchi, *Convenzione e ipotesi*, pp. 16–17. My reasons for dating it thus are given below.

50 For a modern edition of this MS (BL MS Harl. 6796, fos. 193–266), though omitting the diagrams, see Hobbes, "Tractatus opticus," ed. Alessio. For my reasons for this dating, see the section on "missing letters" in *HW* vol. vi, "Textual Introduction"; and see also Tuck, "Hobbes and Descartes."

51 Latin Optical MS, I. 3 (*TO* II, 148).

52 Tuck, "Hobbes and Descartes," pp. 19–20. That the Latin Optical MS was part of a larger project, of at least two "sections," is clear. But it is still unclear whether Hobbes was envisaging, from the outset, that this project would culminate in a treatise on politics. The account of the genesis of *The Elements of Law* given in the dedicatory epistle to that work (quoted below) makes it sound more of a *pièce d'occasion* than the neatly systematic retrospective explanation given in the preface to *De cive* (*HW* vol. ii, p. 82).

53 Aubrey, *Brief Lives*, vol. i, pp. 334–5, 351; *HW* vol. ii, p. 82.

54 *HW* vol. vi, Letters 29, 31–4.

55 Ibid., vol. vi, Letter 27.

56 Latin Optical MS, IV. 14 (Hobbes, "Tractatus opticus," ed. Alessio, p. 207).

57 *OL* V, pp. 249–74.

58 The best modern account is Sharpe, *Personal Rule of Charles I*, pp. 719–30.

59 On Hobbes's candidature, see *HW* vol. vi, Letter 58 n.2; for the speech in parliament by Sir John Strangways, see Cope and Coats, eds., *Proceedings of Short Parliament*, p. 159.

60 *EL* (Tönnies, ed.), p. xvii.

61 Ibid., II. 8. 8 (p. 138).

62 Hobbes, *Mr Hobbes Considered*, p. 5 (*EW* IV, 414).

63 See *HW* vol. vii, Biographical Register, "du Bosc."

64 Chatsworth, MS Hobbes D 8 (£100); MS Hardwick 30, half-yearly payments for midsummer 1638. In these accounts, which go up to Michaelmas 1639, Hobbes was also receiving wages of £50 per annum from the countess of Devonshire.

65 *HW* vol. vi, Letter 35 n. 5.

66 For a typical reaction, see Schino, "Tre lettere di Naudé," p. 707.

67 See *HW* vol. vii, Biographical Register, "Mersenne."

68 On Roberval see Auger, *Gilles Personne de Roberval*; on Gassendi, Abraham du Prat, Sorbière, and de Martel, see *HW* vol. vii, Biographical Register.

69 See Malcolm, "Hobbes's Science of Politics."

70 This MS was referred to above at n. 49. The English passage (from the introductory section of the MS: Hobbes, *AW*, 449) appears in Hobbes's "Answer" to the Preface to Gondibert (see Davenant, *Gondibert*, p. 49; *EW* vol. iv, p. 449). As Rossi noted, the MS also borrows a phrase from Sir Thomas Browne's *Religio medici*, which was published in London in 1642. If we assume that the English in the MS was Hobbes's own, an easy explanation of this link with Browne suggests itself: Sir Kenelm Digby, who had read Browne's book and written a reply to it in London in December 1642, returned to Paris in July 1643 and may well have brought a copy of *Religio medici* with him. That Hobbes should have begun drafting *De corp.* at about this time is also plausible, since he had been occupied with *De cive* in 1641 and with the *AW* in late 1642 and early 1643. However, the planning of *De corp.* was clearly more advanced by the time Sir Charles Cavendish took his notes on Hobbes's latest draft in 1645 (see below). Hence my dating of the National Library of Wales MS to 1643–4.

71 On these MSS, see Pacchi, *Convenzione e ipotesi*, pp. 18–26; for a composite printing of the two, see Hobbes, *AW*, pp. 463–513.

72 Halliwell, ed., *Collection of Letters*, p. 87; Vaughan, *Protectorate of Cromwell*, vol. ii, p. 364.

73 The MS, known as the English Optical MS, is BL MS Harl. 3360.

74 See *HW* vol. vii, Biographical Register, "William Cavendish, first Duke of Newcastle" and "Charles II."

75 See Davenant, *Gondibert*; *HW* vol. vii, Biographical Register, "Waller", "William Cavendish, third Earl of Devonshire", "Payne"; Hyde, *Brief View and Survey*, pp. 6–8.

76 Payne to Sheldon, May 13, 1650 (BL MS Harl. 6942, no. 128).

77 *HW* vol. vi, Letter 61; Hyde, *Brief View and Survey*, p. 7. In late September or early October 1649, Sir Charles Cavendish (who was now in Antwerp) received a letter from Hobbes, in which Hobbes made no reference to *Leviathan*, but said he hoped his "philosophie" (i.e., *De corpore*) would be printed in the following spring: BL MS Add. 4278, fo. 291^v (Cavendish to Pell, Oct. 5, 1649).

78 Hyde, *Brief View and Survey*, p. 7. It was in fact published in London in the following month. The printing had been rapid; the work was entered in the Stationers' Register on Jan. 20, 1651.

79 Hyde, *Brief View and Survey*, p. 8.

80 *HW* vol. vi, Letter 58.

81 *L*, 390.

82 *Mr Hobbes Considered*, p. 20 (*EW* IV, 420–1).

83 Ibid., p. 8 (*EW* IV, 415); Hyde, *Brief View and Survey*, pp. 8–9. See also the comments in *HW* vol. vii, Biographical Register, "James Butler, twelfth Earl and first Duke of Ormonde" and "Charles II."

84 Hyde recalled that Hobbes had fled a "few daies" before his own arrival in Paris, which was on Dec. 25 (*Brief View and Survey*, p. 8; Ollard, *Clarendon*, p. 148).

85 *HW* vol. vii, Biographical Register, "Sir Charles Cavendish."

86 See Malcolm, "Hobbes and the Royal Society," pp. 58–9.

87 *HW* vii, Biographical Register.

88 Isham, ed., *Correspondence of Duppa and Isham*, p. 41.

89 For the motion, see Shapiro, *Wilkins*, p. 97.

90 Wilkins and Ward, *Vindiciae academiarum*; Ward, *In Thomae Hobbii philosophiam exercitatio*. Ward's attack was less extreme than some others, however; he explicitly conceded (p. 340) that Hobbes was probably a theist.

91 See Malcolm, "Hobbes and the Royal Society"; for two important and rather different interpretations, see Skinner, "Thomas Hobbes and the Nature of the Early Royal Society" and Shaffer and Shapin, *Leviathan and the Air-Pump*.

92 For a useful general survey, see Mintz, *Hunting of Leviathan*.

93 BL MS Harl. 7257, p. 220. For the earlier rumor, see Aubrey, *Brief Lives*, vol. i, p. 339.

94 For the treatise on the law of heresy, see Mintz, "Hobbes on the Law of Heresy"; for its dating, see Willman, "Hobbes on the Law of Heresy." For the burning of manuscripts, see Aubrey, *Brief Lives*, vol. i, p. 339, and the letter from James Wheldon to Adam Barker printed in *The Gentleman's Magazine*, vol. 54, pt 2, no. 4 (Oct. 1784), p. 729.

95 For details of all these works, see Macdonald and Hargreaves, *Thomas Hobbes*.

96 See *HW* vol. vi, Letter 94, and my comments in the General Introduction to that volume.

97 Ibid., vol. vii, Biographical Register, "Charles II."

98 Ibid., vol. vii, Letter 208; Macdonald and Hargreaves, *Thomas Hobbes*, p. 29.

99 See their letters in *HW* vols. vi, vii, and the entries in the Biographical Register in ibid., vol. vii.

100 Ibid., vol. vi, Letters 67, 100, 108. Du Verdus also prepared a translation of *De corpore*, which was not published, and a partial one of *De cive*, which was: see ibid., vol. vii, Biographical Register, "du Verdus."

101 *HW* vol. vii, Letters 154, 156, 166, 169.

102 Ibid., vol. vii, Letter 189.

103 Pritchard, "Last Days of Hobbes," p. 184.

104 Aubrey, *Brief Lives*, vol. i, p. 386.

2 Hobbes's scheme of the sciences

More than once in his writings, Hobbes pronounced on the scope and organization of science. He had provocative views about the subjects that could be termed "scientific," about the scientific subjects that were basic, and about the relative benefits of the various sciences. Some of these views reflect his allegiance to the new mechanical philosophy and his opposition to Aristotelianism; others show the influence of Bacon, who was a virtuoso deviser of blueprints for science. Still others belong to a program of self-advertisement: Hobbes wished to be seen as an important scientist himself–an important worker in the field of optics and no less that the inventor of the science of politics. After expounding Hobbes's views about the organization of science and considering some of the problems they raise, I shall suggest that they throw light on old questions about what has been called "Hobbes's system."

THE ACCOUNT IN *DE CORPORE*

Hobbes turns to the organization of science in the preface to the 1647 edition of *De cive*; in *Leviathan*, ch. 9; and in several chapters of Part One of *De corpore*. In other places he broaches the subject in passing, for example, in the *The Six Lessons to the Professors of Geometry* (cf., e.g., *EW* VII, 225–6) and in *De homine* (Ep. Ded.); and there are many passages elsewhere that have implications for the question of what Hobbes takes to be a genuine science (e.g., *L*, chs. 5 and 46). But the principal discussion is in Part One of *De corpore*. It was here that Hobbes introduced his three-volume exposition of the elements of philosophy or science in general, and it was the natural place for Hobbes to identify the recognized sciences and to indicate

45

in a preliminary way how they went together. Again, Hobbes had the opportunity in Part One to present a considered theory of the structure of science, revising, if he wished to, the account that had appeared about five years earlier in *Leviathan*.

The sciences and the non-sciences

Part One of *De corpore* is a sequence of six chapters, and of these the first and last have a particular bearing on our concerns. Chapter 1 defines philosophy or science, explicates some of the terms used in that definition, and then comments on the purpose, utility, and subject-matter of science.

Article 8, on the "subject" of philosophy or science, that is, "the matter that [philosophy or science] treats of," uses the definition of philosophy or science to exclude certain branches of learning from science properly so-called. Theology is the first such branch of learning to be excluded, followed by "the doctrine of angels," civil and natural history, divine knowledge, false or doubtful doctrines or "divinations" such as astrology, and any teaching about God's worship. Hobbes's grounds for these exclusions imply that there are tensions between science, on the one hand, and, on the other, a long list of things: experience, faith, what is doubtful, what is false, the noncorporeal, and the uncaused.

Perhaps it is surprising that religion is not on this list. On the other hand, it is no accident that theology is the first of the would-be sciences to which Hobbes denies scientific status. Hobbes's motivation for excluding it is probably complex. By the time of *De corpore*, he had repeatedly denied in his political writings that churches or churchmen had authoritative views even about how to worship God or about the means to salvation. The point of these denials was to throw into doubt the moral authority of religious officials. But he also wanted to deny intellectual authority to churchmen and church institutions, in particular to the inquisition that had outlawed the writings of his hero, Galileo. In addition, there was an important anti-Aristotelian thrust to the exclusion of theology from the body of science. In Aristotle's scheme of the sciences, pride of place was given to the study of being in general, and theology – identified by Aristotle with metaphysics – was the leading branch of such study.[1] Hobbes always ridiculed the idea that existence could be understood on its own or in the abstract, without reference to the concept of body or location in space. In denying scientific status to theology or a doctrine of God's worship, Hobbes was probably influenced by all of these considerations. His claim is that theology does not have the right subject-matter to be studied scientifically, God being eternal, immutable, and uncaused. Perhaps Hobbes is also implying that neither theology nor the doctrine of God's worship can be "taught" in Hobbes's sense, that is, demonstrated step-by-step to an audience. He is not denying, however, that there can be knowledge with a divine source, or that this knowledge can be about God or salvation or anything else. He says that his definition of *philosophy* excludes such knowledge, not that there *is* no such knowledge.

For Hobbes to deny that something is a science, then, is not necessarily for him to deny that it is a field of knowledge. Nor does he deny that a non-science can promote science. He does not think that only charlatans or quacks practice the non-sciences. For example, when he denies history scientific status, he is not saying that it has no value to science. On the contrary, he says, echoing Bacon, that it is "most useful (nay necessary) to philosophy" (*EW* I, 10). A subject can be nonscientific and yet complement science or aid science. A subject that is nonscientific verges on being valueless only when, as in the case of astrology, it is neither a possible subject of knowledge, being false, nor a possible subject of causal reasoning leading to true and certain conclusions.

Chapter I of *De corpore* is more informative about what lies outside the body of science than about what lies within it. In addition to the list of non-sciences given in article 8, we are told in article 7 that many traditional works of ethics and politics convey no knowledge of any kind, let alone scientific knowledge. Article 7 implies that there are genuine sciences of geometry, mechanics, astronomy, and geography (*EW* I, 7), but does not indicate how they are organized. So it is a vague and unstructured scheme of sciences that Hobbes has presented when he turns in Chapter I of *De corpore* to the benefits of science and to the relative benefits of the two main branches of science, natural and civil.

The benefits of science

Hobbes's view of the benefits of science is unmistakably a scientistic one. Chapter I of *De corpore* implies that virtually all of the best things in life are due to science. The "chief commodities of which mankind is capable" and "the greatest commodities of mankind" are one and all the products of philosophy or science, and it is science alone – in the form of a truly scientific politics or ethics – that can save us from the greatest of avoidable calamities, namely civil war (EW I, 8). Indeed, since we risk losing everything, the commodities of natural science included, through not knowing how to avoid civil war, civil science has a strong claim to be supremely beneficial. It instructs us in things we need to know to do right, and it acts as a kind of insurance that we will continue to have a beneficial science and technology.

The organization of science

Chapter 6 of *De corpore* contains a survey of the genuine sciences and the order in which they should be studied if the elements of science are presented synthetically or in the order of demonstration. This is as close as Hobbes comes in his writings to a full-blown *theory* of the organization of science, and the theory, such as it is, is not very elaborate. There are in fact two similar accounts in Chapter 6, in articles 6 (EW I, 70–73) and 17 (EW I, 87). Both say that science starts from universal definitions. The things that can be demonstrated from such definitions alone constitute first philosophy. After first philosophy comes geometry, or the science that demonstrates the effects of simple motion. Mechanics, or the demonstration of effects due to whole bodies working on one another, comes next, followed by physics: the study of the invisible motions of the parts of bodies, including the effects in the senses of the motions of external bodies. Moral philosophy has to do with the internal effects of sense in the form of passions and voluntary actions. Finally, civil philosophy deduces rules of conduct that secure peace, rules that are able to be followed by creatures with our internal constitutions.

There are many problems of interpretation in connection with the detail of this account. For example, in articles 6 and 7, Hobbes seems both to assert and deny a dependence of moral philosophy on physics. Again, in different places he means different things by "moral philosophy." It is not always clear whether definition-making can be detached from the demonstration of the effects of motion, which makes it hard to know where first philosophy ends and geometry begins. The extent to which geometry and mechanics are autonomous of physics is unclear.[2] And so on. What can be said despite these uncertainties is that most of the sciences are sciences of motion – the apparent exceptions are first philosophy and perhaps civil philosophy – and the most fundamental science of motion is geometry.

Hobbes makes the body of science look remarkably unified and homogeneous in its emphasis on motion, and there is a very big simplification of Aristotle's tripartite division of science into theoretical, practical, and productive branches. Indeed, Hobbes's use of the concept of motion in Chapter 6 allows him to cut across not only Aristotle's tripartite division but also his own neo-Baconian division of the sciences into "natural" and "civil." Sciences on both sides of the natural/civil distinction lend themselves to description as sciences of motion, just as sciences on both sides of the distinction can be described as sciences of body. Whether Hobbes really succeeds in showing that all science has to do with body and motion, however, or whether he even intends to show this, given his consciousness of the differences between the subject-matters of natural and civil sciences, are doubtful matters, as we shall see later on.

THE ACCOUNT IN *LEVIATHAN*

In what ways does *De corpore* depart from claims in *Leviathan* about the content and organization of science? The account in *Leviathan* is in Chapter 9 (*EW* III, 71–3) and consists of three short paragraphs and a table. The main point in the text is that there are two kinds of knowledge, knowledge of fact and knowledge of consequences, registered by books of history and science, respectively. The table purports to record the sort of subjects that books of philosophy are devoted to. In fact, it excludes many subjects that books of philosophy, even books of the new philosophy of the seventeenth century, were devoted to. It excludes the ostensible subject of Descartes's *Meditations*, for example, and it excludes many books of traditional philosophy.

How far does the account in *Leviathan* anticipate that of *De corpore*? Not to any great degree. For one thing, the discussion in *De corpore* is geared to a much more elaborate definition of science or philosophy. In *Leviathan* science is knowledge of the consequences of affirmations; in *De corpore* it is knowledge of effects based on true reasoning from other knowledge of causes, or knowledge of causes based on true reasoning from knowledge of effects (*De Corp*. ch. 1, 2; *EW* I, 3). Second, *Leviathan* seems to exclude less from the scheme of the sciences than *De corpore* does: astrology is recognized as a science in *Leviathan*'s table of the sciences (*EW* III, 73). Third, and more significant, there are some curious assignments of the special sciences to one or another side of the *Leviathan*'s governing distinction between the sciences of natural bodies and the sciences of bodies politic. For example, first philosophy is said to be concerned with the consequences of quantity and motion in general, and not, as in other writings of Hobbes, with the consequences of definitions of the most general terms: 'time,' 'place,' 'body,' 'cause,' etc. So it is reckoned a branch of the science of natural bodies, and not a science preliminary to it. Again, first philosophy, geometry and arithmetic are separated in the table of the sciences from logic, which is classified as a highly derivative rather than a basic science, and as a branch of physics at that. Elsewhere in Hobbes's table there appears to be a double counting of the special sciences. If ethics, rhetoric, and what Hobbes calls "the science of just and unjust" are indeed branches of the science of natural bodies, as the diagram in Chapter 9 of *Leviathan* indicates, then what precisely is the make-up of the supposedly distinct branch of science dealing with "consequences from the accidents of *Politique* bodies"?

The table in Chapter 9 of *Leviathan* suggests a conception of the organization of science that is significantly different from that of *De corpore*, although a mere four years separates the publication dates of the two books. There is more continuity between Chapter 6 of *De corpore* and the Epistle to the Reader in the edition of *De cive* published nearly a decade earlier, in 1647. Hobbes describes there his plan of his trilogy and explains why the volume he had intended to publish last actually appeared before the other two. The passage that bears on our concerns (*HW*, p. 35) runs thus:

I was studying PHILOSOPHY for my minde sake, and I had gathered together its first Elements in all kinds, and having digested them into three Sections by degrees, I thought to have written them so as in the first I would have treated of a body, and its generall properties; in the second of man and his special faculties and affections; in the third, of civill government and the duties of Subjects: Wherefore the first section would have contained the first Philosophie, and certain elements of Physick; in it we would have considered the reasons of Time, Place Cause, Power, Relation, Proportion, Quantity, Figure, and motion. In the second we would have been conversant about imagination, Memory, intellect, ratiocination, appetite, Will, good and Evill, honest and dishonest, and the like; what this last section handles, I have now already shewed you.

This is much the same order of the sciences as one finds in *De corpore*: first philosophy, physics, and psychology, followed by the account of the duties of subjects. First philosophy is not part of or placed alongside physics, but is preliminary to natural science; and the concepts it deals with are not, as in *Leviathan*, quantity and motion simply, but cause, relation, and others.

To accept the account in *De corpore* as giving the official and authorized Hobbesian scheme of the sciences is one thing; to accept it as a defensible account of the structure of the sciences is quite another. There are internal difficulties for the account, especially in regard to understanding the relations there are supposed to be between natural and civil science, and between moral philosophy and physics specifically. I shall return to these presently. Difficulties also emerge when one asks whether Hobbes makes the domain of science too exclusive, even by the standards of a supporter of the new philosophy of the seventeenth century. To expose these difficulties it is useful to compare Hobbes's scheme of the sciences with those of two of Hobbes's contemporaries: Francis Bacon and René Descartes.

OTHER SCHEMES OF SCIENCE: BACON AND DESCARTES

Bacon's *The Advancement of Learning* (1603) predates *De corpore* by more than fifty years. It is no less committed to the reform of learning than Hobbes's writings, but it finds good things to say even about unreformed learning. For example, Bacon admits that such sciences as astrology, natural magic, and alchemy are tainted by credulity on the part of their practitioners, but, on the positive side, he points out that they have also generated some useful experiments.[3] More important, perhaps, he does not deny scientific status to natural magic; it is a science, indeed a science tied to the all-important knowledge of forms. Only it is a deficient science. There is a hugely elaborate branch of science or philosophy that Bacon calls "Human philosophy"[4] and that contains, as a branch of the study of the individual soul, "moral knowledge" and, as a separate branch, "civil knowledge." Although he found these parts of learning underdeveloped and sometimes virtually untouched, Bacon did not dismiss them as utterly prescientific. He also recognized a Divine science or philosophy, defined as such knowledge of God as can be derived from contemplating his characteristics. Not only is this a fully fledged science, according to Bacon, but, virtually alone among the rest of the sciences, it is not deficient.[5]

Is Bacon willing to recognize a wide range of sciences because he is willing to treat just any branch of learning as science? Not at all. He distinguishes history in all its forms from science, and he keeps history and science well apart from poetry. He also recognizes a large body of "Divine learning," including church history, the parables, and Holy doctrine, which occupies a place in the overall scheme of learning alongside natural or divine philosophy.

Hobbes appears to have taken over from Bacon the history/science distinction, but not the tolerant view of natural or civil science to be found in *The Advancement of Learning*. Perhaps Hobbes can also be criticized for producing an overly streamlined scheme of the sciences. *De corpore* fails to mention medicine, even though Harvey is one of the pioneers of the new science praised in the *De corpore*'s epistle dedicatory (*EW* I, viii). Medicine is also left out of the table of the sciences in *Leviathan*. And while civil philosophy is mentioned and even described in some detail in some of Hobbes writing on the organization of science, it is hard not to read Bacon's description of the part of philosophy called "civil knowledge" without concluding that Bacon had thought much more deeply about the limits of the relevant subject matter. Bacon's taxonomy of human learning may be excessively intricate, but at least it finds a place for all of the sciences one might expect to see mentioned, while some of its detail comes of an attempt to be explicit about how far the various sciences had come and what they had still to do.

Descartes's description of the scheme of the sciences comes from the preface to the French edition of the *Principles of Philosophy* (1647).

The first part of philosophy is metaphysics, which contains the principles of knowledge, including the explanation of the principal attributes of God, the non-material nature of our souls and all the clear and distinct notions which are in us. The second part is physics, where, after discovering the true principles of material things, we examine the general composition of the entire universe and then, in particular, the nature of this earth and all the bodies which are commonly found upon it, such as air, water, magnetic ore and other minerals. Next we need to examine individually the nature of plants, of animals and, above all, of man, so that we may be capable later on of discovering the other sciences which are beneficial to man. Thus the whole of philosophy is like a tree. The roots are metaphysics, the trunk is physics, and the branches emerging from the trunk are all the other sciences, which may be reduced to the three principal ones, namely medicine, mechanics, and morals. By 'morals' I understand the highest and most perfect moral system, which presupposes a complete knowledge of the other sciences and is the ultimate level of wisdom.[6]

This is not utterly different from Hobbes's own scheme, but there are major areas of disagreement nonetheless.

The most important of these has to do with the science placed by Descartes at the foundation of philosophy: metaphysics. The subject matter that Descartes assigns to it is expressly excluded from philosophy by Hobbes, excluded by definition. God is incomprehensible and uncaused, and therefore excluded twice over from scientific study. Similarly excluded is any supposedly immaterial human soul. This means that the *Meditations* and Part One of the *Principles* would not have counted as specimens of philosophy for Hobbes. Again, since philosophy in general, and not just physics, is concerned with body for Hobbes, the transition Descartes describes from metaphysics to physics would not have made sense to him. Neither would Descartes's separation of the sciences of man from physics. It is true that, in presenting the elements of philosophy, Hobbes did devote separate "sections" to body and man, apparently mirroring Descartes's scheme. The divisions between body and man do not, however, separate physics from another science. The published version of the section on man, *De homine*, starts with optics, which falls within Hobbes's science of physics, and goes on to discuss matters to do with the passions and good and evil. This means that *De homine* contains some physics and some philosophical psychology continuous with physics. In Descartes, because physics is the study of material things and because human beings are composites of material and immaterial substance, there is no making the sciences of man into mere sub-departments of physics, although they depend on physics. The repeated references to the soul in Descartes' writings about human perception, emotion, and so on would probably have excluded them from science in Hobbes's sense. Even Gassendi's writings on these matters probably present as philosophy material that is disallowed by Hobbes's definition of philosophy,[7] and this despite the fact that Gassendi is another of the founders of genuine science or philosophy mentioned in the Epistle dedicatory of *De corpore* (*EW* I, 9).

What about "morals" in Descartes's sense? Is this another specimen of learning that Hobbes cannot or will not countenance as science? It is hard to be absolutely sure, since very little of this branch of philosophy was developed by Descartes during his lifetime. What can be said is that, like the psychology on which it was intended to draw, it, too, is infected by Descartes's immaterialism, by his commitment to the existence of souls as well as bodies. Hobbes could not have regarded it as a properly scientific ethics.

INTERNAL TENSIONS IN HOBBES'S ACCOUNT

Hobbes's scheme of the sciences may exclude too much, and his description of it may not be explicit enough about where some undoubted sciences, such as medicine, fit into the whole. There are also difficulties in understanding how Hobbes thinks the different sciences depend on one another, in particular how he thinks civil philosophy depends on the natural sciences that lead up to it in the order of teaching the elements of science in general.

Civil philosophy: autonomous or dependent?

In Chapter 6, article 7 of *De corpore*, Hobbes comments on the account he has just given in article 6 of the "synthetical" order of teaching or demonstrating the sciences.[8] His account in article 6 calls for the sort of teaching that starts in geometry and physics and ends in "moral philosophy" (the study of those internal motions of appetite and aversion and related passions) and civil science (the science of citizenly duty and sovereign prerogative). In article 7, he notes that the motions discussed by what he is calling "moral philosophy" are also accessible in a different way, which makes civil science in turn accessible without a grounding in any prior sciences:

Civil and *moral philosophy* do not so adhere to one another, but that they may be severed. For the causes of the motions of the mind are known, not only by ratiocination, but also by the experience of everyman that takes the pains to observe these motions within himself. And, therefore, not only they that have attained the knowledge of the passions and perturbations of the mind, by the *synthetical method*, and from the very first principles of philosophy, may by proceeding in the same way, come to the causes and necessity of constituting commonwealths, and to get the knowledge of what is natural right, and what are civil duties; and, in every kind of government, what are the rights of commonwealth, and all other knowledge appertaining to civil philosophy; for this reason, that . . . they also that have not learned the first part of philosophy, namely, *geometry* and *physics*, may, notwithstanding, attain the principles of civil philosophy, by the *analytical method*, (*EW* I, 73–4)

Hobbes then describes how, by analysis of the concept of justice into the concept of fact against law, law into command of someone with coercive power, coercive power into power conferred by the wills of those wishing to avoid war, and will to avoid war into the passions of fear of encroachment and death, an enquirer would quickly become acquainted with precisely those motions of the mind that moral philosophy, from a starting point in physics, presents as the foundations of politics.

Hobbes's claim that the principles of civil philosophy are accessible from a starting point in acquaintance with the passions, and not only from a starting point in the prior sciences, may be regarded as the claim that civil philosophy enjoys a certain autonomy in the scheme of the sciences. Civil philosophy may seem to depend on the other sciences, but that is an impression created by approaching civil philosophy by the method of synthesis. Anther, analytic method, just as scientific as the synthetic one, provides a shorter route, through the experience of certain passions, to the principles of civil philosophy.[9] This shorter route bypasses the sciences.

Hobbes said something similar in the Epistle dedicatory of *De cive* in 1647 when he was explaining how it was possible for the third section of his *Elements of philosophy* to be understood by readers who had no first and second sections to prepare them for it. The reason the third section section could be approached without preliminaries was that the doctrine of *De cive* was grounded on its own principles, sufficiently known from experience (*EW* II, xx).

Passages like these suggest that, while the truths of civil philosophy may depend on truths that are explained by physics and geometry, *knowledge* of the truths of civil philosophy does not depend on knowledge of physics and geometry, and can indeed be acquired on the basis of a certain self-knowledge, or acquaintance, with human passions in oneself. Hobbes is making this point in his preface to *Leviathan* when he explains how the doctrine spelt out there can be known to be true: all one need do is "read oneself" (*EW* III, xi).

'Motion' and civil philosophy

Is there a significant dependence of civil philosophy on various sciences of motion even when civil philosophy is approached by the synthetic method? Hobbes certainly gives that impression in Chapter 6 of *De corpore* when he connects knowledge of the principles of politics with knowledge of the motions of the typical human mind. But he never shows in his political writings that it is important to know the motions of the mind – the passions – *as* motions of the mind in order to understand the principles of politics. It seems doubtful that any inkling of the supposed mechanical nature of the passions is in fact necessary for grasping the politics. What one needs to know to get political knowledge is that the passions can cause people to go after the same thing; that they lead people to overvalue their intellectual and bodily prowess; that in some people certain passions lead them ruthlessly to appropriate a very large share of goods if there is nothing to stop them; that in the absence of the state there is nothing to stop them; and that there is nothing irrational in acting like them if otherwise they will take your goods and your life. These facts about the passions, taken together with the postulate of the right of nature, help to show people why the state is necessary and why the powers of the sovereign have to be extensive. But the statement of these facts does not draw at all on mechanics, and someone could take in these facts and not know or believe that most passions were species of appetite and aversion mechanistically understood. The idea that Hobbes aimed at stating a "politics of motion" in a pointed sense of mechanistic politics, although it is occasionally encouraged by what Hobbes writes about the scheme of the sciences, and by his insertion of a mechanistic theory of the passions into two of the three major political treatises, does not really stand up to inspection.[10] Indeed, it is significant that the one political treatise in which psychology is absent, namely *De cive*, was always Hobbes's preferred statement of his civil science.

Methodological unity?

Did Hobbes believe that civil philosophy depended on sciences like physics, mechanics, and geometry in the sense that it borrowed its *methods* from these prior sciences? Part One of *De corpore* may once again leave the reader with the impression that the answer is "Yes." The subject matter of science or philosophy is bodies, and of these

two chief kinds of bodies, and very different from one another, offer themselves to such as search after their generation and properties; one whereof being the work of nature, is called a *natural body*, the other is called a *commonwealth*, and is made by the wills and agreements of men. And from these spring the two parts of philosophy, called *natural* and *civil*. (*EW* I, 11).

Natural and civil philosophy are the two chief parts of philosophy, and there is supposed to be a parallel between them. Although the bodies each studies are "very different from one another, "they are for all that bodies, and bodies that have discoverable causes or generations–hence things of which scientific knowledge is possible. No less than natural philosophy, Hobbes seems to be saying, civil philosophy is concerned with the generations and properties of bodies.

Now in *De corpore* the concepts of body, property, and generation are much better defined for natural bodies than for bodies politic or commonwealths. For instance, a body is something that can be conceived of taking up space and having an existence without the mind (*EW* I, 102), while the property of a body is an appearance that a body presents to the senses that allows that body to be distinguished from others (*EW* I, 5). These senses of "body" and "property" are plainly designed for the natural body, as is "generation" in the sense of a "whole progress of motions from an initial change of place to some sensory effect." Did Hobbes mean them to apply to bodies politic? Did Hobbes mean the analogy to go further, so that a causal inquiry into the causes of the properties of a body politic resembles a causal inquiry into the properties of a natural body?[11]

According to this suggestion, one starts with a conception of a "whole" body, either a natural body or an artificial body like a commonwealth; one then takes notice of its "parts" or properties; by the method of analysis or resolution one arrives at the causes of the properties; and from the causes of the properties one reconstructs or "composes" in reasoning the "whole" one began with, the whole thereupon becoming more intelligible than it was initially. Although there is one passage in the preface to the 1647 edition of De cive (EW II, xiv) indicating that in civil philosophy Hobbes aimed at making a whole intelligible, the process is likened by Hobbes to what has to be done to understand a watch – an artificial body, rather than to what has to be done to understand a natural body.[12] There are echoes of this analogy between the state and an artifact in the Introduction to Leviathan, where the commonwealth is compared to an artificial man. Again, the fact that Hobbes was out to show how a state ought to be constructed to last, and not how a short-lived actual state is in fact constructed, throws doubt on the suggestion that even in politics he was out to reconstruct appearances from their causes. He was, on the contrary, as he often pointed out, intent on showing how to devise a form of state that was a great improvement upon, and therefore very different from, any that might be observed. The pattern of rights and duties he deduced from the goal of the commonwealth had yet to be acknowledged, he wrote in Leviathan (L, ch. 20; EW III, 195). Indeed, the disanalogies between the official method of natural science and the official method of civil science, as well as between Hobbes's practice in natural philosophy and his practice as a scientist of politics, reinforce his distinction between natural and civil science.[13]

THE ELEMENTS OF PHILOSOPHY AND
HOBBES'S "SYSTEM"

Hobbes's ideas about the scheme of the sciences were developed in order to systematize the "elements" of science as a whole. He did not regard himself as the inventor of all of these elements. The geometry in De corpore, as well as much of the mechanics and astronomy, not to mention the project of an "Elements" of philosophy, was openly based on Euclid, Galileo, and others.[14] What he claimed as his own were the optics at the beginning of De homine, the chapters on the dispositions and manners of men at the end of *De homine*, the elements of civil philosophy, and of course the framework in which the whole was presented, the framework constituted by the concepts of the first philosophy (Part Two of *De corpore*), the scheme of the sciences, and the definition of science. The fact that the Hobbesian elements of the elements of science occupy a good deal of Hobbes's trilogy should not lead anyone to take the trilogy as an exposition of Hobbes's own system. It is better regarded as Hobbes's systematization of selections from the new science, with his own contributions emphasized so as to underline the claim he makes at the beginning of the trilogy (*EW* I, ix) and elsewhere (*EW* VII, 333) that he was one of the major contributors to the new science. The trilogy being partly an exercise in publicizing Hobbes's own scientific credentials, it is not surprising that it is incomplete as a survey of the new science. The trilogy is also far from being a seamless presentation of the elements, with large discontinuities within at least one of the sections (*De homine*) as well as between them. On the other hand, the fact that the "elements of science" were only partly Hobbes's own raises the question of whether he had an intellectual vision of his own that was comprehensive enough, orderly enough, and sufficiently unified to be called a "system."

Hobbes was a materialist, but did he have a materialist system? He believed that the genuine sciences employed the "methods" of analysis and synthesis, but does this methodological thesis confer unity on his thought? Perhaps it is his conception of philosophy that unifies his thought[15] or, more generally, his theory of reasoning; perhaps it is the style of his repudiation of Aristotelianism.[16] All of these suggestions have something to be said for them, but they probably overestimate the extent to which Hobbes's project of presenting the elements of science was a project of presenting *his* science. It is from the beginning of trilogy that most of the evidence about the character of Hobbes's system is derived, and yet in a certain sense it is at the beginning of the trilogy that its contents are most borrowed. It is true that *De corpore*, *De homine*, and *De cive* were his books, but to the extent that they introduced the reader to the science Hobbes approved of they were only partly introducing the reader to Hobbes's thought; and to the extent that they only introduced the reader to Hobbes's thought, they did not present a very coherent or seamless system of the elements of science. Outside the trilogy, Hobbes's publications certainly mark him out as a systematic writer, but the scientific elements of that writing that are his own do not amount to a total system, and there is much in his output that is not science at all.

Perhaps the right way of getting Hobbes the systematic philosopher into perspective is by reference once again to Bacon and Descartes. Virtually all of the branches of science that Bacon described in *The Advancement of Learning* were supposed to be "deficient" or underdeveloped in some way: Bacon's purpose was to outline the work that an army of investigators, equipped with the right method, had before them if they were to make the sciences progress over a long period into the future. By contrast, Descartes's views about the organization of science were views about a readily completed Cartesian science. He did not believe that all science had to take shape slowly, still less that it depended for its development on a large scientific community with unlimited time and resources. On the contrary, he claimed that with far less than huge sums of money and time for experiments he would have presented a finished philosophy himself. He believed that he had set out the required metaphysics and at least the most general parts of physics; and it is clear from the *Discourse* and other writings that he took himself to have made headway with medicine, mechanics, and morals and the explanation of a lot of particular phenomena in physics.

Hobbes is closer to Bacon than to Descartes. Like Bacon, he thought that science was a communal enterprise, and that it brought together the results of many people over generations. Again like Bacon, he believed that he had the skills to present an overview of the different sectors of science as a whole, at least what had so far developed of it. But the task he undertook was not quite the Baconian one of making a massive report on the progress of learning up to his own day: it was the different one of reducing the mass of existing science to its elements and presenting them so that they could be taken in by others. On the other hand, and now like Descartes, Hobbes believed that he had developed, and even invented, major branches of science. To the extent he had a system it consisted of the systematic presentation of his own contributions to the sciences.[17] The larger system of the new science went far beyond that, and so did its "elements."

NOTES

1 See Aristotle, *Metaphysics* VI, 1.
2 See W. Sacksteder, "Three Diverse Sciences in Hobbes," 739–72.
3 F. Bacon, *Works*, J. Spedding and R. Ellis, eds. (London: Longman, 1858), vol. 3, p. 249.
4 Ibid., p. 367.
5 Ibid., p. 350.
6 *AT* IXB, 14; *CSM* I, 186.
7 See my "17th c Materialism: Gassendi and Hobbes."
8 For useful commentary in this connection, see D.W. Hanson, "The Meaning of 'Demonstration' in Hobbes's Science," 639–74.
9 For a recent account of the relevant notions of analysis and synthesis, see Richard A. Talaska, "Analytic and Synthetic according to Hobbes," 207–37.
10 As even those who emphasize mechanism in Hobbes's philosophy concede: "Hobbes's natural philosophy cannot provide the content of his political theory." See T. Spragens, *The Politics of Motion*, p. 167.
11 The suggestion is associated with *Hobbes's System of Ideas* (London: Hutchinson, 1965), chs. 3 and 4.
12 For an illuminating discussion of the passage from *De cive* in the context of Hobbes's general theory of science, see N. Malcolm, "Hobbes's Science of Politics and his Theory of Science," pp. 145–57.
13 See my *Hobbes*, ch. 2, and "The Science in Hobbes's Politics" in G.A.J. Rogers and A. Ryan, eds., *Perspectives on Thomas Hobbes* (Oxford: Clarendon Press, 1988), pp. 67–80. For a recent and opposed account, see the chapter on Hobbes in R. Woolhouse's excellent *The Empiricists* (Oxford: Oxford University Press, 1988).
14 For Hobbes's modeling of his Elements on Euclid's *Elements* and much else on his system of the sciences, see G. Boss, "Systeme et rupture chez Hobbes," 215–23.
15 See Michael Oakeshott's Introduction to *Leviathan* in his *Hobbes on Civil Association*.
16 See Spragens, *Politics of Motion*, ch. 1.
17 For an interpretation that stresses the importance of *Leviathan* and *De corpore* as vehicles for Hobbes's system, see G. Herbert, *Thomas Hobbes*.

3 First philosophy and the foundation of knowledge

Hobbes's philosophical project is bound up with a rational reconstruction of knowledge. At what point did this reconstruction become associated with a first philosophy that was intended to expli-
cate the most basic concepts and principles of knowledge? Did the
development of the first philosophy coincide with the formulation,
at the end of 1636 or the beginning of 1637, of a complete system of
philosophy: *corpus, homo, civis*,[1] which was to lead to *Elementa
philosophiae*,[2] or did it come later? Did the first philosophy have
something to do with the logic that Hobbes was questioned about in
Kenelm Digby's letters?[3] It is difficult to give firm answers to these
questions because the dating of the manuscripts marking the successive stages of the composition of the first philosophy is for the most
part uncertain.[4]

However the idea of a first philosophy dawned on Hobbes, the
content and function of this subject are clear. Long before the completion of *De corpore* (1655), the *Anti-White* (1643) had defined the
term "first philosophy" and had specified the purpose and scope of
this branch of learning. The threefold definition was spelt out with
reference to Aristotle. Criticizing White's thesis that philosophy
should not be treated according to a method of logic, Hobbes writes,

Now, philosophy is the science of all general and universal theorems, concerning any subject the truth of which can be demonstrated by natural
reason. Its first part, and the basis of all the other parts, is the science where
theorems concerning the attributes of being at large are demonstrated, and
this science is called *First Philosophy*. It therefore deals with being, essence,
matter, form, quality, cause, effect, motion, space, time, place, vacuum,
unity, number, and all the other notions which Aristotle discusses partly in

62

the eight books of his *Lectures on physics* and partly in those other books which some subsequently called *Tôn metà tà physiká* (wherefrom *First Philosophy* got its present name *Metaphysics*).[5]

If in this passage philosophy in general is defined simply by reference to the type of proposition it bears upon and by the faculty of mind it brings into play, irrespective of its purpose or methods, first philosophy and its status are, by contrast, precisely delimited. First, it is concerned with attributes of being in general. These attributes are more or less a throwback to Aristotle's categories.[6] Second, its purpose is to provide a foundation for the other sciences, such as physics, ethics, and politics, that deal with particular existents.[7]

When Hobbes speaks of first philosophy in the *Anti-White*, he refers to Aristotle and his doctrine of the different senses of being. But in 1643 the use and meaning of the terms "first philosophy" had also to be understood in relation to Descartes because two years earlier Hobbes had read Descartes's *Meditationes de prima philosophia* and had prepared a set of Objections. Not that Hobbes's first philosophy resembled Descartes's in content. On the contrary, Descartes's three fundamental propositions – of the immateriality of the soul, the existence of God (in the sense of the demonstrations that Descartes gives of it), and the distinction between mind and body – were all targets of Hobbes's criticisms in the *Third Objections*. Thus, Hobbes denied that there was an ego that grasped its own existence by means of an intellectual "intuition." He insisted that *res cogitans* had to be conceived as a corporeal or material thing. Finally, there couldn't be a proof of the existence of God that proceeded from an idea of God, for we simply have no such idea.[8] Differing clearly from Descartes, Hobbes distances himself still further from those who think that first philosophy is some sort of supernatural science. Scipion Dupleix in particular had given the name "first philosophy" or "first science" to metaphysics, "inasmuch as it considers primary being, the being of beings, the primary causes and principles of things: which, on account of the excellence of its subject matter, is the first of all the sciences."[9] But to define first philosophy in this way as a science above nature is, for Hobbes, to corrupt the sense of the term as well as to give a bad interpretation of the term "metaphysics."[10] It is in these terms that *De corpore* would exclude from the subject matter of philosophy the doctrine of the nature and attributes of God as well as whatever proceeds from revelation. These matters are excluded because they do not lend themselves to the application of natural reason.[11]

Two questions are bound to arise from all this. To begin with, is Hobbes's first philosophy a reversion to Aristotle's, since it refers to Aristotle's physics and metaphysics, and since it parts company so decisively with Descartes? Second, since Hobbes refuses to recognize a first philosophy in the sense of a science that transcends nature, and since he excludes knowledge of God's nature from the scope of philosophy, does it follow that he had emancipated himself entirely from theology? These questions, which are a way of asking how modern and how coherent Hobbes's first philosophy is, lead us to a detailed investigation of the workings of the first philosophy. Before embarking on this investigation, it is important to call attention to the two principal tasks assigned by *De corpore* to first philosophy: (1) to arrive at the most general and universal concepts in use in science; and (2) to state definitions of these concepts that are capable of serving as principles for all the special sciences.[12]

Exactly which highly general concepts are defined by first philosophy, and which philosophical operations do these definitions bring into play? How far does first philosophy discharge its duty of providing foundations? Can it provide a foundation for an ethical and political doctrine as readily as it provides one for a mechanistic physics? We shall see that the answer to these questions is not straightforward and that the task of providing foundations calls upon resources that appear to be far removed from those of first philosophy. In order to make a wide-ranging investigation orderly,[13] we shall conduct it under the following headings: (a) the content of the first philosophy: the principles of a foundation of knowledge; (b) the limits of application of the concepts of first philosophy: the unfinished foundation; and (c) the return of theology: the foundation divided.

THE CONTENT OF FIRST PHILOSOPHY: THE
PRINCIPLES OF A FOUNDATION OF KNOWLEDGE

In Chapter 6 of *De corpore*, entitled *"De methodo,"* Hobbes identified two characteristics of the simplest and most universal concepts applied in human knowledge or science. On the one hand, these concepts can be arrived at by applying an analytical method that consists of resolving complex ideas into their elements; on the other hand, these concepts are common to ideas of singular things. Hobbes also believed that these concepts could be defined. But if definition requires that the terms of the definition are more simple and universal than the terms being defined, it is hard to see how the concepts that are the most universal and simple of all are open to definition. Hobbes recognized this difficulty and tried to overcome it by distinguishing between two types of definition: a genetic definition, which provides the cause of whatever is being defined; and what he calls a definition by circumlocution, which does no more than evoke in the mind a clear idea of what is signified by the term being defined.[14] It is the second sort of definition that is applied to the concepts treated by first philosophy.

Which concepts belong to first philosophy? And isn't some sort of choice about the nature of existence and knowledge involved in Hobbes's candidates for the basic concepts? In fact, at different stages the first philosophy makes use of many different kinds of basic concepts and philosophical operations. We shall confine ourselves to the five first pairs of concepts: space/time, body/accident, cause/effect, power/act (a differentiation of the cause/effect distinction), and identity and difference.[15] The definition of these five pairs of concepts involves four operations: the working out of a distinction between a subjective and an objective order, the working out of a distinction between being and ways of being, the establishment of a deterministic system, and the dismantling of a metaphysical principle of individuation.

The distinction between subjective and objective

We saw earlier that for reasons that distinguish his approach from Descartes's, Hobbes has no theory of the spiritual subject. On the other hand, he does have a theory of subjectivity, or, more precisely, a theory of subjective appearance without a spiritual subject, a theory within a larger theory of representation or phantasm.[16] Against this background, to distinguish between the subjective and the objective is to distinguish what belongs to an appearance from what belongs to the thing it is an appearance of. To effect this separation, Hobbes's first philosophy begins with a thought experiment: the imagined annihilation of the world.[17] This fiction permits

Hobbes to show not only that the whole range of sensible qualities (or at least those known as the "secondary qualities") belong to the sensing subject and not to the things themselves, but also, and more important, that the concepts of space and time are subjective. The hypothesis of the annihilated world assumes two things: that there once existed a world in which events took place, and that there continues to exist a subject who perceived this world and the events that took place in it. The point of the hypothesis can be put by asking what the surviving man can talk about and represent to himself once the world is destroyed. Hobbes's answer:

> I say, therefore, there would remain to that man idea of the world, and of all bodies as he had, before their annihilation, seen with his eyes, or perceived by any other sense; that is to say, the memory and imagination of magnitudes, motions, sounds, colours, &c, as also of their order and parts. All of which things, though they be nothing but ideas and phantasms, happening internally to him that imagineth; yet they will appear as if they were external, not at all depending on any power of the mind.[18]

One can see how the annihilation hypothesis differs from Cartesian doubt. In its content the hypothesis throws no doubt on the existence of the world: On the contrary, what is supposed to remain once the world is destroyed is supposed to show that the world once existed even if it doesn't exist any longer according to the terms of the hypothesis. The hypothesis is not intended to help us to reach an indubitable truth about the subject of thought, but a truth about the structure and content of our representations. Thus, the contents of phantasms or appearances can be considered "either as internal accidents of our mind, in which manner we consider them when the question is about some faculty of the mind; or as a species of external things, not as really existing, but appearing only to exist, or to have a being without us."[19]

In the *Anti-White* the annihilation hypothesis is meant to throw light on limits of the human ability to retain images of objects currently absent or to remember the appearance of a man who is now long since dead.[20] Yet in arriving at these limits, Hobbes establishes that space and time are, in his terms, "imaginary": They belong to what appears to the perceiving or sensing subject and not to the real thing that exists outside us. Thus space is the image or phantasm of a body.[21] Or, as *De corpore* puts it, "space is the phantasm of a thing existing without the mind simply: that is to say, that phantasm, in which we consider no other accident, but only that it appears without us."[22] In the same way, time is the phantasm of motion: "what then can days, months, and years, be, but names of such computations made in our mind? *Time* therefore is a phantasm, but a phantasm of motion."[23] It is important to appreciate that space and time are not particular phantasms among others, but belong to the form of our knowledge of existing and changing things. As time and space depend on our faculty of thinking, one can legitimately speak of the ideality of space and time; on the other hand, this ideality clearly has nothing transcendental about it; space and time have as correlates objectively existing objects, and are caused by the extension and motion of bodies.[24] In its treatment of space and time, the first philosophy establishes the dual order of thing and appearance that one finds throughout Hobbes's work.

Existents and modes of existence

The first philosophy now goes on to establish the real distinction between body and accident. It is from the angle of this distinction that one is able to judge the extent to which Hobbes reinterprets Aristotelian metaphysical concepts,[25] beginning with a double sense of "exist." Things can exist either as bodies or as accidents.

The second stage of the first philosophy begins with the supposition of the re-creation of one of the things from the previously annihilated world.[26] This newly re-created or replaced thing is subject to a number of different appellations or names, each indicating ways in which its existence can be considered.

Hoc autem ipsum est quod appellari solet, propter extensionem quidem, *corpus*; propter independentiam autem a nostra cogitatione *subsistens per se*; et propterea quod extra nos subsistit, *existens*; denique quia sub spatio imaginario substerni et supponi videtur, ut non sensibus sed ratione tantum aliquid ibi esse intelligatur, *suppositum* et *subjectum*. Itaque definitio corporis hujusmodi est, *corpus est quicquid non dependens a nostra cogitatione cum spatii parte aliqua coincidit vel coextenditur.*[27]

The names that express the conception of the newly created thing are either to do with independence from our thought or existence outside us (*subsistens per se, existens*), or else coincidence or coextension with a part of space (*suppositum, subjectum*). These seem to be distinct aspects of the thing, and yet both find their way into the definition of *body*: "*corpus est quicquid non dependens a nostra cogitatione cum spatii parte aliqua coincidit vel coextenditur.*" It is hard to tell from *De corpore* whether the definition of *body* results from a simple adding together of the two aspects, or whether the identification of existent with body is taken for granted from the start. It tells in favor of the latter suggestion that the first name given to the re-created thing is, in virtue of its extension, *corpus*. So the interchangeability of *ens* and *corpus* might have been assumed from the outset. Is there anything to justify the running together of existent and body?

Although the question is not taken up in *De corpore*, it appears to be anticipated in Chapter 27 of the *Anti-White*. Hobbes distinguishes there between two types of existent:

Two kinds of *ens* are recognised. There are the *entia* of which we form an image in the mind. For example, we can imagine a man, an animal, a tree, a stone, in fact any body at all (since the image we conceive of every body is space, a space of a given kind or size corresponding to a body of a given kind or size). There are other *entia* of which we have no picture in the mind, so that a man is quite unable either to perceive them or to imagine them. God and the angels, the good as well as the evil, can be neither conceived nor understood within our imagination. So God is very good, very great, and cannot be understood; neither he nor any angel can have dimensions, or can be circumscribed, either in the whole or in part, by space, not even in the mind.[28]

Since philosophy cannot take into account things that surpass human understanding, the only kind of existent it *can* consider is *ens imaginabile*, the thing we can conceive or imagine. But *ens imaginabile* is nothing other than *id omne quod occupat spatium*,[29] i.e., whatever occupies space. The space in question is imaginary space, which therefore determines what can be represented or understood by us. We have before us a rationale for the identification of *ens* (in the sense of *ens imaginabile*) and *corpus*, and so the interchangeability of the corresponding terms is not simply a matter of stipulation. As Hobbes puts it in the *Anti-White*, "From this definition it appears that *ens* and *body* are the same, for the same definition is universally accepted for 'body'; hence the *ens* under discussion we shall always refer to as 'body', and this is the word we shall use."[30]

Along with the doctrine of accidents, the sense of *esse* preoccupies Hobbes.[31] The modes of being and of being known that belong to body are connected in both *De corpore* and the *Anti-White* to the theory of the proposition, that is, to the theory of the way we say things: "When, for instance, we say: 'man is an animal', those who query the truth of what is said must enquire not only what 'man' and 'animal' are the names of, but also what that 'to be an animal' (*esse animal*) is the name of, in order to know what is meant by this conjunction with the word 'is.' "[32] Yet according to *De corpore*, abstract names, such as *esse aliquid, esse mobile, esse calidum*, which result from propositions, do not denote things: that is the job of the concrete names that function as the subjects and predicates of propositions. Instead, abstract names denote the causes of concrete names. As Hobbes explains, "these causes of names are the same with the causes of our conceptions, namely, some power of action, or affection of the thing conceived, which some call the manner by which any thing works upon our senses, but by most men they are called accidents."[33] Or, as it is put in the *Anti-White*:

The result is that *esse* is nothing but an *accident* of a body (*accidens corporis*) by which the means of conceiving it is determined and signalised. So "to be moved," "to be at rest," "to be white" and the like we call the "accidents" of bodies, and we believe them to be present in bodies (*inesse corporibus*) because there are different ways of perceiving bodies.[34]

On the basis of this much, it is possible to make three comments. First, even though the first philosophy traces the notion of *ens* to that of *corpus*, it traces the notion of *esse* to that of *accidens* in reducing *esse* to *inesse corporibus*.[35] Second, the accidents of a body are modes of this body. This is to be understood in two ways: as mode of conception of a body, and power of a body by which it impresses upon us a conception of itself.[36] The doctrine of accidents therefore has consequences for both the modes of being of things and their modes of being known and stated. Finally, the reduction of *esse* to *accidens* carries with it two further reductions: that of *essentia* and that of *forma*, in the language of traditional metaphysics. The implication is that an essence is nothing other than an accident in virtue of which we give a certain name to a body ("as rationality is the essence of a man")[37], and a form is an essence insofar as a body gives rise to it. Accordingly, a body is named *subjectum* in relation to any accident and *materia* in relation to form.

One can see, then, how Hobbes's first philosophy reinterprets the traditional concepts of metaphysics in order to produce a picture of the world in which there are only bodies and accidents. In addition, the doctrine of accidents is central to the third step in the development of Hobbes's first philosophy, the establishment of a deterministic system or system of absolute necessity.

The establishment of a system of absolute necessity

Hobbes arrives at his determinism by a reinterpretation of the traditional theory of cause and power.[38] Of the four Aristotelian causes, Hobbes retains only the efficient and material, and even these are explicated anew: causation in general can result only from local motion (no effect can be attributed to rest). Thus, the efficient cause (*causa efficiens*) consists of no more than the aggregate of the accidents of the active or moving body, and the material cause (*causa materialis*) consists of the aggregate of the accidents of the body being acted upon. However, efficient and material causes are parts of what Hobbes calls the "entire cause" (*causa integra*):

A CAUSE simply, or an entire cause, is the aggregate of all the accidents both of the agents how many soever they be, and of the patient, put together; which when they are all supposed to be present, it cannot be understood but that the effect is produced at the same instant; and if any one of them be wanting, it cannot be understood but that the effect is not produced.[39]

The concept of the entire cause is important because it guarantees that the cause is necessary and sufficient for the effect[40]: it thus establishes the absolute necessity of whatever happens. Thus "an entire cause is always sufficient for the production of its effect, if the effect be at all possible,"[41] and it is because of this sufficiency that the entire cause is also necessary:

It follows also from hence, that in whatsoever instant the cause is entire, in the same instant the effect is produced. For if it be not produced, something is still wanting, which is requisite for the production of it; and therefore the cause as not entire, as was supposed. And seeing a necessary cause is defined to be that, which being supposed, the effect cannot but follow; this also may be collected, that whatsoever effect is produced at any time, the same is produced by a necessary cause.[42]

This concept of causality permits Hobbes to make a first onslaught on the idea of contingency. He proceeds by reduction. Accidents are called contingent in relation to preceding accidents that did not intervene in their production. On the other hand, in relation to the accidents that did in fact produce them, the accidents are not contingent but necessary. To this first reduction of contingency Hobbes adds another, which presupposes the conversion of the theory of causation into a theory of power. Chapter 10 of *De corpore* redefines the concepts of power and act in terms of cause and effect. What distinguishes the first pair of concepts from the second is that the first pair is used to define a future event and the second describes a past event. Thus, even though the effect is in the future, the efficient cause is called active power (*potentia activa*), and the material cause, passive power (*potentia passiva*). The entire cause becomes the full power (*potentia plena*). This reformulation of the theory of power has an important consequence for the concept of possibility. It turns out that there is nothing in between necessity and impossibility, because whatever is possible is necessary: What is possible is what has occurred, what is occurring or what will occur, and whatever occurs does so necessarily. Hence the second reduction of contingency: Contingency consists of nothing other than ignorance of necessary causes.[43]

In the same way as the establishment of a deterministic system depends on a reinterpretation of theories of causation and power, the definition of identity and individuality follows upon a dismantling of the traditional principle of individuation.

The deconstruction of the metaphysical principle of individuation

Chapter 11 of *De corpore*, entitled "*De eodem et diverso*," completes the fourth stage of the development of the first philosophy. After having defined numerical identity, quantitative and qualitative identity, as well as relation, Hobbes turns to the concept of individuality.

The same body may at different times be compared with itself. And from hence springs a great controversy among philosophers about the *principium individuationis*, namely, in what sense it may be conceived that a body is at one time the same, at another time not the same it was formerly. For example, whether a man grown old be the same man he was whilst he was young, or another man; or whether a city be in different ages the same, or another city.[44]

Hobbes's claim is that there is no unique principle of individuation, provided by matter or form, but that judgments of identity and difference depend on matter, form, or the aggregate of all accidents. If matter individuated things, then a piece of wax would remain the same no matter what changes it underwent, as long as it lost no bulk. Again, one would be unable to define conditions of identity for rivers, men, or commonwealths. If matter provided the principle of individuation, the same man could not be said to have sinned and been punished "by reason of the perpetual flux and change of man's body; nor should the city, which makes laws in one age and abrogates them in another, be the same city; which were to confound all civil rights."[45] On the other hand, if form individuates, then, while one would certainly be able to accommodate the persistence of the same man despite the change in the makeup of his body, two identical ships with interchangeable parts could not be counted as two, but only as the same ship. Finally, if the aggregate of accidents determined identity, nothing could be said to be the same. The man standing would not be the same as the man seated. It follows that the principle of individuating should not be held to reside in the matter or the form, but should be regarded as varying according to the way we consider or name the thing whose identity is in question.

But we must consider by what name anything is called, when we inquire concerning the *identity* of it. For it is one thing to ask concerning Socrates, whether he be the same man, and another to ask whether he be the same body; for his body, when he is old, cannot be the same it was when he was infant, by reason of difference of magnitude; for one body has always one and the same magnitude; yet nevertheless, he may be the same man.[46]

Hobbes is doing nothing less here than transforming a fundamental principle of individuation, turning it from an ontological principle into a semantic one. The question of individuation is no longer tied to the ontological constitution of the individual, but rather to modes of conceiving and designating it. This transformation of the principle of individuation allows Hobbes to relegate to the status of a simple question of physics what the real constitution of an individual is.

We have before us the four stages of Hobbes's first philosophy. We can see that in addition to giving definitions by circumlocution, Hobbes effects a reform that is both ontological and epistemological. The fundamental concepts of philosophy thus bear on the determination of knowledge and being at their most general. What remains to consider is to what extent, if any, the fundamental concepts can provide the foundations for the special sciences: physics, ethics and politics.

THE LIMITS OF APPLICATION OF THE CONCEPTS OF FIRST PHILOSOPHY: THE FOUNDATION UNFINISHED

One could say that the concepts of philosophy are perfectly adapted to grounding the physical sciences, as long as one distinguishes between the science of motion and the science of the sensible world. The science of motion considers in the abstract the effects of one body on another, that is, the laws of impact, and more generally, the laws of the transmission of motion.[47] On the other hand, the science of the sensible world, which Hobbes thinks is physics properly so-called,[48] concerns what appears to the senses and the causes of these appearances. The former science is elaborated a priori from the concepts of first philosophy, while the latter, being concerned with sensible appearance, depends on hypotheses arrived at a posteriori. It is clear, then, that the methods of the two sciences must be distinct. The one proceeds to generate effects known on the basis of causes; the other proceeds to the knowledge of causes based on experience of effects. What is more, the second science depends on the first: the principles of the science of motion help to frame the hypotheses that the science of the sensible world requires.

The application of the concepts of the first philosophy to the science of motion is all the easier because important elements of the latter are already present in the former. Thanks to the theory that existence is corporeal existence and to the reduction of all real causality to motion, Hobbes's first philosophy transforms the categories of traditional metaphysics into categories of physics.[49] This makes it possible to understand how after the definition of motion in its various forms in *De corpore*,[50] one immediately comes upon the definition of force,[51] the principle of inertia, and so on.

The question now before us, however, is that of whether the first philosophy fits the physical sciences at the cost of providing unsuitable foundations for such sciences as ethics and politics. It is true that certain of the concepts of first philosophy are at work in Hobbes's morals and politics. The distinction between appearance and reality, between body and accident, and the theories of causality and identity play an important role. But to what extent can these distinctions and concepts provide a basis for a theory of the passions, natural right, natural law, and, above all, a contractualist theory of the state and an absolutist theory of political power? Hobbes broaches this question in a passage in the chapter on method in *De corpore*.

Civil and moral philosophy do not so adhere to one another, but that they may be severed. For the causes of the motions of the mind are known, not only by ratiocination, but also by the experience of every man that takes the pains to observe those motions within himself. And, therefore, not only they that have attained the knowledge of the passions and perturbations of the mind, by the *synthetical method*, and from the very first principles of philosophy, may by proceeding in the same way, come to the causes and necessity of constituting commonwealths, and to get the knowledge of what is natural right, and what are civil duties; . . . and all other knowledge appertaining to civil philosophy; for this reason, that the principles of the politics consist in the knowledge of the motions of the mind, and the knowledge of these motions from the knowledge of sense and imagination; but even they also that have not learned the first part of philosophy, namely *geometry* and *physics*, may, notwithstanding, attain the principles of civil philosophy, by the *analytical method*.[52]

With regard to method, then, Hobbes sees two possibilities: either a deductive progress from first principles, or a shorter route that approaches politics from principles that can be grasped by experience and the observation of our internal motions. But the disassociation of moral philosophy from politics,[53] which separates politics from other branches of science, does not imply a complete autonomy for politics. Even if immediate experience is able to reveal the principles of politics, these principles themselves can find an ultimate grounding only by being referred to the concepts of first philosophy. So we are back to the question of the extent to which the concepts of first philosophy lend themselves to the grounding of politics. We shall see that they can provide at best a partial or incomplete grounding of politics.

In order to see where the principles of first philosophy give out in relation to politics, it helps to indicate under some definite headings exactly what the scope and limits of the first philosophy are. The limits emerge by asking where the ethics and politics require a *transposition* of the concepts of first philosophy; where they *complete* a treatment of concepts begun in the first philosophy; where the ethics and politics involve a *discontinuity* in the treatment given by the first philosophy; and where the ethics and politics overturn or *invert* the treatment given by the first philosophy.

Transposition

The best example of the transposition of the concepts and distinctions of first philosophy comes in relation to Hobbes's treatment of the physiology and psychology of sensation, imagination, and the passions. There is a place in Hobbes's science of human nature for some attempt at a physical explanation of phenomena involving passion, volition and, more generally, the mind. But precisely because these are matters about the causes and constitution of human mental life, the concepts of first philosophy do not admit of direct application: They need to be transposed or altered to fit these phenomena. So while there are elements in Hobbes of a physics of mental life and of speech,[54] neither mental life nor speech can be reduced to these elements, because neither the quality of mental experience nor meaning is so reducible.

Completion

The treatment that certain concepts receive in Hobbes's first philosophy remains incomplete until Hobbes returns to them in the ethics and politics. For example, the theory of the entire cause and of action only start to cohere with one another in Hobbes's analysis of deliberation and the will. It is in the theory of the voluntary act that the relation established in the first philosophy between the entire cause and the effect can be invoked to determine the time of action.[55] Something similar can be said about the theory of power. It is incomplete until an ethical doctrine of human power is added to the physical doctrine of the power of a body: "The power of a *man* (to take it universally) is his present means, to obtain some future or apparent good."[56] Applied to ethics, the theory of power takes in three new elements: the qualitative dimension – the effect becomes an apparent good; the appearance of purpose in the production of effects that consist of obtaining goods; and the giving way of narrowly physical effects of power to those that result from the desire for domination in human relations.

Discontinuity

One of the clearest examples of discontinuity is in the treatment of body in the politics, on the one hand, and the first philosophy, on the other. Hobbes himself calls attention to it as early as the first chapter of *De corpore*.

The principal parts of philosophy are two. For two chief kinds of bodies, and very different from one another, offer themselves to such as search after their generation and properties; one whereof being the work of nature, is called a *natural body*, the other is called a *commonwealth*, and is made by the wills and agreement of men. And from these spring the two parts of philosophy, called *natural* and *civil*.[57]

Hobbes is pointing to the irreducibility of both the natural body, the subject matter of physics, and the body politic, subject matter of civil philosophy. A natural body, which is material, and a body politic, which is artificial, could never work according to principles of the same kind. Hobbes's political theory has nothing to do with the physics of the state: It concerns institutions, and its sources and implications are quite unlike those of a physical theory. The distinction made by Hobbes between the merely conditional knowledge we have of natural things and the certain knowledge we have of things we made[58] adds to the discontinuity between the concepts of first philosophy and those of politics.

Inversion

The discontinuity by which we are helped to see that the concepts of first philosophy are not suited for grounding politics may indeed alert us to something even more surprising: nothing less than an overturning or inversion of the concepts of first philosophy. Hobbes's ideas of natural right, natural law, social convention, and so on, are conceivable only because Hobbes's ethics quietly turns a philosophy of body into a philosophy of mind, by which I mean a doctrine of mental life dominated by a theory of appearance or the phantasm that has the tendency to detach itself from its supposed basis in a materialistic metaphysics.[59] Is this a way of saying that Hobbes's philosophy breaks down and that one has to recognize that the first philosophy and the politics impose irreconcilable constraints? I don't think so, because the grounding that the first philosophy fails to give to politics may in fact come from a totally unexpected, and one might have thought, excluded source: theology.

THE RETURN OF THEOLOGY: THE FOUNDATION DIVIDED

The return of theology is not a return by stealth because something amounting to theology is always just below the surface in the material we have been examining, even if it is not *called* theology. That an explicitly recognized theology is excluded is proved by the fact that the first philosophy of *De corpore* says nothing about it. Yet, when one turns from statements of Hobbes's own doctrines to polemical writings (involving Descartes, White, and Bramhall), where Hobbes is obliged to take account of other philosophical views, a theological presupposition reasserts itself. The presupposition consists of a theology of omnipotence, and it can be brought out in three ways.

   1. The hypothesis of the annihilated world is stated in the first philosophy of *De corpore* without any reference to theology. On the other hand, in the *Anti-White* Hobbes insists that the annihilation of a body cannot result from a natural process (which can involve only the change of accidents), but that it can be conceived of as an effect of divine omnipotence, even though we cannot know how a supernatural being acts.[60] Of course, the annihilation of a body is not the annihilation of the world, but the explicit theological presupposition of the former provides the implicit theological presupposition of the latter. From start to finish in the theological passages and chapter of the *Anti-White*, the theology of omnipotence supports the doctrine of the contingency of the world. Theology thus flourishes even in places where one would have thought it to be wholly excluded.

In the development of this theology of omnipotence, Hobbes goes as far as to rework certain of the rational categories, taking away from them the sense they have when they are to do with the actions or relations of finite entities, and making them signify something altogether different when they are applied to God. I have shown all of this at length elsewhere.[61] Here it is enough to point out the fundamental changes that the concepts of will and liberty undergo when God is brought under them.[62] Thus, while the human will is necessarily determined by causes, God's will is neither determined by sense nor reason, as is the human will. As a consequence, reason does not make the good known as a notion prior to reason, from which it follows in general that the divine will can't be determined by a principle outside itself.[63] At the same time, the concept of liberty applied to human beings or to any other earthly creature comes down to necessity. Liberty is nothing other than necessity that is not impeded by external obstacles. This reduction of liberty to necessity is seriously put in question when it comes to understanding the divine will, which is wholly independent of necessity: absolute liberty, in fact.[64] Yet this theological reinterpretation of concepts isn't simply set alongside a body of doctrine to which it is alien; the theology of omnipotence plays an important and essential role as much in the scheme of first philosophy as in that of legal and political thought.

2. We saw earlier that the first philosophy consisted in part in the establishment of a deterministic system. This system requires a theological foundation to ensure both its possibility and its limits. The controversy with Bramhall rather than *De corpore* provides the explanation of this point:

Nor does the *concourse of all causes* make one simple *chain* or concatenation, but an innumerable number of chains, joined together, not in all parts, but in the first link God Almighty; and consequently the whole cause of an event, dot not always depend on one single chain, but on many together.[65]

Hobbes's recourse to God permits him to unify the different causal chains in the world, as well as to take into account the process of totalization that, at a given moment, makes up an entire cause of an event. The notion of an entire cause would not be available in the absence of this theological closure. And without the notion of an entire cause, Hobbes would not have materials for determinism. To put it another way, if there were no first cause, there would be an infinite regress of causes, and therefore no possibility of making sense of a given effect.

3. Hobbes's conception of natural law is equally dependent on theology. In the political writings, the concept of divine natural right is formulated explicitly when what is in question is the natural rule of God. This rule is exercised by God over beings who recognize his existence and obey his natural word, that is, the laws of nature. In other words, the kingdom of God is not the same as nature in general. In the order of natural necessity to which all beings are subject, there is a particular order that concerns men only insofar as they are rational. The natural kingdom of God is therefore a subsystem of the total order of natural necessity, concerning which it makes sense to talk of divine justice or divine right. Yet the right in virtue of which God rules over men and punishes those who break his laws also derives from God's omnipotence:

The right of nature, whereby God reigneth over men, and punisheth those that break his lawes, is to be derived, not from his creating them, as if he required obedience, as of gratitude for his benefits; but from his *Irresistible Power* . . . And consequently it is from that power, that the kingdome over me, and the right of afflicting men at his pleasure, belongeth naturally to God Almighty; not as Creator, and Gracious; but as Omnipotent.[66]

It should be clear from this passage that Hobbes belongs to the tradition of theological voluntarism and that his natural and political philosophy depend on it. It is his place in this tradition that enables us to tie together two points that emerge from both his first philosophy and his political philosophy: that the order of the world is not an order in which there is a hierarchy of being or value; and the distinction between good and evil, and just and unjust can only be the product of divine or human will. It is paradoxically this theology that allows for the possibility of conceiving man as self-generating producer of a world in which social convention alone can assure the co-existence of men.

CONCLUSION: THE UNCERTAIN FOUNDATION

The idea of a theologically divided or reinforced foundation may seem perplexing. After all, doesn't Hobbes define God as body?

Doesn't this call into question any suggestion of a theology of absolute transcendence of God? Or, in other words, isn't what I am calling a divided foundation in fact a doubtfully coherent basis for the rest of Hobbes's system, doubtfully coherent because it tries to reconcile the two conflicting claims that God is unknowable and that God is a body? Doesn't the theology of omnipotence, which we have been trying to find traces of from the first philosophy to the politics, turn out to be a pure denial of God, since it ends up by recognizing no more than a material world subject to natural necessity? In a sense this question sums up all that is paradoxical in Hobbes's thought. Hobbes did not think through completely the idea of a theologically divided foundation, and the question of foundations remains to some extent open and uncertain.

Nevertheless, the analysis I have just given of the bearing of the first philosophy on the special sciences does not lead to a wholly uncertain conclusion. For if the foundational status of philosophy is open to doubt, it is no less true that the elements of Hobbes's system – the materialist conception of the world, the theory of natural right and the individual, the idea of the state as the outcome of a social contract – all belong to a tradition of theological voluntarism that goes back to the late Middle Ages.

Translated from the French by Tom Sorell

NOTES

1 Hobbes, *Vita carmine expressa, OL* I, p. xc.
2 The *Elementa Philosophiae* were made up of *De corpore* (1655), *De homine* (1658), and *De cive* (1642).
3 The letters concerned are dated Jan. 17, 1637, and Sept. 11, 1637, and are published in Ferdinand Tönnies, *Studien zur Philosophie und Gesellschaftslehre im 17. Jahrhundert*, pp. 145–7. See also *Corr.* vol. I 42–53 and 50–51. One can reasonably suppose that the logic in question in the letters from Digby is closely connected with Hobbes's first philosophy, since mention is made of definitions "collected out of a deep insight into the things themselves" (*Corr.* vol. 1, 43).
4 Among these manuscripts, one in the National Library of Wales (MS 5297) is customarily called *De principiis*. It was published by J. Jacquot and H.W. Jones as Appendix II of the *Critique du 'De Mundo 'de Thomas White* (Paris: Vrin-CNRS, 1973) pp. 449–60 (subsequently referred to as *Anti-White – AW*). The *De principiis* is taken by its editors as an English

transcription (attributed to Herbert of Cherbury) of a Latin original of
Hobbes. Even if one can be certain that the tenor of the text is authenti-
cally Hobbesian, the date of its composition and the identity of the
transcriber remain altogether obscure. There is a further important La-
tin autograph manuscript A10 from Chatsworth, published as Appendix
III of the *Anti-White* (pp. 463–513), as well as Charles Cavendish's manuscript on a draft (different from MS A10) of *De Corpore*, British Library,
Harleian MS 6083 (the variants that distinguish this manuscript from
MS A10 are taken up in Appendix III to *Anti-White*. According to
Jacquot and Jones, these two manuscripts are supposed to reflect the
state of advancement of *De corpore* around 1645–46. This is also Arrigo
Pacchi's opinion in his *Convenzione e ipotesi nella formazione della
filosofia naturale di Thomas Hobbes.*

Research of great importance is now being conducted by Karl Schuhmann with a view to proposing a more certain dating of the manuscripts
just mentioned. In addition, in an article published in *Hobbes Studies*,
Schuhmann proves conclusively the authenticity of the *Short Tract*,
which is known to be one of the oldest of Hobbes's writings in natural
philosophy, going back as it does to the beginning of the 1630s. The
Short Tract contains many elements that one encounters again in the
philosophia prima, in particular the theory of the sufficient cause as
necessary cause. Until Schuhmann's work reaches its conclusion and
interpretations are adjusted accordingly, the only manuscript whose
date of composition we can be sure of is also the most important in
content and size, namely, the *Anti-White*. Written in the first half of
1643, this text comprises, as we shall see, many of the essentials of
Hobbes's first philosophy.

5 *Anti-White* (hereafter *AW*) I, 1, p. 105/ (English version: pp. 23–4). The
   text of the English translation is very faulty, and has often been altered
   when quoted.
6 In other passages of the *Anti-White* Hobbes tries quite openly to restore
   Aristotle's categories. See *AW* V, 2 p. 129/ p. 57.
7 Just what makes the *philosophia prima* worthy of the name of metaphysics, with all its semantically and theoretical associations, is taken up at
   greater length in *AW* IX, 16, p. 170/ pp. 111–12.
8 Cf. Descartes, *Meditationes de prima philosophia*, AT VII, *Objectiones
   tertiae* (Paris: CNRS-Vrin, 1983), pp. 171–96.
9 Scipion Dupleix, *La Métaphysique* I, II, p. 87.
10 *AW*, X, 16, p. 170/p. 112; "Those books on *Philosophia prima*, i.e. on the
   elements of Philosophy, came to be called the *Metaphysics*. . . . Because
   of this difficulty, and owing to the title *Metaphysics*, since 'meta' means
   not only 'after' but also 'beyond', the ignorant believed that a certain

supernatural doctrine was contained in these books, just as if those who applied themselves to metaphysics were to do in order that, by means of their doctrine, they might step beyond nature's confines."

11 *De Corp.* I, 8; *OL* I, 9/*EW* I, 11.

12 *De Corp.* VI, 6; *OL* I 62/*EW* I, 70.

13 To see what is at stake in Hobbes's first philosophy, one must take account not only of the second part of *De corpore* and of preparatory works such as the *Anti-White*, but also the texts that punctuate the polemic with Bramhall over liberty and necessity, in which the theological theme surfaces explicitly. Also relevant is the *Six Lessons.*

14 *De Corp*, VI, 13; *OL* I, 71–72/*EW* I, 81: "And names of the former kind are well enough defined, when, by speech as short as may be, we raise in the mind of the hearer perfect and clear ideas or conceptions of the things named, as when we define motion to be *the leaving of one place, and the acquiring of another continually;* for though no thing moved, nor any cause of motion be in that definition, yet, at the hearing of that speech, there will come into the mind of the hearer an *idea* of motion clear enough."

15 These pairs of concepts are examined in Chapters 7 to 11 of *De corpore.*

16 Cf. Y.C. Zarka, "Le vocabulaire de l'apparaître" and K. Schuhmann, "Le vocabulaire de l'espace," in Zarka, *Hobbes et son vocabulaire*, pp. 13–29 and pp. 61–82, respectively.

17 For the significance of the fiction of the annihilated world, see Arrigo Pacchi, *Convenzione e ipotesi*, and Y.C. Zarka, *La décision métaphysique de Hobbes*, pp. 36–58. See also K. Schuhmann, "Thomas Hobbes and Francesco Patrizi," *Archiv für Geschichte der Philosophie* 68 (1986).

18 *De Corp.* VII, 1; *OL* I, 81–82/*EW* I 92.

19 Ibid.

20 *AW* III, 1, p. 116/p.40

21 Ibid., p. 117/pp. 40–41: "Spatium igitur *imaginarium* nihil aliud est quam *imago*, sive *phantasma corporis*... Manifestum hinc est existentiam spatii dependere non ab existentia corporis sed ab existentia imaginativae facultatis."

22 *De Corp.* VII, 2 *OL* 183/*EW* I, 94.

23 *De Corp.* 3; *OL* I, 84/*EW* I, 94–95

24 In using the inverse of the fiction of the annihilated world in the *Anti-White* (that is, the hypothesis of the non-existence of the thinking and imagining being), Hobbes speaks of an extension inhering in bodies or *spatiam reale;* one encounters this expression again in *De Corp* VIII, 4; *OL* I, 93/*EW* I, 205. Here is the text from the *Anti-White* (III, 2, p. 117/p. 41); "It follows, therefore, that bodies would exist even if there were no

mind-picture at all. Next, it is impossible to admit the existence of any certain body without at the same time realising that it possesses its own dimensions, or spaces. So this space which, when inherent in a body, as the accident in its subject, can be called 'real', would certainly exist even if there were no being to imagine it. I define 'real space', therefore, as corporeity itself, or the essence of body taken *simpliciter*, insofar as it is body'. Hence a body is to imaginary space as a thing to the knowledge of that thing, because our entire knowledge of existing things consists in that mind-picture produced by the action of these things on our senses. 'Imaginary space', therefore, which is the mind-picture of body, is the same thing as our knowledge of existing body."

25 Cf. M Pécharman, 'Le vocabulaire de l'être dans la philosophie première," in Zarka, *Hobbes et son vocabulaire*, pp. 31–59.

26 *De Corp.* VIII, 1; *OL* I, 90/*EW* I, 101–2. "Having understood what imaginary space is, in which we supposed nothing remaining without us, but all those things to be destroyed that, by existing heretofore, left images of themselves in our minds; let us now suppose some one of those things to be placed again in the world, or created anew. It is necessary, therefore, that this newly created or replaced thing do not only fill some part of space above mentioned, or be coincident or coextended with it, but also that it have no dependence on our thought."

27 *De Corp.* VIII, 1; *OL* I, 90–91/*EW* I, 102. I give the original Latin text, as the English version contains a significant mistranslation. The English text (with mistranslation in brackets) runs as follows: "And this is that which, for the extension of it, we commonly call *body*; and because it depends not upon our thought, we say it is a *thing subsisting of itself*; as also *existing*, because without us; and, lastly, it is called the *subject*, because it is so placed in and *subjected* to imaginary space [that it may be understood by reason, as well as perceived by sense]. The definition, therefore of a *body* may be this, a *body is that, which having no dependence upon our thought, is coincident or coextended with some part of space*."

28 *AW* XVII, 1, p. 312/pp. 310–11.
29 Ibid., p. 312/p. 311.
30 Ibid.
31 Ibid.
32 Ibid., p. 313/p. 312; cf *De Corp.*, VII, 3, *OL* I, 28–29/*EW* I, 31–33.
33 *De Corp.* III, 3; *OL* I, 29/*EW* I, 32–33.
34 *AW* XXVII, 1, p. 313/p. 312.
35 Cf. Pécharman, "Le vocabulaire."
36 *De Corp.* VIII, 2; *OL* I, 91/*EW* I, 103.
37 *De Corp.* VIII, 23; *OL* I, 104/ *EW* I, 117.

38 Cf. *De Corp.*, chaps. 9 and 10.
39 *De Corp.* IX, 3; *OL* I, 107–08/*EW* I, 122.
40 This theory of the interchangeability of the sufficient cause and the necessary cause was present, as indicated in the *Short Tract* (I, Conclusion 11), but its final formulation was not arrived at until the controversy with Bramhall, who countered Hobbes's absolute necessity with what was in effect the idea of a hypothetical necessity.
41 *De Corp.* IX, 5; *OL* I, 108/*EW* I, 122
42 Ibid., *OL* I, 108–9/ *EW* I, 123.
43 Ibid., X, 5; *OL* I, 116/*EW* I, 130: "For men commonly call that *causal* or *contingent* whereof they do not perceive the necessary cause."
44 Ibid., XI, 7; *OL* I, 120–1/*EW* I, 135.
45 Ibid, *OL* I, 121/*EW* I, 136.
46 Ibid.; *OL* I, 122/*EW* I, 137. For the influence of this position of Hobbes's on Locke's concept of identity, se Y.C. Zarka, "Identité et ipséité chez Hobbes et Locke", 5–19.
47 *De Corp.* VI, 6; *OL* I, 63/71–72.
48 Ibid. XXV, I; *OL* I, 316/*EW* I, 388: "Seeing, therefore, the science, which is here taught, hath its principles in the appearances of nature, and endeth in the attaining of some knowledge of natural causes, I have given to this part the title of *Physics* or the *Phenomena of Nature*. Now such things as appear, or are shown to us by nature, we call phenomena or appearances."
49 A comparable physical reinterpretation of metaphysical categories is to be found in Gassendi. Cf. O Bloch, *La philosophie de Gassendi*.
50 *De Corp.* VIII, 10; *OL* I, 97/*EW* I, 109.
51 Ibid., 18; *OL* I, 101–02/*EW* I, 115. 'Wherefore *motions are said to be simply equal to one another, when the swiftness of one, computed in every part of its magnitude, is equal to the swiftness of the other computed also in every part of its magnitude: and greater than one another, when the swiftness of one computed as above, is greater than the swiftness of the other so computed; and less, when less.* Besides, the magnitude of motion computed in the manner is that which is commonly called FORCE'.
52 *De Corp.*, VI, 7; *OL* I, 65/*EW* I, 73–74.
53 This dissociation poses many specific problems. For example, Hobbes assumes, no doubt rashly, that moral philosophy can be deduced without difficulty from first philosophy and physics.
54 Cf. André Robinet, "Pensée et langage chez Hobbes," pp. 452–83.
55 Cf. Martine Pécharman, "Philosophie première et théorie de l'action selon Hobbes," pp. 47–66.
56 LX, p. 150.

57 *De Corp.* I, 9 *OL* I, 10/*EW* I, 11.

58 *D H.* X, 4–5, *OL* II 92–94.

59 Cf. Y.C. Zarka, "Le vocabulaire de l'apparaître."

60 Cf. *AW*, XXVII, 1, p. 314/p. 313, and many other passages.

61 Cf. Y.C. Zarka, "Leibniz lecteur de Hobbes."

62 Hobbes says often that we say what we do about God not in virtue of the thing itself (*rei ipsius causa*), but in virtue of the honor that we owe him (*honoris causa*), (*AW* XXXIV, 7, p. 385/p. 418). This does not, however, alter the fact that he needs, as we shall see, a rational theology in order to complete his system both in the area of the doctrine of necessity and in that of natural law.

63 Cf. *AW* XXXI, 3, p. 368 *in fine*/p. 393.

64 Cf. *AW* XXXIII, 5, p. 378/pp. 408–9.

65 *L&N, EW* IV, 246–7.

66 *Lev.* XXXI, p. 397.

4   Hobbes and the method of natural science

Hobbes's philosophy of natural science is dominated by the idea that all true knowledge must arise from an understanding of causes, so that a genuinely scientific account of a phenomenon requires knowledge of the process by which it was produced. This emphasis on the scientific priority of causal knowledge was by no means a methodological novelty in the seventeenth century. Aristotle's *Posterior Analytics*, the source for the traditional Scholastic understanding of science, declares that scientific understanding must be rooted in the knowledge of causes.[1] Aristotle and his Scholastic followers conceived of substances as composites of form and matter, and their methodology distinguished between formal, material, efficient, and final causes. Thus, a causal explanation in the Scholastic tradition might include reference to a substance's form (the formal cause), its matter (the material cause), the process that produced it (the efficient cause), and the end or purpose for which it was produced (the final cause).[2] The Scholastic way of thinking about nature was rejected by the leading scientific figures of the seventeenth century, who championed a mechanistic conception of the world and insisted that natural phenomena be explained exclusively as the result of the motion and impact of material particles.

Hobbes was a devotee of the new "mechanical philosophy," and he combined his insistence on the causal nature of scientific knowledge with the mechanistic maxim that "Nature does all things by the conflict of bodies pressing each other mutually with their motions" (*DiPh*. Ep. Ded.; *OL* IV, 238). His methodology therefore dictates that the scope of natural science be restricted to the investigation of the mechanical causes of natural phenomena, and it entails the rejection of a Scholastic–Aristotelian natural philosophy grounded in the con-

86

sideration of such nonmechanical principles as substantial forms or final causes. Hobbes himself was tireless in his denunciation of Scholastic natural philosophy and regarded the overthrow of Scholastic doctrines as an essential part of a program for the reform of learning.[3] To understand the Hobbesian methodology of natural science, it is necessary to begin by contrasting his account of demonstratively certain geometric knowledge with the ineradicably hypothetical and conjectural knowledge available in natural science. With this contrast in hand, we can then proceed to investigate two further aspects of his philosophy of science: the distinction between analytic and synthetic methods, and his claim that scientific reasoning depends on the manipulation of signs.

GEOMETRY AND NATURAL PHILOSOPHY

It is well-known that Hobbes took geometry as the ideal for all demonstrative knowledge, notwithstanding his notable failures at circle quadrature and the solution of other famous problems.[4] Indeed, if we are to believe Aubrey's testimony, Hobbes's chance discovery of Euclid's *Elements* at the age of forty literally changed his life, introducing him to a mode of reasoning that he later sought to transfer to natural and civil philosophy.[5] In Hobbes's estimation, geometry is distinguished from (and elevated above) other branches of human learning by two characteristics. First, its terms are carefully defined and explicated, "which is a method that hath been used onely in Geometry; whose Conclusions have thereby been made indisputable" (*Lev.* ch. 5, 20; *EW* III, 33). Second, the objects of geometric investigation are fully known to the geometer because their causes are completely understood, and this because "the lines and figures from which we reason are drawn and described by ourselves" (*SL*, Ep. Ded.; *EW* VII, 184). The result is that geometry is the "onely Science it hath pleased God hitherto to bestow on mankind" (*Lev.* ch. 4, 15; *EW* III, 23).

It is worth noting that Hobbes intends his claims for the special scientific status of geometry to apply, not so much to the traditional geometry of Euclid, but rather to his own reformulation of the subject that proceeds from definitions that express the true causes of geometric objects. Hobbes felt that traditional geometry had been hampered by its reliance upon definitions that were not grounded in the consideration of causes, and part of his project for geometry was to rewrite the traditional geometric definitions to include the motions by which geometric objects are produced. In the essay *De Principiis et Ratiocinatione Geometrarum*, Hobbes sums up his attitude toward this aspect of his geometry by remarking on the appeal to motion characteristic of his rewritten geometric definitions.

"But" you will ask "what need is there for demonstrations of purely geometric theorems to appeal to motion?" I respond, first: All demonstrations are flawed, unless they are scientific, and unless they proceed from causes, they are not scientific. Secondly, demonstrations are flawed unless their conclusions are demonstrated by construction, that is, by description of figures, that is, by the drawing of lines. For every drawing of a line is motion, and so every demonstration is flawed, whose first principles are not contained in the definitions of motions by which figures are described. (*DPRG* 12; *OL* IV, 421)

Hobbes's faith in the demonstrative efficacy of causal definitions accounts, in part, for his misplaced confidence in his own ability to solve such notoriously difficult (indeed, unsolvable) problems as the squaring of the circle. He imagined that once the true definitions had been introduced and the generation of the circle had been grasped, then all of its properties must be readily demonstrable by one who had understood the relevant definitions. On this view, all geometric problems are solvable, and nothing is completely hidden from the true geometer. It is curious that Hobbes also regarded civil philosophy as properly demonstrable, at least once his account of the generation of the commonwealth had been accepted. The reason here is revealing: Because the commonwealth is created by man, its causes are fully knowable by men, and there is room for a genuinely demonstrative science of the commonwealth.[6]

Although geometry completely satisfies the Hobbesian criteria for genuine scientific knowledge, the natural sciences can only approximate to the certainty of geometry by proceeding from causal hypotheses in place of the secure causal definitions of the geometers. To put the matter another way: Where the geometer enjoys the advantage of dealing with demonstrations founded on knowledge of true causes, the natural scientist must reason *ex hypothesi* and try to explain the phenomena of nature by adducing the most probable cause of the phenomenon in question. The reason for this difference between geometry and natural science lies in the fact that we are generally unacquainted with the causes of natural phenomena, whereas the lines and figures of geometry are produced by the manipulation of instruments. We can literally bring the circle into being by tracing it with a compass, but are left to speculate about the causes that conspire to produce a thunderstorm.

Hobbes confines our knowledge of nature to "phantasms" or "fancies" in the mind, which he takes as mental representations of an external world. These phantasms are therefore caused by things external to us, and the fundamental task of the natural philosopher is to seek a causal explanation of such phantasms. As he puts it in the *Decameron Physiologicum:*

Your desire . . . is to know the causes of the effects or phenomena of nature; and you confess they are fancies, and consequently, that they are in yourself; so that the causes you seek for only are without you, and now you would know how those external bodies work upon you to produce those phenomena. (*DP* ch. 2; *EW* VII, 82)

The science of nature prosecuted on this basis amounts, then, to a systematic attempt to "save the phenomena" with hypotheses detailing their causes.

The hypothetical or conjectural nature of natural science thus falls short of the demonstrative certainty obtainable in geometry, and the matter is further complicated by the fact that the minute corpuscles favored in mechanistic science are themselves unobservable. The result, Hobbes concludes, is that natural science can aspire to nothing more than "to have such opinions as no certayne experience can confute, and from which can be deduced by lawfull argumentation, no absurdity."[7]

Although Hobbes grants that "in natural causes, all you are to expect, is but probability" (*SPP* ch. 1; *EW* VII 11), it does not follow that there are no constraints on the possible explanations of natural phenomena. Stated most generally, Hobbes places two requirements on a causal hypothesis: "the first is, that it be conceivable, that is, not absurd; the other, that, by conceding it, the necessity of the phenomenon may be inferred" (*DiPh, OL* IV, 254). More particularly, Hobbes is concerned to rule out Scholastic–Aristotelian natural philosophy as absurd and unintelligible. He insists that only mechanical causes (namely, those appealing exclusively to the motions and impacts of bodies) can be admitted to account for natural phenomena. This stricture extends even to the explanation of motion itself: Hobbes denies the possibility of a self-moving body and claims that one body's motion must arise from its impact with another body.[8] He further insists that in the search for natural causes, priority must be given to his brand of plenist mechanism, as opposed to the vacuist agenda propounded by prominent members of the Royal Society. Robert Boyle and other champions of vacuism pursued a research program that sought to explain natural phenomena in terms of particle motion in otherwise empty space. According to the vacuists, the same body could be made more or less dense as its constituent particles become closer or farther from each other. Hobbes rejects talk of "rarefaction" and "condensation" of bodies as an exercise in the "Vain Philosophy" of the Schools in which empty terms are bandied about and useless distinctions introduced (such as that between a body and its quantity). Hobbes understands quantity of a body to be the amount of matter it contains, and to allow talk of condensation or rarefaction is to proceed on the unintelligible assumption that the same body could have more or less quantity.[9]

The Hobbesian constraints upon possible causal explanations are set forth in an important list of "Maximes necessary for those, yt from ye sight of an Effect, shall endeavor to assigne its Naturall Cause" among the Classified Papers of the Royal Society.[10] These maxims are a succinct statement of Hobbes's philosophy of science and include the following:

1 There is no Effect of Nature, ye Cause whereof does not consist in some motion. For if all things either stand or move, as they did, they will also appear, as they did.
  This maxime may assure a man, yt when any thing else is assigned for a Naturall cause, besides some motion, wch is able to produce ye Effect, ye cause is false.

2 There is nothing, yt can give a beginning of motion to itself. For there can be no reason given in yt case, why the motion began then, rather yn sooner or later; why just so swift, rather than swifter yn slower; why this way rather, yn another: All wch determinations must proceed from some other movement.
  This maxime wil keep a man from assigning *Natural Appe-*

tite for a Cause (as many do) of motion, in things yt have no
Appetite.

4   The first (tho insensible) beginning of motion (wch is com-
    monly called Endeavor) is motion.
    For, ye very first beginning of any thing is a part of it and ye
    whole being motion, ye part (yt is, ye first Endeavor) how
    weak soever, is also Motion.
    This Maxime serves to guide a man, how to enter into his
    search, and, as it were, to hunt ye cause from its seat.
5   The very same matter hath alwaies ye same quantity. Why?
    Because greater and lesser are never the very same.
    This Maxime will keep a man from being deluded and fob'd
    of by others, with ye insignificant Termes (as they are now a
    dayes used) of Rarefaction and Condensa[ti]on.
6   Two bodies cannot be at ye same Time, in one place, or one
    Body in 2 places, Why? Because tis the one place, yt makes it
    true, yt ye Body is one. And ye two places yt makes it true, yt
    they are two Bodies.
    This Maxime serves also to confute Rarefaction and Conden-
    sation. Besides some other false philosophy, wch a man may
    light up on in ye writing of School-divines.[11]

It is important to recognize that even within these constraints
there may well be several causal hypotheses that can serve as explanations of a particular phenomenon. Hobbes was prepared to settle for
such an indeterminacy in scientific explanations, and pronounced
the assignment of a possible cause "all that can be expected" in natural philosophy, because "there is no effect in nature which the Author
of nature cannot bring to pass by more ways than one." (*DP* ch. 2; *EW*
VII, 88) Indeed, Hobbes's own practice in developing his physics testi-
fies to his willingness to pursue several possible explanations for a
given phenomenon.[12] Such indeterminacy of explanation need not, of
course, be permanent or universal. In any given case it may happen
that further empirical investigation rules out one or more competing
explanations, but there is no guarantee that we can always narrow the
field in this way. This further highlights the contrast between geometry and natural philosophy in Hobbes's system: the geometer, having

access to true causes, need concern himself only with rigorous deductions from causal principles to guarantee the truth of his results; but the natural philosopher must accept that, however rigorous his deductions, he may nevertheless have failed to give a proper derivation of the phenomena.

ANALYSIS, SYNTHESIS, AND NATURAL SCIENCE

Hobbes's emphasis on the role of causal principles in the philosophy of natural science figures prominently in his well-known distinction between analytic and synthetic methods. Some kind of contrast between analytic and synthetic modes of reasoning was standard fare well before the seventeenth century, especially in the treatment of mathematics.[13] In Hobbes's day, many writers claimed a classical pedigree for this distinction. François Viète, for example, held that

There is a certain way of searching for the truth in mathematics that Plato is said first to have discovered. Theon called it analysis, which he defined as assuming that which is sought as if it were admitted [and working] through the consequences [of that assumption] to what is admittedly true, as opposed to synthesis, which is the assuming what is [already] admitted [and working] through the consequences [of that assumption] to arrive at and to understand that which is sought.[14]

These remarks echo the comments of the Greek mathematician Pappus, who defined analytic and synthetic procedures as follows:

[A]nalysis is the path from what one is seeking, as if it were established, by way of its consequences, to something that is established by synthesis. That is to say, in analysis we assume what is sought as if it has been achieved, and look for the thing from which it follows, and again what comes before that, until by regressing in this way we come upon some one principle. . . . In synthesis, by reversal, we assume what was obtained last in the analysis to have been achieved already, and, setting now in natural order, as precedents, what before were following, and fitting them to each other, we attain the end of the construction of what was sought.[15]

Although Hobbes is hardly original in distinguishing between analytic and synthetic methods, he adds a slightly different twist to the old methodological contrast by phrasing it in terms of causes and effects. In the Hobbesian scheme, the difference between analysis and synthesis lies in the comparison between the order of reasoning and the order of cause and effect: To reason analytically is to proceed from effects to (possible) causes, whereas the synthetic mode of reasoning follows the natural causal order and moves from causes to effects. Hobbes himself expresses the contrast in *De corpore*:

ANALYSIS is ratiocination from the supposed construction or generation of a thing to the efficient cause or coefficient causes of that which is constructed or generated. And SYNTHESIS is ratiocination from the first causes of the construction, continued through all the middle causes til we come to the thing itself which is constructed or generated. (De Corp. ch. 20.6; EW I, 312)

Because Hobbes defines all philosophy as *"such knowledge of effects or appearances as we acquire by true ratiocination from the knowledge we have first of their causes or generation. And again, of such causes or generations as may be from knowing first their effects"* (*De Corp.* ch. 1.2; *EW* I, 3), we should expect him to hold that both analytic and synthetic methods can be employed throughout all branches of philosophy. Indeed, Hobbes claims that both modes of reasoning are necessary in the investigation of causes.[16] Mathematics, for example, can employ both analysis and synthesis in the classical sense: One proceeds analytically by first assuming what was to be proved and then by investigating the conditions necessary for its proof. Then, provided that all of the steps in the analysis are reversible, a synthetic demonstration from first principles can be effected. Here, the analytic method functions as a preface to synthesis and is intended to aid in uncovering causal principles that can then be used to generate true demonstrations. Should it happen that the analysis leads to an absurdity, then the supposition at the beginning of the analysis is shown to be false.

In the natural sciences we begin with phantasms or fancies in the mind whose existence is not in question.[17] Thus, unlike the mathematical case, an analysis in natural science does not run the risk of terminating in absurdity. Analysis in natural science will lead from observed phenomena or phantasms to their possible causes, and synthesis will proceed from causal hypotheses (namely, particular motions of bodies) to derivations of their effects (i.e., the phenomena to be explained). But because the causes of natural phenomena can only be the matter for hypothesis or conjecture, the synthetic procedures of the natural scientist will fall short of the demonstrative certainty obtainable in mathematics. In other words, the synthesis available to the natural philosopher will typically be no more than a synthesis from a hypothetical cause, whereas the geometer enjoys the advantage of demonstrating from true causes.

This conception of analysis as a preface to synthesis is in keeping with the traditional characterization of analysis as the "method of invention or discovery" and synthesis as the true "method of demonstration." Hobbes explicitly endorses this representation of the distinction, holding that it is by analysis that we are led "to conceive how circumstances conduce severally to the production of effects," whereas synthesis serves "for the adding together and compounding of what they can effect singly by themselves" (*De Corp.* ch. 6, 10; *EW* I, 79).

Hobbes offers his explanation of light as an example of the proper employment of analysis and synthesis: first we observe that there is a "principal object" or source of light whenever light is observed; by analysis, we take such an object as causally necessary to the production of light; further analysis shows that a transparent medium and functioning sense organs are required for the phenomenon to present itself. As the analysis continues, we infer that a motion in the object is the principal cause of light, and that the continuation of this motion through the medium and its subsequent interaction with the "vital motion" of animal spirits in the sense organs are contributing causes. The result is that "in this manner the cause of light may be made up of motion continued from the original of the same motion, to the original of vital motion, light being nothing but the alteration of vital motion, made by the impression upon it of motion continued from the object" (*De Corp.* ch. 6, 10; *EW* I, 79). The analysis must stop somewhere, and Hobbes holds that it will terminate in simple, universal things which are self-evidently known and causally sufficient for the explanation of the phenomena. In the case of natural science, the motion of bodies is that self-evident principle upon which the explanation of physical phenomena depends.[18]

Once the analysis has been completed and the phenomenon to be explained is traced back to certain motions, the way is open for a proper synthesis from first principles. Hobbes actually characterizes the synthetic method as the proper method of teaching, as it begins with uncontestable first principles and proceeds by proper syllogisms to the required result: "The whole method, therefore, of demonstration is *synthetical,* consisting of that order of speech which begins from primary or most universal propositions, which are manifest of themselves, and proceeds by a perpetual composition of propositions into syllogisms, till at last the learner understands the truth of the conclusion sought after" (*De Corp.* ch. 6, 12; *EW* I, 81).

The picture of science that emerges from this discussion has a strong similarity to the methodological doctrine of "resolution and composition" developed in the sixteenth century by Italian philosophers known as the "School of Padua," whose most famous exponent was Jacopo Zabarella (1532–89). On this conception of scientific method, true knowledge comes from first resolving something complex into its constituent parts, and then retracing the steps to recompose the complex whole from the simple constituents. Thus, to understand fully the workings of a clock, one first disassembles it into its simpler gears, springs, etc. From knowledge of the simple parts and their mutual connections, one can then reconstruct the clock and acquire insight into its ability to keep time. Of course, the method of resolution and composition is intended to do more than facilitate clock repair. Properly applied, it should extend to all of nature, because the gears and springs of the clock can themselves be resolved into more basic material constituents. Ultimately, the process of resolution should take us to the fundamental causes or first principles from which all of the phenomena of nature can be derived. (It is important to stress that the resolution or dissection involved here need not be taken as literal. Especially in the investigation of the most basic aspects of nature, it is sufficient to perform a "thought experiment" in which natural phenomena are resolved only in thought.)

Galileo was strongly influenced by the Paduan school, and some commentators see Hobbes's conception of analysis and synthesis as an inheritance from Galileo.[19] Although the evidence for any direct connection between Hobbes and Galileo on this issue is inconclusive, there is no doubt that Galileo employed the technique of analysis and synthesis. The most famous example is his explanation of a projectile's path as arising from the composition of several simple motions. Galileo took the complex motion of a projectile such as a cannon ball and first resolved its path into combinations of simpler rectilinear motions, including gravitation toward the earth as well as the horizontal and vertical components of the velocity imparted by the cannon. He then applied previous results concerning such rectilinear motions to the determination of the complex motion of the projectile. Finally, he reversed the analysis to show (synthetically) how the parabolic flight path arises from the composition of these different fundamental motions.[20]

Whatever the extent of Hobbes's intellectual debt to Galileo or the School of Padua, his account of analysis and synthesis is fundamental in his approach to the method of natural science. Science, for Hobbes, requires knowledge of causes, and the analytic method is that by which causes are to be uncovered. Synthesis is the method to be employed in moving from causal principles to their consequences, and demonstrative synthesis is the preferred form of a scientific explanation. But this is not the whole of the story of Hobbes's account of natural science, for we must also investigate his claims to the effect that all science, and presumably all natural science, depends upon the manipulation of arbitrarily imposed signs.

SIGNS, SCIENCE, AND SYLLOGISMS

Hobbes's philosophy of natural science is closely linked to his conception of language and its role in human reasoning. Man derives many benefits from the possession and use of language, but chief among them is the fact that language makes science possible.[21] Science, as opposed to prudence, depends upon the imposition of signs and the use of reasoning to determine what effects will follow what causes; true scientific understanding thus gives us insight into the ways of nature, and from this we acquire a power over natural events. Prudence, which Hobbes equates with accumulated experience, involves the interpretation of natural signs and is something we share with the beasts. Where prudential considerations show that dark clouds are a likely sign of rain, scientific reasoning unerringly informs us that action and reaction must always be equal and opposite. Another point of contrast between these two kinds of knowledge is that science is infallible and universally applicable, whereas prudence is fallible and depends upon an extrapolation from past cases.[22]

The practice of science must begin with the creation of a scientific language, which amounts to the imposition of names. Names can be either proper or general: proper names are "singular to one onely thing," while general names are "*Common* to many things" (*Lev.* ch. 4, 13; *EW* III, 21). Once names have been imposed, they serve to call to mind the things named and can function either as marks or signs. A mark is a private name used only to remind the speaker of his previous thoughts, and a sign is a name accepted by others and used in communication. The business of science is to employ reason in establishing true propositions about the world, a proposition being "a speech consisting of two names copulated, by which he that speaketh signifies he conceives the latter name to be the name of the same thing whereof the former is the name; or (which is all one) that the former name is comprehended by the latter" (*De Corp.* ch. 3, 2; *EW* I, 30). Hobbes employs a similar account of truth, in which the truth or falsehood of a proposition is a matter of the relationship between names.

When two Names are joyned together into a Consequence, or Affirmation; as thus, *A man is a living creature*; or thus, *if he be a man, he is a living creature*, If the latter name *Living Creature*, signifie all that the former name *Man* signifieth, then the affirmation, or consequence is *true*; otherwise *false*. For *True* and *False* are attributes of Speech, not of things. (*Lev.* ch. 4, 14; *EW* III, 23)

The reasoning by which true propositions are to be established is, on Hobbes's account, a kind of arithmetic involving the addition and subtraction of mental contents. "When a man *Reasoneth*, hee does nothing else but conceive a summe totall, from *Addition* of parcels; or conceive a Remainder, from *Subtraction* of one summe from another" (*Lev.* ch. 5, 18; *EW* III, 29). This addition and subtraction is performed most easily by the manipulation of signs or words, but it is possible to compute without them, in which case our computations will be performed on phantasms. In *De corpore* ch. 1, 3 (*EW* I, 4), he illustrates this part of his doctrine by an example: Suppose a man sees something in the distance, but so indistinctly as not to discern precisely what it is. At this stage he has only the idea of body, for he knows that it must be some kind of visible body. On approaching he sees that the body moves itself about "now in one place and now in another," and he adds the idea "animated" to his previous idea of body. Upon closer investigation of the animated body, he "perceives the figure, hears the voice, and sees other things which are signs of a rational mind, though it have yet no appellation, namely, that for which we now call anything *rational."* The three ideas of body, animated, and rational are then drawn into a sum by seeing that all three pertain to the same thing; thus arises a new idea (namely, the idea of man) compounded out of the three ideas of body, animation, and rationality.

So described, this mental arithmetic is performed on particular ideas and (at least on Hobbes's understanding of the matter) without the use of words. But the more usual case of reasoning will involve words rather than ideas of particular things named by words. In this case, reasoning involves the drawing of consequences from the manipulation of general names:

Reason, in this sense, is nothing but *Reckoning* (that is, Adding and Substracting) of the Consequences of generall names agreed upon, for the *marking* and *signifying* of our thoughts; I say *marking* them, when we reckon by our selves; and *signifying*, when we demonstrate, or approve our reckonings to other men. (*Lev.* ch. 5, 18; *EW* III, 30)

The use of general names in reasoning is es.ential if the consequences drawn are to be truly scientific and to apply beyond the range of past experience. Hobbes insists that "experience concludeth nothing universally" (*HN* ch. 4, 10; *EW* IV, 18) and stresses the crucial role of names in the formation of generalized knowledge. By the imposition of general names, "we turn the reckoning of the consequences of things imagined in the mind into a reckoning of the consequences of Appellations" (*Lev.* ch. 4, 14; *EW* III, 21), and such consequences of appellations can be extended beyond the scope of experience and made general or universal. Hobbes illustrates the universality of reasoning from names by an imaginary case: suppose that a man entirely ignorant of speech reasons about a particular triangle and two right angles placed beside it; suppose further that he concludes that, in this particular case, the interior angles are equal to the two right angles. Hobbes claims that the man's inability to use words will make it impossible for him to generalize this result to cover other cases, whereas a man who has mastered the appropriate geometric vocabulary will acquire truly scientific (that is, universal) knowledge that the same result holds in all cases.

But he that hath the use of words, when he observes, that such equality was consequent, not to the length of the sides, nor to any other particular thing in his triangle; but onely to this, that the sides were straight, and the angles three; and that that was all, for which he named it a Triangle; will boldly conclude Universally, that such equality of angles is in all triangles whatsoever; and register his invention in these generall termes, *Every triangle hath its three angles equall to two right angles.* (*Lev.* ch. 4, 14; *EW* III, 22)

The drawing of consequences from general names is the concern of logic, and Hobbes models his account of scientific inference on the deductive structure of classical syllogistic logic. A syllogism, in Hobbes's idiom, is "A SPEECH, consisting of three propositions, from two of which the third follows" (*De Corp.* ch. 4. 1; *EW* I, 44). In keeping with his account of reasoning as computation, Hobbes treats syllogistic inferences as a kind of mental addition in which the conclusion is drawn as a sum from the two premises (*De Corp.* ch. 4. 6; *EW* I, 48). Because science aims to "establish universal rules concerning the properties of things," the syllogisms appearing in a scientific demonstration must contain only general names, for it is "superfluous to consider any other mood in direct figure, besides that, in which all the propositions are both universal and affirmative" (*De Corp.* ch. 4. 7; *EW* I, 49).

These doctrines result in a conception of science that places a heavy burden on purely linguistic activities such as the imposition of names, the analysis of meanings through definitions, and the construction of syllogisms. Indeed, Hobbes often writes as if the main concern of the scientist is simply the unpacking of definitions and the proper ordering of terms. The universal affirmative propositions appearing in scientific syllogisms would seem to depend for their truth only upon speakers' arbitrary conventions about the meanings of general terms, and this fact suggests that the scientist need tend only to the proper arrangement of terms in his syllogisms. In *Leviathan*, for example, Hobbes comes very close to the implausible claim that science involves nothing more than the correct ordering of names:

Reason is not as Sense, and Memory, borne with us; nor gotten by Experience onely; as Prudence is; but attayned by Industry; first in apt imposing of Names; and secondly by getting a good and orderly Method in proceeding from the Elements, which are Names, to Assertions made by Connexion of one of them to another; and so to Syllogismes, which are the Connections of one Assertion to another, till we come to a knowledge of all the Consequences of names appertaining to the subject in hand; and that is it, men call SCIENCE. (*Lev.* ch. 5, 21; *EW* III, 35)

The "Elements" of science, then, are names arbitrarily imposed by the scientist, and the whole enterprise appears to involve little more than investigating the consequences of such names. Accounting for scientific knowledge in this way does have the virtue of making it completely certain: If science is created by the arbitrary imposition of names and confined to the analysis of names and their interconnections, then (barring inconsistency or ambiguous names) there is no danger that our reasoning might lead to falsehood. It is worth observing that the term "science" in this passage is intended to encompass more than the natural sciences, and would also include both the science of politics and geometry. But even taking this into account, it seems that Hobbes is tempted toward an improbable conception of science that secures the truth and certainty of scientific knowledge at the cost of restricting it to the analysis of language. Furthermore, Hobbes's stress on the arbitrariness with which names are "imposed" on the world seems to commit him to a strongly conventionalist conception of scientific truth in which the truth of a scientific statement will amount to nothing more than speakers' agreement upon the definitions of the terms it contains.[23]

Although Hobbes's stronger statements regarding the role of names may suggest that he conceived of natural science as involving little more than a manipulation of names, this cannot be the dominant theme in his account of the method of natural science. Such an approach clearly conflicts with his other remarks on the importance of causes in scientific demonstrations. As we have seen, Hobbes held that the aim of science is to uncover the mechanical causes of natural phenomena. But the search for causes must surely involve more than simply assigning names to things and analyzing definitions. And indeed, Hobbes himself requires that scientific definitions contain the causes of the things defined, even insisting that "definitions of things, which may be understood to have some cause, must consist of such names as express the cause or manner of their generation" (De Corp. ch. 6, 13; EW I, 81). Definitions of this sort clearly cannot be entirely arbitrary or conventional, because it is possible to have a definition that fails to satisfy such a requirement, either by giving no cause of the thing defined or by falsely identifying its cause. Thus, we should not take Hobbes's comments on the role of names in science as evidence of a purely conventionalist theory of natural science.

What word we use to represent any particular thing is admittedly arbitrary and a matter of the speakers' convention. But this degree of arbitrariness or conventionality is consistent with there being better or worse definitions of scientific terms, and Hobbes holds that the proper definitions for science are those that reveal the causes of the things defined. For example, speakers of English may use the terms "sunrise" or "dawn" interchangeably, and we can agree with Hobbes that it is quite an arbitrary or conventional matter that we use either term to designate a certain type of event. But such arbitrariness in the choice of words does not entail that terms can be defined any way we please. It would be correct but not fully enlightening to define either one as "the appearance of the sun over the horizon." It would be simply incorrect to define either as "the appearance of the sun over the horizon, as a result of the sun's revolution about the earth," and indeed the true definition must be "the appearance of the sun over the horizon, as a result of the earth's diurnal rotation." The last of these three definitions is, on Hobbes's view, the best precisely because it reveals the true cause of the thing defined, and that it does so is not the result of an arbitrary or conventional decision on our part.

Understood in this way, Hobbes's requirements for scientific definitions mesh with his doctrine of analysis and synthesis, as well as his insistence upon the hypothetical nature of scientific knowledge. Ideally, natural science would be cast in the form of syllogisms that start from the most easily understood universal notions, such as body, space, motion, and impact. Through a series of definitions that reveal the causal origins of things, a perfect natural science could derive all the phenomena of nature from unquestionable first principles. It is unfortunate that men in general lack the insight into nature that permits the true causal definitions of things. Instead, the best we can hope for is to employ a process of analysis to lead from the phenomena to be explained to the hypothetical causes of such phenomena. If the analysis is successful and adequate causes are found, then definitions can be introduced and demonstrations set forth by following the method of synthesis. Geometry has achieved this lofty ideal, but the natural sciences require provisional definitions and hypothetical causes. In this context it is worth recalling that Hobbes characterizes geometry as uniquely scientific precisely because its terms are properly defined and carefully explicated. It is the geometers who "begin [their] ratiocination from the Definitions, or Explications of the names they are to use;" and this, Hobbes claims, "is a method that hath been used onely in Geometry; whose Conclusions have thereby been made indisputable" (*Lev.* ch. 5, 20; *EW* III, 33). Geometry's special status among the sciences thus derives from the fact that it satisfies Hobbes's criteria for proper definitions, and any other body of enquiry that could establish true causal definitions would be capable of demonstrative certainty.

THE FATE OF THE HOBBESIAN PROGRAM FOR NATURAL SCIENCE

Hobbes's methodological doctrines had little influence, except insofar as they were the object of attack by members of the Royal Society. Continental scientists working in the tradition of Descartes shared both Hobbes's commitment to plenism and his reliance upon hypotheses in explaining phenomena, but Hobbes had little or no direct influence on the development of Continental science.[24] His conception of natural science gives pride of place to deductions from mechanistic first principles and downplays the role of experiment. Such a program is fundamentally at odds with the "experimentalist" methodology prevalent in Britain in the 1660s and 1670s, and Hobbes failed miserably in his efforts to promote his views in his homeland. The principal form of Hobbes's confrontation with Britain's dominant scientific methodology was his prolonged and bitter dispute with Robert Boyle. Hobbes attacked Boyle's 1660 "New Experiments Physico-Mechanical, touching the Spring of the Air" with his own *Dialogus physicus de natura aeris;* this exchange led to others, and Hobbes's once-considerable reputation as a natural philosopher was destroyed in the ensuing controversy.[25] The reliance upon hypotheses so characteristic of Hobbes's methodology fell out of favor in Britain in the closing decades of the seventeenth century, and by the time of Hobbes's death the word "hypothesis" could serve as a term of abuse. It was a commonplace among British scientists of the era to condemn the baseless and extravagant hypotheses of their Continental rivals and to demand that scientific theories be grounded on experiment and observation. Indeed, Newton's famous pronouncement that "I have not been able to discover the cause of those properties of gravity from phenomena, and I frame no hypotheses" reflects the British scientific community's wholesale repudiation of Hobbes's methodology.[26] Ignored on the Continent and reviled in Britain, Hobbes's methodology of the natural sciences did not outlive its creator.

NOTES

1 As Aristotle puts it: "We think we understand a thing *simpliciter* (and not in the sophistic fashion accidentally) whenever we think we are aware both that the explanation because of which the object is is its explanation, and that it is not possible for this to be otherwise" (*Posterior Analytics* I, 2; 70b 9–12). The "explanation because of which the object is" will, of course, be a causal explanation. I use the translation of Jonathan Barnes in *The Complete Works of Aristotle: The Revised Oxford Translation*, ed. Jonathan Barnes, 2 vols. (Princeton: Princeton University Press, 1984). Citations from Hobbes's works will normally appear in the text, abbreviating '*Leviathan*' as '*Lev.*', '*De Corpore*' as '*De Corp.*', and '*Dialogus Physicus de natura aeris*' as '*DiPh*'. The format includes (abbreviated) title, followed by chapter number, and section number wherever applicable. Citations of the *Opera Latina* and the *English Works* then follow after a semicolon. I use C.B. Macpherson's Penguin edition for the text *Leviathan*, citing the original pagination as given in Macpherson's text; I use Simon Schaffer's English translation of *Dialogus physicus* (Shapin and Schaffer 1988, 345–391), citing the pagination of the *Opera Latina* as given in the translation.
2 See Wallace (1978) for an overview of the philosophical background to medieval science, particularly with reference to the Aristotelian roots of Scholastic scientific methodology.
3 This denunciation of Scholastic philosophy is carried out at greatest length in Chapter 46 of *Leviathan* (*Lev.* ch. 46, 368–81; *EW* III, 664–88), where Hobbes decries the "Darknesse from Vain Philosophy and Fabulous Traditions."
4 Hobbes's failed mathematical career, and particularly his long-running dispute with Wallis, are summarized in Scott, Chap. 10, and Robertson, Chap. 8. See also Chapter 5 of the present volume.
5 Aubrey writes: "He was . . . 40 yeares old before he looked upon geometry. Being in a Gentleman's Library . . . , Euclids Elements lay open, and 'twas the 47 El. libri I. He read the Proposition. "By G--," sayd he, 'this is impossible!' So he reads the Demonstration of it, which referred him back to such a Proposition which proposition he read. That referred him back

to another, which he also read. *Et sic deinceps*, that at last he was convinced of that trueth. This made him in love with geometry" (Aubrey, *Brief Lives*, 1:332).

6 As he explains in the Dedicatory Epistle to the *Six Lessons*, "civil philosophy is demonstrable, because we make the commonwealth ourselves. But because of natural bodies we know not the construction, but seek it from the effects, there lies no demonstration of what the causes be we seek for, but only of what they might be" (*EW* VII, 184).

7 This remark is from a letter dated July 29/Aug. 8, 1636, and addressed to the earl of Newcastle. The entire passage reads: "In thinges that are not demonstrable, of which kind is the greatest part of naturall philosophy, as dependinge upon the motion of bodies so subtile as they are invisible, such as are ayre and spirits; the most that can be atteyned unto is to have such opinions, as no certayne experience can confute, and from which can be deduced by lawfull argumentation, no absurdity." The letter is contained in *The Manuscripts of the Duke of Portland perserved at Welbeck Abbey* (London, 1893), vol. 2, p. 128; I quote from Gargani (1971, 212).

8 Once set in motion, however, a body will remain in motion unless some other body hinders it. As Hobbes puts it in *Leviathan*: "That when a thing lies still, unlesse somewhat els stirre it, it will lye still for ever, is a truth that no man doubts of. But that when a thing is in motion, it will eternally be in motion, unless somewhat els stay it, though the reason be the same, (namely, that nothing can change it selfe,) is not so easily assented to" (*Lev*. ch. 2, 4; *EW* III, 3–4).

9 Thus, in *Leviathan*, he writes: "If we would know why the same Body seems greater (without adding to it one time, than another they say, when it seems lesse, it is *Condensed* when greater, *Rarefied*. What is that *Condensed*, and *Rarefied*? Condensed, is when there is in the very same Matter, lesse Quantity than before and Rarefied, when more. As if there could be Matter, that had not some determined Quantity; when Quantity is nothing else but the Determination of Matter; that is to say of Body, by which we say one Body is greater, or lesser than another, by this, or thus much. Or as if a Body were made without any Quantity at all, and that afterwards more, or lesse were put into it, according as it is intended the body should be more or lesse Dense" (*Lev*. ch. 46, 375; *EW* III, 678–9).

10 The manuscript is cataloged as Classified Papers IV (1), no. 30. It has been brought to light by Schaffer and is reprinted as Schaffer (1988, pp. 297–8). I quote from the reprinted version.

11 Schaffer 1988, 297–8.

12 Schaffer writes that "The provisional basis of Hobbes's causal stories

must be stressed. In the 1660s he often offered alternative accounts of the motions which generated these phenomena [associated with Boyle's air pump]. In his *Dialogus physicus* (1661), for example, Hobbes gave two alternative causal accounts for the rapid ascent of a sucker in the cylinder of the air pump when pulled back and released. One used the simple circular motion of earthly particles in the air, the other the motion of the external air itself. Similarly, whereas in *De corpore* Hobbes accounted for the ejection of a bullet from the wind-gun using simple circular motion of earthly particles flowing into its chamber, in both *Dialogus physicus* and the remarks on "Compression of Air" he accounted for the same phenomenon in terms of the circulation of air inside the barrel. These changes dramatised his view that the same phenomenon could be adequately explained by a variety of different motions. But what was not allowed was talk of entities which violated the rules of philosophy, such as condensation, self moving matter, or vacuum" (Schaffer 1988, 283).

13 See Hintikka and Remes (1974) for a study of the method of analysis and its history. More specifically on Hobbes's conception of analysis and synthesis, see Talaska (1988).

14 Viète 1983 ed. 10.

15 Pappus 1986 ed. 1:83.

16 I leave aside the question of whether Hobbes sees a true unity of method between natural science and political science. Sorell (1986) argues that there is a methodological disunity between natural and civil science, notwithstanding Hobbes's claims that the methodology of analysis and synthesis is universally applicable. To whatever extent Hobbes is serious about his claim that the business of philosophy is the investigation of causes, it seems reasonable that he would see analytic and synthetic procedures as integral to the philosophical enterprise. Thus, his declaration in *De Corpore* that "in the searching out of causes, there is need partly of the analytical, and partly of the synthetical method; of the analytical, to conceive how circumstances conduce severally to the production of effects; and of the synthetical, for the adding together and compounding of what they can effect singly by themselves," (*De Corp.* ch. 1, 6, 10; *EW* I, 79) could be taken as asserting that analytic and synthetic procedures will be part of any scientific investigation.

17 As Hobbes puts it, "The first beginnings, therefore, of knowledge, are the phantasms of sense and imagination; and that there be such phantasms we know well enough by nature; but to know why they be, or from what causes they proceed, is the work of ratiocination; which consists . . . in *composition* and *division*" (*De Corp. 1* ch. 6, 1; *EW* I, 66). The characterization of ratiocination as a process of composition and division will be

examined in the next section when we consider Hobbes's views on the role of language in scientific reasoning.

18 In fact, Hobbes claims that motion is the principle from which absolutely everything can be derived: "but the causes of universal things (of those, at least, that have any cause) are manifest of themselves, or (as they say commonly) known to nature; so that they need no method at all; for they have all but one universal cause, which is motion" (*De Corp.* ch. 6, 5; *EW* I, 69).

19 Macpherson declares that "What was needed was a two-part method, which would show how to reach such simple starting propositions, as well as what to do when one had them. Hobbes found it in the method used by Galileo – the 'resolutive-compositive' method" (Macpherson 1968, 25–6). Similarly, Watkins (1965, Chs. 3–4) argues for a Paduan influence on Hobbes, particularly through Galileo and Harvey. Prins (1990) disputes such a direct linking of Hobbes to the School of Padua, arguing that Hobbes and Zabarella have entirely different conceptions of science. There is no need to decide the issue here, for nothing I say here depends upon whether he is indebted to Galileo or the School of Padua for his methodological distinction between analysis and synthesis.

20 The "Fourth Day" dialogue in Galileo's *Two New Sciences* (Galileo, 1974 ed., 217–60) contains the analytic–synthetic approach to projectile motion. See Watkins (1965, 55–63) for an overview of this case and its relationship to Hobbes.

21 As he puts it in the *Elements of Law*, 1.5.4: "By the advantage of *names* it is that we are capable of *science*, which beasts, for want of them are not; nor man, without the use of them" (*EW* IV, 21).

22 The contrast between science and prudence is explored in Barnouw (1990). Hobbes draws a memorable distinction between science and prudence in *Leviathan*, writing "As, much Experience, is *Prudence*; so, is much Science, *Sapience*. For though wee usually have one name of Wisedome for them both; yet the Latines did always distinguish between *Prudentia* and *Sapientia*; ascribing the former to Experience, the latter to Science. But to make their difference appear more cleerly, let us suppose one man endued with an excellent naturall use, and dexterity in handling his armes; and another to have added to that dexterity, and acquired Science, of where he can offend, or be offended by this adversarie, in every possible posture or guard: The ability of the former, would be to the ability of the later as Prudence to Sapience; both usefull; but the latter infallible." (*Lev.* ch. 5, 22; *EW* III, 37).

23 Sorell (1986, 45–9) argues that Hobbes is not committed to a thoroughly conventionalist theory of scientific truth, although he employs slightly different considerations from those in play here. For an extended study

of the role of conventionalism in Hobbes's treatment of science, particularly in the works before *De corpore*, see Pacchi (1965).

24 This is not to say that Hobbes was a complete unknown among scientific circles on the Continent. In the 1630s and 1640s he was active in the circle around Marin Mersenne. During this period he acquired his reputation as a natural philosopher, eventually publishing his *Tractatus opticus* as Book VII of Mersenne's *Cogitata physico-mathematica*, and contributing part of the preface to Mersenne's *Ballistica*. But after his return to Britain in 1651, Hobbes's influence on Continental science was negligible.

25 See Shapin and Schaffer (1985) for the most comprehensive study of this dispute and its effect on Hobbes's reputation as a natural philosopher and methodologist.

26 The remark is from Book III of Newton's *Principia* (Newton [1727] 1934, 2: 547). Although Newton's declaration is not directed specifically against Hobbes, it is indicative of the methodological suspicion with which British scientists regarded hypotheses.

5   Hobbes and mathematics

I

Posterity has not looked admiringly on Hobbes's ventures into mathematics. Modern historians, aware that the untutored philosopher made no contribution to the subject and that he claimed success in problems now known to be insoluble, tend to view his efforts with dismay or to pass over them in silence. Jean-Etienne Montucla set the pace by publishing (1758) a large two-volume history of mathematics that contrives not to mention Hobbes even once. Later writers, when they have noticed him at all, have often exhibited only the unrepentant circle-squarer or the obtuse opponent of his century's revolutionary application of algebra to geometrical problems. Julian Lovell Coolidge's enchanting book on the mathematics of "great amateurs" gives chapters to such peripheral figures as Piero della Francesca the painter and Denis Diderot the man of letters, but finds no space for the author of *Leviathan*. Petr Beckmann's history of the number π – a number that, as we shall see, figures implicitly in much of Hobbes's geometry – introduces the philosopher's name only to dismiss it with a sneer.[1] Occasionally a more sympathetic voice has been raised, as by Augustus de Morgan (1872): "Hobbes . . . was not the ignoramus in geometry that he is sometimes supposed. His writings, erroneous as they are in many things, contain acute remarks on points of principle."[2] But such defenders have been few.

The story of his *contemporary* mathematical reputation is complex, and is tangled by extrinsic factors. In large measure it is a poignant tale of steep decline from high stature. As late as the 1640s, when Hobbes was in late middle age, he commanded much respect both in England and abroad – as a scientist rather than as a philosopher.[3] I shall explain below how his involvement, during his Paris exile, in one of the great mathematical issues of his time was taken seriously by at least some of the participants, and how his own efforts, though mistaken, may have served as one catalyst of eventual progress. During the same period he had the honor to act as mathematical tutor to the Prince of Wales, later Charles II. Back in England after 1651, he continued to enjoy acclaim. Henry Oldenburg, later famous as the first secretary of the Royal Society, respectfully sought Hobbes's advice in mathematics, and one Ralph Bathurst wrote a laudatory poem that did not scruple to compare the philosopher with Archimedes. Even his arch-enemy John Wallis conceded that Hobbes "had in his younger years some little insights in Mathematics; & which at that time (when few had any) passed for a great deal."[4]

The last decades of Hobbes's long life saw immense progress in mathematics, especially toward the calculus, and the aging philosopher was simply left behind by that historic advance. Worse, Hobbes's persistent attempts to square the circle, and his rash assaults on Wallis's own mathematics, touched off (1655) two decades of weird and pathetic intellectual warfare, in which the philosopher repeatedly broke lances against his rival's superior skill and sophistication. Invective aside – in that sphere the battle may be scored a draw, an equal contest of grand masters – Hobbes's mathematical weaknesses were relentlessly laid bare, and his star fell accordingly. Motives darker than a disinterested quest for truth spurred Wallis to the destruction of his rival's reputation. To him, as to allies like the chemist Robert Boyle, Hobbes's materialist philosophy posed an obvious threat to Christian teaching; and as that philosophy was explicitly grounded in geometry, what better defense of the faith than a public display of Hobbes's mathematical ineptitude? "Our Leviathan," wrote Wallis to Christian Huygens in 1659, "is furiously attacking and destroying our Universities . . . and especially ministers and Clergy and all religion . . . as though men could not understand religion if they did not understand Mathematics. Hence it seemed necessary that some mathematician should show him . . . how little he understands the Mathematics from which he takes his courage."[5] Thus Wallis's zeal in the mathematical arena must be seen as one facet of the savage opposition, documented by Samuel Mintz in *The Hunting of Leviathan*, that sought to discredit the whole range of Hobbes's philosophical positions. Wallis spared no pains, and the effects were devastating. Lord Clarendon, sometime chief adviser to Charles I, slyly noted that Hobbes had come to offer an example of a type that his own *Leviathan* had declared impossible, a person "who is so stupid, as both to mistake in Geometry, and also to persist in it, when another detects his error to him."[6]

Of course Wallis's campaign was not the sole agent of Hobbes's diminished mathematical stature, for any competent geometer could see the truth for himself. Huygens typifies the general disillusionment: In 1654 he had honored the Englishman with a copy of his *De circuli magnitude,* but in 1661 – after the first rash of circle-squarings – he paid Hobbes the distinctly backhanded tribute of saying that "by his abundance of absurdities he becomes pleasant, and I know not if I do well to contribute to bring him to silence hereafter."[7] Some respect for Hobbes survived the decline. His loyal friend John Aubrey tried to put the best face on Wallis's exposures: "where [Hobbes] erres, he erres so ingeniosely, that one had rather erre with him then hitt the marke with Clavius."[8] From another quarter came admiration that had some real if minor historic importance. As late as 1670 the young Leibniz sought Hobbes's acquaintance by correspondence, and borrowed fruitfully from the old warrior several mathematical ideas, including the immensely powerful notion that reasoning is a kind of calculation, the goal of *proving* such Euclidean axioms as "the whole is greater than the part," and the Hobbesian formulation of another concept that I shall mention later. Still another contemporary estimate was even more favorable, holding that Hobbes had "rectified and explained" the principles of geometry, and was indeed "the first that hath made the grounds of geometry firm and coherent"[9] – but this is our philosopher on himself.

II

In weighing these diverse assessments it is well to remember that they bear on only one aspect of the role of mathematics in Hobbes's life and thought. Praise and scorn alike have focused on what we may call "internal" issues – his attempts to solve specific geometrical problems, and his opinions on the nature and epistemological status of mathematical objects. But alongside these, and much more important, was his sense of the wider relevance of mathematics: his vision of geometry as the model science and as the foundation of his entire philosophy. Moreover, these twin facets of his mathematics, the efforts within the subject and the wider applications, remained essentially independent. The stubborn attacks on particular problems like the squaring of the circle neither reflected nor influenced the roles assigned to geometry in his larger schemes. As this latter aspect of his thought is fully discussed elsewhere in this volume (Chapter 4), I shall concentrate here on Hobbes's ventures into the pleasures and pitfalls of technical mathematics.

For this purpose his formal education availed him very little, for (as he wrote in *Leviathan*) geometry had "till of very late times . . . no place at all" in the universities.[10] Thus his acquaintance with important mathematics was long delayed. Who has not savored Aubrey's tale of the mature philosopher's first wondering encounter with Euclid?

He was 40 yeares old before he looked on Geometry; which happened accidentally. Being in a Gentleman's Library, Euclid's Elements lay open, and 'twas the 47 el. *libri* 1 [i.e., Book I, Proposition 47, the "Pythagorean" theorem]. He read the Proposition. *By G –*, sayd he (he would now and then swear an emphaticall Oath by way of emphasis) *this is impossible!* So he reads the Demonstration of it, which referred him back to such a Proposition; which proposition he read. That referred him back to another, which he also read. *Et sic deinceps* [and so on] that at last he was demonstratively convinced of that trueth. This made him in love with Geometry.[11]

Scholarship now calls into question this familiar scenario of sudden revelation, although not the enduring delight of the anecdote itself. There survives, in Hobbes's handwriting, a reading list containing nearly 900 items. Geometry accounts for some 123 of these, including no fewer than ten different editions of Euclid. The manuscript's editor, Arrigo Pacchi, dates it between 1625 and 1628 – earlier than the incident described by Aubrey.[12] But the general picture – of Hobbes coming late in life to mathematics and teaching himself – remains.

In Hobbes's new passion for geometry, notes Aubrey, "he was wont to draw lines on his thigh and on the sheets, abed, and also to multiply and divide."[13] So enthused, he proceeded to write many pages on mathematics – by one reckoning some 27 percent of his total output.[14] Much of this material is a verbose exposition of basics, and will not repay a modern reader's investment of time. To do

Hobbes justice, it was necessary to the grand design of his life's work to lay out the rudiments of geometry, for he supposed all philosophy to depend on them. But many of his pages carry the stamp of the self-educated inquirer for whom the learning even of fundamentals takes on the exaggerated importance of a new discovery.

At one point, to be sure, Hobbes promised that he would begin only where Euclid, Archimedes, and Apollonius left off, for "to what end is it, to do over again that which is already done?"[15] But he thought he saw in the Greek heritage certain flaws that demanded correction ("as for Archimedes, there is no man that does admire him more than I do; but there is no man that cannot err").[16] His most insistent challenge to the ancient legacy was at its very foundations, the definitions that underlie the *Elements*. Again and again he criticized Euclid's definition of a point as "that which has no part." A geometrical point (he urged) is a visible mark, and so has quantity, and so is potentially divisible into parts, although such parts are "not considered" in demonstrations. Similarly he balked at Euclid's definition of a line as "breadthless length." For "lines are not drawn but by motion, and motion is of body only," so that a line must have a width, although this too is always negligible in practice.[17] These pronouncements encapsulate much of Hobbes's philosophy of mathematics. They place him in sharp opposition to the mainstream view that the objects of geometry are abstractions from, idealizations of, sensory experience. He saw geometry as a quasi-physical science of extended body, and his insistence that its objects are produced by *physical motions* was profoundly characteristic.

Hobbes was closer to ancient orthodoxy in his early approach to the difficult concept of number. At first he recognized as numbers only the positive integers $(1, 2, 3, \ldots)$, a stance dating from classic Greece. In the intervening centuries this severely limited vision had had profound historical repercussions, for it obliged its adherents to regard as *geometrical* many concepts and relations that to us are numerical or algebraic. Thus the number that we call $\sqrt{2}$ appeared to the Greeks as a line segment – the diagonal of a unit square. In the same spirit any *arbitrary* quantity was conceived as a line segment, and the product of two such was then a rectangle (our reference to x^2 as a "square" is a lasting legacy). A familiar algebraic identity like $a^2 - b^2 = (a+b)(a-b)$ appears in Euclid (II, 5) in seeming disguise, as a theorem about rectangles and squares. This geometric coloring of numbers and of algebraic relations is often close to the surface of Hobbes's mathematics, and I shall return to it at several points in what follows.

But if his approach to numbers had the stamp of much history, it naturally reflected also some of his most characteristic philosophical positions. Thus in keeping with his denial of Platonic universals and his physical conception of mathematical objects, he puzzled over how the positive integers can be "exposed" (made accessible) to sense perception and thus be given legitimacy. He saw two possibilities. They might be represented by points, as long as these were not "contiguous," for "number is called discrete quantity" in contrast to continuous geometrical magnitudes like line segments. (This distinction, an obvious consequence of the limited concept of number described above, had been a mathematical commonplace such Pythagoras.) But also, Hobbes went on, the positive integers might be "exposed" by their *names*, for example by the recitation of their names "by heart and in order, as one, two, three, etc."[18]

Hobbes's thoughts about number did not end there, however, for all around him the concept was under vigorous debate. The Greek restriction to positive integers was in retreat on several fronts. Many mathematicians (Wallis, Simon Stevin, Rafael Bombelli) had by this time computed freely with decimal fractions, with negative numbers, with "irrationals" (like $\sqrt{2}$), even with "imaginaries" (like $\sqrt{-1}$), for the interest and utility of these quantities was palpable. Other opinion (Pascal, Barrow, Newton) remained conservative, uneasy over whether and how the existence and properties of these more exotic entities could be coherently conceived. Hobbes was of the latter party. To him, for example, the result of subtracting a number from itself, or a greater from a lesser, was problematic because apparently incapable of physical representability. Perhaps, as Helena Pycior has suggested,[19] this dilemma inclined him toward his alternative of regarding all numbers as names. When we subtract 2 and 3 from 5, he wrote, we can say that "nothing" remains; and although this word is a mere name, and "cannot be the name of any thing," it is "not unuseful" as a permanent record and reminder of our calculation; and similarly for *"less than nothing,"* which remains "when we substract more from less."[20] Hobbes did not much pursue these thoughts, and they had no discernible influence. But they retain some slight interest as one of many contemporary gropings toward a rigorously broadened concept of number, an intellectual struggle not fully resolved until the nineteenth century.

III

Hobbes earned much notoriety, in his own time and later, for his hostility to the mathematicians' rapidly increasing use of algebra. In the third century Diophantus had made a beginning in the systematic use of symbols for quantities and operations, but the renewal of this enterprise in Hobbes's lifetime was wholly new in scale and sophistication. Hobbes never grasped the enormous potential of algebra, with its intrinsic ease of transformation of expressions. He saw the new techniques merely as a trivial extension of arithmetic, "to the theory whereof two or three Days at most are required, though to the Promptitude of Working, perhaps the Practice of three Months is necessary."[21] He had no patience with algebra's "scab of symbols," the shorthand that made a mathematical page look "as if a hen had been scraping there." He conceded that these symbols might be useful, even necessary, aids to demonstration, but "they ought no more to appear in public, than the most deformed necessary business which you do in your chambers."[22]

Of course it sounds deplorably perverse. Yet behind the catchy metaphors lay reservations that merit respect. Hobbes had in fact two distinct though related grounds for skepticism over the new algebra. One of these had ancient roots. He was schooled in a tradition, dating from Plato's day, that described much of mathematical and scientific practice in terms of a pair of related procedures called, respectively, "analysis" and "synthesis." Analysis was the Greek geometers' formalization of an intuitively suggestive strategy for the establishment of theorems or the effecting of constructions. Suppose we suspect that some mathematical statement is true. The method of analysis, as classically conceived, *assumes* the validity of this conjecture and draws conclusions from it. Sometimes this leads to a contradiction, in which case the suspected theorem is in fact false. But often one can reach, by successive deductions, a statement already known or assumed to be true – a theorem previously proved or an axiom accepted at the subject's foundation. In this case a reversal of the chain of inference, if possible, provides a *proof* of the result originally conjectured.

A simple example may make the idea clearer. Students are often invited to prove that if a and b are two unequal positive numbers, then their arithmetic mean $A = (a + b)/2$ is greater than their geometric mean $G = \sqrt{ab}$. Now if, in fact,

$$\frac{1}{2}(a + b) > \sqrt{ab} \quad (1)$$

then, equivalently,

$$a + b > 2\sqrt{ab}$$

or (squaring and subtracting),

$$a^2 + 2ab + b^2 - 4ab > 0,$$

i.e.,

$$(a - b)^2 > 0,$$

which of course is known to be true (the square of any non-zero real number is positive). Reversing the sequence of steps is legitimate and gives a *proof* of (1). Arguments of this second type, from known or assumed truths to the proofs of new theorems, were called "synthesis" by the Greeks, and were regarded by them as the only rigorous way to organize and expound a body of mathematical knowledge; the canonical example is Euclid's *Elements*. Synthesis was thus universally viewed, in antiquity and after, as a higher, more scientific procedure than analysis, a distinction duly repeated by Hobbes.[23]

Now when François Viète (1540–1603) and others developed the new algebra, they tended to identify its use with the ancient method of analysis, which the historical record had left rather obscure. (Viète actually referred to algebra as *l'ars analytique*; hence also the "analytic" geometry introduced later by Descartes and Fermat.) This identification was presumably encouraged by two characteristic features of Renaissance mathematics. The commonest application of algebra in those days was to the solution of equations; and there are certain similarities, logical and psychological, between this activity and Greek analysis. The setting out of an equation (say, $ax = b$) amounts to an assumption about the unknown value of x. The consequences of this assumption are pursued through the series of algebraic manipulations (the "analysis") that eventually isolate x on one side ($x = b/a$). (The corresponding "synthesis" is then the *proof*, by substitution into the original equation, that the value of x so obtained is correct.) And if Renaissance algebra thus recalled Greek analysis in methodology, the two also shared a common sphere of application: geometry. For the equations studied by Viète and his contemporaries retained in their eyes much of the geometric flavor that had underlain ostensibly algebraic relations since antiquity. (This explains, for example, their insistence that any equation be "homogeneous," or, in other words, that all its terms be products of the same number of factors: $x^3 + ax^2$ was admissible in an equation, but $x^3 + x^2$ was not, because *geometrically* the addition of a square to a cube makes no sense.) The upshot of all this was that Renaissance algebra inherited the *secondary* status assigned in Greece to analysis; it long seemed more a *means of discovery* in *geometry* than a subject of interest in its own right. This is the background of Hobbes's remark that a student who has Euclid for his mathematical master will have no need of Viète, but not conversely.[24]

   The second of his two reservations about algebra also rested on the belief that the objects and relations of geometry are the true and only subject matter of mathematics. To some this seemed to imply that when we study a circle by drawing it, we *see* a more or less accurate representation of the object of inquiry and of its properties, whereas the *algebraic* approach of writing $x^2 + y^2 = 1$ shows us only arbitrary symbols. Do these not (Hobbes asked) actually *impede* understanding? Are they not like a foreign language, which we must translate to reach meaning? Do they not end by making demonstrations longer, not shorter? "There is a double labour of the mind," he wrote, addressing Wallis, "one to reduce your symbols to words, which are also symbols, another to attend to the ideas which they signify."[25] When Wallis gave algebraic versions of some of Hobbes's geometric arguments, claiming thus to streamline them, his adversary countered that "though there be your symbols, yet no man is obliged to take them for demonstration. And ... when they are taught to speak as they ought to do, they will be longer demonstrations than these of mine."[26] It was in its time a legitimate protest, which Newton (no less) would echo from a perspective of far greater mathematical penetration. Newton declared that the Cartesians' analytic geometry achieved its results "by an algebraic calculus which, when transposed into words ... would prove to be so tedious and entangled as to provoke nausea."[27] But experience very soon laid all such misgivings to rest. That the verbal equivalent of an algebraic calculation is often intolerably complex and clumsy came to seem a reason not to reject algebra but to embrace it, to exploit the wonderful ease, economy, and power of its manipulations.

IV

Inevitably Hobbes also had his say on two formidably difficult concepts that pervaded the mathematics of his day: the infinitely great and the infinitely small. He wrestled with hoary puzzles like the difference (if any) between the duration of the world until his birth and its duration up to the time of writing: are not both infinite, yet one less than the other? He ended in the view (analogous to "negative" theology's concept of God) that nothing can sensibly be asserted about the infinite save our ignorance; "all this arguing of infinites is but the ambition of school-boys."[28] He found incredible a beautiful result proved by Evangelista Torricelli (1641) that an infinitely long solid may have a finite volume; "to understand this for sense, it is not required that a man should be a geometrician or a logician, but that he should be mad."[29] Rather, of course, it is required that one should see, as Hobbes sometimes failed to do, that mathematics can raise and resolve problems where physical experience is lacking and physical intuition may deceive.

He cut a better figure in his thoughts on the infinitely *small*. The problems that would soon give birth to the calculus – problems like the finding of instantaneous velocities and the computation of areas of curvilinear figures – forced the mathematicians of his age to consider the magnitudes (now called differentials) that are somehow less than any assigned positive quantity yet not zero. Thus Hobbes wrote that the circumference of a circle "is compounded of innumerable strait lines, of which every one is less than can be given."[30] In the same spirit he defined an infinitesimal motion of a body as "motion through space and time less than can be given, that is to say, less than can be determined by exposition or by number."[31] Making such intuitions precise and mathematically useful was far beyond his powers. Yet, strangely enough, his formulations were not without effect, for here was another point at which he gave guidance to the young Leibniz, who took over almost verbatim the definition just quoted.[32]

V

But of course Hobbes's most quixotic and derided foray into mathematics was his long series of futile attempts to square the circle. Here again some background may be in order. The problem goes back to Greek antiquity, and for more than two millennia – from Aristophanes to *Princess Ida* – it was renowned beyond the borders of mathematics as the epitome of the seductively intractable riddle. Its classic form may be phrased as follows. Given a circle, "construct," using *only* a "straightedge" (unmarked ruler) and compass, a square of equal area. In the pursuit of this objective one may use the straightedge to join any two already constructed points, and one may draw with the compass a circle with any constructed point as center and any constructed distance as radius. It would in fact suffice to produce the *side* of the desired square, since then the construction of the square itself would follow trivially. Moreover, since (as Archimedes proved) the area of a circle equals the area of the rectangle whose sides are respectively the circle's circumference and half its radius, it would suffice, for the squaring of the circle, to construct a line segment equal to the given circle's *circumference*, and this last version is in fact the form in which Hobbes always tackled the problem.

Two similar challenges, also Greek in origin, are linked in the history of mathematics with the squaring of the circle. They call respectively for the "duplication" of a cube – that is, the construction of (the side of) a cube with twice the volume of a given cube – and the trisection of an arbitrary angle. The instruments and operations permitted in these two problems are the same as those described above for the squaring of the circle. It is to be noted that in Hobbes's time all three problems took a characteristic form: they were phrased not in terms of the *absolute* measures of *single* magnitudes but in terms of the (simple, whole-number) *ratios* of *pairs* of magnitudes. This formulation was yet another consequence of the restricted concept of number prevalent in Greek and early modern mathematics, and could be readily superseded when that limitation was overcome. In the problem of the squaring of the circle, for example, if the given circle's radius is taken as 1, then (for *us*) its area is π, so the problem can be said to ask for the construction of a line segment of length $\sqrt{\pi}$ (the side of the desired square) or, alternatively, one of length 2π (the circle's circumference); in this sense any claimed circle-squaring entails, at least implicitly, a value of π. But – one must stress – this numerical slant to the problem is modern, and would not have been present to Hobbes's mind.

By 1662 Wallis could count twelve different circle-squaring "solutions" by the tireless philosopher,[33] and still more were to come. No doubt Hobbes's reasons for persisting were diverse. The lure of the famously unsolvable might well have been temptation enough, and victory over his antagonist would only have sweetened his joy. But he claimed scientific motivations. At various times he declared that squaring the circle would make possible the multisection of an arbitrary angle and that it "would very much facilitate the doctrine of spherical triangles"[34] – although he made neither connection clear. How he arrived at his "solutions" remains largely a mystery, for on the example of his beloved Euclid he presented his arguments only in polished and final form, with the dust of the workshop swept away. His published circle-squarings (which are not always explicitly identified as such) vary widely in complexity; some run only a page or two, but others are much longer, and come with diagrams whose clutter puts quite in the shade the "scab of symbols" that Hobbes deplored in contemporary algebra. In these latter cases the detection of errors can prove no mean challenge. But in general one may say that the fallacies are logical rather than mathematical: deductions from false assumptions, "conclusions" that do not in fact follow from what precedes, even (as in the case immediately below) *denial* of a conclusion that *does* follow.

I shall try to convey something of the flavor of Hobbes's "proofs" through one particularly simple example.[35] On the side CD of a square $ABCD$ take $DT = 2/5DC$ and DR the mean proportional between DC and DT (that is, $DC/DR = DR/DT$). Draw the circular arc RS as shown on the following page. Then, according to Hobbes, this arc equals the line segment DC. Now this conclusion, if valid, would indeed amount to a squaring of the circle. But of course it is not valid, and Hobbes's argument for it is very weak. I shall quote his words, in the interests of credibility and fairness. "Suppose," he says, "some other arc, less or greater than the arc RS, to be equal to DC, as for example rs: then the proportion of the arc rs to the straight line DT will be duplicate [i.e., square] of the proportion of [the arc] RS to the arc TV, or DR to DT. Which is absurd; because Dr is by construction greater or less than DR." But the stated equality of proportions, so far

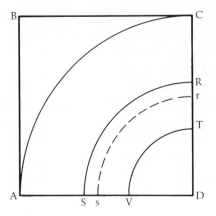

from being absurd, is a perfectly valid consequence of his assumption that $rs = DC$. Nor is this assumption itself absurd; it is actually *true* if, taking $DC = 1$, we choose $Dr = 2/\pi$ (but $2/\pi$ is not constructible!). The muddle in Hobbes's argument shows also in the fact that the number $2/5$ that *defines* the crucial point R plays no role at all in the alleged proof that R serves the purpose. When "some that think themselves logicians" (as he rather testily labeled them) were so unkind as to point this out, the philosopher explained that he took the value $2/5$ from a similar argument, no longer extant, given by the geometers of medieval Islam.[36] It gives his claim (that arc $RS = DC$) the specious plausibility of yielding for π the value $\sqrt{10}$ $(=3.162\ldots)$, an approximation often met in the history of mathematics.

VI

Similar flaws vitiate his proud boast of a duplication of the cube, "hitherto sought in vain."[37] He had his solution published anonymously, in Paris (1661), then asserted his authorship after Wallis's refutation. The reader who has the stamina to follow a rather complex argument[38] will find that Hobbes assumes at a crucial place a result that is actually false, thus undermining the whole venture. DV in the diagram is the side of the original cube. By construction, $AD = 2DV$; $AS = AI = BR$; T bisects SD; a circle (call it K) with center T and radius TV cuts AD in Y and DC in X. Then DX is claimed to be the side of a cube with volume double that of the cube on DV. The proof of this

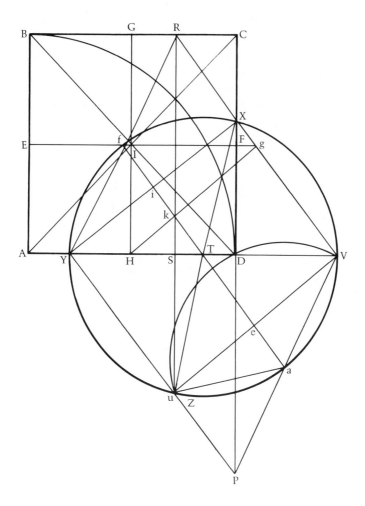

rests on the supposed fact that DX and DY are two mean proportionals between DV and AD ($DV/DX = DX/DY = DY/AD$). One easily checks that this would indeed imply that (taking $DV = 1$) $DX = \sqrt[3]{2}$. Now the cited equality of proportions turns out to require that the three points P, Z, and Y be collinear (where P is on CD produced, $DP = CD$, and Z is the intersection of the circle K and RS produced). Hobbes assumes this collinearity, but it is not quite (though very nearly) true. Showing this would suffice to destroy his argument, but Wallis chose an easier line of attack. If DY is indeed the larger mean proportional in the sense described, then $DY = \sqrt[3]{4}$. It follows from the construction, however, that $DY = 3 - \sqrt{2}$, and Wallis simply showed by direct calculation that the cube of this number is $45 - \sqrt{1682}$, not $45 - \sqrt{1681} = 4$ as required.[39]

One can fairly claim that the sheer ingenuity of Hobbes's construction, and the subtlety of the error, render the effort far from contemptible. But however that may be, the aftermath proved more curious, and more revealing of his mathematical limitations, than the original demonstration. To Wallis's ostensibly clinching counterargument Hobbes offered two defenses that may seem to verge on the bizarre. We have seen that he ascribed "size" to mathematical points; now he wondered (without, to be sure, insisting on it) whether "the point Y will have latitude enough to take in that little difference which is between the root of 1681 and the root of 1682."[40] His other response touched deeper issues. He declared that Wallis's *arithmetical* calculation can not validly be transferred to a *geometrical* context involving magnitudes of different dimensions (like a line segment and a cube). A number (he wrote) is a collection of units, but "when they reckon by arithmetic in geometry, there a unit is sometimes part of a line, sometimes a part of a square, and sometimes a part of a cube"[41] – and these cannot legitimately be combined. In the number $45 - \sqrt{1682}$ reached by Wallis, the 45 represents (according to Hobbes) 45 cubes, "but the square root of 1682, being a line, adds nothing to a cube."[42]

The seeming strangeness of this assertion marks Hobbes not as stupid or perverse but as conservative. His stance reflects the same centuries-old ideas that shaped the Renaissance treatment of equations, described above. The frame of mind behind the words "the square root of 1682, being a line" is the frame of mind that saw the product of a number by itself as *literally* a square, an object of geometry. His insistence that a line cannot be added to a cube was, then, like the algebraists' insistence on homogeneity in their equations, a consequence of the fact that the measures of geometrical magnitudes of different dimensions are strictly incomparable. But now the seventeenth century's growing boldness in the conception and use of exotic numbers was fast dissolving the ancient tie of those numbers to geometry. A pivotal statement, despite its retention of geometric language, was Descartes's urging (c. 1628) that the product of two line segments can – sometimes must – be regarded as another line segment, rather than as a rectangle.[43] Wallis's argument against

Hobbes's cube duplication represents the still greater advance of computing with irrational numbers free of all geometric association. Hobbes himself could rise at times to the same kind of insight, arguing for example that products of more than three factors "are pure numbers, not shapes" ("meri numeri sunt, non figurae sunt").[44] But in the geometric setting of the cube duplication he clung to the older way, and announced that his rebuttal of Wallis's rebuttal was a definitive rout of "the whole herd of them that apply arithmetic to geometry," and that this was his most valuable single service to mathematics.[45]

VII

I turn finally to an aspect of Hobbes's mathematics that may have left a more positive mark on history. He dabbled in a development that became one of the great success stories of his age. Stated in modern terms, the problem was to find the length of a specified portion (an "arc") of a given curve. But Hobbes's contemporaries approached it in a spirit analogous to their formulation (sketched above) of the three classical construction problems: they sought not to calculate the given arc-length in absolute terms, but to demonstrate its ratio to some other magnitude. Ideally, this comparison magnitude was a line segment (or possibly a sum of such), and then the demonstration was called a "rectification" of the given arc (Latin *recta*, a straight line). This problem was bedeviled until the middle of the seventeenth century by a widespread (though not universal) persuasion that the lengths of straight lines and of what we now call algebraic curves are *in principle* incomparable. This view carried the authority of Aristotle,[46] and even Descartes, than whom no man was more impatient with ancient dogmas, lamented in his *Géométrie* (1637) that "the ratios between straight and curved lines are not known, and I believe cannot be discovered by human minds."[47] Hobbes himself reported the quaint notion of the Jesuit mathematician Lalovera (1620) that "since the fall of Adam" the relations of straight lines and curves must remain inscrutable unless through "divine grace."[48]

We owe to Hobbes's interest in this question one of the more vivid vignettes of seventeenth-century mathematics. At some time during the winter of 1642–3 he paid a visit to Marin Mersenne at the latter's Minimite convent in Paris. Present also were Gilles Personne de Roberval and an unnamed fourth person. Mersenne, intellectual gadfly and go-between extraordinaire, was like Hobbes only an amateur in geometry, but Roberval would later hold a chair in mathematics at the Collège Royal. By his own account, which Mersenne corroborated, Hobbes chalked on a wall of the convent an argument for the equality of arcs of a parabola and an "Archimedean" spiral. The latter is the locus of a point that recedes uniformly from a fixed point O along a ray that simultaneously revolves uniformly about O ($r = a\theta$ in modern polar coordinates). Hobbes's claim was that specified arcs of the two curves, spiral and parabola, have equal lengths. While not, of course, a direct rectification of either curve, this result, if valid, would have been of much interest and importance in its own right.

The extent of his originality in this matter is unclear. A suggestive link between spiral and parabola was the fact that each can be regarded as the locus of a point undergoing two simultaneous but independent motions – the spiral in the way already described, the parabola as the resultant of a uniform motion in one direction and a uniformly *accelerated* motion in the perpendicular direction ($y = x^2$ from $x = t$, $y = t^2$). Hence a number of Hobbes's contemporaries brought the two curves together in various investigations. Torricelli found the "quadrature" of (that is, the area bounded by) a spiral from that of a parabola, and vice versa (c. 1640). Gregory of St. Vincent, in work published in 1647 but begun long before, established between the two curves a relation that allowed him to translate results from one to the other.[49] Hobbes's attempt to equate arc lengths was thus to some extent "in the air." Still, no earlier enunciation of this specific idea is on record, and some competent modern opinion grants Hobbes priority.[50] Of his actual argument we know little. But (as befits his whole philosophy's emphasis on motion) it was "kinematic": it tried to show that two particles, starting together and tracing with equal velocities the spiral and parabola respectively, would cover the specified arcs in equal times. The proof that he offered in Mersenne's cell was on his own admission unsatisfactory; Roberval (he tells us) pointed out an error, and Hobbes, throwing down the chalk ("abjecta creta"), conceded defeat. Roberval subsequently – the next day, according to Hobbes[51] – produced his own *valid* demonstration, also kinematic, of the equality of arcs of the parabola and spiral, and there

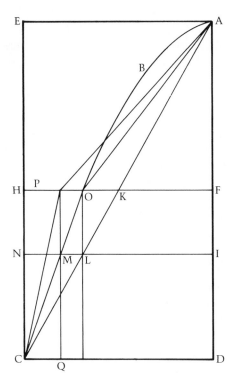

seems no need to doubt that in this successful outcome the exchange with Hobbes, if hardly crucial, was a helpful stimulant.

Nor does the story of his possible influence end there. Eventually he offered his own attempt at a *direct* rectification of a parabolic arc.[52] Let *ABC* be an arc of a parabola with axis *AD*; complete the rectangle *ADCE* and join *AC*. Bisect *AD* at *F* and draw *FH* parallel to *DC*; let *FH* cut *AC* in *K* and the parabola in *O*. Let *FP* be the mean proportional between *FD* and *FH*. Join *AP* and *PC*. Then (Hobbes claimed, incorrectly) the segments *AP* and *PC* are together equal in length to the arc *ABC* of the parabola. The "proof" is again kinematic: it argues that two bodies starting together at *A* and traveling with the same velocity the parabola and the line segments, respectively, would arrive simultaneously at *C*. Hobbes published a first account of this work in *De corpore* (1655), then revised it slightly for the English translation of that treatise (*On Body*, 1656). A note in the *Six Lessons for the Professors of the Mathematics*, appended to *On Body*, explains that the new version corrects a minor error pointed out by Wallis.[53] The altered argument is however still invalid, and was in due course refuted again by Wallis and (independently) by Huygens.[54] But here too Hobbes's efforts seem to have helped spur abler minds to success. The German historian of mathematics Joseph Hofmann, whose command of the seventeenth-century sources was magisterial, judged that the whole complex of rectification problems became "a topic of wider interest" only with the appearance of the *Six Lessons*. In particular, Hofmann added, Hobbes's book "probably" was a key stimulus for the work of William Neil, the short-lived and rather obscure mathematician whose rectification of the semi-cubical parabola $y^2 = ax^3$ (1658) is now widely hailed as a milestone.[55]

To summarize, Hobbes's mathematical activity presents a varied and complex picture, which makes difficult a global judgment of its value. Even his purely technical errors run a wide gamut from the absurd and embarrassing to the subtle. I have tried to suggest that some of his apparently oddest ideas were in fact faithful echoes of the mathematical mainstream of centuries past. But his age moved rapidly away from much of that tradition, and Hobbes himself, though by no means wholly resistant to change, was left behind at many points. On the widest perspective, his grounding of mathematics in the physical and concrete was rendered increasingly inadequate by the swift contemporary push toward ever higher levels of abstraction. Moreover, none of his contributions to specific problems was a *necessary* component of their eventual solution. But he was an amateur of mathematics in the original and best sense of the word, and through his role as a minor stimulant of others' success he merits a modest place in its annals.

NOTES

1   Beckmann, *A History of* π, p. 129.
2   De Morgan, *A Budget of Paradoxes*, p. 67.
3   Malcolm, "Hobbes and the Royal Society," pp. 51–4.
4   Quoted in Reik, *The Golden Lands of Thomas Hobbes*, p. 176.
5   Huygens, *Oeuvres complètes*, Vol. II, p. 296; trans. in Reik, pp. 178–9.
6   Quoted in Rogow, *Thomas Hobbes*, p. 195.
7   In Rigaud, *Correspondences of Scientific Men*, Vol. I, p. 96.
8   Aubrey, *Brief Lives*, p. 151. Christoph Clavius (1537–1612) was a Jesuit mathematician and astronomer.

9 *EW* VII, 185; VII, 242.

10 *EW* III, 670–1; cf. VII, 348–9.

11 Aubrey, *Brief Lives*, p. 150.

12 Pacchi, "Una biblioteca ideale", cf. Jacoby, p. 60.

13 Aubrey, *Brief Lives*, p. 151.

14 Breidert, "Les mathématiques et la méthode mathématique chez Hobbes," p. 416.

15 *EW* I, 204.

16 *EW* VII, 67.

17 *EW* VII, 200–3, 211; quotation, p. 211.

18 *EW* I, 141.

19 Pycior, "Mathematics and Philosophy," pp. 272–3.

20 *EW* I, 17–8.

21 *OL* V, 40, trans. Mandey, p. 125.

22 *EW* VII, 316, 330, 248.

23 *EW* I, 314.

24 Ibid.

25 *EW* VII, 329.

26 *EW* VII, 281–2.

27 Newton, quoted in Westfall, *Never at Rest*, p. 379.

28 *EW* VII, 446.

29 *EW* VII, 445.

30 *EW* I, 216.

31 *EW* I, 206; *OL* I, 177.

32 Bernstein, "*Conatus*, Hobbes, and the Young Leibniz," pp. 25–7.

33 Wallis, "Animadversions," p. 110.

34 *EW* I, 288, VII, 168.

35 *EW* VII, 431–3, 441, 446–7; cf. *OL* V, 18–19.

36 *EW* VII, 446–7. The objectors included Wallis ("An Answer"), p. 630.

37 *EW* VII, 3.

38 *OL* IV, 288–91; *EW* VII, 60–2.

39 *OL* IV, 291.

40 *EW* VII, 64; cf. *OL* IV, 295.

41 *EW* VII, 68.

42 *EW* VII, 64–5.

43 *AT* X, p. 466–8.

44 *OL* V, 96.

45 *EW* VII, 447, 68.

46 References collected and discussed in Heath, *Mathematics in Aristotle*, pp. 140–2.

47 This and other contemporary opinion to the same effect (Viète, Fermat) quoted in Boyer, "Early Rectifications of Curves," pp. 30–1.

48 *EW* VII, 319–20.
49 Moller Pedersen, "Roberval's Comparison," p. 26.
50 Ibid.; Hofmann, *Leibniz in Paris*, p. 103.
51 *OL* IV, 187.
52 *EW* I, 268–70.
53 *EW* VII, 319.
54 Huygens, *Oeuvres complètes*, Vol. I, pp. 439–40.
55 Hofmann, *Leibniz in Paris*, pp. 105, 108.

6   Hobbes on light and vision

I

Like many of his contemporaries, Hobbes showed a keen interest in optics. In fact, the question of the nature of sensory perception was the first philosophical problem he pondered,[1] and his search for an explanation of vision led him to believe that all natural phenomena could be reduced to local motion of material bodies. Hence, from the very start, his theory of light and vision served as a model for his theories of natural phenomena in general.[2] Apart from speculations on light and vision expressed in passing in a number of optical works,[3] Hobbes wrote three specifically optical tracts: the *Tractatus Opticus I* (ca. 1640), the *Tractatus Opticus II* (1644), and *A Minute or First Draught of the Optiques* (1646). Although these works were written in the 1640s, Hobbes conceived the main principles of his optics early in the 1630s.

II

Hobbes's earliest attempt at a systematic account of his natural philosophy probably dates from around 1630. It was published in 1889 by Ferdinand Tönnies as "A short tract on first principles."[4] This text consists of three sections, each composed of one or more principles followed by a number of conclusions. In the first section, Hobbes presents the conceptual building blocks and principles of a mechanical explanation of natural operations. The things constituting nature are defined in terms of their relationship qua being, operation, and generation. Some things – substances – exist by themselves; others, accidents, exist only insofar as they inhere in substances.[5] These substances are related as agents and patients, that is, as substances that either have a "power to move" or a "power to be moved." Agents function as the causes of changes in patients. Some of them act on other bodies by an active power inherent in themselves, others "by motion received from another." By "change" and "motion" Hobbes understands nothing but local motion.

In the second section, Hobbes explains how agents, possessed of an original power to move, act at a distance. The action of one body upon another requires contact. Action at a distance can be effected by successively changing the parts of the medium between agent and patient or by particles emanating from the agent.[6] If a natural agent such as the sun acts at a distance through a medium, the activity of the parts of that medium has to flow from some inherent active power or from an external impulse. In the first case, the parts concerned would exert their influence simultaneously and equally strongly, which implies that objects closer to the sun would be illuminated more strongly than ones farther away, In fact, experience goes against this. In the second case, objects would be illuminated by the local motion of parts of the air whose motion would be disturbed by a contrary agent, such as the wind, or weakened by putting a less movable medium, such as a piece of glass, between air particles and the object. But this, too, contradicts the facts. On the basis of this analysis, Hobbes concludes that at least the sun and other sources of light act at a distance by a continuous emanation of particles called "species." Only on the basis of that assumption can the rectilinear propagation of light be explained. Hobbes attributes the following properties to these particles. They are not propagated instantaneously but with a finite velocity.[7] They move locally and proceed infinitely. The greater the distance to their source, the weaker they are.[8] As the sun is an active substance carrying *lux*, that is, the original light in the luminous body itself, its species are substances too, functioning as carriers of derivative, propagated light referred to as *lumen*.[9]

As the second section is devoted to an explanation of the nature of light and its propagation, taken as an instance of an agent with an inherent power to move, the third and last section of the *Short Tract* is devoted to an explanation of the nature and operation of a number of psychological powers, to wit sense, understanding, and appetite, which derive their power to move from some other agent. These faculties are conceived as accidents, properties of so-called animal spirits, the instruments of sense and motion. In his later works Hobbes describes animal spirit as a three-dimensional, yet imperceptible, substance that is supposed to circulate through the body of an animal organism and, linking the several parts of the body, to produce all operations of the organism by propagating motion from one part of the body to another.[10] Not being endowed with an inherent active power, these spirits can function as agents only after being set in motion by something else. In fact the animal spirits are moved, immediately or mediately, by particles emanating from external objects. The animal spirits in the eye, for example, are set in motion by the particles emanating from a luminous body such as the sun. Accordingly, Hobbes understands by light and the other sensible qualities "nothing but the severall Actions of Externall things upon the Animal spirits, by severall Organs. and when they are not actually perceiv'd, then they be powers of the Agents to produce such actions."[11] Correspondingly, sense is defined as "a passive power of the Animal spirits, to be moved by the species of an externall object, suppos'd to be present,"[12] and the sensory act as nothing but an actual motion of the animal spirits.[13] That motion is transmitted to the brain, giving it the same power to act on the animal spirits as a luminous body has. Hobbes calls an action of the brain thus qualified a "phantasm" and we "are sayd to understand a thing when we have the Phantasma or Apparition of it."[14] Explaining illumination, sensory perception, and imagination as forms of local motion of material bodies, Hobbes has already formulated some of the principles of a mechanical explanation of luminous bodies and visual perception.

III

In the letters Hobbes wrote to the earl of Newcastle, his patron, during his third trip to the Continent (1634–36), natural philosophy, and especially optics, figures prominently. He comments repeatedly on the optical ideas and theories of the mathematician and natural philosopher Walter Warner (ca. 1557–1643), one of Sir Charles Cavendish's learned friends.[15] The correspondence attests to a substantial departure from his views on the nature of light and its propagation formulated in the *Short Tract*. In a letter from October 16, 1636, he wrote that "whereas I use the phrases, *the light passes,* or *the colour passes* or *diffuseth itselfe,* my meaning is that the motion is onely in the medium, and light and colour are but the effects of that motion in the brayne."[16] Apart from the fact that in this letter he does not use the term "light" in the sense of the action of a luminous source, but only in the sense of the effect of such an action on the eye, that is, a motion of the animal spirits, he now apparently also assumes that such an action does not require the emission of active particles, but is effected by a motion of the medium caused by the source of light. He is still in doubt about the nature of that motion, however.[17]

In 1637 Descartes's *Discours* and *Essais* appeared. The *Essais* included *La Dioptrique.* Thanks to his friend Sir Kenelm Digby, Hobbes soon acquired a copy. In 1640 he put a number of objections to Descartes through Mersenne, which in 1641 resulted in a fierce polemic that runs like a continuous thread through his optical writings.[18] In the course of his dispute with Descartes, he sent to the French philosopher a short treatise, virtually identical to a text known to us as the *Tractatus Opticus I* (c. 1640). The treatise concerns light, its refraction in particular, and color.[19] While in the *Short Tract* his ideas about the nature of light, the way it is propagated, and its effects on vision are presented as conclusions from principles, Hobbes introduces the same ideas in the *Tractatus Opticus I* as hypotheses, that is, presuppositions. The tract opens with five hypotheses and is followed by fourteen propositions, plus a few corollaries, definitions, and a postulate. These are used to explain the physical nature of light and refraction, and to derive the sine law of refraction.

The first hypothesis repeats the definitions in the *Short Tract* of agent, patient, action, and passion. "All action is local motion in the agent, as all passion is local motion in the patient." "By the term agent I understand a body by the motion of which an effect is produced in another body; by patient [a body] in which some motion is generated by some other body."[20] Likewise, vision is characterized as a passion in the sensing subject produced by the action of a luminous or illuminated object.[21] The third hypothesis, however, contradicts the second section of the *Short Tract.* As he did in his letter from 1636 to Newcastle, Hobbes now states that vision requires no translation of the luminous body as a whole or of its parts. Its action is propagated to the eye through and by the medium.[22] By now he also has a theory about the kind of motion involved in illumination. From the fact that a luminous body can be seen simultaneously from all directions and

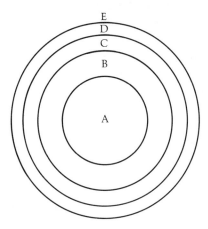

Figure 1

therefore moves simultaneously in all directions without becoming exhausted, he concludes that a luminous body permanently dilates and contracts, a motion perceived by us as scintillation. Dilating the source of light presses aside the directly contiguous parts of the medium, which act similarly on the parts lying directly behind them, etc. Thus the original source of light communicates its diffusing power to all parts of the medium that are illuminated by it. (See Figure 1) As soon as this motion strikes the eye, there occurs a contraction caused by a reactive counterpressure stemming from the brain.[23] With this model, based on the implicit assumption that the universe is filled with an all pervading ether of a uniform density, Hobbes traded his corpuscular theory of the propagation of light for a mediumistic explanation.

As the source and the medium expand at the same time, light is now said to be propagated instantaneously from the source of light through the eye and its nerve to the brain and back again to the eye.[24] Only the velocity of each particle decreases with increasing distance. The greater the distance from the source of light, the smaller the distance covered by the propagated motion. The radiation, in other words, gets weaker and weaker the farther it is removed from the source of light. Further, in view of the fact that there is no such thing as light before there is vision, the motion in question is called light only after it is propagated reactively from the brain through the nerves to the medium between the eye and the source of light.[25] Hence Hobbes understands by light the phantasm of a luminous body, that is, an image conceived in the brain.[26] Like other sensory impressions visual images are not real things existing in the outside world but only motions within the perceiving subject. Sensation, a reaction from the brain to the eye, coincides with imagination. Hobbes thus sets himself against the traditional peripatetic idea that perceptible things send out replicas of themselves, referred to as "species" or "forms," through which their very qualities would appear to us in sensory perception. The denial of the peripatetic idea is repeated in later writings.[27]

Sources of light act through radiation. Like his medieval predecessors, Hobbes understands by a ray the path along which a motion is propagated from a source of light through the medium. As only bodies can move, a ray occupies the place of a body. A ray, in other words, constitutes a solid space.[28] Adding something new, Hobbes transforms this common conception of a ray. Guided by the idea that rays can be considered as nothing but lengths, that is, geometrical lines, the medieval optical scientists opted for a geometrical approach to optics.[29] In Hobbes's view, they incorrectly reduced optics to geometry at the cost of distorting its physical aspects.[30] As appears from his definition of the straight and broken ray as parallelograms, Hobbes believed that rays had breadth as well as length.[31] (See Figure 2) Moreover, he takes into consideration only the motion of a specific part of such a parallelogram referred to as the "line of light": "The line of light from which the sides of a ray begin (e.g., line *AB* from which sides *AI, BK* begin) I call simply a line of light. However, any one of the lines which are derived from the line of light by a continual extension (such as *CD, EF,* etc.) I call a propagated line of light" (see Figure 2).[32] This propagated line of light is always perpendicular to the sides of the ray and represents in fact a propagated pulsefront or a "rayfront" analogous to the idea of a "wave front."[33] Hence, by "ray" Hobbes does not understand a mathematical line or the motion of a body, but the path traversed by a pulse, or rather the successive positions of a pulse front that traces out a parallelogram. With this concept of the ray of light, which helped make available the kinematical description of "wave propagation," Hobbes made an essential contribution to a truly mechanically based optics.[34]

Hobbes's explanation of refraction in the *Tractatus Opticus I* is

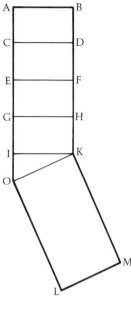

Figure 2

based on the idea that a body does not move equally fast along its whole length but, depending on the resistance of the medium, moves faster at one end than the other. For example, when a ray goes from a rarer to a denser medium and enters the latter perpendicularly, the light will be propagated in a straight line, as in that case all the parts of the ray will be slowed down to the same extent. If, however, it enters the denser medium obliquely it will be refracted toward the perpendicular, for the part of the ray entering the denser medium first will be slowed down, whereas th : rest of the ray will keep moving at the same speed. Conversely, a ray going from a denser to a rarer medium will be refracted from the perpendicular. Hence, in a homogeneous medium the path will be equal to the one traced out by a rolling cylinder where the ray front always has the same length and is perpendicular to the direction of motion. (See Figure 3) When the ray of light enters a medium obliquely, the path traces the figure of a rolling cone or frustrum of a cone, and once the whole ray front is in the same medium, it again follows the path described by a cylinder[35] (see Figure 4).

Thus, with the help of his cone-model, Hobbes gives a mechanical

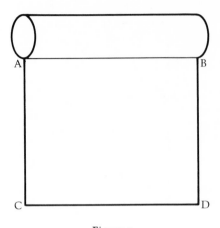

Figure 3

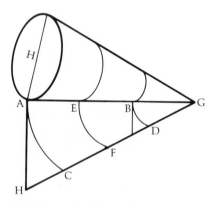

Figure 4

explanation of the refraction of a motion or pulse and shows that the ratio of the sine of the angle of incidence to that of the angle of refraction is independent of the angle of the incident ray and proportional to the different velocities in the two media.[36]

As for color, in *The Elements* Hobbes wrote that "when it [light] cometh to the eyes by reflection from uneven, rough and coarse bodies, or such as are affected with internal motion of their own, that may alter it, then we call it colour; colour and light differing only in this, that the one is pure, the other a perturbed light."[37] In the *Tractatus Opticus I* he is more specific about the kinds of motions involved and

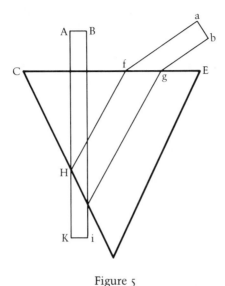

Figure 5

tries to explain color as the product of refraction, including the re-inforcement or restraint of the lateral motion of the ray of light that goes with it[38] (see Figure 5). Looking at a source of light through a trilateral prism, we will see an ovoid patch of light with, at one end, blue, at the other end, red, and in between a few vaguely demarcated zones that, at the red end, are yellow, and at the other end are violet and green, respectively. These colors constitute a subjective representation of the combination of the initial rectilinear motion and the rotating motion of the sides of the ray of light. Faster rotations result in red and yellow, slower ones in green and violet. Hobbes does not tell us how he knows all this. In fact, his explanation comes down to a mechanical interpretation of the Aristotelian theory that colors are modifications of pure light, that the strength of light is related to brilliance, and that all colors are on a scale between the extremes of black and white.[39]

Comparing the ideas in the *Tractatus Opticus I* with those in the *Short Tract*, we see that problems Hobbes still struggled with in the latter have now either disappeared or have been solved. Thus, by replacing the theory of emanation by a mediumistic explanation of the propagation of light, he got rid of the problem of exhaustion of the luminous body.[40] The same idea enables Hobbes to combine the explanation of illumination in terms of local motion with the idea of an instantaneous propagation of light. He is also more specific in the *Tractatus Opticus I* about the weakening of light the farther it is removed from the source of light, and presents an unambiguous explanation of the way in which a source of light acts on the organ of vision. While in the *Short Tract* he still had to demonstrate that sensory perception consists of nothing but motion, in the *Tractatus Opticus I* this is his starting-point. The dynamical explanation of natural phenomena, that is, the explanation in terms of forces, has been replaced in the *Tractatus Opticus I* by pure kinetic mechanics. Finally, the arrangement of the *Short Tract*, a set of principles followed by conclusions, is expanded in the *Tractatus Opticus I* into the format of a geometrical tract.[41]

IV

In many respects Hobbes's ideas in the *Tractatus Opticus I* resemble those of Descartes. Both conceive light as the action of a luminous body, action that is instantaneously yet mechanically propagated through a medium.[42] Both reject the idea that a motion in the optical nerve caused by light requires the emission of particles by the source of light. Consequently, both also reject the idea of "species intentionales."[43] Both deny that sensible qualities are real entities, and drop the idea that with sensory perception, representation requires likeness. Vision is an acquired capacity based on complicated, unconscious inferences, presumably based on comparing experiences through trial and error.[44] In a sense, both Hobbes and Descartes consider the relationship between vision and the visible as the product of an illusion.[45] Finally, they share views regarding the generation of colors and treat linear perspective in similar ways.[46]

The similarities between their views should not blind us to the fundamental differences between their ideas about the nature of light, as well as between their explanations of reflection and refraction. According to Descartes, the parts of the first kind of subtle matter by nature tend to motion in straight lines, but are restrained by the coarser parts. Hence, pressure is exerted on the parts of the second kind of subtle matter making up the medium, and this pres-

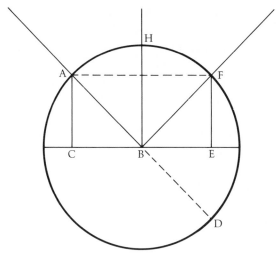

Figure 6

sure constitutes light. In other words, Descartes rejects Hobbes's idea that all action is local motion and understands by light not an actual motion, but only an inclination to motion.[47]

Guided by the belief that all natural phenomena can be reduced to collision phenomena, Descartes explains the equality of the angles of incidence and reflection by comparing the ray of light with a ball. The comparison is supposed to show how a ray of light is deflected when it hits an object. When you throw a ball from A to B, there are two directions to be considered in that motion: a vertical one by which the ball goes down and that is neutralized as soon as the ball hits the ground, and a horizontal one that makes the ball go forward and runs parallel to the ground. The latter motion is not neutralized, but stays as it is. Assuming that the ball keeps moving at the same speed, it will take as much time for it to go from A to B as from B to a point on the circle passing through A and with B for its center[48] (see Figure 6). Essential in this explanation is the idea that the "determination," that is, the direction of motion, is not itself a motion and that the earth does not neutralize the speed of the ball.[49] Hence, in Descartes's view, there is a difference between the force that keeps a ball moving and the force that propels it in a specific direction: motion and direction of motion do not have the same efficient cause.[50] As appears from his idea that the earth does not neutralize the speed of the ball, Descartes also rejected the idea of elasticity and claimed that, like a ball, light rebounds simply because its motion, understood as an absolute quantity, persists. Descartes believed that the velocity of the ball before and after reflection, conceived as an inelastic collision of two bodies, remained the same and that reflection could be explained solely in terms of conservation of motion.[51]

To Hobbes the idea of spherical parts of matter implied by the ball-analogy contradicted Descartes's denial of the vacuum. Hobbes also rejected Descartes's distinction between motion and direction of motion.[52] In his view an agent only can cause motion if it can also determine the direction of that motion.[53] Further, Hobbes explains reflection in terms of pressure and restitution, that is, elasticity. Reflection is a change of the direction of the motion of light caused by resistance, a degree of hardness which in its turn is nothing but motion of the internal parts of the body concerned. An elastic, resisting body, such as a mirror, being acted on by light, will be dented. This indentation elicits an equally strong counter-movement aimed at the restoration of the old shape. This reaction goes with a change of direction in the motion of light, for whereas the horizontal component of the motion stays the same, the vertical component, that is, the downward movement, is neutralized and replaced by an opposite motion. Action and reaction are perpendicular to the surface of the point of contact. The speed of light is left out of consideration. Because the incident and reflected motion are equal, the angles are equal too.[54]

Descartes treats refraction as a special case of reflection and, notwithstanding his notion of light as an inclination to motion, also explains this phenomenon by means of the ball-analogy.[55] Accordingly, in his view there is no substantial difference between the propagation of a body and that of a pulse. Further, assuming that "light can be produced only in matter, where there is more matter it is produced more easily . . . therefore it penetrates more easily through a denser than through a rarer medium."[56] Hobbes criticized that idea as well as Descartes's comparison of light to a body, for whereas light, propagated from a rare to a dense medium, moves toward the perpendicular, a body moves away from it. Descartes replied that "the harder and firmer are the small particles of a transparent body, the more easily they allow the light to pass: for this light does not have to drive any of them out of their places, as a ball must expel those of water, in order to find passage among them."[57] Hobbes was not convinced.[58] In fact, Descartes probably did not quite understand Hobbes's distinction between the propagation of a body and a pulse, for ultimately Descartes condemns Hobbes's physical explanation of refraction as a fiction, taking Hobbes's theory to be about "the motion of a fictitious parallelogram," that is, a body, instead of about the propagation of a pulse or pulsefront tracing out a parallelogram.[59]

V

In 1643 Hobbes completed an extensive commentary on *De Mundo*, an encyclopedic work on natural philosophy by his friend Thomas White. Most of the ideas from the *Tractatus Opticus I* on the nature of light, the way it is propagated and reflected appear once more in this commentary.[60] Hobbes is more specific this time about the cause of the strength of light, as well as about its weakening the farther it gets from its source.[61] Further, the commentary contains a description of the "optical tube" and a discussion of the possibilities of developing it.[62]

In his later writings Hobbes elaborates and embellishes his theory of light without introducing substantial changes. His explanation of sensory perception, however, undergoes a major change. While in *TO* I the central organ of sensory perception is said to be located in the brain, in his later works it is transferred to the heart. His commentary on White's *De Mundo* marks the turning point. Although the brain and animal spirit are still the organs of vision,[63] phantasms are now said to come from the heart.[64]

VI

Early in 1644 Hobbes wrote a sequel to the *Tractatus Opticus I*, the *Tractatus Opticus II* (not published until the twentieth century),[65] in which he further elaborates his optical ideas, including his criticisms of Descartes. The second treatise focuses on the geometrical determination of the relationship between light and vision dealt with in four chapters on, respectively, (1) light, illumination, and the diaphanous; (2) the nature of reflection and refraction; (3) the variety of reflections from convex and concave spherical bodies; and (4) seeing through a simple and direct medium.

The tract opens with a consideration of the specific nature of research in physics. While the causes of artificial objects such as geometrical figures can be known completely and with absolute certainty, as we made them ourselves, in physics we have to be content with probability. Natural phenomena can always be explained in different ways, and we will never know for sure how they actually came to be. We have to make do with hypotheses. We cannot ask more from the philosopher than that his hypothetical causal explanations be imaginable, that they show how the phenomena could have been necessitated, and that no falsehoods can be derived from them.[66]

Accordingly, as he did in the *Tractatus Opticus I*, Hobbes presents his views on the nature and operation of light as the assumptions of optics conceived as a branch not of applied mathematics, but of natural philosophy.[67]

Apart from the doctrines expounded in *The Elements of Law*, the *Tractatus Opticus I* and the 'Anti-White', the *Tractatus Opticus II* also contains a number of new ideas. For the first time Hobbes compares the dilation and contraction of the source of light with the diastole and systole of the heart. New also is the idea that a source of light moves part-by-part and that it only seems to be moving as a whole because of the high speed at which its parts pulsate. Further, he describes a second kind of motion of luminous bodies, the *motus cribrationis* or sieve-like motion. This is a compound motion of the very small parts of a luminous body like that of the grain-particles in a rotating sieve. They have their own rotating motion inside the sieve plus the circular motion of the sieve as a whole. He encountered serious geometrical problems in explaining vision as a result of this kind of motion and eventually abandoned the theory.[68]

The fourth chapter, on vision, begins with an anatomy of the eye and does not deviate significantly from the descriptions current in his day. Hobbes evidently kept abreast of the leading anatomical literature.[69] The organ of vision as a whole includes the eye, the brain, the vital and animal spirit, and the heart. The act of vision is defined as an outwardly directed reaction evoked in the heart by the action of a luminous or illuminated body.[70]

Hobbes dwells on the way the retinal image comes about. In broad outline he follows Kepler, according to whom we see by way of two cones of radiation, one of which is based on the image and the other on the illuminated part of the retina. They share a top at the place in the eye were the visual lines, that is, the lines in which the points of a visible object appear, intersect. The radiation from the points of a luminous object to the retina are refracted in the direction of the optical axis, that is, the line falling perpendicularly from a point of the object on the center of the iris, by the resistance of the humors of the eye as well as its figure. In the retina itself the radiation is refracted away from the optical axis. Thus the perceived object is projected on the retina point by point, upside down and reversed through a double cone of radiation.[71]

We only see distinctly along the optical axis.[72] Hence, in order to see a whole object distinctly, the axis has, as it were, to scan it. The retina remains stationary while the pupil and chrystalline lens move along with the optical axis. Accordingly, seeing is a kind of reading, a successive movement of the optical axes.[73] As was said earlier, Hobbes understands by the visual line the line along which the point of a visible object appears. In fact it is a number of lines constituting a visual cone with its base at the apparent place of the object and its top in the center of the eye. This cone represents a directed resistance produced by the motion of the luminous object. All visual lines intersect in the center of the eye. The lines that are not refracted and go straight through the center of the eye coincide with the optical axis. This happens in all vision where the attention of the observer is fixed on the point he looks at, and only in that case will something actually be seen. Attention depends on our interest, and that in its turn is based on the motions around the heart. Hence, the motions of the optical axes are determined by the will of the perceiving subject.[74]

In his explanation of vision, Hobbes combines the theory of the visual line with what Stroud refers to as the "threshold hypothesis."[75] From the fact that a small object, for example a grain of sand, at a certain distance will become invisible, whereas a heap of sand at the same distance from the observer will be seen, Hobbes infers that a luminous or illuminated object, whatever its size or distance, acts on the eye because that same heap of sand would not be visible if the parts composing it would not irradiate the eye.[76] When we look at an object, the visual line scans it point by point. According to the "threshold hypothesis," the first particles of an object scanned by the visual line will irradiate the eye without actually being seen. When the line goes from the first to the second particle, the motion caused by the former does not cease right away but, as appears from the occurrence of after-images, is stored in the memory: It lingers on for a while and is reinforced by the action of the next particle scanned by the visual line. This process continues until the accumulated action in the organ of vision is strong enough to evoke a reactive motion from the brain, that is, to make us actually see the total object in question.[77] This reaction appears to the observer as an image of the external luminous body. Visual images can be compared with respect to clarity and distinctness; position of the visual line along which it appears in relation to the observer; size; distance and form; motion and rest; color, and with respect to the effect on the observer – pain or pleasure.[78]

VII

Hobbes considered the senses as the origins of all knowledge. Hence, in view of the fact that things often appear smaller or larger and closer or farther away than they really are, Hobbes was greatly interested in the problem of how to determine these properties of the visual image and of how they relate to objective reality. The place of an image is nothing but its size, distance, and shape taken together. The size of an image is judged by the visual angle, that is, the angle constituted by the visual lines from the extreme points of the object in the center of the eye. The distance is determined by the length of the visual lines and by the intensity of light. To determine the shape of an image, it has to be considered as the base of a triangle the vertex of which is the "vanishing point" – the distance at which the object is no longer visible. The shape of the image varies depending on whether the attention is fixed upon a plain, intersecting the triangle, farther or nearer than the natural appearance. Thus, applying the principles of perspective projection, Hobbes accounts for the shape of the image.

According to Hobbes, the image in direct vision is always closer to the observer. Further, the "threshold hypothesis" implies that some part of the object is always invisible. That explains why, as Hobbes believes, the image in direct vision is also smaller than its object.[79]

In the *Tractatus Opticus II*, Hobbes presents an elaborate version of the theory of colors expounded in the first tract. The radiation from a pure luminous body can be corrupted or mixed with other motions in the parts of the body in which it is propagated or by which it is

reflected or refracted. Motions that reach a healthy eye without blend-
ing evoke a clear phantasm called white light. The reflection or refraction of this light results in all kinds of colors. If something is not
illuminated at all, we will not see it, and the stronger it is illuminated,
the more its color will approach white light.

VIII

In 1646 Hobbes completed *A Minute or First Draught of the
Optiques*, his most comprehensive and polished writing on optics.
The book, composed of thirteen chapters dealing with the phenomena of light and illumination, followed by nine chapters on vision,
was not published until three hundred years after his death.[80]
Essentially the theories in this work do not differ from the doctrines in the two foregoing tracts. Seeing is characterized as "the
judgment itselfe of the place, where the object appears to bee."[81]
Hobbes points out that the retinal image should not be confused
with the image we have in the mind when we see an object; for apart
from the fact that the retinal image is reversed and upside down,
nobody can see his own retina.[82]
As for the place of the image after reflection, Hobbes explicitly
rejects the traditional idea, known as the "ancient principle," according to which an image after reflection is located at the intersection
of the reflected ray and the perpendicular from the object to the
mirror.[83]
As in the two foregoing tracts, he explains the generation of colors
by refraction through a prism. Instead of basing his explanation on a
mechanical model differing from the earlier one,[84] he now also
adopts a theory of the generation of black and white attributed to
Honoratus Fabri (1607–88).[85]
Notwithstanding his praise of Descartes[86] and the presentation of
A Minute or First Draught of the Optiques as a mere addition to
Descartes's theories,[87] this work too was directed against his French
rival.[88]

IX

Apart from a few remarks on perception in *Leviathan*,[89] Hobbes
deals extensively with the problems of light and color, reflection and

refraction, and sensory perception in *De Corpore*.[90] In this book he states explicitly that perception as judgment requires memory, and that an outwardly directed motion is experienced as a phantasm only if it repeatedly outdoes other motions.[91] The latter part of *A Minute or First Draught of the Optiques* was published slightly amended in *De Homine* (1658).[92]

X

Hobbes's optical writings suggest that he knew the literature concerned very well. That suggestion is strengthened by a long list of forty-four titles put together by Hobbes about 1630 and containing a section *De Perspectiva*, adequately covering the leading literature at the time.[93] It includes work from Alhazen, Grosseteste, Roger Bacon, Witelo, John Pecham, Aguilonius, and four works by Kepler, to mention only the most familiar names. This literature embodied an Islamic and European tradition that was based on a number of optical theories from antiquity and culminated in the seventeenth century. The main link between antiquity and the seventeenth century was Alhazen (965–1039) who integrated in an original way the physiological, physical, and mathematical optics from antiquity and presents the first mathematical version of the classical intromission-theory, the idea that we see by rays that enter the eyes from outside. Alhazen's theories dominated optics for six hundred years.

Although in the *Short Tract* Hobbes does not explicitly reject medieval optics, and although he uses the traditional term "species," it can be read as an indirect yet fundamental criticism of the Scholastic tradition.[94] That is suggested not only by the corpuscular theory of light but by the characterization of vision in terms of motion and as a pure passion, as well as his theory about the way light is propagated. As opposed to his predecessors, Hobbes understands by "species" no immaterial forces but substances conceived as material corpuscles. Accordingly, they move locally and therefore not instantaneously, as most of his medieval precursors believed.[95] In contrast with them also, he is of the opinion that these species are propagated infinitely. He deems the theory of species applicable to vision as well as hearing, but also relates it to the doctrine of occult powers. Finally, Hobbes does not assume a priori that light is propagated through species, but approaches this topic as a problem, and adopts a species theory in combination with a mediumistic explanation of the propagation of light.[96]

The ideas in the *Short Tract* are allied to those of early seventeenth-century corpuscularists and atomists like Walter Warner (ca. 1557–1643), Thomas Harriot (1560–1621), Isaac Beeckman (1588–1637) and Nicholas Hill (1570–1610/20).[97] As in the *Short Tract*, we find a combination of corpuscularism with the idea of emanating sources of light, the notion of magnetism as manifestation of an active principle, of light and heat as things that are qualities only in relation to the sense, and of senses, imagination, and understanding as powers that follow naturally from each other.[98]

As can be seen from their format, Hobbes's optical writings from the 1640s are modeled on the medieval optical literature.[99] Nevertheless, combining traditional and modern views, he attempted to translate the scholastic explanations of light and vision in mechanical terms. This attempt at a mechanization of optics has had more influence than the histories of optics make us believe. Nearly every writer on optics in the seventeenth century knew Hobbes's theory of refraction. Isaac Barrow's and Emanuel Maignan's explanations of refraction are unmistakably inspired by Hobbes. The same holds true for Hooke's theory of refraction. In the eighteenth century, Hobbes's explanation of refraction was accepted by Giovanni Rizzetti, and Thomas Young put it on a par with that of Huygens and Euler as an alternative to Newton's.[100]

XI

Hobbes presents his optical theories as a break with the Scholastic tradition. He claims to be the first to have developed a doctrine that both "saves the phenomena" and is logically derived from the nature of vision and of light.[101] Apart from being too hard on his medieval predecessors, who were more alive to the physical and psychological aspects of optics than his criticism suggests, his claim is only partly made good. Investigating the frontier between physics and geometry, Hobbes subscribed to the geometrical analysis of optical tradition, but cast it into a new framework by taking the observer as the starting point. Yet, his geometrical proofs are not always consistent with his theory of vision, and he often mixed up geometry and physics.[102] In general, his theory of vision did not benefit from his geometrical and mechanical analysis, and he was unable to provide any new tools with which to decipher the relationship between objects and their images. This does not alter the fact that he made an important contribution to the mediumistic theory of light. Rejecting Descartes's static mediumistic theory and explanation of reflection and refraction based on an analogy with a moving body, Hobbes attempted to give a kinematic description of the rectilinear, reflected, and refracted motion of a pulse. Up to the last decade of the seventeenth century his explanation of refraction was the only viable mechanical alternative to the Cartesian theory.

NOTES

1 Hobbes will be cited from the following works and in the following manner: Aalen's reprint of Molesworth's edition of the *English Works*, referred to as *EW*, and the *Opera Latina*, referred to as *OL*, followed by the numbers of the volume, the title of the work, and the number of the page; *Thomas Hobbes Court Traité des premiers principes. Le Short Tract on first principles de 1630–1631. Texte, traduction et commentaire par Jean Bernhardt* (PUF 1988), referred to as *ST*, followed by the page number; F. Alessio, "Thomas Hobbes: Tractatus Opticus," *Rivista critica di storia della filosofia* XVIII, no. 2 (1963); 147–228, referred to as *TO* II, followed by the page number; Elaine Condouris Stroud, "Thomas Hobbes' A minute or first draught of the optiques: A critical edition," Ph.D. dissertation, The University of Wisconsin–Madison, 1983, referred to as *MDO*, followed by the page number; *The Elements of Law natural & politic*, Ed. Ferdinand Tönnies (1889), reprint with an introduction by Prof. M.M. Goldsmith (London, 1984), referred to as *EL*, followed by the page number; and from *Thomas Hobbes, Critique du De Mundo de Thomas White*, édition critique d'un texte inédit par Jean Jacquot et Harold Whitmore Jones (Paris, 1973), referred to as *AW* ("Anti-White"), followed by the page number. See *OL* I, xx–xxi, and *OL* I, *De Corpore*, 316–17, 320–1.

2 See Brandt, *Hobbes's Mechanical Conception*, pg. 204. Cf. Gargani, *Hobbes et la scienza*, pg. 219–20.

3 The second chapter of *EL* (1640) is devoted to the nature of sensory perception in general and vision in particular. The same subject is glanced at in the first chapter of *Leviathan* (1651). In the *AW* (ca. 1643), Hobbes dwells on the operation of luminous bodies, vision, reflection, refraction, and on problems relating to the telescope. The chapter on the

explanation of natural phenomena in *De corpore* (1655) begins with an explanation of sensory perception.

4 Tönnies published the manuscript as Appendix I to his edition of *EL*. For an exhaustive study of this manuscript, see Bernhardt's commentary in the edition referred to in note 1 and Napoli (1990). For arguments against the attribution of this text to Hobbes, see Pacchi (1978, p. 62, n. 36), and Tuck (1988). See also Prins (1992), p. 241, n. 27.

5 "Substance is that which hath being not in another, so as it may be of it selfe, as Aire or Gold"; "Accident is that which hath being in another, so as, without that other it could not be. As Colour cannot be, but in somewhat coloured" (*ST*, 14).

6 "Every Agent, that worketh on a distant Patient, toucheth it, eyther by the Medium, or by somwhat issueing from it self, which thing so issueing lett be calld Species" (*ST*, 24).

7 The question of whether light is propagated instantaneously or not was hotly debated early in the seventeenth century. Most of Hobbes's contemporaries answered this question in the affirmative.

8 At this early stage of his development, Hobbes still believed that some natural objects attracted or repelled each other at the instigation of occult forces flowing from a natural conveniency and disconveniency of their species (see *ST*, pp. 36–7).

9 Cf. Buridanus: "Lumen non est nisi sicut specis et repraesentatio lucis multiplicata a luce usque ad visum per quam species lux videtur" (*De Anima* II, 17, fo. 14v, cited in Vescovini, p. 157, n. 64). In the sixteenth century, the distinction between *lux* and *lumen* still had not disappeared. Thus with J.C. Scaliger we read "lux . . . dicta est haec vis, quae esset in corpore lucido . . . At huius divini accidentis sive speciem sive effectum, qui in aere ita videtur, ut alibi terminetur, et faciat visibile superficiem per colorem: hanc inquam affectionem, lumen appellarunt" (Scaliger, 1557, exer. lxxi). Kepler (1939) refers to this passage in the *Paralipomena ad Vitellionem* (see *Gesammelte Werke*, Band II, 40) but, as opposed to Descartes (see *AT* II, 204, 205 and 213), no longer makes the distinction himself. Most writers on optics in the seventeenth century shared Kepler's view.

10 "a body natural, but of such subtilty, that it worketh not upon the senses; but that filleth up the place which the image of a visible body might fill up. Our conception therefore of spirit consisteth of figure without colour; and in figure is understood dimension, and consequently, to conceive a spirit, is to conceive something that hath dimension" (*EL*, 60–1.); "neque spiritus in corpore animalis saltem *vegeto* . . . omnino gravitat, sed cursu quodam circulari ad servitia singulorum membrorum circumcursat" (*AW*, 350). See also *Lev.*, *EW* III, 380–3.

11 *ST*, 44.

12 Ibid., 48.

13 Ibid., 46.

14 See *ST*, 48.

15 See *Historical Manuscripts Commission 13th report*, pp. 126, 128–9. (In the following this publication will be referred to as *HMC*.) On Warner Jacquot (1952), see Kargon (1966), pp. 35–40, and Prins (1992), pp. 1–57.

16 See *HMC* 130.

17 In 1646 he claimed to have taught already by 1630 that "Light is a fancy in the minde, caused by motion in the braine, which motion againe is caused by the motion of the parts of such bodies, as we call lucid" (*MDO*, 76–7). See also note 26.

18 See *AT* 3, 287–92, 300–13, 313–18, 318–33, 341–, 353–7. Hobbes's first two letters to Descartes are lost.

19 *OL* V, *TO* I, 216–48. (The text was published by Mersenne, *Cogitata* [1644], 549–66.) See also Brandt (1928), pp. 93–7.

20 "Omnis actio est motus localis in agente, sicut et omnis passio est motus localis in patiente: '*Agentis* nomine intelligo *corpus*, cujus motu producitur effectus in alio corpore; *patientis*, in quo motus aliquis ab alio corpore generatur" (*OL* V, *TO* I, 217).

21 Ibid.

22 "In visione, neque objectum, neque pars ejus quaecunque transit a loco suo ad oculum. Ut motus possit motum generare ad quamlibet distantiam, non est necessarium ut corpus illud a quo motus generatur, transeat per totum illud spatium per quot motus propagatur" (Op. cit., 217–8).

23 See op. cit., 219. Cf. *EL* 5–6: "that that motion, whereby the fire worketh, is dilation, and contraction of itself alternately, commonly called scintillation or glowing, is manifest . . . by experience. From such motion in the fire must needs arise a rejection or casting from itself of that part of the medium which is contiguous to it, whereby that part also rejecteth the next, and so successively one part beateth back the other to the very eye; and in the same manner the exterior part of the eye . . . presses the interior. Now the interior coat of the eye is nothing else but a piece of the optic nerve, and therefore the motion is still continued thereby into the brain, and by the resistance or reaction of the brain, is also a rebound in the optic nerve again, which we not conceiving as motion or rebound from within, think it is without, and call it light."

24 See *OL* I, *TO* I, 220.

25 Accordingly, he now also uses the terms *lux* and *lumen* in another sense. "Light" in the sense of a reaction in the perceiving subject is referred to

as *lumen*; *lux* refers to "light" meaning the action of a luminous body. To Mersenne he wrote (in 1641) that he had taught the same in 1630 to the brothers Cavendish (see Mersenne, *Correspondance*, Vol. 10, 568 Nr. 994). This seems incompatible with the idea that the *ST* was written at that time, for in the *ST* he understands by light the active power and action of a luminous body and believes that the propagation of light takes time. The main similarity, of course, is that light is motion causing, in the perceiving subject, nothing but motion.

26 See op. cit., 221. In *EL* he says: "That the subject wherein colour and image are inherent is not the object or thing seen. That there is nothing without us really which we call an image or colour. That the said image or colour is but an apparition unto us of that motion, agitation or alteration, which the object worketh in the brain or spirits, or soe internal substance of the head. That as in conception by vision, so also in the conceptions that arise from other senses, the subject of their inherence is not the object, but the sentient" (p. 4).

27 "Because the image in vision consisting in colour and shape is the knowledge we have of the qualities of the object of that sense; it is no hard matter for a man to fall into this opinion, that the same colour and shape are the very qualities themselves . . . And this opinion hath been so long received, that the contrary must needs appear a great paradox; and yet the introduction of species visible and intelligible (which is necessary for the maintenance of that opinion) passing to and fro from the object, is worse than any paradox, as being a plain impossibility" (*EL*, 3–4). Cf. *TO* II, 206; *MDO* 335–6, 621; and *L, EW* III, 3.

28 Cf. Witelo: "Omnis linea, qua pervenit lux à corpore luminoso ad corpus oppositum, est linea naturalis sensibilis, latitudinem habens" (*OT*, 63).

29 "quoniam lux minima procedit ad minimam corporis partem, quam lux occupare potest: necesse est quot processus eius fit secundum lineam mathematicam, quae est in medio lineae sensibilis, et secondum lineas extremas equidistantes lineae mediae: neque cadit lux minima in punctum mathematicum corporis oppositi, sed in punctum sensibilem correspondentem omnibus punctis mathematicis indivisibilibus, ad quos lineae mathematicae ipsius lineae sensibilis possunt terminari: et ob hoc utemur in demonstrandis passionibus lucis figuratione linearum mathematicarum in processu" (Risner, *Opticae Thesaurus*, Witelo, 63–4).

30 "Do not you tell me now, according to your wanted ingenuity, that I never saw Euclid's, Vitellio's or many other men's *Optics*; as if I could not distinguish between *geometry* and *optics*" (*EW* IV, *Considerations upon the reputation*, 437).

31 "A straight ray is a ray which, having been cut by a plane through its axis, is a parallelogram (as *AK*). A refracted ray is a ray formed from two

straight rays making an angle with an intermediate part (ray *AM* is a refracted ray because it is formed from the straight rays *AK* and *KL*, with part *IKO*)." (Translation quoted is from Shapiro, 1969, 142.)

32 Ibid.

33 Ibid., 143.

34 See Shapiro (1969): 7, 134–5.

35 See *MDO*: 39, 136–46.

36 Ibid., 136. The proof of the sine law of refraction in the *TO* I, rather confusing and incomplete, is based on the false assumptions that the line of light always has the same breadth, which implies that a ray must curve when passing from one medium to another, that a source of light only radiates from its center, and that all rays are perpendicular to the surface of the source of light. (See Shapiro 1969, 156, 160. Cf. *MDO*, 145.)

37 *EL*, 6. Cf. the definition in the *ST* of color as "Light diversified by the species of diverse bodyes" (*ST*, 32).

38 The following is taken from Blay (1990).

39 See Aristotle, *Minor Works*, 791–9.

40 See *ST*, 34. In his letters from that time to Charles Cavendish, Hobbes still is in search of an explanation of the fact that even when sources of light contract, perception goes on. They stay visible thanks to the fact that contraction follows so fast after dilatation that the effect of the latter is still present during the contraction. The cause of that reciprocal motion itself is inscrutable (see *EW* VII, 459–60).

41 See Brandt (1928), 161.

42 "La lumière n'est autre chose . . . qu'un certain mouvement, ou une action fort promte et fort vive, qui passe vers nos yeux, par l'entremise de l'air et des autre corps transparens, en mesme façon que la mouvement ou la résistance des corps, que rencontre cet aveugle, passe vers sa main, par l'entremise de son baton" (*AT*, VI, 84).

43 "Et par ce moyen vostre esprit sera delivré de toutes ces petites images voltigeantes par l'air, nommées des especes intentionelles, qui travaillent tant l'imagination des philosophes" (ibid., 85).

44 See Caton, 85.

45 See *OL* V, *TO* I, 220–1; *AT* VI, 112–14, 130.

46 See *MDO*, 330–1; and Zarka, "La matière et al representation: Hobbes lecteur de la Dioptrique de Descartes" in *Actes du Colloque CNRS sur Descartes du juin 1987*, Paris. Vrin. 1988 81–98, 95. Hence, according to Brandt the polemic between Descartes and Hobbes did not flow from a philosophical difference of opinion, but was based on a priority-claim concerning the notion of a *materia subtilis* and the idea of the subjectivity of sensible qualities, i.e., two essential ingredients of a mechanical explanation of nature (see Brandt, 140). Although it is possible that inde-

pendently of each other they hit on the idea that sensible qualities are subjective, Galileo was the *auctor intellectualis* of this idea (see *AT* VI, 130–1, 112–3; and Galileo, *Opere* VI, *Il Saggiatore*, 347–50). As for the second point of controversy, Descartes not only rejected Hobbes's identification of the notion of the animal spirit with his idea of a *materia subtilis*, but was also convinced that Hobbes, if he used this idea at all, took it from him. (see *HMC*, 128). Descartes's *Essais* did not appear until 1637. Hobbes's notion of this spirit as a subtle, fluid body does not differ substantially from Descartes's *materia subtilis* (see *AT* III, 301).

47 See *AT* VI, 88, and *AT* III, 315–6. See also Bernhardt (1979), 435.

48 See *AT* VI, 95–7, 102–3.

49 See Brandt, 115–16.

50 See Sabra (1981), 69–92.

51 See Knudsen/Pedersen (1968), 185.

52 See *AT* VI, 94, and *AT* III, 342–3. On the interpretation of Descartes's notion of "determination" see Sabra, 120–1.

53 See Brandt, 114–15; Zarka, 88.

54 See *AT* III, 303–9; and Brandt (1928), 116–18.

55 See Sabra (1981), 103, 116.

56 *AT* X, 242–3. Quoted in the translation from Sabra (1981), 105. See also *AT* III, 315–6; and *AT* VI, 96–103.

57 AT VI, 103. Quoted in the translation from Shapiro (1970), 148.

58 See *AT* III, 310, and *EW* VII, 460–1. See also Shapiro, (1970) 152.

59 See *AT* VI, 316–7.

60 See *AW*, pp. 160–81. In the *AW* he uses the terms *lux* and *lumen* as synonyms.

61 The speed of light does not diminish in the same proportion as that in which the distance from the source grows (see *AW*, 162).

62 See *AW*, 171ff.

63 "eodem . . . instante quo movetur quaelibete pars lucidi versus oculum . . . fit ut motus impingat in oculum, id est lucidum agat in oculum; atque eodem modo etiam derivatur actio usque ad interna capitis ubi est cerebrum & animalis spiritus, quae sunt videndi organa" (*AW*, 162).

64 "fieri per actionem objectorum . . . per medium continuò a parte in partem propagatum . . . usque ad cerebrum, atque etiam ad ipsum cor . . . Hi motus repulsi sive retro procreati per reactionem & resistentiam cordis usque ad partes animalis extimas, sunt phantasmata illa externè apparentia" (ibid., 326).

65 F. Alessio, "Thomas Hobbes: Tractatus Opticus (Harl. Mss. 6796, ff. 193–266)." *Rivista critica di storia della filosofia*, XVIII, no. 2 (1963), 147–228.

66 See *TO* II, 147. See also the quotation from *HMC*, 128 in note 52. Cf.:

"you enquire not so much, when you see a change of anything, what may be said to be the cause of it, as how the same is generated . . . which is always a hard question, and for the most part impossible for a man to answer. For the alternations of the things, we perceive by our five senses are made by the motion of bodies, for the most part, either for distance, smallness or transparence, invisible" (*DP, EW* VII, 78).

67 See *MDO*, 26, n. 59.

68 See ibid., 27–8, and *TO* II, 152–3.

69 See n. 93. This is not to say that there are no interesting differences with the current opinion. In contrast with most of his contemporaries, Hobbes was convinced, for example, that the optical nerve is not hollow and that the eye, although having to move in order actually to see something, never moves as a whole (see *MDO*, 58–64, 87–9, and 91–2).

70 "reactionem a Corde per Cerebrum & nervum opticum et Retinae crassitiem versus externea procreatum ab actione corporis Lucidi sive illuminati propagata per medium diaphanum ad oculum et per oculum, Retinam, nervum opticum, cerebrumque usque ad Cor" (*TO* II, 206).

71 See *TO* II, 204. Cf. Kepler (1939), 152–3.

72 Hobbes notes in this connection that when an object and the eye move parallel to each other and at the same speed, the object will not be seen. Thus, for example, you cannot see that, as is admitted nowadays by the best of philosophers, the earth moves (*TO* II, 225).

73 See *TO* II, 202.

74 See *TO* II, 213–4.

75 See *MDO*, 62–4.

76 See *TO* II, 216. Cf. *ST*, 30.

77 See *TO* II, 215.

78 See *TO* II, 210. See also Prins (1987), 306.

79 See *TO* II, 218–19, and *MDO*, 62–8.

80 See *MDO*.

81 Ibid., 341.

82 Ibid., 268.

83 Ibid., 459. Cf. Alhazen: "Imago in quocunque speculo, videtur in concursu perpendicularis incidentiae & lineae reflexionis" (Risner, *Opticae Thesaurus*, Alhazen, p. 131). Hobbes does not refer in this connection to Kepler, who was the first to reject this principle. (See Kepler [1939], 61–4.) Kepler demonstrated that the image is located at a convergence of the cone of rays reflected from the mirror. Hobbes's own geometric alternative does not differ essentially from the Scholastic tradition. The crucial difference is that with Hobbes, even in direct vision, the object and the image occupy a different place (see *MDO*, 465, 533, and 537).

84 On the differences between the model in *TO* I and II and the one in the
    MDO, see repeated in *De corpore* (*OL* I, 374–9), Blay.

85 See *MDO*, 185–6. See, on Fabri, *Dictionary of Scientific Biography* (E.A.
    Fellmann), 505–7.

86 "And seeing Mons. desCartes who only hath sett forth the true principle
    of this doctrine, namely that the Images of objects are in the Fancie and
    that they fly not through the aire, under the empty name of Species
    intentionales but are made in the braine by the operation of the objects
    themselves" (*AM*, 335).

87 See *MDO*, 336.

88 New in the *MDO* is his criticism of Descartes's idea that cats see by
    extramission (see *AT* IV, 487) as well as his rejection of Descartes's
    identification of "body" with "extension" as an argument against the
    existence of the vacuum (see *MDO*, 96, and Brandt, 189).

89 See *EW* III, 2–3.

90 See *OL* I, 305–334, 362–379.

91 Ibid., I, 320–22.

92 The anatomy and physiology of the eye get less attention in *De homine*,
    but the text is clearer about the physical role of the center of the eye in
    vision. Also Hobbes elaborates in this book on the causes of confused
    vision, the perception of motion, and on conic sections. Apart from a
    few terminological changes he presents another way to determine the
    place of the image in case of reflection from curved mirrors as well as
    seeing through a telescope, seeing objects after one refraction and in a
    rare medium, and regarding the analysis concerning lenses. Descartes
    and Kepler are no longer mentioned in this book. (See *OL* II, *D.H.*, chaps.
    2 to 9; Maurin and *MDO*, 372.)

93 See Pacchi (1968). For Hobbes's interest in the optical work of Grosseteste
    and Roger Bacon, see Pacchi (1965).

94 Brandt suggests the influence of Suarez (pp. 68–72).

95 See Grosseteste (Baur, 54–5) and Witelo (Risner 1972, *Opticae Thesau-
    rus*, Witelo, 63). Alhazen and Roger Bacon constitute the exception to
    the rule (see *MDO*, 171).

96 Cf. R. Bacon: "a species is not a body, nor is it moved as a whole from
    one place to another; but that which is produced [by an object] in the
    first part of the air is not separated from that part, since form cannot be
    separated from the matter in which it is unless it should be mind; rather
    it produces a likeness to itself in the second part of the air, and so on.
    Therefore there is no change of place, but a generation multiplied
    through the different parts of the medium . . . it is not produced by a
    flow from the luminous body but by a drawing forth out of the potential-
    ity of the matter of the air" (Lindberg 1976, 113).

97 See Jacquot (1974), Bernhardt (1987), McColley and Prins (1992). See also Brandt, 73–6.

98 See Hill, *Philosophia epicurea*, aph. 56, 116, 125, 132, 133, 136, 186, 209, 284, 299, 321, 334, 357, 386, 391, 397, 400, 410, 492.

99 See Shapiro, 142; Bernhardt (1977), 13 ff.; *MDO*, passim; Prins (1987).

100 See Shapiro, p. 134 and chaps. V and VI.

101 *MDO*, 530 and 621–22.

102 See *MDO*, 38–9.

7   Hobbes's psychology

Many of Hobbes's philosophical views about psychology appear quite up-to-date. Views very similar to Hobbes's are still being maintained by many, although often in a slightly more sophisticated form. In what follows I shall discuss only Hobbes's philosophical views concerning psychological topics, not his empirical speculations. With regard to matters of sense, this is explicitly in accordance with Hobbes's view of philosophy, for he says, in talking of phantasms involved in sense, we can only know "some ways and means by which they may be, I do not say they are, generated" (*De Corp.* ch. 25, 1; *EWI*, p.388).[1] Hobbes was quite inventive to say that "phantasms seem to be without, by reaction of the endeavour outwards, so pleasure and pain, by reason of the endeavour of the organ inwards, seem to be within" (*De Corp.* ch. 25, 12; *EWI*, 406. See also *Lev.* ch. 1, *EWIII*, 2; and *D.H.* ch. 11, 1). Hobbes knew, however, that this was empirical speculation, and it should be distinguished from what would now be classified as his philosophical views concerning sense.

SENSE AND IMAGINATION

Hobbes's philosophical position is clearly and explicitly a materialist one. The mind consists of motions in the body. Hobbes did not know what these motions are like, nor do we, although we know more than Hobbes about these matters. Different aspects of the mind involve different motions; for example, "Sense, therefore, in the sentient, can be nothing else but motion in some of the internal parts of the sentient; and the parts so moved are parts of the organs of sense" (*De Corp.* ch. 25, 2; *EW* I, 390). Hobbes defines imagination

157

as "sense decaying, or weakened, by the absence of the object" (*De Corp.* ch. 25, 5; *EWI*, 396, see also *Lev.* ch. 2). This definition is often condescendingly quoted, but all that is of philosophical significance is that Hobbes regards imagination as a motion that is related to the motions of sense, an eminently sensible view.

Sense is important to Hobbes, for he holds the standard empiricist view that "there is no conception in a man's mind, which hath not at first, totally, or by part, been begotten upon the organs of sense. The rest are derived from that original" (*Lev.* ch. 1, *EW* III, 1) Hobbes differs from standard empiricism in that he appreciates that language is included in that which was at first begotten upon the organs of sense, and he explicitly says of understanding that it is "nothing else but conception caused by speech" (*Lev.* ch. 4 *EW* III 28; see also *Lev.* ch. 2, *EW* III 11) Thus, to view Hobbes as holding that thought consists of a succession of phantasms, that is, pictures, is to impose on Hobbes the more restricted view of what counts as "begotten on the organs of sense" held by later empiricists. Hobbes, much more than other empiricists, recognized the extraordinary impact of language on thought, remarking that "A natural fool that could never learn by heart the order of the numeral words, as *one, two,* and *three,* may observe every stroke of the clock, and nod to it, or say *one, one, one,* but can never know what hour it strikes" (*Lev.* ch. 4, *EW* III 22).

Hobbes claims that his philosophical view of sense is a direct consequence of his materialist view. This is brought out most clearly when he uses the basic principle "that when a thing is in motion, it will eternally be in motion, unless something else stay it" (*Lev.* ch. 2, *EW*III 4) to explain imagination. This explanation consists primarily in making an analogy between present sense obscuring imagination in the way that the sun obscures the stars. This analogy may, however, lead to Hobbes's most interesting philosophical discovery concerning sense: that sense, or what we would call perception, requires variety. "Sense, therefore, properly so called, must necessarily have in it a perpetual variety of phantasms, that they may be discerned one from another" (*De Corp.* ch. 25, 5; *EW* I 394). Hobbes points out that to see one thing continually and not to see at all both come to the same thing. But Hobbes, like all other materialist philosophers both before and after him, never provides a satisfactory account of phantasms or appearances, that is, an account of the fact that we are aware of something related to the motions of sense.

Hobbes does attempt to explain how the motions of sense are involved in voluntary motion. According to Hobbes, "There be in animals, two sorts of *motions* peculiar to them: one called *vital;* begun in generation, and continued without interruption through their whole life; such as are the *course* of the *blood*, the *pulse,* the *breathing,* the *concoction, nutrition, excretion,* &c., to which motions there needs no help of imagination; the other is *animal motion,* otherwise called *voluntary motion;* so as to *go,* to *speak,* to *move* any of our limbs, in such manner as first fancied in our minds. . . . And because *going, speaking,* and the like voluntary motions, depend always upon a precedent thought of *whither, which way,* and *what;* it is evident, that the imagination is the first internal beginning of all voluntary motion" (*Lev.* ch. 6; *EW* III 38–39).[2]

Here again Hobbes puts forward a rather crude picture of the interaction of the various motions in the body, but he knows that this picture is speculative. His philosophical purpose is to explain how the motions of sense provide the basis for a distinction between two kinds of observable motion in the body. The first, which he calls vital motion, has no need of sense; it is an essential feature of the human organism. These are the kinds of motions that go on even during sleep. Were these motions to stop, the organism would be dead, which is why Hobbes calls them the vital motions. Hobbes has no great interest in these motions. They are relevant to his concerns only because they provide a plausible explanation of appetite and aversion, pleasure and pain. They allow him to show that a materialist account is compatible with an accurate explanation of human behavior, but it is not important to his projects to provide that accurate explanation.

APPETITE, AVERSION, PLEASURE, PAIN,
AND THE PASSIONS

Hobbes wants to show that there is a plausible explanation of all of the features of human psychology – sense, imagination, dreams, appetites, and aversions – in terms of the motions in the body (*Lev.* ch. 6). Thus he wants to show that the motions of sense and imagination can interact with the vital motion in order to provide a plausible explanation of voluntary motion. The motions of sense interact with the vital motion in such a way that they produce voluntary motion by means of a purely theoretically derived motion that Hobbes called endeavor. Endeavor is the key concept in Hobbes's attempt to show the compatibility of his philosophy of motion with the explanation of voluntary behavior. Having shown the plausibility, perhaps even the necessity, of invisible and insensible motions, Hobbes continues, "These small beginnings of motion, within the body of man, before they appear in walking, speaking, striking, and other visible actions, are commonly called ENDEAVOR" (Lev. ch. 6, EW III 39). Hobbes then goes on to use endeavor to define the more common psychological terms that he will use in his analyses of particular passions. "This endeavor, when it is toward something that causes it, is called APPETITE or DESIRE.... And when the endeavor is fromward something, it is generally called AVERSION" (Lev. ch. 6, EW III 39; see also D.H. ch. 11, 1).

Hobbes attempts to relate appetite and aversion to pleasure and pain in two somewhat different ways. In Leviathan he says "This motion which is called appetite, and for the appearance of it delight, and pleasure, seemeth to be a corroboration of vital motion" (Lev. ch. 6, EWIII 42). Here, pleasure is a phantasm of the motion of appetite, just as sense is really "only motion, caused by the action of external objects, but in appearance; to the eye, light and color, to the ear sound, to the nostril odour, &c." (Lev. ch. 6, EW III 42) In De homine, however, although he still compares delight to the senses, he now says that "Appetite and aversion do not differ from delight and annoyance otherwise than desire from satisfaction of desire, that is, than the future differs from the present" (D.H. ch. 11, 1). Appearances have largely disappeared, and delight simply becomes having an appetite for what you now have; annoyance, having an aversion to the situation one is now in. This latter account seems to be a more thoroughgoing materialism than the epiphenomenalism of the former account.

In both works (Lev. ch. 6 and D.H. ch. 13), once Hobbes has the concepts of appetite and aversion, pleasure and pain, his account of the individual passions completely ignores the relation between human behavior and his materialist philosophy. He simply proceeds by way of introspection and experience, along with liberal borrowings from Aristotle's account of the passions. In the Introduction to Leviathan, Hobbes admits that he does not use his materialist philosophy to explain either the individual passions or human behavior in general, stating "that for the similitude of the thoughts and passions of one man, to the thoughts and passions of another, whosoever looketh into himself, and considereth what he doth, when he does *think, opine, reason, hope, fear,* &c. and upon what grounds; he shall thereby read and know, what are the thoughts and passions of all other men upon like occasions" (*Lev.* Intro, *EW* III xi). Hobbes is quite clear that introspection and experience, not a materialist philosophy, provide the key to understanding human behavior. This is made explicit in the final sentences of the Introduction: "when I shall have set down my own reading orderly, and perspicuously, the pains left another, will be only to consider, if he also find not the same in himself. For this kind of doctrine admitteth no other demonstration" (*Lev.* Intro., *EW*III xii).

Hobbes's definitions of the particular passions are noteworthy for their conciseness. For example, "appetite, with an opinion of obtaining, is called HOPE. The same without such opinion, DESPAIR" (*Lev.* ch. 6, *EW*III 43). These definitions seem reasonable, but obviously they are not to be taken as serious attempts at analyses of the concepts of hope and despair. Thus when Hobbes defines DIFFIDENCE as "*constant* despair" (*Lev.* ch. 6, *EW*III 43), it is clear that this definition will not be very useful in explaining Hobbes's famous remark in Chapter XIII of *Leviathan:* "So that in the nature of man, we find three principle causes of quarrel. First competition, secondly, diffidence; thirdly, glory" (*Lev.* ch. 13, *EW*III 112). Recognizing this, Hobbes explains what he means in the next paragraph; "The first, maketh men to invade for gain; the second for safety; and the third, for reputation." Hobbes should have used fear, instead of diffidence, for not only does fear actually fit better with what he says in this latter paragraph, it also fits better with his own definition of FEAR as "*Aversion,* with opinion of HURT from the object" (*Lev.* ch. 6 *EW*III 43). It may simply be that it is because Hobbes wanted to use the passion of fear as one of "the passions that incline men to peace" (*Lev.* ch. 13, *EW*III 116) that he decided to use a different word when he wanted a passion that led to war.

Hobbes's definition of GLORY as "Joy, arising from imagination of a man's own power and ability" (*Lev.* ch. 6, *EW,* 43) does fit in somewhat better with his use of glory as one of the causes of quarrel. But clearly on this definition, it is the desire for glory, not glory itself, that is a cause of quarrel. Here again, it would seem that

Hobbes did not use the right term, even given his own definition. It probably would have been more correct to use "pride," rather than "glory," but it is surprising that Hobbes does not even list pride in the list of passions that he defines in Chapter VI of *Leviathan*. This is all the more surprising, for he does define SHAME as "*Grief* for the discovery of some defect of ability" (*Lev.* ch. 6 *EW*III, 46). In one normal sense of "pride," however, pride does seem to be a cause of quarrel. What this shows is that Hobbes did not take the definitions that he offered in Chapter VI of *Leviathan* very seriously. Both he and his readers knew what was meant by these terms, and his definitions were merely an attempt to show that all of the passions could be explained by relating them to some simpler passion.[3]

Finally, it does not seem that "competition" is the right term for the first cause of quarrel. In Chapter VI he had already defined COVETOUSNESS as "Desire of riches" (*Lev.* ch. 6, *EW* III 44), which seems to be close to what he means. In that definition, however, he had noted that covetousness was "used always in signification of blame," and it may be that he did not want to use a term that he himself had said was of inconstant signification. This examination of Hobbes's use of "competition," "diffidence," and "glory" as the three causes of quarrel shows that although he is not using these terms correctly, this does not create any misunderstanding. Hobbes's explanations of what he means by these terms in the following paragraph makes his point as clear as if he had used exactly the right terms. Also, it is important to note that of the three causes of war, only diffidence or fear is a passion that naturally leads to peace as well as war. The other two passions, competition or covetousness, and glory or pride, do not naturally lead to peace. This may explain, in part, why Hobbes thought a strong state, the Leviathan, was needed to rule over the kingdom of the proud.

Hobbes's definition of deliberation as "the whole sum of desires, aversions, hopes and fears, continued till the thing be done, or thought impossible" (*Lev.* ch. 6, *EW*III, 48) is another example of a not quite successful analysis of a concept. His folk etymological analysis that this process is "called *deliberation*; because it is putting an end to the *liberty* we had of doing, or omitting, according to our own appetite, or aversion" (*Lev.* ch. 6, *EW* III 48) may be partly responsible for the inadequacy of his definition. Although his definition does explain why we cannot deliberate about the past, and of things thought impossible (ibid.), it makes deliberation sound more like a succession of emotional states than a consideration of the consequences of the various alternative courses of actions.

Although Hobbes claims that definitions are the beginning of all science (*Lev.* ch. 4, *EW*III 23-4; ch. 5, *EW*III 31), we have seen that many of his own definitions, especially of the passions, were not carefully formulated. What was really important for Hobbes was to use words in such a way that everyone would agree that the terms referred to the same thing. He did not want to use terms that were primarily expressions of the attitudes of the person using them (*Lev.* ch. 4 *EW*III 28). He anticipated many of the views of the philosophers of language of the early twentieth century; for example, he realized that language was used to express our attitudes and not merely to describe the world (*Lev.* ch. 4, *EW*III 28) and recognized the performatory nature of promising. (*Lev.* ch. 14, *EW*III 121f). He maintained that language was a human invention and denied that there was some natural relationship between words and the world. (*D.H.* ch. 10, 2).

Although Hobbes often equates emotions or passions with appetites and desires, when he is more careful, he is aware that the former are only a subclass of the latter (see *D.H.* ch. 12, 1). In addition to our emotional desires, we also have rational desires, our long-term desires for real goods. Hobbes is referring to these rationally required desires when he says, "the greatest of goods for each is his own preservation. For nature is so arranged that all desire good for themselves. Insofar as it is within their capacities, it is necessary to desire life, health, and further, insofar as it can be done, security of future time" (*D.H.* ch. 2, 6). Hobbes is not claiming that everyone desires self-preservation more than anything else because he explicitly notes that "most men would rather lose their lives (that I say not, their peace) then suffer slander" (*De Cive* ch. 3, 12, *Lev.* ch. 15 *EW* III 140). Hobbes explicitly refers to the distinction between the rational desires and the emotional ones in the Dedication to *De Cive:* "Having therefore thus arrived at two maxims of human nature; the one arising from the *concupiscible* part, which desires to appropriate to itself the use of those things in which all others have a joint interest; the other proceeding from the *rational*, which teaches every man to fly a contra-natural dissolution, as the greatest mischief that can arrive to nature" (*M&C* 93).

The objects of the rational desires are the same in all persons, but

Hobbes is aware that the objects of the emotional desires or the passions differ from person to person. In the Introduction to *Leviathan*, right after claiming that introspection tells us that the passions "are the same in all men," he points out that this is not true of "the *objects* of the passions, which are the things desired, feared, hoped &c.: for these the constitution individual, and particular education, do so vary, and they are so easy to be kept from our knowledge" (*Lev.* Intro. *EW*III xi). It is the universality of the objects of the rational desires that allows Hobbes to use reason as the basis for his arguments concerning morality and the proper ordering of the state. All of the premises about human nature, which Hobbes claims are true of all persons and which he uses in arguing for the necessity of an unlimited sovereign, are in fact statements about the rationally required desires, and not, as most commentators have taken them, statements about the passions.

Since only the rationally required desires are universal, when Hobbes talks about any other desires he is only talking about those that are widespread enough to have an effect on the organization of the state. Hobbes is one of the few philosophers to realize that to talk of that part of human nature that involves the passions is to talk about human populations. He says in the Preface to *De Cive*, "Though the wicked were fewer than the righteous, yet because we cannot distinguish them, there is a necessity of suspecting, heeding, anticipating, subjugating, self-defending, ever incident to the most honest and fairest conditioned" (*M&C* p.100). This kind of passage shows that Hobbes is aware that premises about the passions do not need to apply to each and every person in order to play the role that he wants them to play in his moral and political philosophy. It also shows that he is aware that people are quite different in their psychological characteristics, including the degree to which their behavior is governed by the passions rather than "good education and experience" (ibid.; see also *De Cive* ch. 3, 26, 27).

MENTAL DISORDERS

In our own day there is a debate among psychiatrists about whether deviant behavior is a sufficient condition for a mental disorder, or whether there also needs to be some suffering of an evil. It is surprising that Hobbes seems to support both sides in this debate. He says, "to have stronger and more vehement passions for any thing, than is ordinarily seen in others, is that which men call MADNESS" (*Lev.* ch. 8, *EWIII* 62). But later he says, "if the excesses be madness, there is no doubt but the passions themselves, when they tend to evil, are degrees of the same" (*Lev.* ch. 8, *EWIII* 63). I suspect that just as those current psychiatrists who seem to regard deviance as a sufficient condition for mental disorder think that deviance leads to suffering, Hobbes also regards the more vehement passions as tending to evil.

Hobbes also anticipates modern psychiatry's view that mental disorders can have either mental or physical causes. "Sometimes the extraordinary and extravagant passion, proceedeth from the evil constitution of the organs of the body, or harm done them; and sometimes the hurt, and indisposition of the organs, is caused by the vehemence, or long continuance of the passion. But in both cases the madness is of one and the same nature" (*Lev.* ch. 8, *EWIII* 62). This view shows how little Hobbes's materialism restricts his views about human nature. But it is important to see that it is not inconsistent with that materialism either. Hobbes can be taken to say that sometimes a defective bodily part produces unusual motions, and sometimes the unusual motions of the passion injure the bodily part.

Hobbes's discussion of madness also makes clear that he did not hold some simple view that everyone is most strongly motivated by the desire to avoid death. He tells the story about the fit of madness in a "Grecian city which seized only the young maidens; and caused them to hang themselves. . . . But one that suspected, that contempt of life in them, might proceed from some passion of the mind, and supposing they did not contemn also their honour, gave counsel to the magistrates, to strip such as so hanged themselves, and let them hang out naked. This the story says, cured that madness" (*Lev.* ch. 8, *EWIII* 65). Hobbes was aware that the natural rational desire to avoid death can be much weaker than the learned social desire to avoid shame.

HUMAN NATURE AND PSYCHOLOGICAL EGOISM

The clearest and most complete statement of Hobbes's view about the sources of human behavior is in chapter 13 of *De homine*. In the first section of that chapter he says: "Dispositions, that is men's inclinations toward certain things, arise from a six fold source: namely from the constitution of the body, from experience, from habit, from the goods of fortune, from the opinion one has of oneself, and from authorities." In the remainder of the chapter he elaborates on each of these six sources. Among the more interesting remarks there are the following: "among all peoples religion and doctrine, which everyone hath been taught from their early years, so shackle them forever that they hate and revile dissenters" (sec. 3) and "the dispositions of youths are not less, but much more disposed to bad habit by example than they are to good habits by precept" (sec. 7).

Hobbes's view about human nature is rather ordinary. Although he admitted that infants were born with neither a moral sense nor concern for anyone other than themselves, he held that education and training could make them act in a wide variety of ways and from a wide variety of motives, from very good to very bad, from selfish to unselfish (see *De Cive* preface; *M&C* p.100). Hobbes was also aware that the constitution of the body affected people's behavior, and even discusses such mental disorders as depression (see *Lev.* ch. 8) *EW* III, 620. Once one realizes that Hobbes was aware of the wide variety of human behavior, it becomes quite clear that his remarks about human nature, especially human nature in the state of nature, should not be taken as remarks about actual persons in the real world, but merely as remarks about some common features of the human population. Interpreting Hobbes in this way does not take away any premise about human nature that he needs for building his political theory and allows one to account for many apparent inconsistencies.

The failure to realize that when Hobbes talks about human nature, he usually does not mean to be saying something that he thinks true of each and every human being, but only something that holds for a significant portion of the human population, viz., something that must be taken into account when constructing a workable political theory, is one explanation of the standard practice of claiming that Hobbes subscribed to psychological egoism, the view that all people care only about their own welfare. In fact, like all keen observers of the human scene, Hobbes was aware that real people behave as they do not primarily because of the way they are born, but because of the way that they have been trained. This point is made in many places, such as where he says that children "have no other rule of good and evil manners, but the correction they receive from their parents and masters," and then adds that "children are constant to their rule" (*Lev.* ch. 11; *EW*III 91; see also *D.C.* Pref.; *M&C* p. 100, and I,2, n).

Psychological egoism is also inconsistent with several of the passions that Hobbes defines in *Leviathan*, such as "*Anger* for great hurt done to another, when we consider the same to be done by injury, INDIGNATION." "*Desire* of good to another, BENEVOLENCE, GOOD WILL, CHARITY. If to man generally, GOOD NATURE." "*Love* of persons for society, KINDNESS." "Love of one singularly, with the desire to be singularly beloved, THE PASSION OF LOVE" (*Lev.* ch. 6, *EW*III 43–4). There is great difficulty in even stating psychological egoism so that it is a plausible view, but on a standard formulation, "No person is ever motivated by any passions other than those that have benefit to their own self as an object." Not only is it obviously false; as the above quotations make clear, it is not a view that Hobbes held.

Hobbes did hold that psychological egoism was true of infants. He says in the Preface to *De Cive:* "Unless you give children all they ask for, they are peevish and cry, aye, and strike their parents sometimes; and all this they have from nature" (*M&C* p. 100). Since people in the state of nature are assumed to be like infants, without any kind of education or training, psychological egoism would be true of them (see Ibid. and *De Cive* I, 2 n.). But Hobbes's claim that in the state of nature we are considering people "as if but even now sprung out of the earth, and suddenly, like mushrooms, come to full maturity, without all kind of engagement to one another" (*De Cive*, ch. 8, 1) shows that he knew that no person was ever actually in the state of nature. Hobbes never claims that actual persons, those who were raised up in families, are psychological egoists. Indeed, as the above quotes indicate, he denied such a view.[4]

Attributing to Hobbes the view that no one is ever motivated by concern for others is not only inconsistent with the definition of benevolence quoted above; it is also inconsistent with his remarks about charity, where he characterizes a lack of charity as "a mind insensible to another's evils" (*D.H.* ch. 13, 9). Numerous passages concerning friends and family members also show that Hobbes did not deny people were ever motivated by love and concern for others (e.g., *De Cive* ch. 2, 19; and ch. 6, 5). What Hobbes does deny is that people naturally love all other human beings (see *De Cive*, ch. 1, 2).

Limited altruism is all that Hobbes uses in order to support his claim that there is a need for unlimited sovereign power. Indeed, given that Part Two of *Leviathan* is concerned with the danger posed by popular men, such as Julius Caesar, it would be absurd for Hobbes to hold that people are never motivated by their concern for others. Hobbes was quite aware that the danger to the state did not arise solely, or even primarily, from the self-interest of individuals.

Attributing to Hobbes the view that no one is ever motivated by his or her moral views is not only inconsistent with the definition of indignation quoted above; it also makes nonsense of his distinction between a just person and a guiltless one, the former being one who is "delighted in just dealings, to study how to do righteousness, or to endeavor in all things to do that which is just" (*De Cive*, ch. 3, 5; see also *Lev.* ch. 15 *EW* III 135–6). More centrally, it is in conflict with Hobbes's claims that false moral views were one of the main causes of the civil war (*De Cive*, pref; *M&C* 96–7). It not only makes nonsense of Hobbes's claim that a person "is obliged by his contracts, that is, that he ought to perform for his promise sake;" (*De Cive*, ch. 14, 2 n.), it renders pointless all of his efforts to show that the obligation to obey the laws rests upon the subjects' promise of obedience.

One reason why Hobbes is often regarded as having such a distorted account of human nature is traceable to his political rhetoric. Consider his use of the term "power." When he says, "So that in the first place, I put for a general inclination of all mankind, a perpetual and restless desire of power after power, that ceaseth only in death" (*Lev.* ch. 11; *EW*II 85–6) this sounds as if he is claiming that all people are like Saddam Hussein or other power-hungry dictators. Yet when we look at his definition of power, "THE POWER *of a man*, to take it universally, is his present means to obtain some future apparent good" (*Lev.* ch. 10, *EW*II 74), we see that this is quite misleading. What he is really claiming is that "the voluntary actions, and inclination of all men, tend, not only to the procuring, but also to the assuring of a contented life; and differ only in the way" (*Lev.* ch. 11, *EW*II 85). Hobbes's disturbing statement about power is only a claim that all people tend to be concerned about their future; it explains pensions funds and medical checkups more than it does anti-social power grabs. Indeed, for Hobbes, the former are not only more common than the latter; they are also more rational.

RATIONALITY AND THE GOOD

Although Hobbes did not hold that all natural desires were rational (*Lev.* ch. 11; see also *De Cive* Pref.; *M&C* 100, and I,2, n.), he did hold that the rationally required desires were natural (*De Cive* Ded.; *M&C*) He holds the latter because if these desires were the result of training and education, they could not be taken as universal. Hobbes's view of rational behavior loosely resembles psychological egoism. He held what may be called "rational egoism," viz., that the only rationally required desires are those that concern a person's own long-term benefit, primarily their preservation. The emotions or emotional desires are not in themselves irrational; they only become irrational when they conflict with reason, that is, what can be seen to be necessary to satisfy the rationally required desires (*D.H.* ch. 12, 1). Hobbes does not regard all sacrifice for others as irrational; on the contrary, he lists charity together with justice as encompassing all of the virtues (*D.H.* ch. 13, 9). He thinks, however, that there is a limit to rational altruism, and that limit is the sacrifice of one's own life.

Hobbes's claim that sacrifice of one's life is always irrational sounds exaggerated, and it is stronger than he needs for any of the conclusions that he draws from the concept of reason. He could hold the slighter weaker but much more plausible view – that it is almost always irrational to sacrifice one's life – without affecting any of his other claims. Indeed, given his use of rhetorical exaggeration and his general failure to make minor qualifications, it may be that this is the view he actually held. For he explicitly says that risking one's life for the proper cause is not irrational, making it a law of nature, that is, a dictate of reason, "that every man is bound by nature, as much as in him lieth, to protect in war the authority, by which he is himself protected in time of peace" (*Lev.* A Rev and Con, *EW* III 703).

Even if Hobbes held that all people always act rationally, psychological egoism would not follow from his rational egoism, for his rational egoism only rules out acting contrary to one's long-term interests, primarily one's preservation. But, of course, Hobbes does not hold that people always act rationally. He is constantly lamenting the power of the irrational appetites (see *De Cive* ch. 3, 32; and *Lev.* ch. 15, *EW* III 140). He explicitly states, "The definition of the will, given by the Schools, that it is a *rational appetite*, is not good.

For if it were, then there could be no voluntary act against reason" (*Lev.* ch. 6, *EW*III 48). Hobbes is aware that people are naturally motivated as much, if not more, by the emotions than they are by reason. This is why he holds that "man is made fit for society not by nature, but by education" (*De Cive,* ch. 1, 2, n.) and places so much stress on the need of the sovereign to educate (*Lev.* ch. 30, *EW* III 330ff).

Many philosophers do not seem to like Hobbes' view of human nature because, unlike Aristotle, Mill and many other philosophers, he not only does not put forward the life of the philosopher as the best life; he does not put forward any view of the best life. Although his observation of the way we use language leads him to agree with Aristotle in defining "*good* as that which all men desire" (*D.H.* ch. 11, 4), it also enables to him to realize it does not require that one accept that there is a universally agreed upon objective good. In fact, he explicitly states that "there is no such *finis ultimus,* utmost end, nor *summum bonum,* greatest good, as is spoken of in the books of the old moral philosophers" (*Lev.* ch. 11, *EW*III 85). Hobbes is aware that people have a wide variety of positive goals, and although he has his personal preferences, he denies that there is any objective ranking of these goals. So while Hobbes does not stress tolerance as a political virtue, intellectually he is probably more liberal and tolerant than all other moral and political philosophers, including Mill. On the other hand, he is not a relativist: he realizes that it is compatible with complete tolerance toward different positive goals to regard desires for death, pain, and disability as irrational. To say that there is a limit to the goals that are rational, but that within this limit there is no ranking of goals, is a very sophisticated view, and it may be a correct one.

Hobbes does seem to place severe limits on what is valued, but closer examination shows that these are not real limits. Thus he says that "nothing but goodness, power and felicity are valued" (*Lev.* ch. 10), but when we look at what is meant by these three terms, we see that, except for death, pain, and disability, almost nothing is ruled out as a possible object of value. We have already noted that "The common name for all things that are desired, insofar as they are desired, is *good*" (*D.H.* ch. 11, 4) and that power is simply a person's "present means to obtain some future apparent good" (*Lev.* ch. 10, *EW*III 74). When we add to that his account of FELICITY as "*Continual success* in obtaining those things which a man from time to time desireth, that is to say, continual prospering" (*Lev.* ch. 6, *EW*III 51), we see that Hobbes's supposed severe limits on what is valued are almost no limits at all.

Even though Hobbes holds that "good is said to be relative to person, place, and time" (*D.H.* ch. 11, 4), he realizes that this is not incompatible with holding that some things are good for everyone. In one sentence he makes both of these points. "At times one can also talk of a good for everyone, like health: but this way of speaking is relative; therefore one cannot speak of something as being *simply* good; since whatsoever is good, is good for someone or other" (ibid.). Hobbes realizes that people often desire what is not good for them, and this leads him to note that "good (like evil) is divided into *real* and *apparent*" (*D.H.* ch. 11, 5), "although the real good must be sought in the long term, which is the job of reason, appetite seizeth upon a present good without foreseeing the greater evils that necessarily attach to it" (*D.H.* ch. 12, 1). Hobbes is aware that people desire many different things, but unlike Hume, Hobbes does not regard reason as the slave of the passions. Rather, he regards the passions as being properly subservient to reason, as when he says that, "for the natural state hath the same proportion to the civil (I mean liberty to subjection) which passion hath to reason, or a beast to a man" (*De Cive,* ch. 7, 18).[5]

When Hobbes talks about human nature, it is clear that he views reason not only as determining how to achieve one's goals, but also as having the long-term goals of "life, health, and insofar as it can be done, security of future time" (*D.H.* ch. 11, 6). These common goals of reason allow Hobbes to make a list of those things that are real goods, as opposed to those things that are only apparent goods (see *D.H.* ch. 11). And it is these common goals of reason that supply the foundation of both the right of nature and the laws of nature (See *De Cive* ch. 1, 7 and ch. 2, 1; see also *Lev.* ch. 14, *EW*III, 116–17).

FREE WILL

Hobbes's materialist views make it almost inevitable that he would hold a deterministic position, but since his primary goal in writing was to provide arguments that were designed to persuade people to act in the appropriate ways, it is not surprising that he also accepts that people have free will. Hobbes may have been the first to hold

what is now called a compatibilist view: that on the proper understanding of free will, it is compatible with determinism. Hobbes
defines the will as follows: "The last appetite (either of doing or
omitting), the one that leads immediately to action or omission, is
properly called the will" (*D.H.* ch. 11, 2; see also *Lev.* ch. 6, *EW*III
48). Thus to will is simply to have an appetite that one acts on; if one
does not act on it, it is simply an inclination (*Lev.* ch. 6, *EW*III 49).
Given this understanding of will, Hobbes concludes that "Whenever
we say that someone hath free-will to do this or that, it must always
be understood with this necessary condition, if he wills. For to talk
of having free-will to do this or that whether one wills or not is
absurd" (*D.H.* ch. 11, 2).

It is surprising how modern-sounding is Hobbes's proposed solution to the alleged incompatibility between free-will and determinism. He examines the ordinary uses of the terms "free" and "liberty"
to show that when "applied to any thing but bodies, they are
abused" (*Lev.* ch. 21, *EW*III 197). He applies his analysis of 'free' to
the problem of determining what is meant by free will, concluding
that free will does not mean anything about the liberty "of the will,
desire, or inclination, but the liberty of the man; which consisteth in
this, that he finds no stop, in doing what he has the will, desire, or
inclination to do" (ibid). His compatibilist view that "*Liberty* and
necessity are consistent . . . in the actions which men voluntarily
do" (*Lev.* ch. 21, *EW*III 197) is not merely applied to the supposed
incompatibility between the determinism that is derived from his
materialism; he also applies it to the supposed incompatibility between the liberty of men and the necessity that is the result of God's
power.

Hobbes is usually more careful in describing the use of language
than in formulating his definitions. He realizes that "when the im-
pediment of motion is in the thing itself, we use not to say; it wants
the liberty; but the power to move" (*Lev.* ch. 21, *EW*III 196). What
Hobbes does not realize is that when we talk of free will, we may, in
fact, not be talking about freedom in the normal sense at all, but
rather of the ability of a person to will. His account of free will as the
freedom to do what one wills, not the ability to will, is based upon a
language that was not yet influenced by Freudian notions of phobias
and compulsions. As in Hume and some linguistic philosophers of
the early twentieth century, this attempt to abide by ordinary usage

sometimes resulted in a trivialization of philosophical problems. But in those cases where the language was not suffering from a deficient scientific understanding, Hobbes's attention to ordinary usage was often quite enlightening.[5]

NOTES

1 My references to the works of Hobbes are to chapter and section number, when there are sections.

2 This may conflict with what Hobbes says in that part of *The Elements of Law* known as *Human Nature*. Nevertheless, I do not think that what is said in *Human Nature* should be used to determine Hobbes's views on any subject. That work was an early draft of *De cive* and *Leviathan* and was not intended to be published. Either what is said there is also said in these later works, in which case it is unnecessary, or it conflicts with (or is absent from) what is said there, in which case it indicates that he had changed him mind. I do not quote from that work at all. Those who rely on it are much more likely to mistakenly attribute to Hobbes views like psychological egoism. I do refer quite often to *De homine*, Hobbes's latest writing on human nature. This work was translated into English just twenty years ago (See M&C, edited by Bernard Gert, 1991, Hackett [first published in 1972 by Doubleday Anchor] pp. 35–85, containing Chapters X–XV of *De Homine*, the earlier chapters being primarily about optics) and has seldom been used, although it represents Hobbes's considered views on human nature far better than *Human Nature*. If that work had been consulted more frequently, it is unlikely that the distorted view of Hobbes's account of human nature would have lasted quite so long.

3 Indeed, in Chapter XII of *De Homine*, where he offers a somewhat more detailed account of somewhat fewer passions, he explicitly says in the last paragraph, "There would be an almost infinite number of passions, if we gave different names to all of them, however insignificant the difference between them. But since none there be that are not related to some one of those that we have described, we shall be content with what we have said concerning them."

4 For almost three centuries the standard view of Hobbes was that he held psychological egoism (See Peters, *Hobbes*). In the last several decades, this view has been increasingly challenged. It is now generally held that he does not hold such a view (see e.g. Kavka, *Hobbesian Moral and Political Philosophy*), but there is disagreement about how close to standard psychological egoism his view is. There is universal agreement that he regards unrestricted altruism as very rare or completely nonexistent,

but this view seems to be held by most philosophers and other students of human nature. He certainly held that most people are more motivated by concern for self, family, and friends than they are by concern for strangers, but this too is very commonly held.

5 The Humean view of reason is probably the standard contemporary view of reason, and this may account for the fact that most contemporary commentators view Hobbes as holding such a view (see especially Gauthier, *The Logic of Leviathan*, and Jean Hampton, *Hobbes & the Social Contract Tradition*). However, just as this view of reason is coming under attack, there is increasing recognition that much of what Hobbes says about reason cannot be reconciled with this view.

8   Hobbes's moral philosophy

Hobbes's whole philosophical enterprise, coming as it did so late in his life, has the character of mature reflection on an entire culture with which he was already completely conversant. Nowhere is this truer than in the area of moral philosophy, in which Hobbes looked back in all his great philosophical works at the way in which he and his contemporaries had actually discussed moral issues, and at the rich and complex ethical culture of Renaissance humanism. Accordingly, in this essay I will deal not only with the philosophical reflections in their own right but also with the way in which they drew upon and interacted with that earlier world of practical moral discourse.

'MORAL PHILOSOPHY'

The first issue to consider is just what Hobbes himself understood by "moral philosophy," and in particular how he differentiated it from politics. On a number of occasions he tried formally to define the place of "ethiques" or "moral philosophy" inside his grand system of human knowledge. The correct way to divide up philosophy as a whole was of course one of his constant concerns, and the work on which he labored for about twenty years, his Latin *Elementa Philosophiae* (published as *De corpore, De homine,* and *De cive*) represented in its three separate volumes a sensitive and sophisticated new division of human knowledge. The reasonableness of Hobbes's approach is usually taken for granted, particularly since it corresponds in some ways to a modern common sense; but it was in fact sharply and self-consciously setting itself against the traditions of both antiquity and the Renaissance.

175

The correct division of philosophy had been a matter of great interest in the ancient world, and the view that came to prevail was traced back in antiquity to Plato (although it was apparently first argued for clearly by his pupil Xenocrates),[1] that all philosophy should be divided into three sections: Physics, Ethics, and Logic. Ethics, according to this scheme, comprehended Politics, the most vivid expression of this being the fact that Aristotle's *Ethics* and his *Politics* were in effect two parts of a single work.[2] Various dissenters in antiquity argued that either one or two of these subdivisions should be dropped – for example, it could be argued that since Physics and Logic contributed nothing to human happiness, they were unworthy of the attention of a true philosopher[3] – but the only major thinker who appears to have queried the logic of the division was Epicurus, who argued that Physics and Ethics together were one subject, and Logic the other. For him, too, however, Ethics and Politics went together as a single science.

Roman writers agreed with this Greek division of philosophy; for example, Quintilian accepted that philosophy should be divided into "natural, moral, and rational" parts – "rational" meaning "to do with reasoning," that is, Logic. As is now well known, the Romans' principal dissent from the Greeks was over the role of rhetoric vis-à-vis philosophy: whereas the Socratic tradition had sought to separate rhetoric sharply from philosophy, the Romans insisted that it must be seen as part of each of the subdivisions of philosophy. Even Physics, Quintilian argued, involved rhetoric, for when the physicists talked about such things as the rule of the world by providence, they were using notions like "rulership" about which the rhetoricians were expert.[4] This was a view not totally removed from the Greeks', since Aristotle in his *Rhetoric* had (albeit somewhat grudgingly) accorded a place to rhetoric in both Ethics and Logic. In Logic it formed the logic of probabilities or "dialectic" in the Aristotelian sense of the term, as contrasted with "apodeictic" logic, the logic of certainties. But the Romans insisted on a much greater role for rhetoric than any Greek had done, something in which they were followed by many Renaissance writers. It became conventional in the Renaissance to argue that Logic meant anything to do with words, and that the rhetorician was more knowleddgable about language than the traditional logician.

With this proviso about rhetoric, the account that early Renaissance writers gave of the divisions of philosophy stayed faithful to the Platonic tradition. At the end of the sixteenth century, however, we find a generation of dissatisfied anti-Arisotelians who sought in various ways to supplant traditional philosophy with more-or-less visionary schemes of their own, and these schemes (such as those of Patrizi, Telesio, or Bruno) usually involved some new analysis of the component parts of philosophy. The most important such scheme for our purpose – important because of its relevance to Hobbes – was put forward by Francis Bacon in his *Advancement of Learning* (1605). Bacon argued that philosophy should be divided into a *Philosophia Prima* consisting of universal propositions, common to all sciences, and followed by three separate sections: "Divine philosophy" (i.e., natural theology), "natural philosophy," and "human philosophy".[5] Human philosophy, on Bacon's account, was itself divided into two subsections, "either Simple and Particular, or Conjugate and Civil." The former was a blend of conventional physics and ethics, the novelty of which Bacon recognized:

I do take the consideration in general and at large of Human Nature to be fit to be emancipate and made a knowledge by itself; not so much in regard of those delightful and elegant discourses which have been made of the dignity of man, of his miseries, of his state and life, and the like *adjuncts of his common and undivided nature;* but chiefly in regard of the knowledge concerning the *sympathies and concordances between the mind and body,* which being mixed, cannot be properly assigned to the sciences of either.[6]

Into this branch of human philosophy Bacon put the theory of perception, conventional ethics, much conventional logic, and the whole of conventional rhetoric. Into the other branch, "civil knowledge," he put the study of "Conversation, Negotiation, and Government," and he sharply distinguished it from the first branch: "moral philosophy propoundeth to itself the framing of internal goodness; but civil knowledge requireth only an external goodness; for that as to society sufficeth."

THE DIVISION OF ETHICS AND POLITICS

It is worth stressing that Bacon's scheme did not treat civil knowledge as *following from* the knowledge of human nature: it was a science *parallel* to that of human nature, although within the general category of "human philosophy." It is also worth stressing that he treated rhetoric as a vital part of moral philosophy; he praised Aristotle's *Rhetoric* rather than his *Ethics* as a true textbook of morals, along with the works of "poets and writers of histories" which show how

to set affection against affection, and to master one by another; even as we use to hunt beast with beast and fly bird with bird, which otherwise percase we could not so easily recover: upon which foundation is erected that excellent use of *praemium* and *poena*, whereby civil states consist: employing the predominant affections of *fear* and *hope*, for the suppressing and bridling the rest. For as in the government of states it is sometimes necessary to bridle one faction with another, so it is in the government within.[7]

It is against this background that we should read Hobbes's proposals about the division of philosophy. The best-known of these proposals is the table of the sciences attached to Chapter IX of *Leviathan*, in which there is a fundamental division between the study of natural bodies (including man seen as a natural creature) and the study of artificial bodies or political constructions. *Ethics* is defined as the science or knowledge of "Consequences from the Passions of Men," a subdivision of the general science of natural bodies; its neighbors in the array of sciences based on the study of man as a natural creature are the bodies of knowledge drawn from the consequences of speech, namely *Poetry* ("Magnifying, Vilifying, &c."), *Rhetoric* ("Perswading"), *Logic* ("Reasoning"), and *The Science of Just and Unjust* ("Contracting"). Civil Philosophy, according to the same scheme, is an extremely distant relative of Ethics, since it belongs to the other wing of the sciences, the enquiry into artificial bodies. Broadly speaking, this is clearly the Baconian division, with rhetoric, ethics, and even logic part of a free-standing science of man; but it has the difference that politics is not (so to speak) a sibling of the science of man, but is its most remote cousin.

Hobbes was aware of the oddity of such a thoroughgoing separation of ethics from politics, a separation that was of course to some extent belied by his own practice, and when he returned to the business of laying out the map of human knowledge in his *De corpore* of 1655, he observed that

The principal parts of philosophy are two. For two chief kinds of bodies, and very different from one another, offer themselves to such as search after their generation and properties; one whereof being the work of nature, is called a *natural body*, the other is called a *commonwealth*, and is made by the wills and agreement of men. And from these spring the two parts of philosophy, called *natural* and *civil*. But seeing that, for the knowledge of the properties of a commonwealth, it is necessary first to know the dispositions, affections, and manners of men, civil philosophy is again commonly divided into two parts, whereof one, which treats of men's dispositions and manners, is called *ethics;* and the other, which takes cognizance of their civil duties, is called *politics,* or simply *civil philosophy.* (ch. 1. 9)

But this was probably the closest Hobbes ever came to endorsing something like the Aristotelian notion of a "civil philosophy" divided into ethics and politics, and later in *De corpore* he once again emphasized the distinction between them, remarking that *"Civil* and *moral philosophy* do not so adhere to one another, but that they may be severed" since (he argued) *moral* philosophy, "in which we are to consider the motions of the mind, namely, *appetite, aversion, love, benevolence, hope, fear, anger, emulation, envy,* &c.; what causes they have, and of what they be causes," had to be arrived at on the basis of a deduction from fundamental principles (what he termed a "synthetic" approach). *Civil* philosophy, on the other hand, could be based (although it did not have to be) on "analysis," reasoning from the implications of the common experience of men about both their own psychology and political conflict (*De Corp.* ch.6, 6)

The most important illustration of the division between ethics and politics in Hobbes's eyes was the break between the second and third volumes of his *Elementa philosophiae.* These volumes were published eventually as *De homine* (in 1658) and *De cive* (in 1642) but as I have suggested elsewhere, they were most probably already in a draft form by 1640, and certainly the distinction between the volumes was already in Hobbes's mind then.[8] Thus in the *Anti-White* (1642/3) which summarized much of the *Elementa* as they existed at that date, he observed that one part of philosophy

concerns the passions, the manners [*mores*] and the aims or purposes of men, and is called ethics or moral philosophy. Another concerns human society and discusses civil laws, justice and all the other virtues; it is called politics or civil philosophy. (f.5v, trans. p.24)

This sharp distinction between ethics and politics, expressed in these terms, illustrates the heterodoxy of Hobbes's view of ethics.

The contents of moral philosophy according to both the old tradition and our own view of the matter are, after all, precisely such things as "justice and all the other virtues," which Hobbes assigned to the domain of *civil* philosophy; whereas ethics, for him, was conversant instead with the passions and manners of men. To see what he understood by this, we should first look carefully at the structure and argument of *De homine*, since only there did he specifically and exclusively address the issue of ethics as distinct from politics.

THE BENEFITS OF *ORATIO*

In *De homine* Hobbes distinguished between moral and civil philosophy, the study of men and the study of citizens, in the following terms.

Dispositions [*ingenia*], when they are so strengthened by habit that they beget their actions with ease and with reason unresisting, are called *manners* [*mores*]. Moreover, manners, if they be good, are called *virtues*, if evil, *vices*. Since, however, good and evil are not the same to all, it happens that the same manners are praised by some and condemned by others, that is, are called good by some, evil by others, virtues by some, vices by others. So, just as the proverb hath it, "So many men, so many opinions," one can also say, "Many men, many different rules for vice and virtue." Nevertheless, what is to be understood about man insofar as they are men, is not applicable insofar as they are citizens; for those who are outside of a state are not obliged to follow another's opinions, while those in a state are obliged by covenants. Whence it is to be understood that they, who consider men by themselves and as though they existed outside of civil society, can have no moral science because they lack any certain standard against which virtue and vice can be judged and defined. For all sciences begin with definitions, or otherwise they must not be called sciences, but mere verbiage. (ch. 13, 8)[9]

If a conventional moral language, with notions of duty or virtue, is inapplicable outside a particular civil society, then of course there can be no traditional ethics. Its place must be taken by an account of *manners* or *mores* understood in the nonethical sense, that is, by an account of man's desires and passions as modified or influenced by habit and other considerations. Such an account will also, of course, include an explanation of *why* it is not possible for men outside a civil society to agree on their evaluative descriptions. In particular, Hobbes had first to address the obvious question about an anti-realist account of this kind, namely, why should a language apparently expressing fundamentally subjective evaluations lead to conflict? If "good" means "what I prefer," then my description of something as "good" simply does not contradict your description of it as "not good."

The answer to this question was provided by the first nine chapters of the book, which consist of an explanation of vision.[10] This has often been seen as an incongruous introduction to a book on moral philosophy, but the connection in Hobbes's mind is clear enough: vision, and in particular the phenomenon of optical illusion, is a prime example of the way in which we have a profound conviction in the reality of what is in fact a wholly subjective experience. As he said at the beginning of his account of vision, in Chapter 2,

It is implanted by nature in all animals that at first glance they think an image of something is the thing itself being seen, or at least that it is some material object exactly reproducing the thing itself in its spatial properties. And men definitely think that an image is the object itself (if we except the few who have corrected the judgment of their senses by reason), nor without instruction can they come to believe that the Sun and stars are larger and further away than they seem.[11]

Since the first and most important function of speech is to assign names to the "idea or concept" (*ideam sive conceptum*) (ch.10, 1), language itself immediately takes on this false realism, and throughout his discussion of moral matters Hobbes assumes that the actual moral language that human beings employ presupposes (wrongly) the real existence of the entities with which it is concerned – and therefore presupposes the possibility of conflict over the correct description of the entities. To make this point clearer, Hobbes devoted the first part of Chapter 10, *De sermone et scientiis,* to a contrast between the lives of animals and of men. Animals respond to things in a wholly subjective and unmediated fashion: by their calls and other noises

they are warned of danger so that they may flee, are summoned to feeding, aroused to song, solicited to love; yet these calls are not speech since they are not constituted by the will of these animals, but burst forth by the strength of nature from the peculiar fears, joys, desires, and other passions of each of them; and this is not to speak ... (ch. 10, 1)

Men, on the other hand, are led by language both to new capacities and to new sources of error and conflict. To illustrate this, Hobbes turned to a theory about the power of language embodied in the tradition of the Roman oratorical writers (we shall see the full significance of this later).[12] The Roman writers had asserted that it was the power of "clear" or "informed" *oratio* that led men to leave the woods and fields, and to have a civilized and social life.[13] Hobbes agreed: the benefits *ab oratione* were, first, the capacity to use numerals and hence to create technologies – "all of these proceed from numbering, but numbering proceeds from speech" (*sermone*). Second, *oratio* enabled men to teach one another, and, third, it allowed men to give and receive commands. This

is a benefit of speech (*sermonis*), and truly the greatest. For without this there would be no society among men, no peace, and consequently no disciplines; but first savagery, then solitude, and for dwellings, caves. For though among certain animals there are seeming polities, these are not of sufficiently great moment for living well; hence they merit not our consideration; and they are largely found among defenseless animals, not in need of many things,; in which number man is not included . . . From this it is easily understood how much we owe to *oratio*, by which we, having been drawn together and agreeing to covenants, live securely, happily, and elegantly . . . (ch.10, 3, trans. p.40)

This is a half-ironic version of the Roman theory, in which the power of *oratio* rests upon the brutality of command rather than the suavity of persuasion, but it shares with its ancient sources the conviction that *oratio* is the key element in moral life. But Hobbes then went on to stress the *dangers* of *oratio*, and to show how it was simultaneously the solution to the problem of social life and the cause of the problem.

But *oratio* also hath its disadvantages; namely because man, alone among the animals, on account of the universal signification of names, can create general rules for himself in the art of living just as in the other arts; and so he alone can devise errors and pass them on for the use of others. Therefore man errs more widely and dangerously than can other animals. Also, man if it please him (and it will please him as often as it seems to advance his plans), can teach what he knows to be false from works that he hath inherited; that is, he can lie and render the minds of men hostile to the conditions of society and peace; something that cannot happen in the societies of other animals, since they judge what things are good and bad for them by their senses, not on the basis of the complaints of others, the causes whereof, unless they be seen, they cannot understand. Moreover, it sometimes happens to those that listen to philosophers and Schoolmen that listening becomes a habit, and the words that they hear they accept rashly, even though no sense can be had from them (for such are the kind of words invented by teachers to hide their own ignorance), and they use them, believing that they are saying something when they say nothing. Finally, on account of the ease of speech, the man who truly doth not think, speaks; and what he says, he believes to be true, and he can deceive himself; a beast cannot deceive itself. Therefore by *oratio* man is not made better, but only given greater possibilities. (ibid.)

The corruption of man by language, and by the intuitive but false realism with which he interpreted his sense impressions, was thus at the heart of Hobbes's discussion of *mores*. Man's immediate responses to his environment were (unlike those of animals) constantly mediated by an interpretative framework constituted by a language that might be radically misleading, and this potential corruption reached into the heart of man's actions, since human passions themselves had (for Hobbes) an essentially cognitive component. This was made clearest not in the somewhat sketchy discussion of the passions in the final version of *De homine*, but in the much richer discussion in the *Elements of Law* of 1640. This was (as we have already seen) essentially an English version of *De homine* and *De cive* as they existed at that date, and in Chapters 9 and 10 Hobbes gave an account of the passions that constituted (in his eyes) the essential meat of ethics. It was preceded (in Chapter 8) by a distinction between three kinds of "conception," "whereof one is of that which is present, which is sense; another, of that which is past, which is remembrance; and the third, of that which is future, which we call expectation" (Pt.I.ch 8, 2). The latter conception is the most important from the point of view of moral philosophy:

Conception of the future is but a supposition of the same, proceeding from remembrance of what is past; and we so far conceive that anything will be hereafter, as we know there is something at the present that hath power to produce it. And that anything hath power now to produce another thing hereafter, we cannot conceive, but by remembrance that it hath produced the like heretofore. Wherefore all conception of future, is conception of power able to produce something; whosoever therefore expecteth pleasure to come, must conceive withal some power in himself by which the same may be attained. And . . . the passions whereof I am to speak next, consist in conception of the future, that is to say, in conception of power past, and the act to come. (Pt.I.ch.8, 3)

THE PASSIONS

All human passions, according to Hobbes in the *Elements*, are fundamentally to do with power, and with *honour*, which is "the acknowledgement of power" (Pt.I.ch.8, 5). But power is itself a matter of belief, as is shown by his discussion of the concepts (central to his ethical project) of *glory, false glory* and *vain glory* in I.9, 1, in which glory or "imagination of our power and worth [may be] an assured and certain experience of our own actions [or it may] proceed . . . from fame and trust of others, whereby one may think well of himself, and yet be deceived [or it may consist in] the fiction (which also is imagination) of actions done by ourselves, which never were done" – that is, vain glory. Passion thus, for Hobbes, is in part a matter of cognition: it involves beliefs about what sort of power we possess and what we can do with it. A good example of how this can operate and of its connection to his work on rhetoric, which we will be considering later, is provided by his discussion of *pity* and *indignation* (Pt.I.ch.9, 10–11).

PITY is imagination or fiction of future calamity to ourselves, proceeding from the sense of another man's present calamity; but when it lighteth on such as we think have not deserved the same, the compassion is the greater, because then there appeareth the more probability that the same may happen to us. For the evil that happeneth to an innocent man, may happen to every man . . .

INDIGNATION is that grief which consisteth in the conception of good success happening to them whom they think unworthy thereof. Seeing therefore men think all those unworthy whom they hate, they think them not only unworthy of the good fortune they have, but also of their own virtues. And of all the passions of the mind, these two, indignation and pity, are most easily raised and increased by eloquence; for the aggravation of the calamity, and extenuation of the fault, augmenteth pity. And the extenuation of the worth of the person, together with the magnifying of his success (which are the parts of an orator), are able to turn these two passions into fury.

Most commentators on Hobbes's moral and political theory fall into one of two categories. The first (probably also the larger) con-

sists of people who believe that, broadly speaking, Hobbes is concerned with the clash of individual *interests* and their reconciliation
in various ways by the political process. An example of this would
be the line of argument found in Gauthier and Hampton, which
seeks to construe Hobbes's theory in terms of games theory, and
which assumes that the men in Hobbes's state of nature have given
interests and are then faced with the problem of their potential or
actual conflict. The second category (in which my own earlier work
on Hobbes is to be located, along with that of Johnston and, most
recently, Lloyd) consists of people who think that Hobbes was principally concerned with the clash of *beliefs*. But as we can now see,
there is no valid distinction in Hobbes to be drawn between interests
and beliefs, at least when it comes to understanding conflict: the
desires men have which lead them to conflict are not simple and
basic desires such as the requirement of enough food for their survival. Indeed, Hobbes on a number of occasions expressly says that
in the world as it is at present (although not necessarily in all future
ages) there are enough material resources for everyone.

The multitude of poor, and yet strong people still encreasing, they are to be
transported into Countries not sufficiently inhabited: where neverthelesse,
they are not to exterminate those they find there; but constrain them to
inhabit closer together, and not range a great deal of ground, to snatch what
they find; but to court each little Plot with art and labour, to give them their
sustenance in due season. And when all the world is overcharged with
Inhabitants, then the last remedy of all is Warre; which provideth for every
man, by Victory, or Death. (*Lev.* p. 239)[14]

Instead, conflict arises as a result of men's differing beliefs about
their own power, and in particular about the means by which they
might come to preserve themselves – self-preservation being (as we
shall see) the aim that can most plausibly be attributed to them.
Hobbes gave an extremely wide definition of the area of epistemic
conflict that was relevant to ethics: this was most vividly expressed
in a remarkable passage at the end of the *Elements of Law*, which
also no doubt drew on a lost draft of *De homine.*

In the state of nature, where every man is his own judge, and differeth from
other concerning the names and appellations of things, and from those
differences arise quarrels, and breach of peace; it was necessary there should
be a common measure of all things that might fall in controversy; as for

example: of what is to be called right, what good, what virtue, what much, what little, what *meum* and *tuum*, what a pound, what a quart, &c. For in these things private judgements may differ, and beget controversy. This common measure, some say, is right reason: with whom I should consent, if there were any such thing to be found or known *in rerum natura*. But commonly they that call for right reason to decide any controversy, do mean their own. But this is certain, seeing right reason is not existent, the reason of some man, or men, must supply the place thereof; and that man, or men, is he or they, that have the sovereign power . . . ; and consequently the civil laws are to all subjects the measures of their actions, whereby to determine, whether they be right or wrong, profitable or unprofitable, virtuous or vicious; and by them the use and definition of all names not agreed upon, and tending to controversy, shall be established. As for example, upon the occasion of some strange and deformed birth, it shall not be decided by Aristotle, or the philosophers, whether the same be a man or no, but by the laws. (Pt.II.ch.10, 8)

All these things had indeed historically been the object of debate (the question of "much" and "little," for example, being the Sorites paradox in the form discussed by Cicero in his *Academica*); what is particularly striking about the list from the point of view of a modern moral theory is that it goes well beyond the domain of purely "ethical" evaluations to include (for example) problems of prudence – what is "profitable" and "unprofitable."

FROM PASSIONS TO MORAL AGREEMENT

As this passage illustrates, and as his defense of the distinction between moral and civil philosophy in *De homine* confirms, Hobbes regarded politics as the solution to the conflicts characteristic of *mores*. Hobbes's argument began in effect with the observation that there are, as a matter of fact, propositions that all men agree on, and that this is as much a matter of fact as their disagreements. He set this out most clearly in his discussion of the distinction between "teaching" and "persuading," that is, between (one might say) the legitimate and the illegitimate use of rhetorical skill.

The infallible sign of teaching exactly, and without error, is this: that no man hath ever taught the contrary; not that few, how few soever, if any. For commonly truth is on the side of the few, rather than of the multitude; but when in opinions and questions considered and discussed by many, it happeneth that not any one of the men that so discuss them differ from another, then it may be justly inferred, they know what they teach, and that otherwise they do not. And this appeareth most manifestly to them that have considered the divers subjects wherein men have exercised their pens, and the divers ways in which they have proceeded; together with the diversity of the success thereof. For those men who have taken in hand to consider nothing else but the comparison of magnitudes, times, and motions, and their proportions one to another, have thereby been the authors of all those excellences, wherein we differ from such savage people as are now the inhabitants of divers places in America . . . Yet to this day was it never heard of, that there was any controversy concerning any conclusion in this subject . . . The reason whereof is apparent to every man that looketh into their writings; for they proceed from most low and humble principles, evident even to the meanest capacity; going on slowly, and with most scrupulous ratiocination (viz.) from the imposition of names they infer the truth of their first propositions; and from two of the first, a third; and from any two of the three a fourth; and so on, according to the steps of science. (Pt.I.ch.13, 3)

By simply asserting that there are some principles, "evident even to the meanest capacity," the mark of which is precisely that there is no disagreement about their truth, Hobbes side-stepped the problem of how to establish the foundations for agreed moral judgments. One way of seeing this is to contrast Hobbes's approach to foundationalism with that of Hume, with whom he is often (and plausibly) compared. For Hobbes, as we shall see, one of the chief objectives of moral philosophy was to answer the moral relativist such as Montaigne, who recognized the sheer diversity of actual moral beliefs; this relativist could be answered satisfactorily by the empirical observation that there are limits to that diversity, and that human beings of all times and places do agree about certain things. For Hume, an agreement of this kind was beside the point: one of his most famous arguments, after all, was directed precisely against such a widespread belief, namely that we have a life after death, and his hostility to deriving any moral conclusions from empirical observation is well known. A great deal of twentieth-century argument about Hobbes (including particularly the so-called "Taylor–Warrender" thesis and its critics) has mistakenly tried to attribute a modern, post-Humean kind of foundationalism to Hobbes, whereas the essence of his kind of response to the relativist is its refusal to employ this kind of argument.

But the ethical principles evident even to the meanest capacity are likely to be of an extremely exiguous kind, since they cannot include any of the propositions standardly in debate among moral philosophers, nor those found to vary among different societies. The most prominent candidate, and indeed the foundation of Hobbes's theory, was the conviction that each man has a right to preserve himself.

> Forasmuch as necessity of nature maketh men to will and desire *bonum sibi*, that which is good for themselves, and to avoid that which is hurtful; but most of all that terrible enemy of nature, death, from whom we expect both the loss of all power, and also the greatest of bodily pains in the losing; it is not against reason that a man doth all he can to preserve his own body and limbs, both from death and pain. And that which is not against reason, men call RIGHT, or *jus*, or blameless liberty of using our own natural power and ability. It is therefore a *right of nature:* that every man may preserve his own life and limbs, with all the power he hath. (Pt.I.ch.14, 6)

Here, we must note that what "men call" something plays a key role in the construction of Hobbes's argument. We do not have to suppose that Hobbes's theory here turns on the claim that men *actually* always avoid death (as various commentators have noted, this is clearly not true, and was not even thought by Hobbes himself to be true); instead, it turns on the claim that it is always *justifiable* or *understandable* to avoid death, and that all men will recognize this fact (or, more strictly, that their universal acceptance of this description constitutes it a "fact").

Self-preservation was indeed an extremely plausible candidate for a universal principle. There had been very little disagreement throughout the history of Western moral philosophy that people, all other things being equal, are always entitled to defend themselves against attack, and Hugo Grotius had recently used this principle as one of the foundations of his own minimalist moral enterprise.[15] There had of course been disagreement over when all things *were* equal: for example, was a criminal entitled to defend himself? Were preemptive strikes justified on the grounds of protection, as many Roman authors appear to have thought? Hobbes captured this disagreement in his further observation that in a state of nature, "every man is judge himself of the necessity of the means, and the greatness of the danger" (Pt.I.ch.14, 8), and that there was a right to "all things," that is, that any thing might serve the cause of self-preservation; it was in this sense that there could be disagreement about what was "profitable or unprofitable," as he said in Pt II.ch.10, 8. Argument about the scope of the right of self-preservation was at the heart of Hobbes's theory, for he recognized that even with the common accceptance of this moral principle, men would not live in peace: opinions would differ about what actually threatened each man's security, and men would act on the basis of these disparate opinions. The consequence would be the state of war: "in the state of nature, where every man is his own judge, and differeth from other concerning the names and appellations of things, . . . from those differences arise quarrels, and breach of peace" (Pt II. ch.10, 9).

THE LAWS OF NATURE

Hobbes added to this universal right another set of principles, which were more contentious, and have been the subject of extensive discussion among subsequent commentators. He described them as the "laws of nature", but (at least in the *Elements of Law*) they were in fact presented as an implication of the principle of self-preservation: the closing paragraph of Part 1 chapter 14 of the *Elements* (in which self-preservation is discussed) introduced the idea, before Hobbes turned in chapter 15 to describe the laws of nature. What Hobbes said in 1.14, 14. was that

since it is supposed from the equality of strength and other natural faculties of men, that no man is of might sufficient, to assure himself for any long time, of preserving himself thereby, whilst he remaineth in the state of hostility and war; reason therefore dictateth to every man for his own good, to seek after peace, as far forth as there is hope to attain the same; and to strengthen himself with all the help he can procure, for his own defence against those, from whom such peace cannot be obtained; and to do all those things which necessarily conduce thereunto.

Only in 1.15.1 did Hobbes say that this "dictate" is a general description of the laws of nature – "there can therefore be no other law of nature than reason, nor no other precepts of NATURAL LAW, than those which declare unto us the ways of peace, where the same may be obtained, and of defence where it may not."

At the same time, he recognised that these precepts are *not* universal, at least in the same sense as self preservation is:

[Some writers] make that against the law of nature, which is contrary to the consent of all mankind; which definition cannot be allowed, because then no men could offend against the law of nature; for the nature of man is contained under the nature of mankind. But forasmuch as all men, carried away by the violence of their passion, and by evil customs, do those things which are commonly said to be against the law of nature; it is not the consent of passion, or consent in some error gotten by custom, that makes the law of nature. Reason is no less of the nature of man than passion, and is the same in all men, because all men agree in the will to be directed and governed in the way to that which they desire to attain, namely their own good, which is the work of reason.

And Hobbes proceeded in Chapters 14 through 17 to give an outline of the various laws of nature that went some way beyond the principles that all men might be thought to agree on, and which included such propositions as *"That every man is obliged to stand to, and perform, those covenants which he maketh"* (Pt.I.ch.16, 1). The first and most important of the laws, indeed, was precisely the negation of something that in the previous chapter had been presented as an agreed and universal principle, for it prescribed that *"every man divest himself of the right he hath to all things by nature."* It might thus seem that Hobbes had reintroduced via the notion of the laws of nature an idea of rationally apprehended and objective moral truth quite inconsistent with his proudly borne relativism.

There has, as a consequence, been a great deal of argument among commentators on Hobbes about the status of the laws of nature; indeed, this is the fundamental argument about Hobbes's moral and political thought. Some people have argued that they consist of principles that, if followed, will conduce to men's preservation; they are thus prudential imperatives, on a par with "doctors' orders."[16] Observing that this does not always seem to be true, and that, in particular, it might often benefit people to (for example) break their word, other writers have argued that Hobbes is a kind of "rule egoist," outlining general principles that provide a better guide to preservation than any other general principles.[17] Still others have denied that there is any element of prudence here at all: according to Warrender, for example, the proposition that we should seek peace is more like a

Kantian categorical imperative, with no necessary relation to our prudential interests.[18] My own view is that none of these interpretations quite captures Hobbes's fundamental idea, although all of them have some merit.

The first point to make, which has often been overlooked because of its very obviousness, is that the laws of nature in Hobbes are not just an arbitrary selection of rules that, if followed, will conduce to our preservation; they do not, for example, contain any propositions such as "take regular exercise." They are *exclusively* rules about what conduces to social "peace," and to the maintenance of the kind of agreement that permits a sovereign to assign meaning to disputed terms. (It was in part his observation of this exclusivity that prompted Warrender to put forward his interpretation of Hobbes.) The only thing Hobbes appears to deem plausible as a general obligation is the proposition that we should successfully coordinate our judgments about what conduces to our preservation. Other than this, he does not put forward any potentially universal principles of preservation. Indeed, it would clearly have been inconsistent for him to have done so; even regular exercise is, after all, of debatable value.

But was it no less inconsistent for him to have argued that it is obviously true that we should coordinate our moral judgments, flying thereby in the face of the clear fact that we do not? This question takes us to the heart of Hobbes's moral theory (in our sense of the term), and to the reason for the widespread puzzlement about it on the part of modern commentators. What is special about this particular universal injunction is that its force arises precisely from the *absence* of objective and rational standards. It is in fact an example of the familiar paradox, especially beloved in the seventeenth century, that reason might be called upon to destroy itself, and that the path to wisdom might consist in not thinking that one has the path to wisdom. The literature of late sixteenth- and early seventeenth-century moral philosophy, particularly in its skeptical mode, is full of arguments that the wise man should suspend his own judgment about the truth or falsehood of any of his beliefs in order to live a psychologically and socially secure life. The most familiar example of this to modern readers is probably Descartes's "provisional moral code" in his *Discourse on the Method*, in which he basically reproduced (at that juncture in his disquisition) the contemporary skeptical view:

Lest I should remain indecisive in my actions while reason obliged me to be so in my judgements, and in order to live as happily as I could during this time, I formed for myself a provisional moral code consisting of just three or four maxims . . .

The first was to obey the laws and customs of my country, holding constantly to the religion in which by God's grace I had been instructed from my childhood, and governing myself in all other matters according to the most moderate and least extreme opinions – the opinions commonly accepted in practice by the most sensible of those with whom I should have to live. . . .

My second maxim was to be as firm and decisive in my actions as I could, and to follow even the most doubtful opinions, once I had adopted them, with no less constancy than if they had been quite certain . . .

My third maxim was to try always to master myself rather than fortune, and to change my desires rather than the order of the world. In general I would become accustomed to believing that nothing lies entirely within our power except our thoughts, so that after doing our best in dealing with matters external to us, whatever we fail to achieve is absolutely impossible so far as we are concerned.[19]

(The fourth maxim was a resolution to continue with the life of a philosopher.)

But as striking, and no doubt as influential on Hobbes, was Montaigne's essay "That the taste of goods or evils doth greatly depend on the opinion we have of them" (Essay 40 of Book I), in which he wrote

Men (saith an ancient Greeke sentence) *are tormented by the opinions they have of things, and not by things themselves.* It were a great conquest for the ease of our miserable humane condition, if any man could establish every where this true proposition. For if evils have no entrance into us, but by our judgement, it seemeth that it lieth in our power, either to contemne or turne them to our good . . . If that which we call evill and torment, be neither torment, nor evill, but that our fancie only gives it that qualitie, it is in us to change it.

This is the closest to Hobbes's position that any predecessor came, for it involves the same idea that because "good" and "evil" are matters of opinion and judgment, it ought to be possible for us to change our judgment about them in ways that will lead us to greater tranquillity of mind than we currently possess.

Renunciation of our existing judgments was therefore not, for Montaigne, Descartes, or Hobbes, inconsistent with moral relativism. Moreover, both Montaigne and Descartes accepted that bringing our moral judgments into line with those of the rest of our community was a good reason for renouncing our existing ones and accepting a range of new evaluations; seen in this light, Hobbes was simply making more precise and self-aware the process whereby such an alignment might be secured. Hobbes's predecessors had supposed that renunciation would be practiced by a skeptical sage living in a society of unskeptical believers, and that the direction of the renunciation was therefore unproblematical. Hobbes, however, raised the question of how an entire society of skeptics might coordinate its renunciations round a single figure in order to create a set of moral beliefs for the society.

THE REPLY TO 'THE FOOLE'

A number of commentators (including Gauthier and Hampton) have supposed that modern coordination problems such as the Prisoners' Dilemma are to be found embedded in Hobbes's theory, and it might be indeed be thought supposed that there is a puzzle of this kind about a coordinated renunciation of moral and prudential beliefs. Why should I not take back my own belief when it suits me (rather as a person in a group who have bound themselves to stop smoking can sneak an occasional cigarette)? Hobbes himself was clear, in a famous passage of *Leviathan*, that it would be the act of a "Foole" to do this

The Foole hath sayd in his heart, there is no such thing as Justice; and sometimes also with his tongue; seriously alleaging, that every mans conservation, and contentment, being committed to his own care, there could be no reason, why every man might not do what he thought conduced thereunto: and therefore also to make, or not make; keep, or not keep Covenants, was not against Reason, when it conduced to ones benefit. (ch.15, Tuck, ed. p. 101)

The reason for Hobbes's confidence that this is foolish may be as follows (although it must be admitted that this passage, with its further remarks about winning "the Kingdome of God" by violence, is notoriously obscure). He repeatedly stated that we could not renounce our judgment about self-defense in extreme and obvious cases:

there be some Rights, which no man can be understood by any words, or other signes, to have abandoned, or transferred. As first a man cannot lay down the right of resisting them, that assault him by force, to take away his life; because he cannot be understood to ayme thereby, at any Good to himself. The same may be sayd of Wounds, and Chayns, and Imprisonment; . . . because a man cannot tell, when he seeth men proceed against him by violence, whether they intend his death or not. (*Lev.* ch. 14, 93)

Again, Hobbes's technique is to ask what can or cannot be understood or described in a certain way: it is not possible to describe certain kinds of behavior, notably a feeble acceptance of direct injury, as a means of self-preservation. But if it is not possible, then it is not possible for the *sovereign* to describe them as such. Since the sovereign's job is to decide which of various contested descriptions is to apply in a particular situation, there is no possibility of his describing someone's acceptance of injury to themselves as being a means to their preservation. So even if an individual were to renounce *all* judgment to the sovereign, what he would do in these situations would be identical to what he would have done if he had continued to follow his own judgment. The sovereign would have to concede that the subject would best preserve himself by taking direct personal action. It is true that he might also judge that other subjects would be best preserved by such action being prevented, and the state of war might thereby inevitably be recreated between the subject and his sovereign, but that does not affect Hobbes's general argument. He expressed this thought most clearly in another famous passage of *Leviathan,* when he said that

man by nature chooseth the lesser evill, which is danger of death in resisting; rather than the greater, which is certain and present death in not resisting. And this is granted to be true by all men, in that they lead Criminals to Execution, and Prison, with armed men, notwithstanding that such Criminals have consented to the Law, by which they are condemned. (ch. 14, 98)

What is "granted to be true by all men" again plays the critical role in the argument.

If one cannot lose the right to defend oneself against "certain and present" danger, and the status of all other presumed dangers is contestable, then (on Hobbes's account) there cannot be any real risk attached to the renunciation of right, and therefore no problem about reclaiming rights. It is indeed the case that only a "Foole" would suppose that he should take back his right to private judgment in contestable cases, since the whole point of wisdom consists in the recognition of one's own fallibility in such situations. This view of the matter obviously makes it appear very different from a Prisoners' Dilemma, in which the individual agent's own preferences among all the outcomes is canonical for him, and in which the dilemma arises precisely from that fact.

MORAL PHILOSOPHY AND RHETORIC

As I said at the beginning of this essay, Hobbes's moral philosophy has much the character of a philosophical reflection on a pre-existing ethical culture, and many of its central concerns derive from that fact. In particular, its stress on the fragility and malleability of beliefs corresponds to the great weight put on the alteration of belief by the moral writers by whom he was most influenced. These writers were not, in general, the obvious ones from the point of view of modern histories of ethics; instead, as a number of recent authors have begun to realize, they were above all the writers working within or close to the tradition of *classical rhetoric*.[20] (Hobbes himself indicated as much when he remarked to Aubrey that "Aristotle was the worst teacher that ever was, the worst polititian and ethick – a countrey-fellow that could live in the world would be as good: but his rhetorique and discourse of animals was rare").[21] That tradition, however, was as complex and multiform as everything else in Renaissance humanism, and Hobbes's own position within it was undeniably rather idiosyncratic.

We can see this clearly in his *A Brief of the Art of Rhetorick*, published (with the printers who later published *Leviathan*) in February 1637, just after he came back from France, and at the very beginning of the period during which his most creative thinking on philosophical matters seems to have taken place.[22] The book (which has some claim to be Hobbes's first published work on moral philosophy, as he understood it) consists of an extremely simplified and characteristically immoderate presentation of a view of rhetoric that, although genuinely present in Aristotle's *Rhetoric*, upon which the work was based, was by no means a commonplace among either ancient or Renaissance writers on rhetoric.

Hobbes accepted the Aristotelian point that the techniques of rhetoric, its "proofs," consist of examples and *enthymemes*, the latter being syllogisms "out of which are left as superfluous, that which is supposed to be necessarily understood by the hearer." He also accepted the threefold division of orations into *Demonstrative*, *Judicial*, and *Deliberative*, the first "to Prove a thing *Profitable*, or *Unprofitable*," the second "*Just*, or *Unjust*," and the third "*Honourable*, or *Dishonourable*." But he then proceeded to claim that

The *Principles* of *Rhetorick* out of which *Enthymemes* are to be drawn; are the *common Opinions* that men have concerning *Profitable*, and *UnProfitable*; *Just*, and *Unjust*; *Honourable*, and *Dishonourable*; which are the points in the several kinds of *Orations* questionable. For as in *Logick*, where certain and infallible knowledge is the scope of our proof, the *Principles* must be all *infallible Truths*: so in *Rhetorick* the *Principles* must be *common Opinions*, such as the Judge is already possessed with: because the end of *Rhetorick* is victory; which consists in having gotten *Belief*.

These "common Opinions" he also termed "Colours."

Aristotle had indeed accepted that in some circumstances it might be right for an orator to be merely parasitic upon the existing beliefs of his audience, and in particular to describe vices in terms suggesting that they were the corresponding virtues – "the choleric and passionate man may be spoken of as frank and open, the arrogant as magnificent and dignified; those in excess as possessing the corresponding virtue, the foolhardy courageous, the recklessly extravagant as liberal."[23] But when discussing the foundations of rhetoric, Aristotle was clear that the orator should seek to promote the truth (which mankind has a "sufficient natural capacity" to recognize) (I.1.11), and he argued that the foundation of emphythemes were objectively valid propositions about the world, albeit of a non-necessary kind (like the principles that practical reason in the *Ethics* works from in order to draw ethical conclusions). Although the orator's job was to vindicate his subject's conduct to an audience, part of that job might consist of revising the audience's beliefs through a deductive argument from first principles. At that point, the orator would be behaving more like a conventional philosopher.

Later writers on rhetoric, such as the Romans, were explicitly critical of Aristotle for even going as far as he did in *Rhetoric* I.9.[24] Indeed, the Roman rhetoricians isolated a figure of speech, *paradiastole*, which consisted in drawing attention, through the use of a contrastive definition, to the fact that an opponent had diverted in this way from the truth.[25] Cicero argued (clearly against Aristotle) that saving ourselves "from being deceived by those vices which seem to imitate virtue" ("for cunning masquerades as prudence, boorish contempt for pleasure as temperance," etc.) had to be a central feature of the rhetorical practices of panegyric and reprehension.[26]

So when Hobbes rather recklessly asserted that rhetoric was solely concerned with winning victory through the manipulation of existing opinions, he was consciously opposing himself to the mainstream of ancient rhetorical discussion. Quintilian had in fact attacked one of his contemporaries for saying that "the reward of the party to a suit is not a good conscience, but victory . . . if this were true, only the worst of men would place such dangerous weapons at the disposal of criminals or employ the precepts of their art for the assistance of wickedness" (II.xv.32). Hobbes's deviation from this tradition is also signaled by his extensive use of the notion of the "color." This was a technical term in Roman rhetoric for a twist given to the interpretation of something by the manipulative skill of the orator. Cicero does not use the term, and Quintilian (our principal source for its meaning among the theorists of rhetoric) describes it roundly as a "falsehood" (falsa expositio) or something we "make up" (fingemus), although he endorsed its use in certain circumstances (IV.II.88–96). The elder Seneca in his Controversiae used the term most extensively, usually in the sense of conjectural features of a situation that might confirm the particular line an orator was taking (for example, a Vestal virgin was thrown off the Tarpeian Rock for unchastity; she survived the fall, and there was a discussion about whether she should be thrown off again. One orator alleged that she had hardened her body with drugs, and Seneca describes this completely imaginary allegation as a "colour.")[27]

Moreover, no other Renaissance writers on rhetoric used the term as a foundational part of their exposition, with one extremely interesting exception. This was Francis Bacon, who published Of the Coulers [sic] of Good and Evill in 1597, in a volume also containing the first ten of his Essayes and his Meditationes Sacrae (which are also essays, on less secular matters). Bacon's purpose in The Coulers was identical to that of Hobbes forty years later – that is, to reconstruct Aristotle's discussion of common opinions in Book I of the Rhetoric in terms of the language of "colour." Bacon acknowledged in the dedication that his presentation of the material was scarcely Aristotelian, and his other writings reveal a considerable debt to the elder Seneca.[28]

By stressing that the orator secured a change in belief on the part of his audience by manipulating their existing opinions in this way, both Bacon and Hobbes signaled their conviction that there was nothing objective to which the orator could draw attention in order to persuade. The *"common Opinions that men have concerning Profitable, and UnProfitable; Just, and Unjust; Honourable, and Dishonourable"* could not, in Hobbes's eyes, be based on anything objective, and therefore there could be no hope (at least in normal circumstances) of any "infallible Truth" about these topics. It is clear that, broadly speaking, this was the view of the late sixteenth-century skeptics from whom both Bacon and Hobbes drew a great deal, and we find in (for example) the *Essays* of Montaigne the same combination of skepticism about objective moral properties and awareness of the manipulative character of rhetoric.[29] Thus Montaigne could write, as we have seen,

Men (saith an ancient Greeke sentence) *are tormented by the opinions they have of things, and not by things themselves.* It were a great conquest for the ease of our miserable humane condition, if any man could establish every where this true proposition. For if evils have no entrance into us, but by our judgement, it seemeth that it lieth in our power, either to contemne or turne them to our good . . . If that which we call evill and torment, be neither torment, nor evill, but that our fancie only gives it that qualitie, it is in us to change it . . . (I.xl, "That the taste of goods or evils doth greatly depend on the opinion we have of them").

He could also write

A rhetorician of ancient times, said, that his trade was, to make small things appeare and seeme great. It is a shoemaker, that can make great shooes for a little foot. Had he lived in *Sparta,* he had doubtlesse beene well whipped, for professing a false, a couzening and deceitfull art . . . Those common-wealths, that have maintained themselves in a regular, formal, and well-governed estate, as that of *Creete* and *Lacedemon,* did never make any great esteeme of Orators. . . . It is an instrument devised, to busie, to manage, and to agitate a vulgar and disordered multitude; and is an instrument imployed, but about distempered and sicke mindes, as Physicke is about crazed bodies. And those where either the vulgar, the ignorant, or the generalitie have had all power, as that of *Rhodes*, those of *Athens*, and that of *Rome*, and where things have ever beene in continuall disturbance and uproare, thither have Orators and the professors of that Art flocked. (I.li, "Of the vanitie of words")

Hobbes's first discussions of substantive moral issues drew on these ideas, particularly as put forward by Bacon. In his 1597 volume, Bacon had followed his general remarks on rhetoric in *The Coulers* with examples, namely the *Essayes*, in which there was constant appeal to the existing beliefs and experiences of the audience. Hobbes and his pupils in the Devonshire household followed this precedent in a highly Baconian, and Montaigne-like, set of essays that they appear to have composed between 1610 and 1640.[30]

The essays also include an extensive discourse on Tacitus, clearly modeled on the *discorsi* which were a central feature of contemporary European Tacitism, and again with various themes familiar from Hobbes's work. These include the remark (p. 269) that a *"Popular state . . .* is to the Provinces not as one, but many tyrants" (compare, e.g., *Leviathan* ch.19, p. 135 in the Tuck edition); the fierce attack on ever buying-off political opponents – "to heape benefits on the sullen, and averse, out of hope to win their affection, is unjust and prejudiciall" (p. 266; compare ch. 30, 241–2; *De Cive* ch. 13, 12); and the observation that all men are "of this condition, that desire and hope of good more affecteth them than fruition: for this induceth satiety; but hope is a whetstone to mens desires, and will not suffer them to languish" (p. 291; compare *Leviathan* ch.6, 46, *EL*, Pt.I. ch.7, 6). The central theme of the work is again the power of opinion, with a prince being urged to govern his people by manipulating their beliefs.

We can find the same attitude in a long letter of moral advice that Hobbes wrote in 1638 to Charles, the eighteen-year-old brother of Hobbes's employer William, third earl of Devonshire (William himself was only twenty-one, and had just come of age).[31] Hobbes had been responsible for the education of both the earl and his brother, and had accompanied the older boy on a tour of the Continent that has become famous among historians of seventeenth-century philosophy, since on that tour Hobbes first made the acquaintance of Mersenne and Gassendi, and indirectly of Descartes. Charles was now touring the Continent with another "governor" while Hobbes stayed in England, and disturbing news had come to the former tutor about the young aristocrat's behavior in Paris. Hobbes felt himself obliged to set out his views on how a young nobleman should comport himself.

First . . . I must humbly beseech you to avoyd all offensive speech, not only open reviling but also that Satyricall way of nipping that some use. The effect of it is the cooling of the affection of your servants, and the provoking of the hatred of your equalls. So that he which useth harsh language whether downright or obliquely, shall be sure to have many haters, and he that hath so, it will be a wonder if he have not many just occasions of Duell[32] . . . To encouradge inferiors, to be cheerfull with one's equalls and superiors, to pardon the follies of those one converseth withall, and to helpe men off, that are fallen into the danger of being laught at, these are signs of noblenesse and of the master spirit. . . . Secondly I beseech you take no occasion of quarrell but such as are necessary and from such men only as are of reputation. For neither words uttered in heate of Anger, nor the words of youths unknown in the world, or not known for virtue are of scandall sufficient to ground an honourable duell on. When two boys go out of the Academie to Pre aux clercs, no man but thinks them boys as before. Nor is their act valour. For having engaged themselves rashly they are forced to the feild with shame, and expect their adversary with cold hartes, and praying that he may be prevented. Does the world call this valour?

Lastly I think it no ill counsell, that you profess no love to any woman which you hope not to marry or otherwise to enioy. For an action without designe is that which all the world calls vanity.

This letter reminds us that Hobbes's views on morals were formed in an aristocratic milieu, in which issues such as how to respond when threatened with a duel were important, and in which even fundamental questions of political theory might appear with an unusual twist.[33] But it also shows us that in practice as well as in theory, for Hobbes and his circle, moral matters were inextricably bound up with what "the world" says. What "the world" called valor, or vanity, mattered most to Hobbes and (he appears to have thought) to his pupil. A perceived agreement on moral matters was the foundation of morality.

When Hobbes himself came to write works directly and exclusively on moral philosophy, this style of rhetorical moralizing remained. We find many echoes not only of these early essays, but also of Bacon himself, both in passages that reproduce Bacon's views or turns of phrase and in passages that criticize him. One of the clearest comes in his discussion of vainglory in the *Elements of Law*, a subject that (his 1638 letter to Charles Cavendish reveals) was at the heart of his moral thinking.

> The fiction (which also is imagination) of actions done by ourselves, which never were done, is glorying; but because it begetteth no appetite nor endeavour to any further attempt, it is merely vain and unprofitable; as when a man imagineth himself to do the actions whereof he readeth in some romant, or to be like unto some other man whose acts he admireth. And this is called VAIN GLORY: and is exemplified in the fable by the fly sitting on the axletree, and saying to himself, What a dust do I raise! (Pt.I.ch.9, 1)

Bacon's essay *Of Vaine-Glory* begins,

> It was prettily Devised of *Aesope; The Fly sate upon the Axletree of the Chariot wheele, and said, What a Dust doe I raise?* So are there some *Vaine Persons*, that whatsoever goeth alone, or moveth upon greater Means, if they have never so little Hand in it, they thinke it is they that carry it.[34]

Similarly, Hobbes said of anger that "it hath been commonly defined to be grief proceeding from an opinion of contempt; which is confuted by the often experience we have of being moved to anger by things inanimate and without sense, and consequently incapable of contemning us" (Pt.I.ch.9, 5). Bacon in his essay *Of Anger* wrote that one of the chief causes of anger was "the Apprehension and Construction, of the Injury offred, to be, in the Circumstances thereof, full of *Contempt*. For *Contempt* is that which putteth an Edge upon *Anger*, as much, or more, then the *Hurt* it selfe."[35] Here Hobbes is clearly criticizing Bacon.[36]

Out of this rich soil of essay-reading and writing, the composition of moral epistles, and (no doubt) the actual giving of moral advice to his pupils grew Hobbes's philosophical reflections on the nature of ethics. They represent in effect the most profound philosophical analysis of the practice of late Renaissance humanists, and the centrality of language and opinion in Hobbes's philosophy follows naturally from its origin in these reflections. Fortunately for us, it is also one of the things that makes Hobbes's philosophy peculiarly relevant to the late-twentieth century and to the problems of cultural conflict and incomprehension that are likely to be the basic material of politics for the rest of our lifetime.

NOTES

1 See Sextus Empiricus, *Against the Logicians* I.16 (Loeb, ed., II p. 9).

2 Aristotle himself seems to have thought that the correct term for this comprehensive science was Politics rather than Ethics, and this may have been what Cicero had in mind when he talked about a "civil science" (*De Inventione* I.6), although this was a far from common expression. Quintilian (II.15.33) glossed Cicero's remark with the phrase "civil science is the same as *sapientia*," by which he probably meant *phronesis*; practical wisdom, the mode of ethical thinking according to Aristotle.

3 Ibid. I.11, p. 7.

4 Quintilian, XII.2.10, 21.

5 *Works* vol. III, ed. Spedding and Ellis, pp. 346–9.

6 Ibid., p. 367.

7 Ibid., p. 438.

8 See Tuck, "Hobbes and Descartes," pp. 11–42. The division is already adumbrated in the earliest version of *De Corpore*; see Hobbes, *Critique du De Mundo de Thomas White*, ed. J. Jacquot and H.W. Jones (Paris 1973), p. 464.

9 The translation is from *M&C* 68–9.

10 This was already true of the first draft of the book: see Tuck, "Hobbes and Descartes." It is also true of the *Elements of Law* (1640), which was largely (it seems) an English version of the drafts of *De Homine* and *De Cive*. It too begins with an account of perception and optical illusion.

11 My translation. The original reads *Natura autem insitum est omni animali, ut primo intuitu imaginem illam, ipsam rem visam esse putent, vel saltem aliquod corpus quod ipsam rem simili situ partium exacte referat. Imo homines (si valde paucos qui judicia sensuum ratione correxerunt, excipias) imaginem illam putant esse objectum ipsum, nec sine disciplina in animum inducere possunt Solem & Astras majora esse aut remotiora quam videntur (De Homine* II.1, Hobbes, *Opera Philosophica, quae Latine scripsit, Omnia* [Amsterdam 1668] II p. 8). The only English translation of *De Homine* (by Gert, above, n. 7) omits the chapters on optics "since they are irrelevant to Hobbes's moral and political philosophy" (p. 35 n.).

12 For a full discussion of this tradition and of Hobbes's relationship to it in his other works, see Quentin Skinner, " 'Scientia civilis' in classical rhetoric and in the early Hobbes," pp 67–93.

13 See Cicero, *De Inventione* I.II.2 (where he uses the term *eloquentia* to describe this power) or Quintilian, II.16.9–10 (who uses the terms *docta vox* and *claritas orationis* to describe it).

14 This is strikingly similar to the justification for the annexation of ab-

originals' land provided by Locke. See J.H. Tully's "Rediscovering America: The Two Treatises and Aboriginal Rights" in his *An Approach to Political Philosophy*, pp. 137–76.

15 See Tuck, *Philosophy and Government 1572–1651*, ch. 6.

16 This is true of J.W.N. Watkins in his *Hobbes's System of Ideas*.

17 See, in particular, Gregory S. Kavka, *Hobbesian Moral and Political Theory*.

18 Howard Warrender, *The Political Philosophy of Hobbes*.

19 *AT* VI. 22–5; *CSM* I 122–3.

20 The best example of this new view is provided by Quentin Skinner in his perceptive article "Thomas Hobbes: Rhetoric and the Construction of Morality," pp, 1–61.

21 Aubrey, *Brief Lives* I, p. 357.

22 A modern edition is by John T. Harwood, *The Rhetorics of Thomas Hobbes and Bernard Lamy*, although he is insufficiently attentive to the differences between Hobbes and Aristotle. The *Brief* is effectively an English translation of a Latin MS in the hand of the young third earl, though presumably dictated by Hobbes, dated to c. 1633: see Peter Beal, *Index of English Literary Manuscripts* II (1987), p. 583.

23 *Art of Rhetoric*, ed. J.H. Freese (Loeb) I.ix.29–31, pp. 97–9.

24 See, e.g., Quintilian, *Institutio Oratoria* III.vii.25 (Loeb ed.I), p. 477.

25 Quentin Skinner, in his article "Thomas Hobbes: Rhetoric and the Construction of Morality," was the first to draw attention to the importance in Hobbes of the kind of equivocation mentioned by Quintilian, although it would be wrong to conclude (as he implies) that the figure of *paradiastole* was particularly central to the discussion of the issue, either in antiquity or for (most) Renaissance writers. The clearest ancient definition of *paradiastole* is in Rutilius Lupus, a contemporary of Cicero:

This figure [*schema*] distinguishes two or more things, which seem to have the same force, and, by assigning each its proper meaning, shows how far they differ. [For example,] Hyperides: "By trying to deceive the minds of others you defeat your own ends. In fact you are unconvincing when you call yourself wise instead of cunning, brave instead of conceited, careful of your money instead of mean, and stern instead of disagreeable. There is no fault of which you can boast simply by praising virtue." The same figure is customarily used more impressively, when a reason is given for the proposition. Such as in this way: "You must not so often call yourself frugal, when in fact you are greedy. For he who is frugal, uses what is enough: you on the other hand, because of your greed, use more than you have. So the result will not be the fruits of carefulness, but rather the miseries of poverty" (*Rhetores Latini Minores* ed. Carolus Halm [Leipzig, 1863] p.5.

The translation is my own, except for the quotation from the Attic orator Hyperides, which is from the Loeb ed. *Minor Attic Orators* II, ed. J.O. Burtt, p. 575). Quintilian said essentially the same thing (IX.iii.64–5). As Rutilius's quotation from the Greek orator Hyperides shows, they clearly took the view that it was *paradiastole* for an orator to distinguish between wisdom and cunning, etc.

When Renaissance scholars read Rutilius and Quintilian, many of them, and certainly the most authoritative, took the same view. The fullest discussion of *paradiastole* available to Hobbes was undoubtedly the famous *Oratoriarum Institutiones* of G.J. Vossius, first published in 1606, and praised to the skies by both Scaliger and Casaubon, in which Vossius clearly treats *paradiastole* as a kind of definition – what he called in the enlarged essay on the subject in the 1635 edition a "linked" definition, "when we remove the false name of something, and give it its true name" (see Vossius, *Tractatus Philologici* [Amsterdam, 1697], p. 258). The one tradition in which this was denied was that which Professor Skinner has traced, stemming largely from the textbook of the German school-teacher Johannes Susenbrotus, in which *paradiastole* was defined as the actual practice of substituting a favorable connotation for an unfavorable one; but this tradition was out of line with both the ancient texts and the modern experts, and there is little evidence that Hobbes was particularly influenced by it. There is, however, plentiful evidence that he was very interested in the kind of practice that *paradiastole* was used to expose.

26 *De Partitione Oratoria*, ed. H. Rackham (Loeb) xxiii.81, p. 371.

27 *Declamations*, ed. M. Winterbottom (Loeb); *Controversiae* I.3.11, I p. 103.

28 See Karl R. Wallace, *Francis Bacon on Communication and Rhetoric*, pp. 69, 206.

29 For a fuller discussion of the relationship between both Bacon and Hobbes and late Renaissance skepticism, see Tuck, *Philosophy and Government*.

30 The earliest example is a long *Discourse against flatterie*, which was published in 1611. This was an earlier version of a discourse with the same name which appeared in a group of four discourses as an adjunct to a collection of very Baconian essays, in an anonymous volume entitled *Horae Subsecivae* in 1620. The essays (it is known from a manuscript at Chatsworth) were by William Cavendish, later the second earl, and Hobbes's first "pupil" (though that is rather a misnomer – Cavendish was only two years younger than Hobbes, had graduated from Cambridge the same year that Hobbes graduated from Oxford and became his "tutor," and had married in the same year). The *Discourse against flatterie* is dedicated to Cavendish's father-in-law in terms that are entirely appropri-

ate for Cavendish himself, and there is no reason to suppose that it, and the other three discourses in the 1620 volume, are not by him. The MS volume of *Essayes* at Chatsworth is dedicated by "Your Lordships mos[t] observant and dutifull sonne W. Cavendishe," presumably to the first earl by his son, Hobbes's pupil, in Venice. The MS is in Hobbes's hand (Peter Beal, *Index of English Literary Manuscripts* II [London and New York 1987], p. 583), and also contains some annotations by Hobbes (Rogow, pp 249–52). This need not mean very much, however: the Latin version of the *Brief of the Art of Rhetorique,* which no one has denied to be by Hobbes, is to be found in a Chatsworth MS in the hand of William Cavendish, the third earl (Beal, *Index*, p. 583). Clearly, it was a matter of some indifference whether Hobbes or his pupil wrote out these treatises. The MS essays are published in Friedrich O. Wolf, *Die neue Wissenschaft des Thomas Hobbes* (Stuttgart 1969). The 1620 volume is *Horae Subsecivae: Observations and Discourses.* Malcolm (op. cit.) is the best account of this question, and includes the announcement of the discovery of the 1611 discourse. Leo Strauss's overenthusiastic attribution of the MS to Hobbes himself and the debacle of his proposal to publish it (see Wolf, p. 133) has deterred subsequent scholars from taking it and the discourses as seriously as they deserve as evidence for the intellectual life within the Cavendish household, and for the context out of which (at the very least) Hobbes's own ideas developed. Hobbesian themes surface in these essays and discourses, however, and there seems to have been a complex intellectual relationship between Hobbes and his pupil (acknowledged by Hobbes himself, for example in the dedication of his translation of Thucydides).

I have recently learned from Professor Reynolds of Brigham Young University, whose team has conducted an exhaustive statistical analysis of Hobbes's works, that there are strong reasons for supposing that the MS essays are indeed not by Hobbes, but that three of the four supplementary discourses (the long discourse on Tacitus referred to below, the discourse on laws, and the discourse or travel guide to Rome) do seem to be by him. This corresponds both to the circumstantial evidence and to a plausible intuitive assessment of the prose style. The team's full account is shortly to be published by Chicago University Press.

31   The letter was printed by Ferdinand Tönnies in his "Hobbes-Analekten," pp. 294–6. Tönnies identified the recipient as William Cavendish the elder son, but the letter is addressed to "Mr. Cavendish," not to Lord Cavendish (William's style). It is known that Charles was at that date on a tour of the Continent (see the D.N.B article on him), while William seems to have come home with Hobbes in October 1636 (see Hobbes's letter of Oct. 16 to the earl of Newcastle, in Historical Manuscripts Commission, *13th Report II* (1893), p. 129).

32 There seems to have been some duel, or threatened duel, in the background to the letter.

33 This was first pointed out by Keith Thomas with great insight in his essay "The Social Origins of Hobbes's Political Thought," pp. 185–236. The most remarkable example of this is perhaps the fact that in April 1639 Hobbes drafted a statement on behalf of the earl complaining about the way the earl's mother had managed his inheritance during his minority, a legal struggle that, among other things, illustrates the weakness of normal familial relation in Hobbes's world. The document refers to the various causes of the earl's suspicion of his mother "which are not necessary to be here mentioned, because every man may lawfully seeke to secure himself upon his owne suspitions, whether they be well or ill grounded" (quoted in Arnold A. Rogow, *Hobbes*, p. 264 n.22). This sentence is in effect the fundamental proposition of Hobbes's political thought!

34 *Essayes* p. 161. As Kiernan points out (p. 302), this is not Aesop, but Laurentius Abstemius.

35 *Essayes*, pp. 170–1.

36 The relationship between Bacon and the Cavendish family even became a matter of public interest: Bacon was himself well-known to the family, and when Hobbes and the future second earl of Devonshire visited Venice during a Continental journey between 1610 and 1615, their acquaintance with Bacon was one of the things that most excited their hosts in that city. Fulgenzio Micanzio, the aide to and biographer of the Venetian statesman Paolo Sarpi, wrote to Cavendish shortly after their return to England that "I am exceedingly bound to you for relating to Sir Francis Bacon how much I esteem his judgements and learning, having not a long time met with any writing that has given me greater content and having taken such a conceit of the Author from his Essays that I find myself very much carried away to love and honour him" (Vittorio Gabrieli, "Bacone, la riforma e Roma nella Versione Hobbesiana d'un Carteggio di Fulgenzio Micanzio," p. 203). The letters from Micanzio to Cavendish (under various pseudonyms, although Gabrieli says that there is "no doubt" [p. 244] that they are all by Micanzio) were translated from Italian into English by Hobbes so that his master could read them easily. The seventy-five letters date from 1615 to 1628 and were copied for circulation to other people interested in Anglo-Venetian affairs. Despite Noel Malcolm's doubts ("Hobbes, Sandys, and the Virginia Company," pp. 319–20), there is good reason to think that Hobbes and Cavendish were abroad continuously from 1610 to 1615; see my *Philosophy and Government*, pp 280–1.

In 1623 Micanzio urged on Cavendish the thought that "the service of the sciences requires that he [Bacon] should have helps to write not only what he says but also what passes through his mind if it were possible"; it was presumably because of this suggestion that Hobbes was seconded to wait on Bacon at Gorhambury near St Albans and take notes of his ideas (Gabrieli, p. 215; Aubrey, *Brief Lives*, p. 331). Aubrey says that it was "after his first lord's death," i.e., after 1626 (Bacon himself died in that year, so this is unlikely to be literally correct), but Aubrey clearly knew that it was toward the end of Bacon's life. Bacon's *Essayes* particularly excited Micanzio, and he was especially keen to have them translated into Italian; Hobbes also seems to have assisted Bacon in translating some of the *Essayes* into Latin, as part of the same campaign to get him international recognition. The translations appeared posthumously as part of Bacon's *Operum Moralium et Civilium Tomus* in 1638 (Gabrieli, pp 207–11; Aubrey, I 331).

9   Hobbes's political philosophy

This chapter discusses some large questions in Hobbes's political philosophy. My aim is to identify what, if anything, Hobbes thought to be *the* central problem, or problems, of politics and to link the answer to an account of why the state of nature is so intolerable, of how we may leave it, and whether the manner of our leaving is well explained by Hobbes. I then turn to the implications for Hobbes's account of the rights and duties of the sovereign, and then to the contentions issue of the subject's right, in extremis, to reject his sovereign and rebel. In the course of that discussion, I also consider Hobbes's account of the nature of punishment and the question whether his two rather different accounts are not one too many. In answering these questions, I shall say something about Hobbes's conception of the law of nature, his theory of political obligation, and the role (or lack of a role) of religious belief in his political system.[1] I say a little about Hobbes's account of liberty and link its oddities to the politics of his own day.

HOBBES'S CAREER

It would be otiose to say much about Hobbes's career here; that has been done elsewhere. I will only emphasize some features of his life to frame the discussion of the central arguments of his political philosophy and the interpretative problems they present. Hobbes observed that fear and he were born twins into the world, because his mother had gone into labor upon hearing the (false) rumor of the approach of the Spanish Armada in the spring of 1588. "His extraordinary Timorousness Mr Hobs doth very ingenuously confess and attributes it to the influence of his Mother's Dread of the Spanish

208

Invasion in 88, she being then with child of him," says Aubrey.[2] Hobbes made much of this, treating caution as one of the primary political virtues, arguing that anxiety was the main stimulus of religious belief, and thinking that religious belief gave fear a useful focus.[3] We shall see below how important fear is in explaining the causes and character of the "war of all against all" in the state of nature, in motivating persons in the state of nature to contract with one another to set up an authority to "overawe them all" and make peace possible, and in persuading them to obey that authority once it has been established.

Hobbes's education at his grammar school in Westport and at Oxford was a literary one; in Oxford it was literary and "philosophical" in a traditional and non-Hobbesian sense. His first employment as a tutor and confidential secretary in the Devonshire household made use of the skills of a man of a literary and historical education; those are what he taught his charge, the young earl of Devonshire, and Hobbes's first published work was a translation of Thucydides' *History of the Peloponnesian War*. The publication was in part a compliment to Hobbes's employer. It was not the only possible choice for a man who translated Homer into passable English verse in his extreme old age and wrote his autobiography in Latin verse (and much of his philosophy in Latin prose), as he did when he celebrated the marvels of the Peak District.[4] He might have chosen many other ways to compliment his employer; the choice of Thucydides was a meaningful one, and its meaning was plain enough. "Thucydides is one, who, though he never digress to read a lecture, moral or political, upon his own text, nor enter into men's hearts further than the acts themselves evidently guide him; is yet accounted the most politic historiographer that ever writ."[5] As to the implications of Thucydides' work, Hobbes stressed that as far as Thucydides' opinions of forms of government were concerned, "it is manifest that he least of all liked the democracy."[6]

Twentieth-century readers admire Athens more than seventeenth-century readers did, and today we admire Pericles' famous Funeral Oration without reflecting on the fact that Alcibiades (who urged the Athenians into the disastrous Sicilian expedition, the overwhelming defeat of which cost Athens the war) exerted more influence over Athens than Pericles ever did. We try not to notice when Thucydides observes that, under Pericles, Athens was a democracy in name only and a monarchy in fact because of the authority that Pericles could exercise. Hobbes emphasises what we flinch from. "And upon diverse occasions he noteth the emulation and contention of the demagogues for reputation and glory of wit; with their crossing of each other's counsels, to the damage of the public; the inconsistency of resolutions caused by the diversity of ends and power of rhetoric in the orators; and the desperate actions undertaken upon the flattering advice of such as desired to attain, or to hold what they had attained, of authority and sway among the people." Not that Thucydides was a friend to aristocracy either. "He praiseth the government of Athens when it was mixed of *the few* and *the many*; but more he commendeth it, both when Peisistratus reigned (saving that it was an usurped power), and when in the beginning of this war it was democratical in name, but in effect monarchical under Pericles."[7] Hobbes took to heart Thucydides' message that democracies collapse into factionalism and chaos as their search for freedom and glory ends in civil war and self-destruction. Hobbes's first work was historical and so was the work of his last years. *Behemoth* is perhaps a strange example of its genre, inasmuch as it takes the form of a dialogue in which the two parties exchange hypotheses about the causes of the English Civil War. Nonetheless, it was historical in form and in purpose; it was intended to unravel the course of particular events and to draw a moral from them: "the principal and proper work of history being to instruct and enable men, by the knowledge of actions past, to bear themselves prudently in the present and providently towards the future."[8] Since this chapter considers Hobbes's *science* of politics, and Hobbes explicitly contrasted that science with a historically based *prudence*, it is worth keeping in mind the fact that Hobbes also wrote history.

One last aspect of Hobbes's career worth mention is his connection with the law during his brief career as ammanuensis to Francis Bacon, inductivist and Lord Chancellor, and in his later excursion into jurisprudence in the *Dialogue Between a Philosopher and a Student of the Common Law*. I shall argue that Hobbes's political philosophy is "absolutist" in a slightly curious sense, namely that perhaps his greatest wish was to show that a political system had to settle the question *What is the law?* with a clear, unambiguous, and indisputable answer; the way to achieve that was to secure universal agreement that only *one* source of law existed, and that whatever that source declared as law *was* law. The so-called Hobbesian problem of order was cast by Hobbes in a particular light: how to escape from a situation in which there were no clearly enunciated and scrupulously enforced rules of conduct into a situation where a determinate, ultimate, omnicompetent authority laid down the law and enforced it. Any authority with that standing and intended to perform that task must be legally absolute, that is, unchallengeable in the name of any other legal authority.[9]

There were many problems in the way of establishing such an authority; one was the arrogance of the common lawyers who held that "the law is such a one as will have no sovereign beside him." The greatest of the common lawyers of Hobbes's day, Sir Edward Coke, held that the "High Court of Parliament" was the only authority able to change the common law by statute, but he fell under the same Hobbesian anathema. The High Court of Parliament on Hobbes's account of the matter could change the law only to the extent that the sovereign empowered it to do so. Qua court, its authority was derivative. Other obstacles included the foolishness of those who believed that only a republican or "free" government could be legitimate, and who therefore complained that the laws of a monarchy limited their freedom and had no binding force. They had simply failed to understand that all law limited freedom. The liberty at which republics aimed "is not the Libertie of Particular men; but the Libertie of the Commonwealth," that is, its independence as a sovereign state, as to which "[w]hether a Common-wealth be Monarchicall, or Popular, the Freedome is still the same."[10] A greater obstacle still was the arrogance or madness of religious fanatics who believed that God had spoken to them in their dreams, licensing them to legislate for others according to their inspiration, or absolving them from the decrees of the unrighteous. Hobbes's view of unauthorized inspiration is well known: "To say that he hath spoken to him in a Dream, is no more than to say that he hath dreamt that God spake to him;"[11] his skeptical criticism of dissenters and enthusiasts reflected his view that religion must be subordinate to law so that law would not be subordinated to the ambition of priests. For Hobbes the dividing line between *religion* and private fantasy was to be drawn by the sovereign authority as a matter of "law not truth." It was to establish one unequivocal source of law, not in order to demonstrate the truth of some particular religious creed, that Hobbes waged his campaign to undermine the credibility of the unofficial prophets.

POLITICAL SCIENCE VS POLITICAL PRUDENCE

The final feature of Hobbes's life to be borne in mind was his acquaintance with the greatest scientific minds of the day. He quarrelled with several of them and was on the losing side on several occasions.[12] Nonetheless, he was as deeply conscious of living in the middle of an intellectual revolution as he was of living in a period of political and religious revolution. The bearing of this fact on this chapter's concerns is simple: Hobbes's political philosophy was distinctive in its ambition to be a *science* of politics. Hobbes's positive understanding of what this involved is a matter of controversy. Hobbes explained what a science of politics was by contrasting it with political prudence; the latter was practical wisdom, practiced in the light of the best advice that we can draw from a storehouse of historical examples. Thucydides was a model of political prudence, as well as the source of instructive examples, but Hobbes proposed to improve on him. The Romans, Hobbes remarks, rightly distinguished between *prudentia* and *sapientia*; we call both wisdom, but we ought to follow the Romans and distinguish them.[13] "As much Experience, is *Prudence*; so, is much Science, *Sapience*. For though we usually have but one word of Wisedome for them both; yet the Latines did always distinguish between *Prudentia* and *Sapientia*; ascribing the former to Experience, the later to Science." Prudence is the knowledge of events and affairs that comes from wide experience and reflection and from recapitulating the experience and reflection of others as recorded in history. Prudence is *essentially* experiential; its method is historical – whether it is a matter of retrospective reflection upon our own experience or upon that of mankind in general – and its object is sound judgment in particular cases. The best evidence of prudence is continual good judgment. Prudence is a genuine form of knowledge, yet it is always knowledge of particulars; it is a knowledge of how things have worked out in the past and what *has* happened, not of how they *must* work out nor of what *must* happen. Generalizations based on such experience are always in danger of being falsified by a novel, unexpected event.[14]

Sapientia is based on science. Science is hypothetical, general, and infallible. Most commentators have found nothing very surprising about the thought that science deals in hypothetical generalizations. Modern analyses of causal laws (water boils at 100°C, say) as universal propositions of the form (x) Ax → Bx ("If anything is water, it boils at 100°C") treat them as just that. Yet nobody has offered an entirely persuasive account of Hobbes's view that science is infallible; modern accounts of causal laws emphasize their fallibility, finding their empirical content in their capacity for falsification.[15] Hobbes's account becomes no clearer with his insistence that the only science we possess is geometry. For our purposes, we may decently avoid controversy and suggest that Hobbes's assimilation of geometry and politics is best understood by analogy with economic argument. Economic theory explains the conduct of a rational economic agent by laying out the optimal strategy for such an agent to pursue. It is normative as much as descriptive because its explanations of what actors *do* do are parasitic on its accounts of what for them is the thing *to* do.[16] I shall use an analogy I have used before and try to place no more weight on it than I must. Hobbes's science of politics is a form of blueprint making; it sets out a rational strategy for individuals placed in the dangerous and anxiety-ridden state of nature, individuals whose goal is assumed to be self-preservation and whose means of survival are minimal. Politics so understood is a normative discipline, and in this resembles modern economics.[17] The blueprint sets out what rational individuals *must* do if they are to form a political society; it does not predict that they *will* do. Far from offering a disconfirmable prediction of what they will in fact do, Hobbes's politics relies for its rhetorical power on the fact that men have so often failed to do what the blueprint dictates and have thus caused themselves appalling misery.

Political science sets out what men rationally must do. Its relationship to empirical accounts of human psychology, anthropological investigations of nonpolitical societies, political socialization, and a great deal else that the twentieth century embraces under the general heading of "political science," is thus complex. It plainly has *some* vulnerability to factual considerations. If mankind were empirically so constituted as inevitably to fail to follow Hobbes's prescriptions, we should at least lose interest in them – as we should lose interest in a theory of pedestrian safety that enjoined us to rise vertically ten feet above onrushing traffic. Short of that, it is hard to set out general rules for adjusting Hobbes's science to the facts or the facts to Hobbes's science. To the extent that actual agents pursue the recommended strategy, whether knowingly or unknowingly, their behavior will be both explained and justified by the theory; and to the degree that the world matches the world posited in the theory, their actions will "infallibly" produce the results predicted. The practice of modern economics suggests that Hobbes was right to link geometry and politics. Hobbes's account of the horrors of the state of nature has in recent years often been interpreted as a prisoners' dilemma problem, and contemporary economics places the analysis of strategic interactions at the very heart of its concerns.[18]

Hobbes's contemporary Sir James Harrington, the author of *Oceana*, began the tradition of accusing Hobbes of slighting the historical understanding of politics in favor of his own scientific understanding.[19] It is surely true that Hobbes thought that the scientific understanding of politics was superior to an historical one, and in that sense preferred "modern" prudence to "ancient" prudence.[20] But this is far from implying that he despised historical analysis. What he despised was the habit he saw in many of his contemporaries of flaunting their historical erudition not to advance their understanding of their own age's dilemmas, but to show off their learning. This was particularly foolish because it amounted to retailing second-hand experience in preference to their own.

And even of those men themselves, that in the Councells of the Commonwealth, love to shew their reading of politiques and History, very few do it in their domestique affaires, where their particular interest is concerned; having Prudence enough for their private affaires; but in publique they study more the reputation of their owne wit, than the successes of anothers businesse.[21]

He also despised the habit of taking past political actors, beliefs, or systems as authoritative models in current conditions. That the Athenians had practiced democracy was their misfortune; that the citizens of ancient republics had thought their governments free and all others servile was their mistake. To follow them blindly was to repeat their errors and to refuse to learn from experience. Learning from experience was not to be despised, particularly since it reinforced the lessons Hobbes's political science taught. If Hobbes had not thought so, he would hardly have wasted his time writing *Behemoth*. Nor, for that matter, could he have published *De Cive* ahead of the rest of his projected system, on the grounds that it was "grounded on its owne principles sufficiently knowne by experience."[22]

There was much that science could not prove. It could tell us that no society without an ultimate and absolute legal authority possessed a *sovereign*, and that it was to that degree not a state at all; but it could not demonstrate that a monarch would make a better sovereign than an assembly. Experience tells us it is highly probable that monarchy is the best form of government, but Hobbes did not think he had demonstrated this conclusion, and he may well have doubted that it could be demonstrated.[23] Demonstration handles large structural features of political life and leaves experience to deal with particularities. The science of politics tells us that anything we can properly regard as a state must have a certain constitution; to learn what a prudent empirical implementation of that constitution is, we must turn to experience. It could tell us what laws are, but not what the laws of any particular country are.[24] Hobbes cannot have thought that a feckless monarch would be better than an assembly of thoughtful and prudent senators, any more than he could have thought that science could tell us whether a given judge would take bribes or listen to a case carefully. Science tells us what law *is*. In the light of that we can appreciate the qualities to look for in a judge, such as a willingness to subordinate his private judgment to the commands of the sovereign. It cannot tell us whether Francis Bacon, Lord Verulam and a noted bribe-taker, was a wise choice for Lord Chancellor.

This leaves much of the methodological detail of *Leviathan* unresolved. In particular, it leaves unclear why Hobbes should have devoted so much of the first two books of *Leviathan* to an elaborate account of human beings considered as elaborate automata. The emphasis on a speculative physiological reduction of the most important emotional and intellectual qualities of human beings does not on the face of it add much to what Hobbes might have achieved by starting with persons in the state of nature and elucidating the dangerousness of their condition, as a preliminary to offering the only secure way out of it.[25] To the extent that this physiological and psychological speculation provides a foundation for later arguments, it is by leading us to think, in a broadly constructivist way, that *were* we in the position of God, first creating the world, then man, and then exploring the consequences of putting man in such a world, there would be only one rational route to self-preservation available to man. This captures Hobbes's talk of the way we create the state on an analogy with God's creation of the entire natural world; it is, after all, the very first thing he tells us: "Nature (the Art by which God hath made and governed the World) is by the *Art* of Man, as in many other things, so in this also imitated, that it can make an Artificial Animal."[26] It also leaves a great deal untouched. In particular, it leaves untouched Hobbes's own skepticism about our knowledge of just how God rules the world. Hobbes elsewhere stresses that *we* can never know what God's perspective on his creation is. We might draw up a system that seems rationally compelling to us, but God's free choice cannot be limited by what seems rationally compelling to us.

THE NATURAL CONDITION AND ITS HORRORS

Perhaps the most famous single phrase in Hobbes's entire oeuvre is his observation that life in the state of nature is "solitary, poore, nasty, brutish, and short."[27] The interest of Hobbes's view emerges by contrast with the views of his predecessors and successors. Aristotle, whom Hobbes savaged throughout *Leviathan*, sometimes by misrepresenting him for the purpose, had claimed that "The polis is one of those things that exist by nature, and man is an animal made to live in a polis."[28] Hobbes's break with the teleological perspective of Aristotle's *Politics* made this claim not only false but absurd. States exist by convention, and conventions are manifestly manmade, so states are self-evidently artificial and thus nonnatural. But Hobbes dissented from Aristotle on the substance of human nature, too, even though he cheated in his statement of the difference. Men, said Hobbes, were not political by nature as bees and cattle were; their association depended on an agreement to observe justice among men who disagreed about who ought to receive what, and thus they needed common standards of right and wrong to regulate their affairs.[29] This was hardly a hit against Aristotle. He had claimed that bees and cattle were sociable or gregarious, but not *political* – for just the reason Hobbes cited against him.[30] Bees and cattle simply congregated together, but men could live together only on the basis of agreed principles.

Still, the difference persists; Aristotle thought that there was some kind of natural attraction toward the good, and toward life in society. Hobbes thinks that at best there is a common aversion to the *summum malum*, or death, and that we become "apt" for society only by being socialized into decent conduct. Almost equally important is Hobbes's insistence on the natural equality of mankind. For Aristotle the social order can, and when things go well, does, mirror a natural hierarchy in which the better sort of person is plainly distinguished from the less good: aristocrats from their inferiors, men from women, adults from children, free men from slaves, and Greeks from barbarians. Hobbes rejected this view of the world. Not only was it false, it violated two conditions of political peace: one, that we should reckon everyone our equal and demand no more from them than we allow them to demand from us; the other, that everyone should acknowledge the sovereign as uniquely the fount of honor.[31] An aristocrat was anyone the sovereign declared to be an aristocrat, no more and no less.[32] The pride of descent that aristocrats displayed was a threat to peace; it made them think they were entitled to demand political preferment, it made them touchy about their honor, and it provoked needless fights. Thinking of humanity as morally, politically, and intellectually on a level reinforced the view that the state rested on universal consent rather than on a tendency toward a natural hierarchy.

Hobbes's successors held a variety of views about the state of nature, ranging from the view that there had never been a state of nature, so that considering what it was like and how we might have emerged from it was a waste of time, to Rousseau's view in *Discourse on the Origins of Inequality* that it was a peaceful condition, pre-human in important respects, and perhaps a model for a kind of innocence that we might hope to recover in a social setting at the end of some very long process of change.[33] I shall contrast Hobbes's account of the state of nature with Locke's and Rousseau's accounts, and will in passing mention Filmer's patriarchalist theory of government as a contemporary, but diametrically opposite, view.

Hobbes writes of the "condition of mankind by nature" without anxiety about its historical accuracy. He is quite right. As he says, the heads of all governments live in a state of nature with respect to one another. The state of nature is simply the condition where we are forced into contact with each other in the absence of a superior authority that can lay down and enforce rules to govern our behavior toward each other.[34] Like many of his contemporaries, Hobbes thought that the Indians of North America were still living in the state of nature. More important, the inhabitants of Britain had been in that condition during the Civil War; so not only was the state of nature a historical fact but relapse into it was a standing danger. Indeed, the state of nature with which Hobbes is concerned is more nearly the condition of civilized people deprived of stable government than anything else. This can be seen by a simple thought experiment.

There are many societies that anthropologists call acephalous. They have no stable leadership; there is nothing resembling law or politics in their daily life. Such societies persist for long periods. They have no apparent tendency to self-destruction, although they are easily wrecked by contact with more advanced societies. Hobbes seems to suggest that their existence is impossible to explain. In the state of nature, he says, we are governed by no rules, recognize no authority, are therefore a threat to each other, and must fall into the state he describes as a war of all against all. But, we counter, if that were so, acephalous societies would self-destruct. It is easy to think of reasons why they might not. Hobbes plays down such possibilities by saying only that the concord of the American Indians "dependeth on naturall lust" and by going on to observe that they live in a "brutish manner."[35] The brutishness of their existence is, however, not the decisive point. The decisive question is whether they can – at least on a small scale – get by with the laws of nature alone. On the face of it, they can. Hobbes never suggests that we cannot know what rules we *ought*, both as a matter of prudence and as a matter of morality, to follow. The members of acephalous societies can understand the laws of nature.

For enforcement the institutionalized practice of the blood feud may serve well enough. If you murder me, I cannot revenge myself, but my brother can do so on my behalf. In a small society, it is likely that the murderer would be immediately obvious; if he has killed me only because he is murderously inclined, he will not find allies to help him resist vengeance. The knowledge that he faces the vengeance of my family will, one may hope, act as a powerful deterrent when he contemplates murder, so that the whole process of taking revenge need never start. For this to work, several things have to be true that will *not* be true in large and complicated societies. It is crucial that my death must be known at once to my family, on whom the burden of revenge falls, and the probable killer must be easily discovered and brought to justice. This is not true in larger societies: if I am traveling on business and am robbed three hundred miles away from home, I must depend on institutionalized police power for help or on my own unaided force. Many people have suggested that Hobbes's state of nature is peopled with the men of the seventeenth century; properly understood, this may not be a defect in the theory. That is, the theory may be designed around the problem of sustaining and policing a *large*, prosperous society, where most people are known well only to a few friends but want to transact business and hold intellectual converse with distant strangers.

What is Hobbes's theory? We are to consider men in an ungoverned condition. They are rational, that is, able to calculate consequences; they are self-interested, at any rate in the sense that they ask what good to themselves will be produced by any given outcome; they are vulnerable to one another – you may be stronger than I, but when you are asleep I can kill you as easily as you can kill me; they are essentially *anxious*.[36] They are anxious because they have some grasp of cause and effect, understand the passage of time, and have a sense of their own mortality. It is these capacities that Rousseau, for instance, denies that we possess merely qua human animals, and in their absence, he claims, we would be like other animals, heedless of any but present danger. Hobbesian man is heedful of the future. This means that no present success in obtaining what he needs for survival can reassure him. I pick apples from the tree now, but know I shall be hungry in six hours; my obvious resource is to store the surplus apples somewhere safe. But the logic of anxiety is remorseless. Will the apples remain safe if I do not find some way of guarding them? I find myself in a terrible bind. In order to secure the future I have to secure the resources for my future; but to secure them, I have to secure whatever I need to make them safe. And to secure it. . . . This is why Hobbes puts "for a generall inclination of all mankind, a perpetual and restless desire of Power after power, that ceaseth only in Death."[37]

Such creatures encounter one another singularly ill equipped in the natural condition. Each appears to the other as a threat, and because each appears as a threat, each is a threat. This is not because of any moral defect in us. Hobbes wavers somewhat on the subject of original sin, but the miseries of the state of nature would afflict people who do not suffer from original sin, but who do have the anxieties that Hobbes ascribes to us. Nor does our knowledge of the moral law, that is, of the laws of nature, make any difference. Each of us has the natural right and the natural duty to preserve ourself. This right is an equal right. You have no greater right over anything than I have, and I have no greater right over anything than you have. In the absence of a secure system of law to protect us from each other, we all have a right to all things; that is, we have no obligation to defer to anyone else or yield to them. This equality of right is matched by a rough equality of capacity, and therefore an equality of hope. It is this combination that brings us to grief.

Each of us is a potential threat to everyone else because each of us faces a world in which other people *may* cause us harm. The reasons for this are threefold. First, the state of nature is a state of scarcity. You and I may both want the same apple, or even if we do not, we both want to be sure of having enough to eat. This sets us at odds. This is the condition described by Hobbes as *competition.* However modest we may be in our wants, we face the fact that other people's use of the world may deprive us of what we need. I may be happy to drink water rather than champagne, but if your anxiety about future water supplies has led you to sequester all the local water supply, I shall have to do something to extract from you enough water for my needs.

The second cause of trouble is fear or *diffidence.* The logic of fear is something with which humanity has become extremely familiar during the past fifty years. It is the logic of interaction between two persons or two societies who can each annihilate the other, and neither of whom possesses second-strike capacity, that is, the ability to revenge himself on the other *post mortem.* Two nuclear powers who can wipe out the other side's nuclear forces *if they strike first* and therefore cannot revenge themselves on the other side if they do *not* strike first would be the post–World War II illustration of Hobbes's theory. The point to notice is that the horrors of the situation do not hinge on either party's wishing to attack the other. People in this situation are driven to attack one another by the logic of the situation, no matter what their motives. Thus, I look at you and know that you can kill me if you have to; I know that you must have asked the

attack by
the logic
of situation

question whether you have to. Do you have to? The answer is not entirely clear, but a plausible reason is that you will have looked at me and have understood that I have every reason to be afraid of you, because you *might* need to attack me. But if that's true, you do need to attack me, and if I know that about you, I can see that I must attack you. If I let you strike first, my loss is complete. So, however little I incline to attack you, I have a strong incentive to do so. Or, as Hobbes puts it: "from this diffidence of one another, there is no way for any man to secure himselfe, so reasonable, as Anticipation.[38]

Both these first two reasons for conflict can be dealt with fairly easily. Competition can be dealt with by the achievement of prosperity; if I can be sure that my efforts to gain a subsistence will indeed secure my continued existence, I have no further reason to fight. It is sometimes suggested that Hobbes failed to understand that markets help to overcome scarcity, but this is surely as false as the equally common view that Hobbes's politics are only about maintaining markets. The obvious reading of Hobbes is that once *mine* and *thine* are defined and enforced, we shall successfully look after our own welfare: "Plenty dependeth (next to Gods favour) meerly on the labour and industry of men."[39] Similarly, once there is a system of police, fear makes for peace rather than conflict. I see that you have every reason not to attack me, so think you will not; you see that I have every reason not to attack you (because we are both threatened with the same sanctions by the sovereign) and think I will not; now we both know that neither of us has any incentive to attack, so we both have even less of an incentive, and peace is established.

The third cause of conflict is not so easily dealt with. This is pride or vainglory. Hobbes insists that a peculiarity of human desire is its indeterminacy. Not only do we constantly change our ideas about what we want; we are chronically unsure whether what we want is worth having. There is no tendency to gravitate toward the truly good, for our desires are the psychological outcrop of a physiological mechanism that is in constant flux. But one crude test of value is the envy of other men.[40] This presents a worse problem than the other causes of conflict. "Vain Glory" is satiable only when we come top of the heap, and the criterion of success is universal envy; vainglory cannot be slaked by prosperity, and it creates a competition that security cannot defuse. There logically cannot be more than one top position; if that is what we seek, the conflict between ourselves and others is absolute. It is not surprising that Hobbes treats pride as the worse threat to peace, and assails it both in aristocrats who take pride in their descent, and in their social inferiors who strive for riches and social position. It is the one attitude that has to be suppressed rather than merely assuaged or diverted, and it is apt that *Leviathan* is the story of the genesis of the creature who was king over the children of pride.[41]

The combined pressure of competition, diffidence, and glory leads to the war of all against all, and to a life that is poor, solitary, nasty, brutish, and short. To escape this condition, men must devise institutions that will enforce rules of conduct that ensure peace. To discover what those rules are is to discover the law of nature. We are so familiar with such an argument that we may fail to see how different its assumptions were from the political assumptions on which most of Hobbes's contemporaries relied. Sir Robert Filmer, for instance, argued in his *Patriarcha* that men had never lived outside government; the Bible and secular history concurred in tracing political history to life in small, clanlike groups governed by the absolute authority of the father. The Roman *patria potestas* was much like the authority of Old Testament fathers; it was a power of life and death, a power to sell one's children into slavery. It was the proper model of political authority. Although few modern readers think much of Filmer's history, there is something deeply engaging about his response to state of nature theory's assertion that men are born free and equal: they aren't. Many others of Hobbes's contemporaries would have thought it simply needless to stray outside English history in looking for the foundations of government. The realm of England had a traditional structure: it was an organic community to be governed according to familiar principles by the King, the Lords Spiritual and Secular, and the Commons. Hobbes thought that it was essential to go behind these debates. The polity had to be founded on the laws of nature, not on habit or on local myth.

Hobbes's account of the laws of nature is distinctive. "A LAW OF NATURE (*lex naturalis,*) is a Precept, or generall Rule, found out by Reason, by which a man is forbidden to do, that, which is destructive of his life, or taketh away the means of preserving the same; and to omit, that, by which he thinketh it may be best preserved."[42] Hobbes sees that their standing as *laws* is problematic; both in *Leviathan* and *De cive*, Hobbes insists that a law is the word of someone who by right bears command. The laws of nature, conceived as deliverances of reason, are thus not in the usual sense *laws*. Hobbes sees this; he calls them "theorems," which they surely are. Laws, properly, are commands rather than theorems, and thus exist only when someone issues them as commands.

These dictates of Reason, men use to call by the name of Lawes, but improperly: for they are but Conclusions, or Theoremes concerning what conduceth to the conservation and defence of themselves; whereas Law, properly, is the word of him, that by right hath command over others. But yet if we consider the same Theoremes, as delivered in the word of God, that by right commandeth all things; then are they properly called Lawes.[43]

This approach contrasts in an interesting way with that of Locke. For Locke, the argument runs *through* the inferred wishes of God and could not be sustained otherwise. That is, in the Lockean state of nature a man first comes to the view that he is sent into the world about His business, as the creation of an omnipotent maker, and then concludes that such a maker requires him to preserve himself and others as far as that is consistent with his own preservation.[44] This is a process of ratiocination, and to that extent is like the process Hobbes invokes; but it is not the same process.

Hobbes, then, claims that we can see that the rules we ought to follow lay down that we must preserve our lives, and that we have an absolute right to do whatever conduces to that end. What most conduces to it is to seek peace, and that is accordingly the first law, just as the statement that we have the right to do anything necessary to preservation is the fundamental right of nature. We can then infer that the way to achieve peace is to give up as much of our natural right as others will. It appears that we must renounce *all* our rights, save only the right to defend ourselves *in extremis*. It is to be noticed that Hobbes does not suggest that we shall generally have any psychological difficulty in seeking peace. Some people have bolder characters and perhaps a taste for violence; they will present a problem, since they will not be moved by the fear of death that moves most of us to desire peace.[45] Most of us are not like them, but wish to be protected against them. Hobbes's account of the way we are forced into conflict explains the conflict not as the result of our wish to engage in aggression, but as the result of our wish to lead a quiet life.

Moreover, we can see why it is a mistake to assimilate too closely

Hobbes's account of our situation to the prisoner's dilemma of recent game-theoretical discussions. The prisoner's dilemma is superficially very like the Hobbesian state of nature. The dilemma is that each of the two parties to the dilemma faces a situation in which, should he do the cooperative thing and the other person not, he suffers a great loss, whereas if they both do the noncooperative thing, they both do badly. A Hobbesian who, say, disarms himself without being sure others do so also may now be killed more easily by others; so he had better keep his weapons, even though everyone will be worse off if all are armed than they would be if all were disarmed. This looks very like the problem of a noncooperative, aggregatively inferior outcome dominating a cooperative, aggregatively superior one.

		B	
		adheres	violates
	adheres	2,2	4,1
A			
	violates	1,4	3,3

The matrix above does not put values on the outcomes, only on their ranking in the eyes of self-interested participants. Each participant ranks as his favored outcome the one in which the other party (party B) keeps his agreement and he (party A) benefits from that agreement while violating it. For example, the other person disarms himself, and I take advantage of his unarmed condition to take what I want from him. Hobbesian man is supposed to repress this desire. This is why the state of nature is not a true prisoner's dilemma. The essence of a prisoner's dilemma is that the parties to it are utility-maximizers, so that opponents in the game will always try to exploit each other and they know it. Hobbesian man will not. He is not a utility maximizer, but a disaster-avoider. The proper response to my disarming myself is to disarm yourself, not to kill me: to seek peace, not to maximize advantage. I do wish to be vulnerable not because I know you will exploit me if you can, but because I am not certain that you will not exploit me. In modern discussions, utility-maximizing assumptions ensure that none of the obvious ways of getting out of the dilemma

will work. The most obvious is to agree to follow the cooperative
route and to set up an enforcement system to enforce the agreement.
But if we are utility-maximizers, it will both be overstretched (because everyone will rat on their agreements when they can profit
from doing so) and underoperated (because its personnel will not do
their job as enforcers if they think they can do better by sloping off). In
a manner of speaking, utility-maximizers are rational fools, for they
cannot but ignore agreements if it profits them. Hobbesian man is
obliged to keep his agreements unless it is intolerably dangerous to do
so, and Hobbes does not suggest we will be tempted to stray, as long as
we keep our eyes on the need to avoid the state of nature. Once
Hobbesian men have agreed on the cooperative path, they will follow
it not only until they can see some advantage in not doing so, but
unless and until it threatens their lives.[46] Hobbes relies heavily on his
subjects' fear of the return of the state of nature to motivate them to
keep their covenant of obedience; as he says, fear is the motive to rely
on, and he spent much of *Leviathan* trying to persuade them to keep
their eyes on the object of that fear.

THE CONTRACTUAL ESCAPE ROUTE

The explanation of this demands an account of the Hobbesian contract and its place in his political theory. Hobbes's first two laws of
nature tell us to seek peace and to be ready to give up as much of our
right as others are for the sake of peace. The third law of nature is
"that men perform their covenants made." This law is central to the
entire edifice. It is also a slightly odd law. All the other laws,
whether the basic injunction to seek peace or elaborate corollaries
such as the requirement to give heralds safe conduct, are injunctions
of a clearly moral kind. The requirement that we keep promises is
peculiar because it seems to be both moral and logical. A covenant
says now what we shall do in some future time; if it did not bind us
(*ceteris paribus*), it would not be a covenant. Consider how often we
try to evade an obligation we wish we had not acquired by saying
something on the lines of "It wasn't really a promise, only an expression of hope." To know what a covenant is to know that it is a way
of incurring an obligation. This thought is what lies behind Hobbes's
claim that breach of covenant is like what logicians call absurdity, in
effect saying that we shall and shall not do whatever it may be.[47]

The reason for Hobbes's concern with covenants is obvious enough. If we are to escape from the state of nature, it can only be by laying aside our "right to all things." That is, we can do that only by covenanting *not* to do in future what we had a right to do in the past – mainly, by agreeing not to use and act on our private judgment of what conduces to our safety in contradiction of the sovereign's public judgment, save in dire emergency. Hobbes sees that there are difficulties in the way of contracting out of war and into peace. Since we are obliged not to endanger our lives, we shall not keep covenants that threaten our safety, and a covenant to disarm would do that unless we could rely on everyone else keeping their covenant to disarm too. But how can we do that if there is as yet no power to make them keep their covenants? One of Hobbes's more famous pronouncements was that "Covenants, without the Sword, are but Words, and of no Strength to secure a man at all."[48] It seems that to establish a power that can make us all keep our covenants, we must covenant to set it up, but that the covenant to do so is impossible to make in the absence of the power it is supposed to establish. Hobbes in fact understood the problem he had posed himself.

He did not think that all covenants in the state of nature are rendered void by the absence of an enforcing power. The laws of nature bind us *in foro interno*; they oblige us to intend to do what they require; a person who makes a contract is committed to carrying out his side of the agreement *if* the other party does and *if* it is safe to do so. If upon making a contract he finds that the other party has indeed performed, and that it is safe to perform himself, then he is obliged *in foro externo*, too, that is, as to the carrying out of the act. It is no use pretending to recognize an obligation *in foro interno* but then failing to act when it is safe to do so. The only conclusive evidence of a sincere recognition of the obligation *in foro interno* is acting when it is safe. If I shout across the ravine that keeps us from injuring each other that I will place ten apples at some agreed-on spot if you agree to place five pears there when you pick up the apples, and I then place the apples there and retire to a safe distance while you collect them, you are *obliged* to leave the pears. If I can spare the apples and do not endanger my life by leaving them there, a Hobbesian, though not a twentieth-century games theorist, would think I did well to risk disappointment if you take my apples and leave no pears. Experimentally, of course, people behave as Hobbes suggests and try to create cooperative arrangements by engaging in tit for tat: If you take my apples and leave no pears, I "punish" you by not cooperating the next time; if you leave the agreed-on pears, I leave apples again.[49]

Can this explain the obligation to obey the sovereign and get out of the state of nature? Perhaps it can, even though most commentators have been sure it could not. Remember that we are not all watching for an opportunity to take advantage of other people's compliance with the laws of nature; we are only watching lest they take advantage of our compliance. It is, of course, absurd to imagine that we could *literally* make the sort of covenant that Hobbes describes as a "Covenant of every man with every man, in such manner, as if every man should say to every man. . . ."[50] It is far from absurd to imagine that we could in effect indicate to others that we proposed to accept such-and-such a person or body of persons as an authority until it was proved to be more dangerous to do so than to continue in the state of nature. In a manner of speaking, we do it the entire time inside existing political societies.

Hobbes was not apparently very anxious about such puzzles. Two reasons may be guessed at, although guessing is all it is. The first is that the usual situation in which we find ourselves is not that of setting up a state *ab initio*, but of deciding whether to swear allegiance to an existing government. That is, modern commentators are fascinated by the puzzle of how to create a sovereign by institution, but Hobbes paid more attention to the rights of and duties to sovereigns by acquisition. Hobbes published *Leviathan* when he came back to England and made his peace with the commonwealth established by Cromwell after the deposition and execution of Charles I. He said that he thought the book had framed the minds of many gentlemen to a conscientious obedience, by which he meant that they had been moved by his arguments to understand that they could give allegiance to Cromwell without dishonoring their previous allegiance to Charles. So Hobbes's topic was the "sovereign by acquisition" rather than the "sovereign by institution." The second reason is that Hobbes's most strikingly counterintuitive claim about the contract that binds us to the sovereign is that it is valid even if extorted by force. "Covenants entred into by fear, in the condition of meer Nature, are valid. For example, if I Covenant to pay a ransome, or service for my life, to an enemy; I am bound by it. For it is a

Contract, wherein one receiveth the benefit of life; the other is to receive mony, or service for it; and consequently where no other Law (as in the condition, of meer Nature) forbiddeth the performance, the Covenant is valid.[51]

What Hobbes imagined was the situation in which we find ourselves after the end of a war or the end of a decisive battle at the absolute mercy of the victor. He is entitled to kill us if he wishes; we are in a state of nature with respect to him; we are, to use Hobbes's terminology, an *enemy*. This does not mean someone actually engaged in fighting him, but someone who is not pledged not to fight him. The victor has the right of nature to do whatever seems good to him to secure himself, and killing us to be on the safe side is no injustice to us. In Hobbes's unusual terminology, it cannot be unjust, since all injustice involves breach of contract and there is no contract to be breached. He may offer us our lives on condition that we submit to his authority. Now we have a choice: to refuse to submit and so draw our death upon us, or to submit. What Hobbes insists is that if we submit, we are bound. To cite the fact that we submitted out of fear is useless, because we always submit to authority out of fear. "In both cases they do it for fear: which is to be noted by them, that hold all such Covenants, as proceed from fear of death, or violence, voyd; which, if it were true, no man, in any kind of Commonwealth, could be obliged to Obedience."[52] The only thing that can void a contract is an event *subsequent* to the contract that makes it too dangerous to fulfil it. Nothing that we could take into account when we made the contract counts against its validity. Most readers find Hobbes's view quite shocking, but it is, after all, true enough that when we go and buy food at a grocery, we regard ourselves as obliged to pay for what we purchase even though we are ultimately driven to eat by fear of starvation. Hobbes's point was that both contracts – the contract of all with all, and the contract of the individual with the person who has his life within his power – are based on fear; and both are valid.

CONTRACTUALISM AND OBLIGATION

In some ways, the greater oddity of Hobbes's work is the insistence that each of us is obliged only because each of us has, implicitly or explicitly, contracted to obey the sovereign. Of all the routes to obligation, contract is at once the most and the least attractive. It is the most attractive because the most conclusive argument for claiming that someone has an obligation of some kind is to show them that they imposed it on themselves by some sort of contract-like procedure. That route is uniquely attractive because promising is a paradigm of the way we voluntarily acquire obligations. It is unattractive for the same reason; few of us can recall having promised to obey our rulers for the very good reason that few of us have done so. (American schoolchildren, who are obliged to pledge allegiance to the Stars and Stripes and "the Republic for which it stands" most mornings of the school year, are an exception to this. It is odd that schools tend to drop this ceremony when children reach the age of reason and might be held to account for their promises.)

The example of the pledge made by American schoolchildren shows one or two other problems. The most obvious is just what Hobbes tried to defuse with his claim that fear does not invalidate covenants. If we had approached a flag-burning dissident at the time of the Vietnam War and reminded him that he had once pledged allegiance, he would not have been much moved. For one thing, he might have said, he had no option; if he wanted to attend school, he had to say the pledge or face expulsion. How could a pledge extorted by such methods have any binding force? For another, students might plausibly complain that they had had no idea what was involved in pledging allegiance. How were they to know that the Republic for which the flag stood would subsequently turn out to be intent on sending them to get killed in Vietnam? Here, too, Hobbes's response is that what we pledge is *obedience* to a person or body of persons, and in doing so we renounce any right to discuss the terms of that obedience thereafter. It is just because we renounce *all* our rights that Hobbes's theory has the character it does. It is also what made it vulnerable to the complaints of Locke, who observed that it would be folly to defend ourselves from polecats by seeking the protection of lions; leaving the state of nature by exposing ourselves to the absolute, arbitrary power of the sovereign appears less than rational.

It seems odd that Hobbes should insist that obedience rests on a covenant, and that he should have argued himself into a corner where he had to give a very counterintuitive account of the way in which coercion does and does not affect the validity of contract. One wonders what drove him to do so. Some aspects of his argument seem easily explicable; they were driven by the political needs of the day. It is part of his argument that when the person whom we acknowledge as sovereign can no longer protect us, we may look for a new ruler. The bearing of this on the situation of anyone who was formerly a loyal royalist and now had to consider whether to acknowledge Cromwell's commonwealth is obvious enough. To do this, though, he had to defuse the objection that a person who joined the service of a sovereign out of fear would feel himself permitted to leave it whenever things got hot. Hobbes denies this twice over. In the "Review and Conclusion" of *Leviathan*, he says

To the Laws of Nature, declared in the 15. Chapter, I would have this added, *That every man is bound by Nature, as much as in him lieth, to protect in Warre, the Authority, by which he is himself protected in time of Peace.* For he that pretendeth a Right of Nature to preserve his owne body, cannot pretend a Right of Nature, to destroy him, by whose strength he is preserved: It is a manifest contradiction of himselfe.[53]

But he had earlier said clearly enough that what we do when we promise to recognize a given person or body of persons as sovereign is to sustain that authority in all necessary ways, particularly by paying our taxes willingly and by not quibbling over ideological issues.[54]

Less explicable is Hobbes's insistence that obligation is self-incurred. Sometimes this insistence is diluted, as when Hobbes claims that by accepting our lives, property, and liberties from a sovereign who can lawfully kill us, we have in effect contracted to obey him. More commonly, it appears to have reflected a deep conviction that everything in the last resort hinges on the thoughts and actions of individuals. Hobbes, we might say, saw himself as addressing his readers one by one, trying to persuade each of them to accept his case for obedience to an absolute sovereign. It is a vision that seems on its face not wholly consistent with his view that persons possessed of sufficient power can simply force others to subscribe to their authority. "The Kingdome of God is gotten by violence," he observes; what that seems to mean is that because God's power is irresistible, only He has unique authority not based on our contracting to obey him.[55] But even then one wonders whether God's dissimilarity to any human authority may not be the true point of Hobbes's observation. At all events, Hobbes's individualism is in the spirit both of the methodological tactics of the opening chapters of *Leviathan* and of the concentration on each individual's fears for himself and his own concerns that underpins Hobbes's account of the state of nature. And it is important in Hobbes's insistence that the limits of our obligation to obey the sovereign are set by our inability to give away our lives. We may say to him or them, "Kill me if I do not perform," but not "If you try to kill me, I shall not resist." It is one of the many peculiarities of Hobbes's cast of mind that he insists that the rights of despotic sovereigns are just the same as those of sovereigns by institution, and still says that "It is not therefore the Victory, that giveth the right of Dominion over the Vanquished, but his own Covenant. Nor is he obliged because he is Conquered; that is to say, beaten, and taken, or put to flight; but because he cometh in and submitteth to the Victor."[56]

RIGHTS AND DUTIES OF THE SOVEREIGN

When the sovereign is instituted, or acquires his power by succession or conquest or some other conventional route, a strikingly lopsided situation arises. We the subjects have nothing but duties toward the sovereign, but he is not in the strict sense under any *obligation* to us. Hobbes's argument for these alarming conclusions is a *tour de force*, but it has always struck critics as more bold than convincing. In the case of the sovereign by institution, Hobbes points out that we covenant *with each other*, not with the sovereign. Strictly, we are contractually obliged to one another to give up our natural rights in the sovereign's favor. The sense in which we are obliged to the sovereign is somewhat tricky to elucidate. In one sense he is the beneficiary of our contracts but not a party to them, as would be the case if you and I promised one another to look after a neighbor's child. Are we obliged *to* the child as well as in respect of the child? Opinions vary. In Hobbes's theory, it is a moot point, for the sovereign is the beneficiary of our promised intention to do whatever he tells us, which is just the position he would be in if our obligation was *to* him as well as to each other in respect of him. In any case, the central issue is Hobbes's determination to show that the sovereign has no obligations to us.

Almost every commentator is so intrigued by this argument that it usually passes unnoticed that in the case of the sovereign by acquisition, the contract is made with the sovereign, who does there-fore have – momentarily – an obligation to us. The step to be at-tended to is that the sovereign's obligation can be instantly fulfilled. The sovereign in effect says to us, "If you submit, I will not kill you." When he spares us, he has fulfilled his obligation. Our obliga-tion, on the other hand, endures indefinitely. So the same situation comes about as comes about in the more complex case of sover-eignty by institution. "In summe, the Rights and Consequences of both *Paternall* and *Despoticall* Dominion, are the very same with those of a Sovereign by Institution; and for the same reasons.[57]

Nonetheless, the sovereign has duties. Indeed, he has obligations to God, although not to any earthly authority. For the natural law binds the sovereign, and as long as his or their subjects are more-or-less well behaved, this law binds the sovereign not only in con-science but in action.

The Office of the Sovereign, (be it a Monarch, or an Assembly,) consiseth in the end, for which he was trusted with the Soveraign Power, namely the procuration of *the safety of the people*; to which he is obliged by the Law of Nature, and to render an account thereof to God, the Author of that Law, and to none but him. But by Safety here, is not meant a bare Preservation, but also all other Contentments of life, which every man by lawfull Industry, without danger, or hurt to the Common-wealth, shall acquire to himselfe.[58]

The inference is hard to shake: We are obliged to obey the laws of nature except when it is too dangerous to do so, and if the sovereign is moderately effective, it will not be dangerous for him to do so. No doubt a conversation might be imagined between Machiavelli and Hobbes in which the question were debated as to what the sovereign should count as danger and how scrupulous he should be in follow-ing natural law.

For all that, Hobbes insists quite energetically *both* that there is no question of our holding the sovereign to account for anything he might do, *and* that he should be guided by the moral law. It is not too much to claim that Hobbes's ideal sovereign would be absolute in principle, but indistinguishable from a constitutional sovereign in practice. Or, to put it otherwise, we cannot demand a constitutional government as a matter of right, which is why Hobbes is never going to turn into a Lockean; but a ruler, when it is safe to do so, ought to govern in a constitutional fashion. This is, to belabor a point, a place where the coincidence of utilitarian and deontological consider-ations is very apparent. What other writers might demand as a mat-ter of right, Hobbes derives from such obvious considerations as the fact that threats of punishment, say, will only enhance the well-being of society if people know what will happen to them under what conditions, and know how to avoid them. Retroactive punish-ment is thus contrary to the purpose of civil society, and so is to be deplored regardless of whether we have a *right* not to suffer it. Hobbes, in fact, comes close to letting a right not to be so punished back into his lexicon by a sort of conceptual sleight of hand.

Harme inflicted for a Fact done before there was a Law that forbad it, is not Punishment, but an act of Hostility: for before the Law, there is no transgres-sion of the Law: But Punishment supposeth a fact judged to have been a transgression of the Law; therefore Harme inflicted before the Law made, is not Punishment, but an act of Hostility.[59]

The sovereign's duties under the law of nature fall into three roughly distinct categories. On the one hand, there are restraints on his actions that stem from the nature of sovereignty, of which the most important are those that forbid the sovereign to divide or limit his sovereign authority. He can transfer it whole and undivided, set out rules for its transfer to his successor, and do whatever does not destroy it, but any action that seems to part with a vital element of sovereignty is void.[60] The second class of actions embraces those things that the law of nature forbids or enjoins. A Hobbesian sover-eign who observes these requirements will go a surprisingly long way toward recognizing everything that human rights advocates de-mand of governments, except for one thing – conceding subjects a share in government as a matter of right. I shall return to that point almost at once, since it bears on Hobbes's understanding of freedom. It is perhaps not surprising that the requirements of the law of na-ture coincide with the requirements of most human rights theories; but it is worth noticing that they forbid disproportionate punish-ments, forbid the *ex post facto* criminalization of conduct, forbid anyone to be a judge in his own case, and much else besides.

The final class of actions occupies most of Hobbes's attention in the Second Book of *Leviathan*, where Hobbes discusses what one might call the standard political tasks that a prudent and effective sovereign will have to perform. For the most part, they contain no surprises. We might wonder at the vanity that leads Hobbes to suggest that the sovereign would be well advised to have the doctrines of *Leviathan* taught to the entire population in order to keep their minds on the horrors of war and the blessings of order, but these chapters are in general not unpredictable in their concentration on the need for adequate taxation, security of property, and so on. They do contain two possible surprises for the modern reader. One is the prominent place Hobbes gives to the sovereign's role in judging what doctrines may be publicly taught and defended. It is, says Hobbes, against the sovereign's duty to give up the right of "appointing Teachers, and examining what doctrines are conformable, or contrary to the Defence, Peace, and Good of the people."[61] Hobbes's view on religion were very complex, but two simple things can be said of them. The first is that Hobbes was so appalled by the way religion led men into civil strife that it was obvious to him that the secular powers had to control religious institutions and decide what might and might not be preached in the pulpit. Hobbes was in general an anti-pluralist, in the sense that his insistence on the sovereign's unique standing as the source of all law meant that no subordinate body such as a church or university could claim any independent authority over its members, other than the state might grant it. But what they could not claim as a right, they might well be given as a license to engage in harmless and possibly useful enquiry. As far as the church went, Hobbes was entirely opposed to ecclesiastical claims to the right to impose secular penalties. Hobbes anticipated Locke's *Letter on Toleration* by arguing in his essay on heresy that a church should have no power over its members beyond that of separation from the common worship and, more contentiously, that the first secular laws against heresy were intended to apply only to pastors, not to the laity.[62]

The other thing one can say of Hobbes's view was that he saw that the degree of religious uniformity the state needed to impose would vary with the temper of the people. If there was much doctrinal dispute, the state must settle at least the externals of behavior, such as whether altars were or were not to be used and whether we must pray bare-headed. These were conventional signs of honor, and it was a proper task of the state to set those conventions. Beyond that, Hobbes hoped that with the return of common sense, men might return to the condition of the early church and to "independency."[63] Too much intervention would be destructive of felicity.

The second surprise is not at what Hobbes proposes to regulate in a way we might think excessive, but at what he proposes not to regulate. Hobbes was not a "capitalist" thinker, nor a theorist of commercial society, and in many ways he was hostile to the life of money-making and had a thoroughly uncapitalist preference for leisure over labor. Nonetheless, he advised the sovereign to concentrate on defining property rights, cheapening legal transactions by such devices as establishing registered titles to land – something not achieved for another two and three quarter centuries – and encouraging prosperity by leaving his subjects to look after their own well-being. This was not a pure *laissez-faire* regime. Hobbes's proposal was much nearer what we would call a welfare state, with provision for the sick, the elderly, the infirm, and the unemployed.[64] Yet it shows once more how insistent Hobbes was that the central task of politics was to settle who had the ultimate legal authority, and to make sure that the possessor of authority could get the law enforced. It did not follow that busybody legislation was prudent or useful. Indeed, once the matter was framed in such terms, it clearly was not.

All this is set out with no suggestion that the sovereign's political self-control reflects the subject's rights. Indeed, Hobbes is at pains to deny it. As we have seen, the subject, having given up his rights, cannot now appeal to them. Moreover, the one area in which Hobbes breaks entirely with later writers on human rights is his insistence that we have no right to have a share in the sovereign authority, and that any system in which we try to set up a collective sovereign embracing many people will almost surely be a disaster. His grounds for so thinking are partly historical; that is, he believed that democracies characteristically collapsed into chaos and factionalism, and doubtless thought himself vindicated by the behavior of parliament in his own day. Even more interesting, he broke with the tradition that held that one form of government, and one form only, pursued *freedom*. His view was summed up in a sentence from a passage we have quoted already: "There is written on the Turrets of the city of *Luca* in great characters at this day, the word *LIBERTAS*; yet no man can thence inferre, that a particular man has more Libertie, or Immunitie from the service of the Commonwealth there, than in *Constantinople*. Whether a Common-wealth be Monarchicall, or Popular, the Freedome is still the same."[65]

Hobbes defines liberty in two not entirely consistent ways. First, in the state of nature, "Liberty, is understood, according to the proper significance of the word, the absence of externall impediments."[66] Second, civil liberty, under government, is the *absence* of law or other sovereign commandment. "The Greatest Liberty of Subjects, dependeth on the Silence of the Law."[67] Both accounts make it entirely possible to act voluntarily but from fear, and neither suggests that freedom has anything to do with the freedom of the will. Hobbes disbelieved in free will and conducted a running battle with Bishop Bramhall on the contentious issue of freedom, necessity, and foreknowledge. His two chief purposes are clear enough. As we have seen already, he wanted to argue that a contract made out of fear for our lives is made freely enough to be a valid contract; the common view that coerced contracts are invalid *ab initio* he explained as a reflection of the fact that we are normally forbidden to force people into making contracts by the positive law of the sovereign. That civilized societies will forbid coerced contracts makes perfect sense. It is clear that there are sound reasons of policy for keeping force out of economic transactions.

The second great aim was to enforce the claim that freedom was not a matter of form of government. In one sense, freedom and government are antithetical, because we give up all our rights when we enter political society, save, as Hobbes observes in his discussion of the liberty of subjects, the right to defend ourselves against the immediate threat of death and injury. Had we reserved any rights upon submitting to a sovereign, we should have left open endless occasions for arguments over the question whether a given law does or does not violate one of those reserved rights. This would have frustrated the object of entering political society in the first place, so would have been absurd. Once we are members of political society there is a further issue, which is the extent of the control our sovereign wishes to exercise over us. A despot who largely leaves us alone leaves us more liberty than a democracy in which the majority is constantly passing new legislation. This is the point of Hobbes's reference to Constantinople. Being part of the sovereign does not add to one's liberty; Hobbes is not Machiavelli, nor is he Rousseau. He felt strongly that the classical education of his day and religious enthusiasm could in this area combine to delude people into thinking that they could only be free in a republic. "And as to Rebellion in particular against Monarchy; one of the most frequent causes of it, is the Reading of the books of Policy, and Histories of the ancient Greeks, and Romans."[68]

The thought that killing one's king is not murder but *tyrannicide* is, says Hobbes, an encouragement to anarchy. To the degree that classical republicans talk sense at all, the freedom they have in mind must be the freedom of the republic as a whole from domination by outsiders. This plainly was a large part of what Machiavelli admired in the Romans, but hardly all of it. Here as elsewhere, Hobbes is not entirely scrupulous about painting his opponents in the colors that most flatter them.

RESISTANCE

Hobbes was not a liberal, and this statement goes beyond the observation that "liberal" is a term not employed in English politics until around 1812; Hobbes was strenuously opposed to many of the things that define liberalism as a political theory. Nonetheless, many things about his political theory would sustain a form of liberalism, and he held many of the attitudes typical of later defenders of liberalism. It is easy to feel that as long as nobody talked about their "rights," a Hobbesian state would be indistinguishable from a liberal constitutional regime. The sovereign has excellent prudential reasons for listening to advisers, allowing much discussion, regulating the affairs of society by general rules rather than particular decrees, and so on indefinitely. Allied to the natural law requirement to respect what we might call the subjects' moral rights, something close to a liberal regime emerges.

Still, the antipathy to claims of right is a real breach with liberal political ideas. Where Locke insists that we enter political society only under the shadow of a natural law whose bonds are drawn tighter by the creation of government, Hobbes relegates that law to the realm of aspiration. If the sovereign breaches it, we are not to resist but to reflect that it is the sovereign whom God will call to account, not ourselves. It is an unlovely view, for it suggests all too unpleasantly that if Hobbesian subjects are told to kill the innocent, or torture prisoners for information, they will do so without much hesitation. They may think it very nasty, but they cannot engage in conscientious resistance, or, if they do they must not incite others to resist with them. They may embrace martyrdom, but not engage in rebellion.

This is the aspect of Hobbes that many readers find repugnant. It cannot entirely be got round either. Still, we may in conclusion see whether even in this area there is something to be said for Hobbes's views. We may approach an answer by way of Hobbes's account of punishment. Hobbes has two accounts of punishment; they serve much the same purpose, but they are very different. The purpose they serve is to insist *both* that there is a real difference between legal punishment and the treatment of "enemies," and that we are not obliged to submit to punishment without a struggle. The difference lies in whether the right to punish is a right the sovereign has gained upon the creation of the state or a right we all had in the state of nature that everyone but the sovereign has relinquished on submission. The first view would be an ancestor of Rousseau's and Kant's; the second view would be very like Locke's were it not for the fact that Hobbes does not anticipate Locke in distinguishing the state-of-nature right to *punish* from the state-of-nature right to do whatever we need to defend ourselves from our enemies.

The first view follows from Hobbes's discussion in Chapter 30 of the nature of the obligation to obey the sovereign. He says unequivocally that the obligation imposed by civil law rests on the prior natural duty to keep covenants: "which naturall obligation if men know not, they cannot know the Right of any Law the Sovereign maketh. And for the Punishment, they take it but for an act of Hostility."[69] The second is offered in Chapter 28, where Hobbes insists that "to covenant to assist the Soveraign, in doing hurt to another, unless he that so covenanteth have a right to doe it himselfe, is not to give him a Right to Punish. It is manifest, therefore, that the Right which the Common-wealth (that is, he, or they that represent it) hath to Punish, is not grounded on any concession or Gift of the Subjects."[70] In the state of nature, we all have the right to subdue, hurt, or kill anyone we think we need to in order to secure our own preservation; what the covenant does is commit us to helping the sovereign to employ that right. What then distinguishes punishment from hostility is the regular, predictable, lawful, and public nature of the harm so inflicted.

The reason why any of this matters is straightforward. On the one hand, Hobbes must mark a difference between our vulnerability to punishment if we enter political society and then violate the rules and our vulnerability to being treated as an enemy if we remain in a state of nature with those who have entered. Unlike Rousseau, who suggested that we might remain in something like state-of-nature relations and still be treated decently, Hobbes insists that if we were to remain in this situation, we could be treated in any way the sovereign thought fit, ignoring his own insistence that the law of nature at least urged the recognition *in foro interno* of acting with no more than the barely necessary force. By signing up for political membership, we sign up to suffer no more than the penalties prescribed by law, if we break the law at some future point. This supposes that punishment is something other than the ill treatment properly applied to enemies for our own protection.

The view that punishment rests on the sovereign's state-of-nature right of self-defense has some awkward consequences. One is that we appear to remain in the state of nature vis à vis the sovereign, and that legal relations are always, as one might say, horizontal, holding between subject and subject, but not between subject and sovereign. It is a complex operation to analyze the ways in which we do and do not leave the state of nature in our relations with the sovereign. At one level, it is harmless enough to suppose that we do not. The sovereign and ourselves can transact most of our business on the basis of the law of nature, especially since the law of nature would enjoin us to respect the sovereign's laws whether or not we had ever contracted to do so. It is perhaps in the general spirit of Hobbes's account that legal relations in the usual, conventional sense, hold between subjects only. Thus, we must abstain from one another's property, but the sovereign is not bound by the same rules. All the same, there is an awkwardness to it; it fails to distinguish except in a shadowy fashion between the regular, law-governed treatment of the citizens' property by way of such things as properly legislated taxation, on the one hand, and peremptory expropriation, on the other. This case is much like the case of Hobbesian constitutionalism. The sovereign ought to behave as a constitutional sovereign would behave, but there is no suggestion that the sovereign must do so for constitutional reasons. *Ex hypothesi*, the sovereign is the fount of law and "absolute" in the sense of not being bound by his own rules in the same way as his subjects are bound by those he promulgates; nonetheless, he ought to consider himself bound *in foro interno* and by the law of nature.

Many later writers, perhaps overimpressed by the difference between punishment and mere ill-treatment for a purpose, have suggested that the fact that the subject willed the punishment was a morally significant aspect of the institution.[71] Hobbes was very much not of that camp. It was clear enough that the rational person had to commit himself to the existence of a system of sanctions: other people would not sign a contract of submission to sovereign authority unless he signed up as well, and they would not believe he was bound unless they saw he was vulnerable to sanctions. He must, therefore, say something equivalent to "if I do thus and such, you may try to kill, imprison or fine me." What he could not say was "I will endorse your doing so as you do it." He could not refuse to resist.

And here Hobbes's system encounters its moment of truth. Hobbes is eager to say three things, and they may not be entirely compatible. The first is that as long as the sovereign preserves my life and possessions, I must assist him to retain his power. If he calls an army together, I must fight or pay for a soldier to serve in my place.[72] If the enemy is at the gate, I must fight regardless. Useless sacrifice is certainly useless, but readiness to take risks on behalf of the power that protects us is indispensable. The second is that I am in the last resort entitled to do whatever seems best to me to save my life. I need not, and probably cannot, give myself up to prison and death. I have a right to self-preservation that overrides everything I may have formerly said. But, third, we cannot encourage others to resist the sovereign with us.

The conjunction of these last two claims presents problems. The absence of the first claim would amount to the dissolution of the whole political system upon the first crime committed against it. The absence of the second would not only, as we have seen, make it impossible to see why the formerly loyal subjects of Charles I might later swear allegiance to Cromwell with a whole heart and a clear conscience. The absence of the third would come close to admitting that people might foment revolution when it seemed to them that revolution was to be preferred to submission. But the third is inconsistent with the obvious possibility that the best way to secure myself against the sovereign's ill will is to ally myself with others who can resist him. If we are, for whatever reason, enemies to the sovereign, we must seek the best way we can find to our own safety.

At that point, Hobbes requires some much less formal way of

explaining what forms of resistance are morally acceptable and which are mere criminal conspiracies. It is not hard to see the ingredients of such an explanation in his own writings, but it would be wholly at odds with the spirit of his political philosophy to seek them out and elaborate anything we might call a "Hobbesian theory of resistance." The point of his system was to discredit any such theory. The genius of Hobbes was to produce a theory that, because it was built on individualist and rationalist foundations, must, in spite of its author's intentions, leave room not only for individual resistance but also, *in extremis*, for fully fledged revolution. *Leviathan* may well have framed the minds of many gentlemen to a conscientious obedience, but it also framed in many other minds a disposition to ask whether the sovereign had failed to secure our peace and safety or was visibly about to do so. In so doing, it was inadvertently a prop to the revolutionaries of the next fifty years.

NOTES

1 On religion, see Springborg, Chapter 14, this volume. I have written on this elsewhere: see "Hobbes, Toleration, and the Inner Life" and "Hobbes and Individualism." Two much more extended and very useful recent accounts, differently oriented but not wholly at odds with one another, are S. A. Lloyd's *Ideals as Interests in Hobbes's Leviathan*, and A. P. Martinich's *The Two Gods of Leviathan*. David Johnston's *The Rhetoric of Leviathan* is an elegant argument for the view that Hobbes's purpose in his discussion of religion is to remove religious controversy from politics. My general perspective on Hobbes is not unlike that of Michael Oakeshott in *Hobbes on Civil Association*.

2 *Brief Lives*, ed. Oliver Lawson Dick (Harmondsworth: Penguin Books, 1972) p. 316; everyone comments on the fact that Hobbes's physical timidity was quite at odds with his intellectual boldness. Leslie Stephen's *Hobbes* is still a very engaging account of its subject.

3 *Lev.*, Tuck, 76–7.

4 *de Mirabile Pecci.*

5 *EW* VIII, viii.

6 Ibid., xvi.

7 Ibid., xvi–xvii, 221: "It was in name, a state democratical; but in fact a government of the principal man." For two very different views of the place of Thucydides in Hobbes's political thought, see Leo Strauss, *The Political Philosophy of Hobbes*, and J. W. N. Watkins, *Hobbes's System of Ideas*.

8 *EW*, vii.

9 *A Dialogue between a Philosopher and a Student of the Common Laws of England.* See below, Ch. 11.

10 *Lev.*, 149.

11 Ibid., 257.

12 See Steven Shapin and Simon Schaffer, *Leviathan and the Air Pump*, for Hobbes's controversy with Robert Boyle; for Hobbes's (failed) relations with the Royal Society, see Noel Malcolm, "Hobbes and the Royal Society."

13 *Lev.* 38; for the problems of Hobbes's account of science, see Watkins, *Hobbes's System of Ideas.* The best recent account of these is in Tom Sorell, *Hobbes,* and on the bearing of Hobbes's science on his politics, the same author's "The Science in Hobbes's Politics."

14 Karl Popper, *The Poverty of Historicism* (London: Routledge and Kegan Paul, 1957), pp. 115–16.

15 This idea is particularly associated with Karl Popper, *The Logic of Scientific Discovery* (London: Hutchinson, 1957); it sets the context for the discussion in Watkins, *Hobbes's System of Ideas.*

16 See Popper, *Poverty of Historicism,* for an account of situational logic; also see Martin Hollis, *The Cunning of Reason* (Cambridge: Cambridge University Press, 1988).

17 I have long been in Martin Hollis's debt for this insight; see his "Theory in Miniature," *Mind,* 1973.

18 The most sustained discussion from this standpoint comes in David Gauthier, *The Logic of Leviathan* (Oxford: The Clarendon Press, 1969); Jean Hampton, *Hobbes and the Social Contract Tradition.*

19 *The Political Works of James Harrington,* ed. J. G. A. Pocock (Cambridge: Cambridge University Press, 1977), pp. 161–3.

20 Ibid., p. 161.

21 *Lev.* 37.

22 *De Cive* (Warrender, ed.) p. 36.

23 Ibid., 37.

24 Ibid; 36–7.

25 As he did in *De Cive* and *EL*, where he simply presumes the truth of the psychological basis of our problems in the state of nature.

26 *Lev.*, p. 9; incidentally, Martinich's view that Hobbes's use of this analogy shows how seriously he took religion seems rather forced, especially since Martinich emphasizes the sharpness of the distinction that Hobbes drew between the behavior of human beings and the essentially unintelligible behavior of God.

27 *Lev.* 89.

28 *The Politics of Aristotle*, translated by Sir Ernest Barker, Oxford, The Clarendon Press, 1948, p.6 (I, ii, § 9).

29 *Lev.*, 119; the account in *De Cive*, pp. 87–8 is equally insistent on the role of pride or "eminence" in creating discord.

30 *Politics*, 7 (I, ii, § 10)

31 *Lev.* pp. 107–8

32 Ibid., 126, 128.

33 Jean-Jacques Rousseau, *Social Contract and Discourses* (London: Everyman Library, 1993); Emile Durkheim, *Montesquieu and Rousseau: Pioneers of Sociology* (Ann Arbor: University of Michigan Press, 1961); François Tricaud, "Hobbes's Conception of the State of Nature" in Rogers and Ryan, *Perspectives*, explores ambiguities in Hobbes's account, and especially variations between his accounts in *Elements*, *De cive*, and *Leviathan*, that I do not touch on here.

34 *Lev.*, 89–90; *De Cive*, pp. 32–3, p. 45

35 *Lev.*, 89; Anthony Pagden, *The Fall of Natural Man* (Cambridge: Cambridge University Press, 1982), provides a riveting account of the role of American Indians in European accounts of "natural man."

36 *Lev.* 75–6; incidentally, this passage, founding religion on "some peculiar quality, or at least in some eminent degree thereof, not to be found in other Living creatures," shows how much closer Rousseau and Hobbes were than is commonly thought.

37 *Lev.* 70.

38 Ibid., 87.

39 Ibid., 170.

40 Cf. Hobbes's comparison of life to a race (*EW* IV 53) in which there is no other goal but to come first.

41 Cf. *Lev.* 221.

42 Ibid., 91.

43 Ibid., 111; *De cive*, p. 76; the question whether Hobbes made their status as divine commands central to the analysis of the laws of nature has been much debated. Martinich, *Two Gods*, is the most recent defense of the view that he does. My own view is that he may well have thought that God commanded obedience to them, but that he still thought that they could bring men to agreement in virtue of their status as "convenient articles of peace."

44 John Locke, *Two Treatises of Government* (Cambridge: Cambridge University Press, 1969), II, § 4.

45 *Lev.* 90; *De Cive*, 42–3.

46 This is not to slight the interesting work of David Gauthier and Jean Hampton cited above; it is, however, to say that they discuss some issues

that I do not think *Hobbes's* account in fact raises. That it is too late in the day to deny the label "Hobbesian" to such problems is very likely true, just as it is, as Professor Hampton agrees, too late to relabel Hobbes's argument if it is, as she thinks, not a "contractual" argument in the strict sense at all. See *Hobbes and the Social Contract Tradition*, pp. 186–8, and David Gauthier, "Hobbes's Social Contract" in Rogers and Ryan, *op cit.* In the latter essay, Gauthier agrees that the state of nature is not a pure Prisoners' Dilemma, but he remains (I think) firmly wedded to a utility-maximizing psychology. The title of Gregory Kavka's *Hobbesian Moral and Political Theory* is entirely apt, of course, because he focuses on issues of mutual deterrence that arise whether or not all parties are utility-maximizers.

47 *Lev.* 93; *De Cive*, 63. One of the many insights in Brian Barry, "Warrender and His Critics," is the special status of contractual agreement as an obligation-undertaking device.

48 *Lev.* 117.

49 This is famously spelled out in Rapaport, *The Evolution of Cooperation* (New York: Basic Books, 1984), and discussed in passing in David Gauthier, "Hobbes's Social Contract."

50 *Lev.* 120

51 Ibid., 97–8; cf pp. 138–9.

52 Ibid., 138–9; it is to be noticed that Hobbes's account has a curious internal flaw. I do not follow Don Herzog (*Happy Slaves*) in his cheerful view that Hobbes's contradictions were the small price Hobbes had to pay for the rhetorical effect he wanted to make, so I wish I could see some way out of them. We begin with a "right to all things" in the state of nature; thus we have a right to the obedience of others, but one that they have no obligation to recognize, because they cannot save their lives by recognizing it, and in any case is at odds with *their* equal right to have the obedience of everyone else. Hobbes often suggests that the covenant is necessary only because a human sovereign needs the help of others to exercise his rights; God, whose kingdom is "gotten by violence," needs none. Then the interesting question is whether the victor in battle has a right to my obedience or not. It looks as though he has because I cannot resist, and the victor has that right – that is, to my obedience – in the state of nature. On the other hand, Hobbes insists that I am only under an obligation once I have submitted; that is, I have agreed to obey. This introduces an asymmetry between the right to command and the obligation to obey. The one view of obligation I think we may reject is John Plamenatz's in *Man and Society*, according to which "I am obliged" means "I had better." It is clear this does not make sense of obligations stemming from covenant.

53 *Lev.* 484; Hampton, *Hobbes and the Social Contract Tradition*, in arguing for a noncontractual interpretation of Hobbes, insists that all agreements must be upon terms, therefore cannot confer absolute power;
   Locke argues against the suggestion that we might contract into servi-
   tude in *Second Treatise*, § 8 on that basis.
54 *Lev.* 18, 121–9.
55 Ibid., 101; cf fn 52 above.
56 Ibid., 141; cf fn 53 above.
57 Ibid., 142.
58 Ibid., 231.
59 Ibid., 216.
60 Ibid., 127.
61 Ibid., 231.
62 *An Historical Discourse and Narration Concerning Heresy*; Richard
   Tuck, in "Hobbes and Locke on Toleration," points out that Hobbes and
   Locke were in fact of one mind on toleration in the 1670s. Locke later
   hardened his position on toleration, not in the sense of becoming more
   or less tolerant, but in the sense of refusing to accept toleration as a
   concession from the monarch.
63 *Lev.* 479.
64 Ibid., p. 239; the portrait of Hobbes as the great proto-theorist of market
   society in C. B. Macpherson, *The Political Theory of Possessive Individualism*, is wonderfully imaginative but entirely implausible.
65 *Lev.* 149.
66 Ibid., p. 91; cf p. 145.
67 Marginal note to *Leviathan*, p. 152.
68 *Lev.* 226; Hobbes was certain that the only role of parliament was to give
   advice to the sovereign, and many times said that it was no accident that
   people called their king a sovereign but did not so call parliament – not
   entirely fairly to the usage of "King-in-Parliament." Deborah Baumgold,
   in *Hobbes's Political Theory*, argues a delicate case for the implicit
   constitutionalism of Hobbes's theory.
69 *Lev.* 232.
70 Ibid., p. 214.
71 One interesting place where Hobbes's argument was indeed simply re-
   invented three hundred years later was the 1950s attempt to deal with the
   issue of unjust "punishment" by the definitional manoeuvre of pointing
   out that only a penalty inflicted on the guilty for a crime could *count* as
   "punishment." Here, Hobbes's Chapter 28 surely is three hundred years
   ahead of its time, whatever one thinks of the quality of the argument itself.
72 "Review and Conclusion," *L*, 484–5.

10   Lofty science and local politics

Hobbes claimed that his political theory was a rigorously philosophical, that is, scientific, system. "[C]ivil philosophy," he said, is "no older than my own book *De cive*" (*EW*1,ix). Dedicating that work to the third earl of Devonshire, he argued that recent progress in science was largely the work of students of geometry, who had reasoned correctly from first principles. Moral philosophers, by contrast, had failed to adopt an adequate method, instead contenting themselves with winning the approval of their audiences by rhetorical devices designed to appeal to the emotions. He himself, however, had succeeded in grounding moral and political thinking upon firm foundations. He had begun his investigations, he said, by examining the nature of justice. Justice meant giving every man his own, and that raised the question of how things became one man's rather than another's. The answer, he concluded, was that nature taught people to shun the horrors that resulted from community of goods, and by consent to introduce private property. Through this analysis, Hobbes came to recognize two "most certain postulates of human nature" (*duo certissima naturae humanae postulata*). The first was that through natural cupidity people desire to appropriate for themselves what all hold in common. The second was that reason induces them to avoid the greatest of natural evils, which is death. From these two principles, said Hobbes, "I seem to have proved to myself by a most evident connexion' [*evidentissima connexione videor mihi demonstrasse*] the elements of moral and political duty (*De Cive*, epistle dedicatory, sections 5–10).[1]

Of course, Hobbes's critics – and there were many – did not accept that he had arrived at a true demonstrative science of politics, as he maintained in *De Cive* and elsewhere. "His aime to demonstrate the

246

nature of man and of human actions as distinctly as the mathematicians have done that of quantity in geometricall figures," said Bishop Brian Duppa of Salisbury in 1651, "is the highest reach of mans witt." Duppa went on to observe (quite correctly) that divines and lawyers would be sure to attack Hobbes's system, and he himself found much to criticize in it.[2] John Eachard (later vice-chancellor of Cambridge University) declared in 1672 that despite Hobbes's boasts, his account of human nature was based on no new fundamentals, but on premises readily available from standard textbooks, "besides some small matter that was shirk'd up in France from some of *Cartes*'s acquaintance, and spoyled in the telling." Nor, said Eachard, did Hobbes's pretense that his philosophy was a coherent, watertight system bear scrutiny, for his books were in fact "tailed together by far fetched contrivances."[3] Few modern scholars accept Hobbes's claim that his conclusions flow inexorably from self-evident or readily acceptable premises. Frequently, commentators are happy to discard some of his main conclusions altogether – such as abandoning his contentions that peace may be secured only through absolute sovereignty, and that the sovereign should exercise total control over religion, education, and the dissemination of information. Admitting that Hobbes's system does not work as it stands, they pay little attention to the results that he reached, and instead reconstruct his theory in order to elicit more satisfactory conclusions.

The purpose of this chapter is not to offer another re-writing of *Leviathan*, but to examine some of the things Hobbes in fact said, and to advance historical explanations of why he said them. We shall see that Hobbes's theory, despite its veneer of scientific detachment and its pretensions to universal validity, was constructed to support conclusions that were of the highest relevance to contemporary political circumstances in England. Commenting on *De Cive* in 1643, Descartes remarked that its author's whole aim was to write in favor of monarchy. Grotius likewise took the work to be a defense of the royalist cause.[4] Hobbes was indeed a royalist, and in what follows we shall first examine the relationship between his ideas and those of other English royalists – and anti-royalists. Then we shall turn to an analysis of some of the doctrines expressed in *The Elements of Law* and in *De Cive*, showing that two major points of what Hobbes had to say were to rebut principles commonplace among Charles I's parliamentarian opponents, and to argue for an absolutism more thoroughgoing than most royalists were willing to support. Before and after the beginning of the Civil War, Charles I's adherents included both moderates (who wanted the king to rule as a constitutional monarch) and authoritarians (who wanted him to assert his powers without compromise). Hobbes belonged to the latter group. Finally, we shall turn to *Leviathan* and address the question of what light is cast upon the differences between it and Hobbes's earlier writings by events of the years between 1642 and 1651.

I. HOBBES AND POLITICAL DEBATE BEFORE THE ENGLISH CIVIL WAR

From 1608 on, Hobbes was closely connected with the aristocratic Cavendish family, acting as tutor and secretary in the household of the earls of Devonshire. His translation of Thucydides, first published in 1629, was dedicated to the recently deceased second earl. During the 1630s he participated in the intellectual life of the men of science who gathered at Welbeck Abbey, the home of William Cavendish (a close relative of the earls of Devonshire, and himself earl, marquis, and finally duke of Newcastle). In 1634 Hobbes wrote to Newcastle from London, discussing Galileo's *Dialogue of the Two Chief World Systems* (which the earl had commissioned him to buy), reporting that there "is no newes at Court but of maskes," and thanking his lordship for "continuall favors."[5]

Newcastle had good reason for being interested in events at the royal court, for he hoped to be given office by the king. In 1638 his hope was fulfilled when he was appointed governor to the Prince of Wales.[6] The earl also became a Privy Councillor, and at the time of the Scottish rebellion against Charles I he offered to lend the king the very large sum of £10,000. This was at a meeting of the Council on December 5, 1639. At the same meeting Charles announced his intention of summoning an English parliament to assemble in the following April.[7] Not long afterward the earl of Devonshire unsuccessfully attempted to secure Hobbes's election to the parliament in question – later called the Short Parliament.[8] It met on April 13, 1640, but proved unwilling to finance the king's war against the Scots unless Charles granted large concessions to his subjects. On May 5 the Council advised the king to dissolve the parliament, and he did so at once. Four days later Hobbes penned the dedication to

Newcastle of *The Elements of Law*. He later implied that the book itself had been finished while the parliament was still sitting, asserting that "Of this treatise, though not printed, many gentlemen had copies, which occasioned much talk of the author; and had not his Majesty dissolved the parliament, it had brought him into danger of his life" (*EW* IV,414).

After dissolving the Short Parliament, Charles I found himself unable to raise sufficient funds to defeat the Scots. When a Scottish army entered England, he was forced to summon another parliament – the Long Parliament – which met on November 3, 1640. This body soon began to question people who had too vigorously asserted royal rights, and Hobbes now fled to France. In 1641 a plot was hatched to use military force on Charles's behalf against the parliament, and Newcastle was implicated. Under pressure, the king dismissed him from the office of governor to the Prince of Wales, but continued to show him marks of favor.[9] In January 1642, when civil war looked increasingly probable, Charles authorized Newcastle to take command of the important arsenal at Hull.[10] Not long afterward the earl went to the king at York, and spent a great deal of his vast fortune in raising troops for the royalist cause in northern England. The earl of Devonshire likewise joined Charles at York, and was consequently impeached by parliament and expelled from the House of Lords.[11] In November 1641 Hobbes had dedicated the manuscript of *De Cive* to the earl.

So Hobbes was closely connected to leading royalists on the eve of the Civil War. Newcastle, in particular, was well placed to influence the king's policies. Hobbes's letter dedicating *The Elements of Law* to him makes it clear that the philosopher was fully aware of this, for he declared that the "ambition . . . of this book [was] by your Lordship's countenance to insinuate itself with those whom the matter it containeth most nearly concerneth" (*EL* p. xvi) – in other words, the king and his closest advisers. Hobbes argued that students in the universities should be instructed in his own political principles, and that the seditious doctrines that were currently taught there should be rooted "out from the consciences of men" (*EL* Pt. II. ch. 9, 8; cf. *EL* p. xvi).

In the *Elements*, Hobbes singled out six doctrines that he took to be particularly seditious (*EL* Pt. II ch. 8, 4–10; Pt. II: ch. 9, 8), and he repeated the list (with small additions) in *De Cive* (ch. 12, 1–8) and

Leviathan (ch. 29, 223/168–226/171). He took pains to point out that his own theory refuted all of these false principles. The six doctrines were (1) that the individual should not carry out the commands of the sovereign if they conflicted with the dictates of his conscience (*EL* Pt. II ch. 8, 4–5); (2) that sovereigns are bound by their own laws (*EL* Pt. II. ch. 8, 6; (3) that ' "the sovereign power may be divided' (*EL* Pt. II: ch. 8, 7); (4) that subjects hold rights of property "against the sovereign himself' " (*EL* Pt. II. ch. 8, 8); (5) that the people is a distinct body from him or them that have the sovereignty over them"; and (6) that "tyrannicide is lawful" (*EL* Pt. II ch. 8, 10). It has been said that there is "no trace of polemical purpose" in the *Elements*.[12] This is extremely dubious. For virtually all of the six seditious doctrines were regularly voiced by people who objected to royal policy in the years before civil war broke out in England. Patently, the *Elements* is an attack on the thinking of those who opposed the king's actions in the 1630s.

Rights of conscience

Critics of the king's religious policies commonly argued that Charles – or his wicked bishops – had infringed the subjects' rights of conscience. Recent church government, said the Root and Branch Petition of 1640, had afflicted subjects "in their own consciences."[13] A year later, the Grand Remonstrance affirmed the desire of the House of Commons "to unburden the consciences of men of needless and superstitious ceremonies."[14] The influential puritan William Ames argued that the individual should not obey human commands unless he was persuaded in conscience that they were lawful: "It is not lawfull to doe any thing against a *Practicall* doubt; that is, a doubt whether the thing to bee done be lawfull."[15] In matters of worship, he said, Christ had freed the individual conscience from any duty to obey merely human commandments. Other puritans argued similarly.[16] The effect of such teaching was to impose large limitations upon the subject's duty of obedience to the sovereign – and upon the sovereign's powers. In 1627 the notorious royalist cleric Roger Maynwaring inveighed against "the Phanaticall, and Erronious Spirit" of those who reduced "all things, to the Dictates of a private Conscience."[17] A major reason why the Scots rebelled was that they believed that the religious policies of the king (or his evil advisers) had placed an intolerable burden upon their consciences.

The king and the law

The king's policies were criticized for infringing rights of conscience and also for breaking the law. Kings, it was often said, are bound by the laws of the land. An illegal royal order, declared Speaker Glanville in the Short Parliament, "will be void" and those who carry it out "will stand lyable and exposed to strict examinacion and Just Censures."[18] It was treason, said Sir Francis Seymour in the same assembly, to tell the king that "his prerogative is about all Lawes."[19] Similar reasoning underlay the attitude of many members of the House of Commons who in 1628 supported the Petition of Right, which set down a number of important respects in which the king's authority was limited in England. Royal power, said Christopher Sherland, was circumscribed by law: "I never knew the prerogative but as a part of the common law."[20] Other members remarked that "common law limits prerogative," and that in England royal power "is regular, and regulated by laws."[21] The Roman Catholic church (and not good Protestants), said Sir Dudley Digges, "makes kings above laws."[22] One of the offenses of which the absolutist cleric Roger Maynwaring was guilty, said Francis Rous, was asserting that the king had "power not bounded by human law."[23] Maynwaring had preached in favor of the Forced Loan of 1626–7, which Hobbes had helped to collect. (Hobbes later said that the clergyman had preached his own doctrine.) Maynwaring's sermons led to his impeachment by parliament in 1628. The declaration of the Commons against him included the charge that he had attempted to persuade the king that "his Majesty is not bound to keep and observe the good laws and customs of this realm."[24]

The divisibility of sovereignty

Closely connected with the notion that English kings are bound by the laws of the land were two further principles, both of which were also frequently expressed in parliament. One was that sovereign power does not reside in the king alone. The fifteenth-century lawyer Sir John Fortescue had described the king of England's power as "not only royall, but also politique," specifying that this meant the monarch could "neither change Lawes without the consent of his subiects" nor tax them "against their wills."[25] Members of the Commons frequently appealed to Fortescue's theory early in the seventeenth century. Drawing on Fortescue in the 1628 parliament, Sir Robert Phelips remarked that England was a limited monarchy in which "the King can neither raise taxes nor make laws but by the parliament."[26] Sovereignty, then, lay not in the king alone, but was divided between him and the two houses of parliament. To grant that the king alone held sovereign power, said Edward Alford, would be to acknowledge that he had "a regal as well as a legal power," and he invited his fellow members of the Commons to "give that to the King that the law gives him, and no more."[27] If parliament admitted that Charles I possessed sovereign power, affirmed the great lawyer Sir Edward Coke (against whose ideas Hobbes had much to say in *Leviathan* and in the *Dialogue between a Philosopher and a Student of the Common Laws of England*), it would in effect grant him power above all the laws of the land, including that bastion of the subjects' liberties, Magna Carta. Others said much the same thing.[28]

Property

Another principle that members of the Commons frequently enunciated in the early Stuart period – and which was also closely linked to the idea that kings are bound by the law of the land – was that subjects hold rights of property not only against each other but also against the king. It was often claimed that by the fundamental laws of England, including Magna Carta, the king could not tax without consent. Magna Carta and other statutes, said the Petition of Right of 1628, guaranteed subjects "this freedom, that they should not be compelled to contribute to any tax . . . not set by common consent in Parliament."[29] Although he agreed to the petition, Charles I raised a number of extra-parliamentary levies during the 1630s, of which the most famous and the most hated was Ship Money. In the Short Parliament, the king proposed to withdraw Ship Money in return for a large parliamentary grant with which to fight the Scots. A number of members of the Commons had doubts about the prudence of acceding to this proposal. As long as the king retained the power to take property without consent, said one, it was pointless for subjects to vote him taxes, since (lacking property) they had nothing to give him.[30] Lucius Cary, Viscount Falkland, who became a leading royalist in the Civil War, adopted much the same position. So, too, did John Pym, who was to become a leading parliamentarian.[31] In the event, Charles dissolved the parliament without receiving any taxes from it.

The distinction between king and people

Some held that the king's duty to tax only with consent arose from a covenant between him and the people – a covenant that was recapitulated in the royal coronation oath. "[O]ur Gracious Soveraigne,' said the leading puritan Henry Burton in 1636, "hath entered into Solemne and sacred Covenant with all his people, to . . . maintaine all their just Rights and Liberties, and . . . to demaund of them no other obedience, but what the good lawes of the Kingdome prescribe, and require."[32] "[T]he King and his people make one politicke body," he declared, and drew the conclusion that no one could be for the king who was not also "for his Lawes, and his peoples rights & liberties."[33] In 1641 John Pym similarly claimed that "A King and his People make one Body," using this proposition to argue that those who infringed the people's rights were guilty of undermining the commonwealth.[34] "His Majesty, at his Coronation," said the leading parliamentarian Oliver St. John, "is bound by his oath to execute Justice to his people, according to his Lawes."[35]

Tyrannicide

Burton affirmed in 1640 that the Scots who had taken up arms against Charles I were not rebels, for they had only been trying "to defend their ancient Rights and Liberties' " "which both Prince and People are bound by mutuall Covenant, and Sacred Oath to maintaine."[36] The Scottish Covenanters themselves justified active resistance to royal policy in defense of religion and liberties.[37] Writing against Burton in 1637, the outspoken absolutist Peter Heylin argued that the Puritan faction allowed the deposition of kings, and he cited works by the Calvinists George Buchanan and David Paraeus. Paraeus's commentary on Romans XIII was condemned and burnt at London, Oxford, and Cambridge in 1622.[38] The puritan William Prynne later lamented that the book had been "so solemnly burnt'. . . . with all the ignominie, and disgrace that might bee . . . 'for one meere point of State, against the Supremacy of Kings."[39] Earlier, the influential puritan Paul Baynes had roundly declared that in the case of kings who were "not absolute Monarches, it was never esteemed as absurd, to say that their people had power in some cases to depose them."[40] There is no evidence to suggest that he thought the king of England an absolute monarch. A deposed king was no king but a mere usurper, and it was commonly said that usurpers could licitly be killed by anyone.[41] In 1638 the puritan Jeremiah Burroughes argued that subjects may take up arms against a tyrannical sovereign who violates his coronation oath, and he used the notion to justify the Scottish rebellion against Charles I.[42]

*   *   *

Until the later 1640s few people in England explicitly advocated tyrannicide; it would have been very risky to do so. But the first five of Hobbes's six doctrines were widely endorsed, not least in the House of Commons. Indeed, after the Civil War began, not only parliamentarians but also a number of royalists maintained that England was a mixed or limited monarchy. The most famous argument, Charles I's Answer to the Nineteen Propositions, which was drawn up for the king by his advisers in 1642, admitted that the monarch's power was co-ordinate with that of the Lords and the Commons.[43] Between 1640 and 1642 Charles I gained support by conceding constitutional ground. Men like Edward Hyde and his close friend Lucius Cary, Viscount Falkland, were critics of royal policy at the beginning of the Long Parliament, but they sided with the king when they came to believe that not he but his opponents posed the greater threat to the traditional constitution and the established religion. Hobbes's theory was far removed from the outlook of these moderate royalists and was much closer to the attitudes of a number of absolutists who wrote before 1640.

Justifying the Scottish rebellion, the Scottish cleric Robert Baillie claimed that the king had been misled by a "wicked faction." They had encouraged him to pursue policies that undermined religion and liberties, and that forced his loyal subjects reluctantly to take up arms. The wicked faction, he said, had tried to lead Charles into tyranny by telling him that royal power is "absolute and illim-

itate," that the coronation oath is "no true covenant or paction . . .
betwixt the King and his subjects," and that "the prince alone is
the Law-giver." These were all, of course, principles that Hobbes
held. Baillie attributed them to the wicked faction in general and to
the English clergyman Peter Heylin and a number of Scottish writers in particular.[44] Heylin was a close associate of Charles I's leading minister, Archbishop William Laud, and a friend of Sir Robert
Filmer. In 1637 he argued that the powers of the monarch in England were not limited, that the laws of the land "were made by
the Kings authoritie," and that subjects owed "absolute obedience
unto Kings and Princes."[45]

   Similar opinions were expressed in sermons by the clerics William
Beale, Roger Maynwaring, and Robert Sibthorpe (and in manuscripts
of the laymen Filmer and Sir Francis Kynaston).[46] Kynaston had
scathing things to say against those who held that members of the
Commons discharged their office well if they opposed the king's
requests for taxes and defended "the Liberty of the Subject." Parliament, he asserted, had no authority to bargain with the king, because its powers were derived from and wholly subordinate to the
monarch's will. He inveighed against members who thought that
they did the state good service by giving speeches in favor of the
subject's liberty, and opposing the will of the king – whom God had
made "the immediate Instrument of the peoples harme or welfare."
"[T]oo much affection of popularity," he said, was "a vice condemn'd in all Subjects."[47] The sovereign, Hobbes similarly declared,
should "ordain severe punishments, for such as . . . affect popularity
and applause amongst the multitude" (EL Pt. II ch. 9, 7). Hobbes's
remarks on seditious authors of rebellion, who combined eloquence
with little wisdom (EL Pt. II ch. 8, 12–15), were plainly directed
against members of the Commons. Beale allegedly made some caustic comments about parliament in a sermon preached in 1635. As a
result, he was summoned to appear before the Commons in the
Short Parliament, but the parliament was dissolved before the date
appointed for his appearance.[48] Beale and Maynwaring were imprisoned by the parliamentarians during the Civil War. Heylin and
Sibthorpe succeeded in escaping to the king at Oxford; when parliament won the war they were deprived of their livings. Hobbes may
not have acted precipitately in fleeing to France when the Long
Parliament met.

Heylin, Maynwaring, and the rest derived much of their case from earlier absolutist writers such as Jean Bodin, William Barclay, and Marc' Antonio De Dominis. Hobbes rarely cited sources, but in *The Elements of Law* he drew on Bodin to confirm the crucial doctrine that sovereignty is indivisible (*EL* Pt. II ch. 8, 10). On many points Hobbes's conclusions coincided with those of other absolutists. But on two questions he adopted strikingly novel positions. First, he argued that subjects hold no rights of property against sovereigns.[49] Second, he claimed that the clergy have no authority whatever except as delegates of the sovereign.

Hobbes on property

Bodin stressed that the subject has rights of property that apply even against his sovereign, and most later absolutists agreed. The usual claim made in defense of Charles I's extra-parliamentary levies in the 1620s and 1630s was that the king can justly take his subjects' property without their consent only in cases of necessity – and the king is sole judge of what constitutes such cases. (This argument was used to justify the Forced Loan of 1626–7 and Ship Money in the later 1630s.) But many people in England did not believe that there was any genuine case of necessity in those years. Charles lost a great deal of political support by admitting that he should not tax without parliament except in times of necessity, and then announcing to his unconvinced subjects that such times then existed. Hobbes's theory vindicated the royal levies while avoiding talk about necessity, for he argued that it can never be unjust for sovereigns to take the lands and goods of their subjects, since subjects hold no rights of property against them.

A feature of Hobbes's theory that has perplexed a number of commentators is his talk about covenants. As Howard Warrender noted, some scholars have suggested that "the theory of covenant is largely superfluous to Hobbes's argument" [and that he] 'should have dispensed with it entirely." For in Hobbes's system, "the rights and duties of sovereign and subject" are deductions from the principles enjoining us to preserve ourselves and to seek peace. No fictional pact is required to establish these rights and duties.[50] Arguably,

Hobbes's system would indeed be better calculated to appeal to modern sensibilities if his discussion of covenants were omitted or revised. But from the perspective of early Stuart politics, Hobbes's analysis of covenanting was perhaps the most important part of his theory, because it allowed him to establish the crucial doctrine that the king can always justly take his subjects' possessions even without their consent.

It is sometimes said that in *The Elements of Law*, Hobbes recognized that individuals could possess property (or "propriety") in the state of nature, and that it was only in *De Cive* and especially in *Leviathan* that he definitely ruled out this possibility.[51] But even in the *Elements*, Hobbes insisted that where there was no sovereign power, "the right of men is not propriety to any thing, but a community." Property was possible only where there was a sovereign who used coercive power to ensure that people kept their covenants. It was the sovereign who defined what constituted a person's property; so no one holds rights of property against him: "Propriety therefore being derived from the sovereign power, is not to be pretended against the same," especially since it is only through the sovereign's efforts that individuals are secured in their rights of property against each other. Hobbes hammered home the practical implications of this position. "Those levies therefore which are made upon men's estates, by the sovereign authority, are no more but the price of that peace and defence which the sovereignty maintaineth for them" (*EL* Pt. II. ch. 5, 3).

Early in the seventeenth century it was commonly supposed that property had at first been instituted by contract or consent. Contracts were held to be binding regardless of whether there was a sovereign at hand to enforce them, so rights of property could be set up outside civil society. Hobbes argued that in a contract between two people who "are not compellable" – because they do not live under a sovereign – it would be irrational for either party to perform his part of the bargain first. By doing so he would "but betray himself . . . to the covetousness, or other passion of him with whom he contracteth. And therefore such covenants are of none effect" (*EL* Pt. 1 ch. 15, 10). But it is unclear that first performance of such covenants will always or even usually jeopardize the performer's chances in the struggle of all against all, which is the state of nature. By performing first you signal your trustworthiness to the other inhabitants of that state, and (Hobbes argued in *Leviathan*) to be trusted by them increases your prospects of survival (*Lev.* ch. 15, 102/73). On Hobbes's own account, then, there are reasons in favor of (as well as against) keeping covenants in the state of nature. His claim that outside civil society all covenants are void is not demonstrated. But it was a claim that permitted Hobbes to support the crucial conclusion that rights of property are possible only once a sovereign has been established, and therefore that no one holds such rights against the king.

Hobbes' anti-clericalism

Before 1640, a number of English thinkers vindicated the king's extra-parliamentary levies. Hobbes was one of them. Others included Kynaston and Filmer, two laymen who had little to say about church affairs. But many were clerics who supported the ecclesiastical policies of Laud during the 1630s. Laud and his adherents advocated *jure divino* episcopacy. In other words, they asserted that by God's decree bishops are distinct from and superior to other clerics, and that they draw certain powers (including the power of excommunication) from an immediate divine grant, and therefore not from the will of the sovereign. They admitted, indeed, that bishops are not infallible and that the powers they derive from God are not temporal, but spiritual. If a bishop excommunicated you, it did not necessarily mean that you would go to hell, because bishops could err and only God had the power to damn. Nevertheless, the theory meant that an individual who flouted the authority that his bishop held over him in religious matters would sin, unless the bishop's commands were directly contrary to the express words of Scripture.

People who argued in this way managed to reconcile their views on episcopacy with high notions of royal authority by claiming that bishops could *exercise* their spiritual powers in any commonwealth only with the permission of the sovereign. The powers themselves, they asserted, were derived from God alone. Hobbes rejected such claims. Already in *The Elements of Law* he denied that clerics possess any power independently of the sovereign. True, in that book and again in *De Cive*, there are a few gestures in the direction of *jure divino* episcopacy (e.g., *EL* Pt. II. ch. 7, 8, *De Cive* ch. 17, 24, 28). But in its broad contours, Hobbes's teaching on church–state relations in both works diverged sharply from the thinking of most royalists. The latter held that the Bible contains a clear message that all believers can understand, which tells them (among other things) about the powers of the clergy over them. Hobbes, by contrast, argued that the Bible, like any other text, needs to be interpreted. To grant the power of interpreting Holy Writ to anyone but the sovereign was to destroy the state, for if "kings should command one thing upon pain of death, and priests another upon pain of damnation, it would be impossible that peace and religion should stand together." "It is manifest therefore that they who have sovereign power, are immediately rulers of the church under Christ, and all others but subordinate unto them" (*EL* Pt. II ch. 7, 10). God, he concluded, nowadays spoke to man only through his vicegerents – that is to say, sovereigns (*EL* Pt. II ch. 7, 11; cf. *De Cive* ch. 17, 27). It followed that the sovereign's will defined what powers, if any, were granted to clerics by Scripture and, more generally, what, if anything, the Bible said. Such claims may have pleased the earl of Newcastle, who was reputedly lukewarm toward religion, and did not incline strongly toward any denomination.[52] But it is not surprising that Hobbes's views alienated zealots and clerics of all complexions.

III. THE CHANGED POLITICS OF *LEVIATHAN*

Hobbes and royalist politics during and after the Civil War

In the Civil War, most royalist writers toned down or abandoned the absolutist theories of Maynwaring, Heylin, and the rest. Certainly there were differences of opinion among them, and some undoubtedly still adhered to absolutist ideas. But most emphasized the king's moderation on constitutional questions and, in particular, his respect for his subject's property.[53] Many also stressed their loyalty to the Church of England as it had been established in 1559, and to church government by bishops. Like *The Elements* and *De Cive*, *Leviathan* was a broadly royalist work. But its outspoken absolutism and anticlericalism distinguished it from most contemporary royalist writing. In *Leviathan*, Hobbes did not attentuate his absolutism, but he did accentuate his criticisms of the clergy. He also parted company from most royalists by permiting the English to acknowledge as legitimate the usurping power of the Rump Parliament.

After the Restoration, Hobbes was forbidden to publish anything in England on politics or religion, and his enemies lobbied to inflict more severe punishment upon him. These enemies included the bishops and the Lord Chancellor, Edward Hyde, who became earl of Clarendon. As we have seen, Hyde held that the king was bound to abide by the law of the land. He also regarded episcopacy as the best form of church government and came to believe that it had been sanctioned by God.[54] Hyde had read a manuscript of Hobbes's *Elements*, and in 1647 he expressed his strong disapproval of the philosopher's political principles.[55]

In the opening months of the Long Parliament, Hyde had been a critic of royal policies. Later he sided with the king and became one of his leading advisers in the Civil War. Hyde counseled Charles to abide by customary constitutional arrangements, to uphold the established episcopal church, to grant no concessions that would undermine the monarchy's traditional powers, and not to intrigue to use foreign forces against his English enemies. Some other royalists, including Queen Henrietta Maria, took a rather different line, encouraging the king to do whatever was necessary in order to recover power, even if this involved using foreign military aid and abandoning episcopacy.

When Charles Prince of Wales arrived at Paris in 1646, Hobbes was commissioned to teach him mathematics. The man responsible for getting Hobbes this appointment was probably Henry Jermyn, the secretary and close associate of the queen.[56] There were other connexions between Hobbes and the queen's circle. One member of the group was Sir William Davenant. He took part with Jermyn, Henry Percy, and others in the so-called first army plot of 1641 – a scheme to use military force against the Long Parliament. (This was the plot in which Newcastle had been implicated).[57] Davenant served as a lieutenant-general under Newcastle in the Civil War, and in exile in Paris stayed at the Louvre with Jermyn and the queen, who later sent him on a mission to Virginia. Davenant's preface to his poem *Gondibert* is addressed to Hobbes and records that the philosopher allowed "this Poem a daily examination as it was writing."[58] *Gondibert* was published along with an essay on poetry by Hobbes, with prefatory verses by Edmund Waller and Abraham Cowley.

Hobbes also acted as tutor to Waller's son. Cowley was Jermyn's secretary and Hobbes' friend. In 1652 Sir Edward Nicholas reported to his close ally Hyde that Hobbes had "rendered all the Queen's court . . . atheists."[59]

Another of Hobbes's pupils in Paris was George Villiers, second duke of Buckingham, and a political opponent of Hyde. In 1650 Buckingham, Percy (the former army plotter and a leading member of the queen's group), and Newcastle were among the most important advocates of an alliance between Charles II and the Scots, by which the king would abandon episcopacy and agree to institute presbyterianism in return for Scottish military support to help him recover the English throne. Hyde and Nicholas strongly opposed the alliance. They regarded Percy "as an atheist because he favoured Hobbes" and because he advised the king to ally with anyone who would help him recover his crown.[60] Charles II indeed went to Scotland and officially adopted presbyterianism. (Hobbes later justified these actions on the grounds of necessity.)[61] The Scots raised armies for Charles who were defeated by Oliver Cromwell at Dunbar on September 3, 1650, and then finally at Worcester exactly a year later. *Leviathan* was published in the spring of 1651 and was largely completed before Dunbar.[62]

Charles II returned to Paris on 20/30 October 1651.[63] Shortly afterward, he summoned Hyde and Nicholas to join him. Thereafter Hyde became an increasingly important adviser of the king, and Buckingham, Percy, and Newcastle fell from royal favor.[64] Hobbes himself presented an expensive manuscript copy of *Leviathan* to Charles, but not long afterward he was told by the marquis of Ormonde – another of Hyde's allies – that he had been banned from the royal court, and he then returned to England. Hyde claimed that he had himself been instrumental in Hobbes's exclusion from court. Earlier, he had commented trenchantly on the subject of *Leviathan* in conversation with Newcastle's brother Sir Charles Cavendish. Hobbes, said Hyde, deserved to "be punish'd in the highest degree, and with the most severe penalties."[65]

Leviathan

In what follows, we shall see that some of the new material in *Leviathan* took issue with ideas dear to Hyde and his associates. In

Behemoth, dedicated to Henry Bennet, earl of Arlington, Hobbes once again attacked Hyde's principles. Bennet was a political enemy of Hyde. Along with Buckingham and others he became one of Charles II's leading advisers after Hyde's fall in 1667. Before 1651 and again after 1660, Hobbes enjoyed the patronage of royalist opponents of Hyde. When Hobbes's patrons fell from royal favor in 1651, he was unprotected against the attacks of Hyde and his allies, and returned to England.[66]

Of course, not all of the new material in *Leviathan* was targeted against Hyde. Some of it referred directly to events and debates of the 1640s and expressed attitudes common among royalists. Hobbes launched a trenchant assault on the notion (expressed by Henry Parker and other parliamentarian pamphleteers) that kings are superior to individual subjects, but inferior to the community as a whole (*singulis majores . . . Universis minores:* (*Lev.* ch. 18, 128/93)). He added a new law of nature to his earlier lists, declaring "*That every man is bound by Nature, as much as in him lieth, to protect in Warre, the Authority, by which he is himself protected in time of Peace*" (*Lev.* Review and Conclusion, 484/390). Hobbes highlighted the topical relevance of this law by noting that "the Times require to have it inculcated, and remembered" (ibid.). When these words were published, a royalist army was still in the field, and the law can be read as advocating adherence to the king's cause. Certainly it was sufficient to condemn those who had sided against the king at the beginning of the wars.

Discussing representative assemblies that are subordinate to a sovereign, Hobbes argued that in such bodies "it is sometimes not onely lawfull, but expedient, for a particular man to make open protestation [against the assembly's decrees] because otherwise they may . . . be responsible for crimes committed by other men" (*Lev.* ch. 22, 158/117). In November 1641 the future royalist Geoffrey Palmer requested in the House of Commons that a protest against the Grand Remonstrance be registered on behalf of himself and others. His request led to heated debate and very nearly to violence.[67] Hobbes's insistence that the sovereign alone have control of the militia (*Lev.* ch. 18, 126–7/92–3) alludes to the debate on this question, which preceded the outbreak of civil war in 1642. His principle that soldiers should not desert a defeated sovereign while he still has an army in the field (*Lev.* Review and Conclusion, 484–5/390) was highly relevant to the circumstances of early 1651, when Scots forces fighting for Charles II had been beaten at Dunbar, but the king had not yet suffered final defeat at Worcester.

In *De Cive* Hobbes added to his list of seditious doctrines the idea that holiness is attained not by study but by supernatural inspiration (*De Cive*, ch. 12, 6; cf. *Lev.* ch. 29, 223/169). From the beginning of the Civil War, preachers claimed that the Long Parliament was God's chosen instrument, raised up by the Lord to do His work. Later the same claim was made for the New Model army in its struggle with parliament. Providentialist and millenarian notions were central to the outlook of many who fought the king in the 1640s, and who supported the Rump and then Cromwell in the 1650s. In *Leviathan* Hobbes castigated people who bewitched their fellow-subjects into rebellion by slandering the established government and claiming special access to God's will (*Lev.* ch. 36, 299–300/232). The madness that arose "from an opinion of being inspired" did not always manifest itself in individuals "by any very extravagant action," he said, but when it affected a whole multitude it became apparent enough. Such a multitude, he declared, "will clamour, fight against, and destroy those, by whom all their life-time before, they have been protected, and secured from injury," and he compared "the Roaring of the Sea" with "the Seditious roaring of a troubled Nation." Individual members of the nation might seem sane enough, but the fact that they joined with the rest in claiming divine inspiration showed that they were mad (*Lev.* ch. 8, 54–5/36). In other words, the parliamentarians were literally insane to have taken up arms against Charles I.

In *Leviathan* Hobbes stressed that the subject's duty of obedience lapses if his sovereign fails to protect him (*Lev.* ch. 21, 153/114; ch. 27, 208/156; Review and Conclusion, 484–5/390, 491/395–6). This principle flowed naturally from doctrines expressed in *The Elements* and *De Cive* (*EL* Pt. II. ch. 2, 15; *De Cive* ch. 7, 18). But there were special reasons for emphasizing it in 1651. The republican government that had executed and succeeded Charles I was concerned about the loyalty of the population, because it was well aware that many people believed its actions had been illegal. So in 1650 it required adult males to take an Engagement promising allegiance to the new regime. A number of defenders of the Engagement argued that if a government is in fact protecting you, then you owe it obedience even though it may have acquired power by illegitimate means. This was precisely Hobbes's position, and his teaching on this point certainly annoyed some royalists, who saw it as a betrayal of the Stuarts. It is clear that Hobbes was fully alive to the practical implications of his teaching on protection and obedience. But it by no means follows that *Leviathan* is a defense of England's new republican governors. True, Hobbes argued that individuals who were under the republic's power could promise it allegiance. He also held, however, that the struggle for sovereignty in England was not as yet decided, and encouraged Charles II's soldiers to remain loyal to the king. He argued that royalists who submitted to the Rump would give it less assistance than those whose estates were confiscated for failing to submit (*Lev.* Review and Conclusion, 485/390). Moreover, he made it evident that parliament had acted wrongly in taking up arms against Charles I in 1642, and as we have seen he had some very acerbic things to say about ideas that were commonplace among the supporters of the new republic.

In *The Elements* and *De Cive*, Hobbes reached vigorously absolutist conclusions. He repeated these in *Leviathan* and went out of his way to make clear his disapproval of attitudes common among such moderate royalists as Hyde and his allies. First, he attacked their views on church government and especially on episcopacy (*Lev.* ch. 42, 374/297; Review and Conclusion, 479/384–5). Second, he condemned their constitutional theories. Hyde held that Charles I had erred in the years before 1640 by ruling unconstitutionally and by failing to consult parliament. He argued that any lasting settlement in England would have to be based on the constitutional reforms of 1641, which had dismantled the instruments of Charles's arbitrary government.[68] Hobbes, by contrast, claimed in *Leviathan* that belief in mixed monarchy had been a prime cause of the Civil War (*Lev.* ch. 18, 127/93), and listed "*Want of Absolute power*" as one of the things that weaken a commonwealth (*Lev.* ch. 29, 222/167). It was a ruler's duty, he affirmed, to ensure that his subjects were instructed "in the Essential Rights . . . of Soveraignty." If he failed to do so, it was his own fault, or that of "those whom he trusteth in the administration of the Common-wealth" (*Lev.* ch. 30, 233/177).

In *Behemoth* Hobbes made similar points. During the Civil War, he said, Charles I had been handicapped by his counsellors, who "thought the government of England was not an absolute, but a mixed monarchy" and who believed that if the king totally defeated parliament "his power would be what he pleased." The result was that they continually urged Charles to come to terms with parliament, which discouraged his best soldiers, who thought they would profit by victory but not by a treaty.[69] Although Hobbes said it was "not necessary to name any man," he made it clear which counsellors he had in mind, referring to men who "were in love with *mixarchy* which they used to praise by the name of mixed monarchy, though it were indeed nothing else but pure anarchy." These people "had declaimed against ship-money and other extraparliamentary taxes, as much as any; but when they saw the Parliament grow higher in their demands than they thought they would have done, went over to the King's party.[70] It is obvious that this referred to Hyde, Falkland, and their associates.

In part, then, *Leviathan* and *Behemoth* were intended as attacks upon the principles of Hyde's moderate royalism. Hobbes enjoyed the patronage of some of Hyde's political opponents among the royalists, including Newcastle and Percy. Can we see *Leviathan* as a piece of political propaganda aimed at furthering the policies of such men? While Hobbes was finishing *Leviathan*, Charles II was in Scotland where, on the advice of Hobbes's friends, he had accepted presbyterianism. *Leviathan* is manifestly *not* a defense of presbyterians, but a vigorous attack upon them. Like Roman Catholics, Hobbes said, they arrogated power to themselves by claiming that their church is God's kingdom: "The Authors therefore of this Darknesse in Religion, are the Romane, and the Presbyterian Clergy" (*Lev.* ch. 47, 476/382). Presbyterians, he declared, tried to usurp power over kings in states where they had established themselves, just as the pope did universally (*Lev.* ch. 44, 427/341). Of course, much of *Leviathan* was finished before Charles II went to Scotland. But Hobbes could have excised his more outspoken criticisms of presbyterianism before sending the book to the press. Indeed, as Richard Tuck has shown, Hobbes did tone down some of his remarks about the Independents (who were arch-enemies of the king's presbyterian allies) between completing the texts of the vellum manuscript and of the printed version.[71]

So *Leviathan* was plainly not written, or revised, to justify the king's presbyterian allies. We saw above that Hyde and his associates discouraged the king from making concessions on points of principle, and this was one reason why they opposed the alliance with the Scots (whose presbyterianism they, like Hobbes, strongly disliked). Large concessions were indeed the price of this alliance. In *Leviathan* Hobbes specifically warns that sovereigns should not grant away any of their powers, even to gain a kingdom. They might, he said, calculate that they could later recover power at pleasure, but this was faulty reasoning, for by first making and then retracting concessions they would encourage rebellion, and the rebels would be sure to benefit from foreign aid (*Lev.* ch. 29, 222/167–8). Once again, Hobbes's advice runs counter to the policy of alliance with the Scots. More generally, Charles's chances of recovering his English throne in 1650–1 rested upon royalists rising in his support. But *Leviathan*, although it castigates parliamentarian political thinking, emphatically does not tell royalists to risk their lives by rebelling against the Rump, because it counsels everyone to put self-preservation above all other considerations.

Leviathan, we may conclude, is a *critique* of the thinking of parliamentarians, and also of Hyde and his associates, who stressed the importance of episcopacy in the church and argued for mixed monarchy in the state. Hobbes blamed both groups for the Civil War and held that no lasting peace could be restored as long as men continued to hold their principles. His work is, in part, an attack on Hyde's brand of royalism, but it cannot readily be viewed as propaganda intended to justify the specific policies of Hyde's enemies.

Hobbes combined absolutist attitudes on state power with marked hostility toward the pretensions of the clergy. This was an odd combination in 1640, when many of those who took a high view of royal power were clerics who also argued for *jure divino* episcopacy. In some ways, the combination was less odd in 1651. Events in 1640–2 and 1645–6 strongly suggested that England's political elite was unwilling to adopt any church settlement – whether Laudian or presbyterian – that gave the clergy too great a power over the laity. The mass of England's wealthier classes, who alone were likely to buy and read a large and expensive volume such as *Leviathan*, feared that millenarian and providentialist attitudes and the pretense of divine inspiration on the part of their social inferiors would undermine their own position, and they looked to strong government to curb the nuisance. Hobbes held that the wars had taught people that the rights of sovereigns are indivisible: "there be few now (in *England*,) that do not see, that these Rights are inseparable" (*Lev.* ch. 18, 127/93). So there were grounds for supposing that whoever finally won the war, public opinion (duly shaped by reading *Leviathan*) would ensure that England was henceforth governed on Hobbesian principles. But Hobbes was aware that deeply held prejudices might prevent this from happening. If the book was "generally decryed," he advised Francis Godolphin (to whom he dedicated it), "you may be pleased to excuse your selfe, and say I am a man that love my own opinions, and think all true I say" (*Lev* dedication). *Leviathan* is packed with points that were of immediate practical relevance to the circumstances of 1651. But it is no mere party political manifesto, for Hobbes was too cross-grained and opinionated a thinker to agree wholeheartedly with any contemporary political grouping.

NOTES

1 I am very grateful to David Harris Sacks, Quentin Skinner, Tom Sorell, and Patricia Springborg for comments on an earlier draft of this chapter. My thinking on Hobbes and his historical context is much indebted to a number of important articles by Quentin Skinner (including "History and Ideology in the English Revolution" in *Historical Journal* 8[1965]:151–78; "The Context of Hobbes's Theory of Political Obligation"; and "Thomas Hobbes on the Proper Signification of Liberty" in *Transactions of the Royal Historical Society* 40[1990], 121–51). Also to Hans-Dieter Metzger, *Thomas Hobbes und die Englische Revolution 1640–1660*.

Dates below are Old Style unless otherwise indicated, but the year is taken to begin on January 1. Occasionally both Old and New Style dates are given; for example, 5/15 December 1651, refers to December 5, 1651, Old Style (the system of dating employed in England), which was December 15 New Style (the method of dating used in France and elsewhere on the Continent). Unless otherwise stated, London is the place of publication of books referred to in the notes. The following editions are employed in this chapter:

Thomas Hobbes, *De Cive: the Latin version*, ed. Howard Warrender, Oxford 1983. References are to chapter and section.

Thomas Hobbes, *The Elements of Law Natural and Politic*, ed. Ferdinand Tönnies, 1889; second edition, with a new introduction by M. M. Goldsmith, 1969. References are to part, chapter, and section.

Thomas Hobbes, *Leviathan*, ed. Richard Tuck, Cambridge Texts in the History of Political Thought, Cambridge 1991. References are to chapter, page number in Tuck's edition, and page number in the 1651 edition (recorded in Tuck's edition and in the commonly used Penguin edition of C. B. Macpherson, Harmondsworth 1968).

2 Sir Gyles Isham, Bart., ed., *The Correspondence of Bishop Brian Duppa and Sir Justinian Isham 1650–1660*, 34 (quotation); 41, 91–2, 135 (criticisms).

3 John Eachard, *Mr. Hobbes's State of Nature considered In a Dialogue between Philautus and Timothy*, 26, 34.

4 René Descartes, *Oeuvres*, ed. Charles Adam and Paul Tannery, vol. 4, 67; Hugo Grotius, *Epistolae, Quotquot reperiri potuerunt*, 951–2.

5 Hobbes to the earl of Newcastle, 26 January 1633/4, calendared in H.M.C. Thirteenth Report, Appendix, Part I: The Manuscripts of His Grace the Duke of Portland, preserved at Welbeck Abbey. Vol. II (1893), 124.

6 S. R. Gardiner, *History of England from the accession of James I to the outbreak of the Civil War, 1603–1642*, vol. 8, 243.

7 Gardiner, *History*, vol. 9, 76–7.

8 H.M.C. Twelfth Report, part two (Cowper), 251.

9 Gardiner, *History*, vol. 9,313. Conrad Russell, *The Fall of the British Monarchies 1637–1642*, 356.

10 Gardiner, *History*, vol. 10,152; Russell, *The Fall of the British Monarchies*, 457.

11 *Journals of the House of Commons*, 2,629, 631; *Journals of the House of Lords*, 5, 140, 141, 168, 210, 212, 219.

12 G. P. Gooch, *Political Thought in England from Bacon to Halifax*, 37.

13 S. R. Gardiner, ed., *The Constitutional Documents of the Puritan Revolution 1625–1660*, 137.

14 Ibid., 229.

15 William Ames, *Conscience with the Power and Cases Thereof*, first pagination, 18.

16 Ames, *A Fresh Suit against Human Ceremonies*, [Amsterdam] 1633, first pagination, 151; second pagination ('An Addition'), 35, 41, 60; cf., e.g., Robert Parker, *A scholasticall Discourse against Symbolizing with Antichrist in Ceremonies*, second pagination, 10; Henry Burton, *Englands Bondage*, passim, especially sig. B1b, C2a; *Lord Bishops, none of the Lords Bishops*, 1640, sig. D3a; William Bradshaw, *Twelve General Arguments, Proving that the Ceremonies Imposed upon the Ministers of our Gospel in England, by our Prelates, are unlawfull*, sig. A3a-b.

17 Roger Maynwaring, *Religion and Alegiance: in two sermons* (1627), second pagination, 50.

18 Esther Cope with the collaboration of Willson H. Coates, eds., *Proceedings of the Short Parliament of 1640*, 1977, 127; cf. Judith D. Maltby, ed.,

The Short Parliament (1640) Diary of Sir Thomas Aston, Camden fourth series, vol. 35, 1988, 1; and Glanville's similar remarks in 1628 in R. C. Johnson et al., eds., *Proceedings in Parliament 1628,* 6 vols. (New Haven, 1977–83), vol. 4, 393; and in 1629: Wallace Notestein and Frances Helen Relf, eds., *Commons Debates for 1629* (Minneapolis, 1921), 164, 230.

19 Cope, ed., *Proceedings of the Short Parliament,* 142; cf. 253, and Maltby, ed., *The Short Parliament (1640) Diary of Sir Thomas Aston,* 5.

20 Johnson et al., eds., *Proceedings in Parliament 1628,* vol. 3, 99.

21 Ibid., vol. 2, 484, 173.

22 Ibid., vol. 3, 405.

23 Ibid., vol. 3, 261.

24 Johann P. Sommerville, *Thomas Hobbes: Political Ideas in Historical Context,* 9–10 (Maynwaring, Hobbes, and the Forced Loan). Johnson et al., eds., *Proceedings in Parliament 1628,* vol. 4, 102 (Commons' declaration against Maynwaring).

25 Sir John Fortescue, *De laudibus legum Angliae,* ed. John Selden (1616), f.25b (*Principatu namque, nedum regali, sed & politico*), f. 26a (*nec leges ipse sine subditorum assensu mutare poterit, nec subiectum populum renitentem onerare impositionibus peregrinis*).

26 Johnson et al., eds., *Proceedings in Parliament 1628,* vol. 2, 109 (limited monarchy), 124 (laws and taxes).

27 Ibid., vol. 3, 494.

28 Ibid., vol. 3, 495; cf., e.g., 3, 531–2 (Browne), 565 (Glanville).

29 Gardiner, ed., *Constitutional Documents,* 67.

30 Cope, ed., *Proceedings of the Short Parliament of 1640,* 178.

31 Ibid., 191 (Falkland); 190 (Pym).

32 Henry Burton, *For God and the King,* 41–2.

33 Burton, *An Apology of an Appeale,* 28.

34 *Speeches and passages of this great and happy parliament,* 1641, 200.

35 Oliver St. John, *Mr S.-John's speech to the Lords in the vpper house of Parliament Ianuary 7. 1640. Concerning Ship-Money* (1640), sig. D2a.

36 Burton, *Lord Bishops none of the Lords Bishops,* sig. K4a.

37 *The intentions of the army of the Kingdome of Scotland, declared to their brethren of England* (Edinburgh, 1640), vol. 7, 10–11, 19; 'The answers of some brethren of the ministerie', in *Generall demands concerning the late covenant: propounded by the ministers and professors of divinitie in Aberdene, to some reverend brethren, who came thither to recommend the late covenant to them . . . Together with the answers of those reverend brethren to the said demands* (Edinburgh 1638), sig. C3b-4a.

38 Peter Heylin, *A briefe and moderate answer, to the seditious and scandalous challenges of Henry Burton* (1637), 156, 118.

39 William Prynne, *A briefe survay and censure of Mr Cozens his couzening deuotions* (1628), 98–9.

40 Paul Baynes, *The diocesans tryall* ([Amsterdam] 1621), 89.

41 For example: the Jesuit Francisco Suarez, *Defensio fidei Catholicae* VI, 4, 7, in *Opera omnia*, 28 vols. (Paris 1856–78), 677; the absolutist Marc' De Dominis, *De republica ecclesiastica pars secunda* (1620) 792 (VI, 10, 60); the Scottish presbyterian Samuel Rutherford, *Lex Rex, or the Law and the Prince* (1644) (Edinburgh, 1843), 33. The doctrine was, indeed, standard.

42 William Hunt, *The Puritan Moment: The Coming of Revolution in an English County*, 278.

43 Extracts printed in J. P. Kenyon, *The Stuart Constitution: Documents and Commentary*, 21–23. The document is discussed in Corinne Comstock Weston, "The Theory of Mixed Monarchy under Charles I and After" 426–33; Weston and Janelle Renfrew Greenberg, *Subjects and Sovereigns: The Grand Controversy over Legal Sovereignty in Stuart England* (Cambridge, 1981), 36–45; Michael Mendle, *Dangerous Positions: Mixed Government, the Estates of the Realm, and the Answer to the xix propositions*, especially 171–83.

44 Robert Baillie, *Ladensium [Greek: AUTOKATAKRISIS], The Canterburians Self-Conviction*, 3rd. ed. (1641), first pagination, 122–3.

45 Heylin, *Briefe and moderate answer*, 32, 156.

46 Sommerville, *Thomas Hobbes*, 9–10, 18.

47 Sir Francis Kynaston, "A true presentation of forepast parliaments," B. L. Lansdowne Manuscripts 213, ff. 146a–76b, at ff.162a, 167b (members, parliament and liberty), f.167a (instrument), f.166b (popularity).

48 Cope, ed., *Proceedings of the Short Parliament of 1640*, 185–6, 204–5; Maltby, ed., *The Short Parliament (1640) Diary of Sir Thomas Aston*, 112–16.

49 William Beale may have claimed that subjects have no rights of property against the king. According to one summary of his 1635 sermon, he argued that 'wee and, our person & our estates are his, wee have property in nothing': Maltby, ed., *The Short Parliament (1640) Diary of Sir Thomas Aston*, 112; cf. Cope, ed., *Proceedings of the Short Parliament of 1640*, 186.

50 Howard Warrender, *The Political Philosophy of Hobbes: his Theory of Obligation*, 242–3.

51 M. M. Goldsmith's introduction to *EL*, pp. xi–xiii, especially p.xiii: "In *The Elements of Law* men are expected to acquire property in the state of nature"; Hans-Dieter Metzger, *Thomas Hobbes und die Englische Revolution 1640–1660*, 39.

52 Gardiner, *History* 8:243–4; cf. 'The earl of Newcastle's letter of instruc-

tions to Prince Charles for his studies, conduct and behaviour', in Margaret, Duchess of Newcastle, *The Life of William Cavendish Duke of
Newcastle*, ed. C. H. Firth, [1907], 184–7, at 185.

53 A useful recent discussion of royalist political thought in the 1640s is in
John Sanderson, *'But the people's creatures': The philosophical basis of
the English Civil War*, especially 38–85. A clearly absolutist work is *The
Divine Right of Government* (1647) by Charles I's chaplain Michael
Hudson; Hudson grants the king the power to tax without consent (sig.
S3b-4a) and to make laws on all civil matters (sig. X1a-2b); he asserts
that God has delegated to kings "an absolute, and unlimited power, over
both our estates and persons" (sig. Z1b).

54 B. H. G. Wormald, *Clarendon: Politics, History, and Religion 1640–
1660*, 310–11 (episcopacy); see also Mendle, *Dangerous Positions*, 184–
6.

55 Martin Dzelzainis, "Edward Hyde and Thomas Hobbes's *Elements of
Law, Natural and Politic*, 303–17. Hyde to John Earles, 1/8 January 1647,
in Thomas Monkhouse, ed., *Clarendon State Papers*, 3 vols (Oxford
1767–86), vol. 2,329.

56 Sir Charles Cavendish to John Pell, Paris, December 7, 1646: 'Mr:
Hobbes his iourney to Montauban was staied, being imploied to reade
Mathematickes to oure Prince; My Lord Jerman did (I beleeve) doe him
that favoure & honor': Cornelis de Waard et al., eds., *Correspondance du
P. Marin Mersenne*, 17 vols. (Paris 1932–88), vol. 14,663.

57 Russell, *The Fall of the British Monarchies*, 292, 356. There are good
discussions of political groupings among the exiled royalists in David
Underdown, *Royalist Conspiracy in England 1649–1660* (New Haven,
1960), 10–12; Ronald Hutton, *Charles II King of England, Scotland, and
Ireland* (Oxford, 1989), 40–1.

58 Sir William Davenant, *Gondibert: An Heroick Poem* (1651), 1. The preface to Hobbes is dated from the Louvre, January 2, 1650 (New Style),
December 23, 1649, Old Style.

59 George F. Warner, ed., *The Nicholas Papers. Correspondence of Sir Edward Nicholas*, vol. 1, 284.

60 C. H. Firth, article on Henry Lord Percy of Alnwick in *Dictionary of
National Biography*.

61 Hobbes, *Behemoth or the Long Parliament*, ed. Ferdinand Tönnies
(1889), 165.

62 Richard Tuck in his edition of *Leviathan*, p.xi, argues that the bulk of the
book was completed before the battle of Dunbar, and this is certainly
correct (it is proved by Robert Payne to Gilbert Sheldon, May 13, 1650, in
'Illustrations of the state of the church during the Great Rebellion', in *The
Theologian and Ecclesiastic* 6(1848), 161–75, at 172). Tuck also suggests

that some passages, and in particular the Review and Conclusion – "with its explicit call for submission to the new regime" – were penned "in the political climate after Dunbar, when the war at last seemed to be over." This is plausible, but Metzger, *Thomas Hobbes und die Englische Revolution*, 153–7, argues that Hobbes continued to hope for a royalist victory after Dunbar, and observes that *Leviathan's* remarks on conquerors can be read as justifying obedience to a conquering Charles II.

63 O. Ogle, W.H. Bliss, and W. D. Macray, eds., *Calendar of the Clarendon State Papers*, 3 vols., Oxford 1869–76, 2:110.

64 Hutton, *Charles II*, 73.

65 Edward Hyde, earl of Clarendon, *A brief view and survey of the dangerous and pernicious errors to church and state in Mr. Hobbes's book, entitled Leviathan* (Oxford, 1676), 8–9, states that Hobbes presented to the king a copy of *Leviathan* "engrossed in *Vellam* in a marvellous fair hand," and that a few days before Hyde arrived there, Hobbes "was compell'd secretly to fly out of *Paris*, the Justice having endeavour'd to apprehend him." The manuscript is almost certainly B. L. Egerton MSS 1910: cf. Richard Tuck's remarks in his edition of *Leviathan*, p. xxxii. Hyde arrived in Paris on Christmas day (15/25 December) 1651 (Richard Ollard, *Clarendon and his friends*, 1987, 148). On 1/11 January 1652 Sir Edward Nicholas wrote to Hyde from The Hague, commenting on Hobbes's exclusion from court (Warner, ed., *The Nicholas Papers* vol. 1,284). On 8/18 January he wrote again reporting that some said that "Wat. Montagu and other Papists (to the shame of the true Protestants) were the chief cause that that grand atheist was sent away" and that it was also alleged that "the Marq. of Ormonde was very slow in signifying the K.'s command to Hobbes to forbear coming to court" (ibid., 285). On 12/22 February Nicholas informed Lord Hatton that "Mr. Hobbes is at London much caressed" (ibid., 286). Writing to Nicholas on 17/27 January 1652, Hyde asserted that he himself "had some hand" in the exclusion of Hobbes from court, that Ormonde had not been slow in telling Hobbes of the king's decision to ban him, and that Catholics were not responsible: Monkhouse, ed., *Clarendon State Papers*, vol. 3, 45. A letter from Ormonde to Nicholas of 5/15 December 1651 makes no mention of Hobbes (Warner, ed., *Nicholas Papers* vol 1,282–3), which may suggest but does not prove that Hobbes was excluded from court after that date.

We may tentatively infer from this evidence that Hobbes was excluded from court and left Paris a little before 15/25 December. Hyde shared in responsibility for this, but since he was not yet in Paris it is perhaps doubtful that he was solely or chiefly responsible. Hobbes arrived in England a few weeks after 15/25 December, making his way to London by early February 1652.

Hyde, *A brief view and survey*, 8, records his conversation with Sir Charles Cavendish.

66 That Hobbes's fall from royal favor resulted solely from Hyde's growing influence is difficult to show; Hobbes's views had already been criticized by royalist clergy (including Bramhall), and it is possible that even if Newcastle and the others had retained favor they would have been unable to save Hobbes once *Leviathan* had been published.

67 Gardiner, *History*, vol. 10, 77.

68 Wormald, *Clarendon*, 172–4.

69 Hobbes, *Behemoth*, 114–15; cf. 125, and also Hobbes's comments on the Oxford parliament at 131; this parliament was Hyde's brainchild: Wormald, *Clarendon*, 133–5.

70 Hobbes, *Behemoth*, 116–17.

71 Hobbes, *Lev.* ed. Tuck, p. xxxiv. Doubts about the extent to which it makes sense to see *Leviathan* as a defense of Independency are expressed in Sommerville, *Thomas Hobbes*, 26, 121.

11 Hobbes on law

Discussions of law occupy a prominent place in all three of Hobbes's principal works on political philosophy: *The Elements of Law, Natural and Politic,*[1] *De cive,*[2] and *Leviathan.*[3] He also wrote a *Dialogue between a Philosopher and a Student of the Common Laws of England.*[4] Remarks on law sometimes occur in other works by Hobbes. Discussions of law recur in his writings because law and legal theory are deeply involved in his moral and political philosophy through his conceptions of sovereignty and the state.

I. THE DEFINITION OF LAW

In *Leviathan* Hobbes defines law as a command "addressed to one formerly obliged to obey" the commander. A command addressed to someone not obligated is not law. Nor is advice or counsel law, since its recipient is not obligated to follow it. So, "CIVILL LAW, *is to every Subject, those Rules, which the Common-wealth hath Commanded him, by Word, Writing, or other sufficient Sign of the Will, to make use of, for the Distinction of Right and Wrong; that is to say, of what is contrary and what is not contrary to the Rule."*[5] A similar definition is given in the *Dialogue:* Law is the command of the person or persons having sovereign power, to the subjects, "declaring Publickly, and plainly what every of them may do and what they must forbear to do."[6]

Hobbes's definition of law clearly makes him a command theorist. Nevertheless, the commonwealth through its sovereign legislator does not simply issue direct orders – do this, do not do that – but rather what the subject is commanded are rules about property, right and wrong, just and unjust actions, and what is to be called good and evil.[7] Because Hobbes regards the sovereign's commands as being formulated not as prohibitions or mandates, but as rules that tell the subject what may be done as well as what must or must not be done, he does not face the problem, raised by H. L. A. Hart in relation to John Austin's legal philosophy, of having no place in his scheme for empowering laws.[8]

Hobbes is not only a command theorist but also a legal positivist. Legal positivism denies that general principles of justice, morality, or rationality (as such) are criteria of the validity of law. Crudely, it denies that laws need be just, right, moral, or good in order to be laws. Instead, law is distinguished by a procedural (or, in Ronald Dworkin's term, a pedigree) test: viz., it has been perceptibly signified as the legislator's command.[9] In *De cive*, both civil law, commanded by the sovereign, and natural law, commanded by God, are described as passing the test of having been commanded and promulgated by an authority to which the subject is already obligated.[10]

Although Hobbes's discussion provided some of the inspiration for John Austin's later version of legal positivism, Hobbes's theory varies in significant ways from that of Austin as well as from those of other legal positivists.

To begin with common ground, both Hobbes and Austin are command theorists. According to Austin, "laws are a species of command," and a command is an expression of desire backed by the power and the purpose to inflict an evil if the wish be not complied with. Laws are general commands of a superior to an inferior. In any society there is some supreme commander, a determinate person or aggregate of persons (a sovereign) who is habitually obeyed by the bulk of the society and who in turn habitually obeys no one.[11] Thus we have what Hart caricatured as a "gunman theory" of law: law is a command backed by a threat of a forceful infliction of some evil. The issuer of the command, the sovereign, is very like a gunman who demands obedience and threatens harm to those who disobey.[12]

Even though Hobbes, like Austin, requires that the sovereign be an identifiable person or organization of persons, Hobbes differs from Austin in several ways. For Austin, laws must refer to a general class of actions, not to particular or occasional actions. They are usually, although not necessarily, addressed to all, or to a class of, subjects, not to a specific individual or individuals.[13] Hobbes too regards law as normally addressed to an unspecified set of subjects and as general rules rather than specific orders. Yet, unlike Austin, Hobbes includes as law some types of particular commands as well as some commands addressed to particular subjects: law is for each subject those rules which the commonwealth has commanded be used to distinguish right from wrong actions. In that sense Hobbes seems even more of a command theorist than Austin.

Second, Hobbes differs from Austin in the role he ascribes to penalties. Whereas Austin makes the sanction or threat of penalty an essential characteristic of law, Hobbes does not.[14] Not that penalties are unimportant: enforcement is required for an effective system of law. (A system lacking enforcement would lack one of the two most significant characteristics of a commonwealth – a power to enforce obligations.) Nonetheless, Hobbes does not hold that the existence of a sanction is part of the meaning of a "law." In all of his discussions, Hobbes distinguishes between aspects of laws that guide subjects and those that set penalties; the former provide the existence of laws, and the latter their efficacy.

In *Leviathan* Hobbes distinguishes between distributive and penal laws. Distributive laws set out the (legal) "Rights of the Subjects," providing rules about property ("propriety in lands, or goods") and actions ("right or liberty of action"). "*Penal* [laws] are those, which declare, what Penalty shall be inflicted on those that violate the Law; and speak to the Ministers and Officers ordained for execution."[15] Nonetheless, the two types of laws are often combined, both in the general form of legislation and in the particular form of sentences in individual cases.

Hobbes had made a similar distinction in *De cive*. There he denied that these were two species of laws; instead they were two parts or aspects of the same law, providing the two functions or duties of the legislator: to judge, and to enforce the judgment. The first sets out the rules of property and of action; the second provides their enforcement. The first are prohibitory, addressed to all; the second are vindicative or mandatory and speak to public officials. But the first aspect of law is inadequate without the second; defining rights is insufficient unless others are effectively excluded from interfering with those rights or in hindering their holder in their use. Consequently, laws without penalties are in vain.[16]

In the *Elements of Law*, Hobbes distinguished between laws addressed to all ("simply laws") and those addressed to magistrates declaring penalties, such as "thou shalt not steal" as contrasted with "he that stealeth an ox, shall restore four-fold."[17]

The three accounts maintain a similar distinction between rules for guidance about property and action rights and rules that provide penalties and are primarily addressed to judges and officials. Before *Leviathan*, Hobbes's examples of laws addressed to particular subjects are confined to those addressed to officials. In *Leviathan* he also mentions judgments in cases that are law for the parties.

Unlike more recent writers,[18] Hobbes regards laws as providing guidance for *all* those subject to them. He even specifically discusses whether someone breaks a law when that person acts contrary to the law but willingly undergoes the prescribed penalty – as if the penalty were the price of a licence. Hobbes points out that there are two possible interpretations. The first takes the law to have two parts, a prohibition and a punishment; the other takes the law as conditional. While pointing out that it is not possible for humans to obligate themselves willingly to accept some penalties, such as death, Hobbes declares that the interpretation of which way a law is to be taken is to be left to the sovereign.[19]

Thus for Hobbes, laws are rules commanded and promulgated to subjects by an authority superior to them. Some (aspects) of these rules are directed primarily to officials, setting out penalties to be imposed on those who do not comply with them. The legislative, rule-making, and promulgating authority for civil law is the sovereign.

II. SOVEREIGNTY

According to Hobbes, only the state (or commonwealth) can make laws and "The Legislator in all Common-wealths, is only the Soveraign."[20] The state, like any artificial body, can act only through its representative – a human being or group of human beings. It is thus the sovereign who commands through a sign of his will what is to count as law.[21] Similarly, only the sovereign can annul or abrogate law, for that is done by a further law "that forbiddeth it to be put in execution." Again, the sovereign is "not Subject to the Civill Lawes." For, suppose the sovereign were subject to a law. Since the sovereign has the power to make and repeal laws, the sovereign can "when he pleaseth, free himselfe from that subjection, by repealing those Lawes that trouble him . . . and consequently he was free before." If one can free oneself, one is not bound, for no one can be bound to oneself. Thus, on this account, the sovereign is *"legibus solutus"* – not bound by the law.[22]

The contention that the sovereign is always free because he cannot ultimately be bound seems odd. The door is not unlocked before I unlock it. Similarly, the sovereign will be free at time$_2$ when he repeals the restrictive law at t_1; but he is not therefore free at t_1 or at t_0. Is the sovereign not required to follow a normal procedure of repealing a law containing a restriction? Or does Hobbes think that having to follow such a procedure is not really a restriction? What does follow is that a Hobbesian sovereign cannot be restricted by entrenched laws or constitutional restrictions, for those legal restrictions can be removed by the sovereign himself.

Hobbes operates with a conception of legal sovereignty involving two principles. First, laws and authorities have a hierarchical relationship such that the validity of any law or authority is derived from a superior law or authority – the principle of hierarchy. Second, the hierarchical system is closed by a final authority beyond which there is no appeal – the principle of closure.[23] For Kelsen this final authority is the "grundnorm" (whose validity is presupposed), and for Hart it is an ultimate rule of recognition (which is in fact accepted by some society); for Hobbes it is a human being or group, committee, or assembly of human beings.[24] That person or group is sovereign by virtue of a procedure of authorization by the subjects.

For Kelsen and Hart, as well as for Hobbes, this final authority is supreme in the sense that any other rule or authority within the system can be overruled or repealed or altered by it (or by the procedures it embodies), whereas it cannot be altered or overruled by any of them. There is no appeal beyond it. Thus for Hart,

a criterion of legal validity or source of law is supreme if rules identified by reference to it are still recognized as rules of the system, even if they conflict with rules recognized by reference to the other criteria, whereas rules identified by reference to the latter are not so recognized if they conflict with the rules as identified by reference to the supreme criterion.[25]

For Hobbes the sovereign is not only supreme but also unlimited. For an authority to be the highest authority in a system is one thing; for there to be no limits upon his (its) jurisdiction is another. Nonetheless, Hobbes's position is that the sovereign is unlimited as well as supreme. Hobbes seems to deploy three arguments to show that the sovereign is unlimited.

First, he attempts to derive unlimitedness from supremacy (the supremacy argument). Hobbes regarded the legislative power as supreme, and also contended that sovereign powers are unitary: the same person must possess supreme legislative, executive, and supreme judicial power.[26] (No authority can override or repeal the sovereign's enactments.) Thus no authority can declare a law beyond the sovereign's jurisdiction. So the sovereign's authority is unlimited.

Second is the authorization argument. A sovereign could be said to act unjustly or wrongly if he violated a covenant to the subjects. (A covenant or, in *De cive, pactus* is an undertaking to act, or not act, in some way in the future.)[27] But Hobbes contends that no covenants are made by a sovereign with the subjects. The subjects grant unlimited power to the sovereign, or at least the sovereign accepts no limits by any covenant or agreement with the subjects. There are two cases: sovereignty by institution and sovereignty by acquisition:

I. In sovereignty by institution, sovereignty is constituted by covenants among the subjects "when they assemble to make a common Representative." If the individual(s) becoming sovereign were to make covenants, those covenants would have to be made to the whole body as a single entity or severally to the contracting individuals. But the single entity comes into existence only by virtue of the contractual process; it does not exist before that process is complete. (And it is only a single entity by virtue of its single representative.) So a prior covenant to the whole body is impossible.

Covenants made to each contractor could no longer bind the sovereign after he (it) became sovereign, since then his (its) acts are the authorized acts of all the contractors. So the sovereign's supposed violation is authorized by the objecting contractor, and it is also authorized by all the other contractors. It follows that any such prior covenant to an individual is void.[28]

These covenants between the contractors contain no reservations. The subjects authorize the sovereign "simply." Hobbes speaks of the subjects transferring to the sovereign their power to decide how to act. Moreover, the natural individual(s) composing the sovereign retain(s) the natural liberty to do whatever is thought necessary for his/their (or even her) survival. Therefore, even if the sovereign had attempted to agree to limits to his (its) sovereignty, those limits would have no legitimacy.[29] If there were a dispute about the sovereign violating such a supposed restriction, the ultimate judge would be the sovereign.

2. In sovereignty by acquisition, each subdued subject promises obedience to the sovereign. Sovereignty is thus gained by covenants from those subjected to the sovereign authority. Although the sovereign is a party in each of these contractual relationships, he (it) is the recipient rather than the maker of covenants. His (its) part in the contract is to grant life to the subjected in return for the promise of obedience.[30]

So in neither mode of creating sovereignty has the sovereign made a covenant, a contractual undertaking to act or not to act in some way. In sovereignty by institution, such a covenant is impossible or void; in sovereignty by acquisition it does not happen, and if it did it would be void. Thus the sovereign cannot be said to act beyond some limit he has agreed to – he cannot be unjust.

Hobbes does not bother to argue that covenants subsequent to the institution of the sovereign do not bind the sovereign. Even so, Hobbesian arguments for that position seem obvious: if such a covenant were made to the whole body, it could be made only to its representative, the sovereign itself; if covenants were made to the individuals, those covenants would remain subject to the sovereign's overriding authority.[31]

The third argument for the unlimited power of the sovereign is a semantic one. An act is termed unjust if it violates a covenant or if it violates a law. The sovereign makes the rules that define what is to be called just or unjust, right or wrong. So the subjects have no independent criterion by which to declare actions of the sovereign wrong or unjust. The sovereign cannot be unjust.

None of these arguments is convincing. The supremacy argument depends on the logical impossibility of a superior authority to the highest authority. But it also relies on the notion that the absence of a limiting element or procedure is equivalent to the absence of a limit. Nevertheless, there are authorities who have the final say in various matters – like umpires in some games – whose authority is merely to give decisions according to the rules. The absence of appeal is not equivalent to the absence of a limiting standard. Hobbes seems to want to claim that contention about the right decision disrupts peace and so destroys society. If that is true, then having a standard without a procedure to enforce it is impractical and undesirable.

The authorization argument is countered by Jean Hampton. Hobbes's argument for an absolute sovereign who decides all questions (makes all decisions) is invalid. Not only does each individual retain a right of self-preservation, at least in the sense of liberty to defend life, body, and the means of life, but also the sovereign's effective authority depends on at least some subjects obeying the sovereign's commands to punish offenders. Deciding to obey such a command is consequently a decision made by subjects. Thus there are necessarily some decisions that the sovereign cannot make. It follows that the subjects cannot create a sovereign fulfilling Hobbes's specifications. The sovereign can at most be a nearly absolute authorized agent of the subjects. The subjects will continue to obey punishment orders only as long as those orders seem generally more beneficial than ceasing to obey them and thus depriving the sovereign of authority. Hampton contends that this allows substantive limits on the sovereign by express or implied contract.[32]

The impossibility of limits on an instituted sovereign also disappears if the position is thought of as a rule-constructed role. There seems to be no reason why one could not think of prior covenants as constitutional rules within which the sovereign has to act and which might be changed by constitutional procedures. (Would this mean that the sovereign was now the procedure rather than the individual holding the office of ruler?) Despite the claim that it is impossible, limited sovereignty does seem to be countenanced by Hobbes. He treats apparently limited or divided constitutions in several ways. First, the correct ultimate authority must be identified. Where a ruler is elected for a period of time, the electoral body rather than the ruler is sovereign. Similarly, where a ruler exercises limited power, the authority that enforces the limits is sovereign.[33] Second, it is possible to fail to constitute a sovereign. Some arrangements fail to constitute a sovereign. For example, a power divided between two authorities, whether spiritual and temporal or a monarch and an assembly, is self-destructive.[34] Yet Hobbes also recognizes that there are historical instances of limited and divided sovereignty. He admits that sovereigns have accepted limited power – sometimes in ignorance, sometimes hoping to recover full power. But the consequences are internal dissension, with resistance to the putative sovereign often being supported by foreign governments interested in weakening the state. Hobbes gives the examples of William the Conqueror separating the church from royal control and the subsequent support of Becket by the pope against Henry II; of William Rufus allowing too much power to the barons; of the joint sovereignty of the senate and people leading to Rome's civil wars; and the Athenian assembly's self-imposed prohibition on proposing the conquest of Salamis, which was circumvented by Solon pretending madness.[35]

As for the semantic argument, yes, the sovereign cannot be unjust, nor can a law be unjust, but this merely stipulates that this word not be used in this way. Hobbes himself admits that the sovereign can commit iniquity, just as a law may be iniquitous.[36] Law distinguishes what is just from what is unjust, and here Hobbes points out that St. Paul declared that without the law he did not know sin. Moreover, the sovereign cannot commit a wrong with enforceable penalties.

Hobbes is particularly concerned to insist that the sovereign holds the supreme position in the system of law: the sovereign is above, not beneath, the law. Hobbes explicitly attributes the latter doctrine to English common-law judges. While not denying that there is "judge-made" law, he argues that its authority derives from the sovereign, not from the judges. Like previous legislation and like customary law, law that results from decisions by courts remains law by virtue of the sovereign's failure to repeal or replace it. By allowing it to continue, the sovereign authorizes it. Hobbes's argument here relies on the sovereign's full legislative authority. Moreover, the sovereign is not restricted from changing laws previously enacted; if the sovereign were to act, he could repeal or change any existing law. Thus all law exists by the sovereign's authority, either by enactment or by non-repeal.

But if the sovereign acts by non-repeal, he acts by doing nothing and declaring nothing. It must be presumed that the sovereign's inaction is knowing and so authorizing silence. Such a knowing and authorizing silence hardly seems to be the promulgation "by Word, Writing, or other sufficient Sign of the Will" that Hobbes elsewhere requires.[37]

By allowing silence as a sign of the sovereign's authorizing will, Hobbes undermines his position in two ways. First, the test for what is law becomes not "what has been signified as law by the sovereign," but rather "either what has been signified as law by the sovereign or what has been used as law in the courts and has not been repealed." In effect that makes English law what the courts say it is, at least until the sovereign explicitly changes it. Second, it suggests a different conception of sovereignty. Instead of the sovereign being an identifiable individual or set of individuals – a committee or assembly – it becomes a constitutional office held by a succession of individuals. Continuity of law and of sovereignty is assured.[38] Then the enactments that count as laws according to the rules of the system, legislation by previous holders of the office of sovereign, and determinations of officials exercising appropriate delegated powers, all remain law until they are altered or repealed according to the rules of the system.

III. THE CHARACTERISTICS OF A LEGAL SYSTEM

Despite Hobbes's attempt to construct an absolutist theory, he conceives of the state as a *rechtstaat* operating by the rule of law rather than as a despotism. Hobbes's version of legality is evident from his exposition of what follows from his definition of law and from some of the things he says about its administration.

1. Laws provide standards of conduct for the members of a society by prohibiting certain kinds of actions, by permitting others, and by assigning property rights.
2. The system is meant to be univocal: the subordination of authorities and legislative supremacy tend toward the absence of conflicting guidance of equal authority.[39]
3. These standards apply to those capable of following such guidance. (Incapacity, insanity, and immaturity are excuses from legal responsibility.)[40]
4. Laws are explicitly promulgated by word, writing, or other act; their content is publicly available, and their authenticity is publicly verifiable.[41] Ignorance of the law is an excuse for non-compliance where the law cannot be easily discovered (and the action is not contrary to the law of nature); ignorance of the penalty is no excuse, nor is ignorance of the existing authority.[42]

5. Laws are prospective.[43]
6. Laws are to be administered congruently to their meaning.
7. Laws are to be interpreted impartially, consistently, and in accordance with the intention of the legislator. That intention is to be understood as always in conformity with equity.

Hobbes is particularly concerned with what he regarded as unreasonable and unjustifiable positions put forward by common-law writers and practitioners. The authoritative interpretation is always that of the sovereign, or of those authorized by the sovereign. Unreasonable and inequitable interpretations cannot provide a precedent for future cases or change the law. Judges (indeed the sovereign) are required to be impartial by the law of nature itself.[44] That requirement overrides the authority of a decision in a particular case being authoritative in further cases.

Nevertheless, Hobbes always reserves an ultimate power to the sovereign. While English kings (whom Hobbes takes to have been and to be sovereign rulers) may have granted by statute such liberties to their subjects as not to be taxed without parliamentary consent, they are "bound to make them good, so far as it may be done without sin." The sin here would be committed by the sovereign's interpreting those grants to have disabled himself (itself) from acting as might be necessary to perform the functions of providing internal peace and external defense. The powers to levy money and command armed force are essential to the maintenance of the state.[45] In the *Dialogue* the Philosopher even approves of such grants "as creating some kind of Difficulty" for kings obsessed with the glory of conquest, while at the same time holding that all such grants should be understood as having an implicit exception reserving regal (sovereign) powers.[46]

Although the sovereign is above the law, Hobbes clearly contemplates the sovereign acting (when not acting as legislator) within and according to law. He specifically mentions legal disputes concerning debt, rights to property, services and corporal or pecuniary penalties, between the sovereign and a subject proceeding according to the ordinary course of law. He distinguishes these cases from those where the sovereign demands not by virtue of a law, but of his power.[47]

But suppose a sovereign did command something utterly iniquitous. Suppose that the king is a tyrant, commanding the subject to commit some repugnant act. For example, "What if he should command me with my own hands to execute my father, in case he should be condemned to die by the law?" When this question is put in *Behemoth*, Hobbes has the other speaker respond by distinguishing between laws and other commands. Laws are made before their application to any particular person, and the king "commands the people in general never but by a precedent law, and as a politic, not a natural person." Moreover, there never has been an instance "of any King or tyrant so inhuman" to have made such a law, and surely there never will be. So the situation would never actually arise. Nonetheless, if such a command "were contrived into a general law," a subject would be obligated to obey it – avoiding the obligation only by leaving the country after the passing of such a law and before the father's judicial condemnation. Thus Hobbes does accept the implications of his own position.[48]

IV. NATURAL LAW AND CIVIL LAW

But despite Hobbes's emphasis on positive law, what he calls "the law of nature" plays an important part in his legal philosophy. He tells us that natural law is always binding, that where there are no promulgated civil laws, natural reason, or equity, is to be followed.[49] Indeed, he identifies law with reason, even agreeing that English common law is reason.[50]

Civil law and natural law, claims Hobbes, "contain each other, and are of equall extent,"[51] by which he seems to mean that the civil law is the authoritative exposition of the law of nature for any society. According to the *Dialogue*, it is a dictate of the law of reason that statute laws are necessary to the preservation of humans and that they are to be obeyed.[52] If one wishes to know what the law of nature requires, one first consults the laws of the society insofar as those laws are publicly promulgated. But there may be some natural law precepts that have not been enacted – rules that are implicit in the conditions for a peaceable, social order. These will be laws of nature and reason in any society. Civil law thus becomes an explicit and promulgated content for the law of nature. It is in that sense that civil law implies and depends on the laws of nature: the justification for the bindingness of civil law is the natural-law obligation to justice: the subject has covenanted to obey the sovereign.[53] Where there are no promulgated or implicit rules, the subject remains at liberty.

Nevertheless, the law of nature is said to provide some restrictions in addition to the positive law. Any restriction that is not a publicly promulgated law must be a law of nature or reason. These restrictions are of two types. First are principles that apply to all, summed up in the negative formulation of the Golden Rule. The precepts of the law of nature require that the rules applying to others apply also to one-self, that one should not seek special exemption or advantage at the expense of others. These seem to be the kind of principles that Hobbes believes that judges should follow in cases involving equity. Second are principles implicit in particular roles. For example, judges are to judge impartially; they are to follow the intention of the legislator in interpreting statutes; ambassadors and officials are to act for the sover-eign's interests where they have no written instructions.

Nonetheless, the laws of nature do not provide substantive grounds for judging that laws are unjust. Nor, even if they are iniqui-tous, does the law of nature provide a justification for disobedience. Hobbes does hold that subjects retain some elements of their natural liberty: for example, they cannot be obligated to kill, wound, or maim themselves, or to resist assault, or to abstain from the necessi-ties of life, or to kill another, or to confess to a crime without an assurance of pardon; and they may sometimes refuse to perform dangerous or dishonorable duties. But there is no implication that where the subject retains natural liberty, the sovereign lacks a right to command. On the contrary, Hobbes holds that the sovereign's commands (laws) generally encroach on liberty.[54]

Although Hobbes deploys the language of natural law, he denies the crucial implication of the usual and traditional substantive natural-law position, viz., that some positive laws are not truly laws and consequently impose no (moral) obligation. The most influen-tial medieval version of that position, combining elements from Cicero and Aristotle with others from the fathers of the church, was set out in the thirteenth century by Thomas Aquinas. He defined law as an ordinance of reason, for the common good, made by the community or the person who has command of the community, and promulgated.[55] Purported laws that lack one or more of these charac-teristics are not truly laws. They may fail by not being made by persons with appropriate authority, but they may also fail by being substantively unjust – either in not being directed to the common good or by imposing burdens inequitably or disproportionately.[56]

Instead of a law of reason that sets moral limits to what can be law, Hobbes provides a different type of law of nature. It prescribes that humans seek peace, where that is possible, and that they may otherwise exercise the right of nature. But effectively seeking peace rationally prescribes adopting certain types of conduct set out in Hobbes's law of nature. And it also prescribes a sovereign state and obedience to its laws. The law of nature forbids actions that disturb social peace and order; it forbids theft, murder, and adultery. But what counts as someone's property and so what taking is theft, which killings are forbidden, and what acts are adultery are all determined by civil law.[57] Thus it seems that (virtually) every civil order will be an instantiation of the requirements of the law of nature.

V. ENGLISH LAW

Hobbes's most extensive consideration of the law of England is in the *Dialogue*, although *Leviathan* contains a number of similar remarks, sometimes quoting the same passages for criticism. In fact, the *Dialogue* is less a survey and exposition of the law than it is an attempt to show how it should be understood on Hobbesian lines and an attack on English legal theorists, especially Edward Coke, who adopted a position that Hobbes regarded as theoretically wrong and politically pernicious.

The *Dialogue* takes the form of a set of discussions. According to the subtitle on the first page, the participants are a "Philosopher" and "a Student of the Common-Laws of *England*" – who is referred to in the body of the text as "Lawyer". These characteristics echo Christopher St. German's *Dialogues betwixt a Doctour of Divinitie and a Student in the Lawes of England*, usually known as *Doctor and Student*.[58] Neither work involves instructing a learner in the rudiments of the law. Both the Student and the Lawyer are treated as knowing the law and legal literature. Hobbes's Lawyer can authoritatively state what the law is, what is contained in the statutes, and what the legal definitions of various terms are; he can quote Sir Edward Coke's *Institutes* and other legal treatises. In other words, the Lawyer and the Student are students in the sense of one who has studied, and does study, the law – experts rather than beginners.

In his first dialogue, St. German sought to give an account of the grounds of English law in terms of scholastic legal theory. The Doctor explains the four types of law: eternal law – God's law for the created world embodied in it; natural law – the rational creature's participation in the eternal law, available through the use of reason; human law – mainly the positive law of particular states; and divine law – the revealed law guiding humans to eternal felicity. Here the Doctor refers principally to the writings of Jean Gerson, but clearly relies also on Aquinas, who in any case was Gerson's main source. The aim is show how English law is in accord with reason and, thus, natural law, which is often referred to in the work as the law of reason. *Doctor and Student* is thus concerned to show that English law is consonant with reason and so with equity, in the sense of legal procedure producing a just result and also in the sense of the development by the chancellors of a jurisdiction, with procedures and rules, by which they claimed to intervene in common-law cases to produce such a result.

It should be remembered that chancellors, being clerics, had a canon law background. Common law might be best characterized as a law primarily focused on real property, in which claims had to be subsumed under a formal writ that alleged some type of damage. The chancellors claimed the power to intervene where injustice would result from the standard application of a common-law rule. Considerable areas of what now would be regarded as private law lay outside the common law in the sixteenth and seventeenth centuries. For example, originally, contractual obligations were a chancery matter – a matter of conscience. Common law only recognized actions on a sealed instrument (a covenant). (Vestiges of this restriction remain in many common-law–based legal systems where land transactions involve greater formality than other types of contracts: they are valid only when the documents are signed, sealed, and delivered.) Yet for the chancellors, a contract involved a promise, a vow before God. It was thus a matter of faith, or as *Doctor and Student* puts it, "trouth." So the discussion is concerned with the extent to which the law ought to recognize less formal agreements.

Doctor and Student attempts to explain when the chancellor should enforce such agreements, explicating the notion that there should be some reason (*causa*) for the promise with the notion of "consideration," that is, that something of value was given in exchange for the promise (which was to become central to common law), or at least that the party attempting to get legal redress on the basis of the agreement should have relied upon that agreement to his detriment. The work thus attempts to reconcile English law with scholastic philosophy and canonistic legal thought. As Holdsworth says, "the English version of the first Dialogue put into an intelligible form the current learning of the canonists as to the nature and objects of law, and the different kinds of law and their respective functions."[59]

St. German's *Doctor and Student* provided Hobbes with a model.[60] First there is the obvious similarity in form: both are dialogues; both involve a lawyer in discussion with a learned layman. Both works aim at a theoretical account of English law; both works show how English law is based on reason and the law of nature. There is even considerable similarity between what St. German and Hobbes regard as required by the law of nature; *Doctor and Student*, while giving a normal scholastic account, points out that the aim of the law is the felicity of this life and emphasizes that it requires that we live in peace, keep agreements, and follow the Golden Rule in both its positive and negative versions. It forbids murder and slaying of the innocent, prescribes that we love benefactors, and allows us to use force to defend ourselves and our goods from force.[61]

The *Dialogue*'s philosopher replaces St. German's theologian, just as Hobbes's philosophy replaces scholastic thought and Hobbes's law of nature that of Gerson and Aquinas. There is even some similarity in another aspect of the two works: St. German, following a line of thought that can be traced to Marsilius of Padua, is concerned with vindicating the jurisdiction of English law and the powers of England's rulers in relation to the claims of Rome. The supremacy of the sovereign in both civil and ecclesiastical matters is a foregone conclusion for Hobbes, who is more concerned in the *Dialogue* to vindicate the powers of the sovereign king against the claims put forward on behalf of the courts and the lawyers.

While the Lawyer's main role in the *Dialogue* is to state and defend the legal, especially the common-law, point of view while the Philosopher expounds Hobbesian views about law and corrects legal errors, both participants agree on important elements of Hobbes's political philosophy. What the Lawyer refers to as the "irregular appetites" will, if unrestrained, master reason; thus, without the law provided by a sovereign state, "all things would be Common, and this Community a cause of Incroachment, Envy, Slaughter, and continual War of one upon another" – a state of nature. Peace within a nation, if not between nations, can be established when what is one's own and what is another's is publicly declared in laws. These laws must be "Laws living and Armed" – "not the word of the Law, but the Power of a Man that has the strength of a Nation, that makes the laws effectual." So what is needed is a sovereign individual or assembly to compel obedience to "reason" as it is embodied in law. The means that conquered a nation (it seems clear that Hobbes is referring to England) are the same means that ensure continued peace. The examples of Rome and Athens as well as England are used. Peace will be assured if the common people are made to see what the Philosopher (identifying himself as one of them) sees, viz., the benefit of adhering to the sovereign and the harm done by taking part with those who promise reformation or change of government.[62]

Thus the two participants agree on Hobbes's contention that a sovereign state is necessary.[63] Hobbes also has them agree on a suitably qualified version of his absolutism. When the Lawyer points out that statutes apparently restrict the powers of the sovereign, for example, to raise money without parliamentary consent and to send troops outside the kingdom, the Philosopher contends that all statutes restricting the powers of the monarch implicitly contain a reservation qualifying the restriction, viz., unless that action is necessary for the preservation of the kingdom.[64] Although the Philosopher agrees that kings ought to respect such restrictive clauses, he nevertheless insists, and the Lawyer agrees, that they are not enforceable.

An important part of Hobbes's aim in the *Dialogue* is to oppose what he took to be the conception of the basis of English law put forward by Sir Edward Coke. At the very beginning of the *Dialogue*, the Philosopher explains how he has read the statutes since Magna Carta, Littleton's book on tenures, and Coke's commentary on Littleton (that is, the first volume of Coke's *Institutes*). He claims to agree with Coke that reason is the soul of the law and that there is nothing in the law that is against reason – indeed, that "the Common Law itself is nothing but Reason." He accepts Coke's definition of equity, that it is right reason interpreting and amending the existing law.[65]

From this apparent agreement, Hobbes's Philosopher launches his attack on Coke in the *Dialogue*.

For Hobbes, written law and so statute law is primary. He can call English common law "reason" because he regards it as an unwritten law that he is prepared to assimilate to his own law of nature. Hobbes holds the view that some actions are by their nature crimes; he mentions treason, murder, robbery, and theft. Treason involves a rejection of the existing order of the state; it attacks the laws and the established authorities. The other crimes seem to be actions sufficiently antisocial so that any society will have to forbid them.[66] In that sense they are against reason and the law of nature.

Statute law is primary because it is the law that clearly emanates from the sovereign's legislative authority. The first thing that reason requires is that there should be statute laws and that they should be obeyed.

It is also a Dictate of the Law of Reason, that Statute Laws are a necessary means of the safety and well being of Man in the present World, and are to be obeyed by all Subjects, as the Law of Reason ought to be obeyed, both by King and Subjects, because it is the Law of God.[67]

So the first requirement of reason is that the rules to guide human action be formulated and promulgated. They are not to be left as vague principles to be worked out in particular circumstances. The legislative action of the sovereign is the embodiment of reason. In the *Dialogue*, the first inquiry about what a particular crime is, is whether it is set down in a statute. For Hobbes, legal reasoning begins with statutes; they are the definitions of legal science.[68] And those definitions are laid down by the sovereign legislator: "there is no reason in Earthly Creatures, but Humane Reason."[69]

Sir Edward Coke gave a rather different account of English law, based upon the primacy of the common law. Coke held that law was "an Artificiall perfection of Reason, gotten by long study, observation, and experience."[70] For Coke, legislation was merely a part of the law. Law's reason is artificial because law is an art, craft, or "mystery" – a highly skilled craft whose practitioners develop their expertise by working through – reasoning about – cases.[71] In working out the law for a case, there is a presumption that the common law does not run out. Judges do not make law anew; they try to find the legal solution for the case; there is no case which is completely new. The existing law is so copious that parallels or analogies can be discovered to any apparently new case. Indeed, Coke used his learning in the yearbooks and legal records both in his *Reports* and his *Institutes* to set out and comment upon what he took to be the law (the legal principles, values, maxims, and rules) embedded in previous decisions. In stating what he took to be the law, Coke profoundly influenced what the law was and what it was to be, although he surely would have rejected any suggestion that he was legislating.

Coke's conception of common law as being exhibited in previous cases and decisions, as existing "time out of mind," differs from the modern doctrine of precedent. On the modern doctrine, the judge is bound by precedent; the judge must follow the rule laid down in previous similar cases. This clearly holds in regard to following decisions of higher courts: on a strict doctrine of precedent, the decisions of the same court (or of courts of equal status) must also be followed. On this theory, the strongest cases in the line of precedent are the most recent ones. For Coke, the principles, values, and maxims of the law are exhibited throughout its history. Older cases, indeed the oldest available cases, testify to what the law is at least as well and usually better than more recent ones. Moreover, previous decisions testify to what the law already was when the decision was made.

Hobbes's view is quite different. When he discusses punishments in the *Dialogue,* he does allow that precedent should be followed. It is to be presumed that the custom of imposing a particular punishment is derived from a judgment of a former king, virtually equivalent to a legislative enactment. Moreover, "the most immediate, antecedent precedents" have the strongest authority; they have the most vigor, being fresh in people's minds and "tacitly confirmed (because not disapprov'd)" by the sovereign. (He explicitly objects to seeking out older customs that were used by the Saxons or the Normans.)[72]

For Coke, legislation does not provide the basic principles and values of the law; where it does not merely confirm what is already law, it may amend, alter, or add particular rules. A statute is seen as adding or altering particular elements while fitting into an existing body of law. Legislation does not provide a set of definitions and axioms; it is not primary to the system of law but merely supplementary and partial. Equally important are the activities of judges and courts. In the process of applying the lawyer's knowledge and art in deciding particular cases, judges and courts reveal what is implicit in the law. Thus the common law is both implicitly complete and explicitly the result of the reasonings and activities of many minds over a long period of time. On this account, it is at least conceivable that a statute might have to be "controlled" by the common law: some enactments might not be capable of being assimilated into the system which, because it was a product of reason working from time immemorial, would have come to embody the principles of reason (or natural law).

Coke's conception of law basically relies on a coherence theory. The rules, principles, and values of the law have been confirmed over a long period of time through many decisions. The lawyer's (or judge's) art involves extensive knowledge of particular cases. These cases reveal the way in which the various principles and values are harmonized into a system.[73] Over the course of time, inconsistencies will be weeded out. In fact, Coke provided a list of statutes that had been repealed, after they had been discovered to be inconvenient. They did not fit in with the system.[74]

From Hobbes's point of view, Coke's theory asserts the authority of judges, courts, and lawyers over that of the legislator. If "artificial" rather than legislative reason decides what the law is, then those claiming possession of that reason are claiming authority to make law (that is, to legislate). In effect, they claim what Hobbes attributes to the sovereign. Hobbes puts forward this objection to Coke's claims both in *Leviathan* and in the *Dialogue*.[75] Law is not what the judges think, but what the sovereign commands. Judges are bound to interpret a statute in accordance with its "meaning and sense" – the preamble, the time when the statute was enacted, and the "Incommodities" aimed at provide the bases of interpretation.[76] The function of the judges in interpreting statutes is not to make them fit into their conceptions of the law. Moreover, erroneous, unreasonable, or inequitable judgments are not precedents that bind courts in the future. Equity, in the common-law courts or in the Chancery, provides a means by which such erroneous judgments may be amended.[77] Ultimately, the king as sovereign controls the jurisdiction and the powers of the courts, rather than, as Coke suggests, the common-law courts that interpret the rights and jurisdiction of the various courts.

Sir Matthew Hale's *Reflections* criticize Hobbes by propounding a skeptical defense and revision of Coke's "artificial reason" as well as by moderating Hobbes's absolutism. First, it is a mistake to rely on general abstract reasoning in moral, political, and legal matters. Not only is all reasoning improved by continuous exercise in relation to a subject, but also moral and legal reasoning is more concerned with particular cases and special circumstances than some other types of more general reasoning. Agreement on general principles does not necessarily result in univocal judgments in particular cases. Consequently there is considerable diversity of judgment on such matters.[78]

Second, although no general rule will be without some inconveniences, having a certain and general rule is preferable to the uncertainties and arbitrariness that would follow from using natural reason anew on each case. Mere rationality cannot draw up general rules for all contingencies. When legislation is considered to remedy a mischief, the widest prospect of the situation is desirable. Nonetheless, while the more central and obvious situations and problems may be envisaged, there are always "other accidentall, Consequentiall or Collateral thinges that may Emerge uppon the Remedy propounded."[79]

Given the variety of circumstances that may occur, it is unwise to rely on speculative theories proposed by anyone or on the reasoning powers of any single human being. It is wiser to rely on accumulated experience – the collective rationality of rules and principles tested over long periods of time. The rationality of laws is not necessarily obvious to natural reason, nor are they always clearly related to a single, simple principle. Common lawyers are not infallible, but they do have the advantage of long study and inculcation in the principles of the law.

Hale's critique of Hobbes is more sophisticated and more developed than Coke's fragmentary remarks. It tends toward an explicit conventionalist notion of the law of any particular jurisdiction. The diversity of particular judgments as well as the variety of circumstances in which they are made suggest that universal principles of rightness (even if they exist) would be too remote to determine what was right or wrong in any actual legal system. It therefore suggests a Burkean perception of collective reason over time.[80]

Hobbes did not see in Coke's conception of the common law's artificial reason the conventionalist, historical alternative to his own conception of rationality that Hale discovered in it. He simply sees Coke as proposing common lawyers and common-law courts as sovereign. So, when Coke asserts that the common-law courts may prohibit the removal of cases to the Court of Chancery, or other courts within the realm, Hobbes takes him as attributing to those courts the position of the sovereign. All courts within the realm, no matter what rules of law they apply and no matter what procedures they employ, are the king's courts – their authority is derived from the sovereign. To attribute to the common-law courts the power to forbid removal of cases is both to misinterpret the historical basis of *praemunire* – it was intended to secure the position of the king's law against the claims of the papacy – and to usurp the sovereign's position as chief judicial authority.[81]

Hobbes is further concerned to criticize Coke's views about punishment. Hobbes regards punishments as conventional. There is no natural measure of the appropriate punishment. "For if the Law of Reason did determine Punishments, then for the same Offences there should be through all the World, and at all times the same Punishments." Since punishments should be certain and previously declared, they cannot be left to be decided by various individuals; they must be defined by authority, like trumps in card playing, and made known before the offence is committed.[82] Allowing judges to decide on punishments would be opting for uncertainty and diversity. Where no punishment is prescribed, the judge ought to consult the king before passing a sentence that irreparably damages the offender.[83]

Coke's definitions of various types of crimes, his account of treason, his explanation of the meaning of felony, and his distinctions among various types of homicide are all criticized by the Philosopher. He regards Coke's etymology of various terms as mistaken, his historical knowledge as deficient, and his distinctions as fanciful. For definitions one must look at the statutes, not at particular cases or the views expressed by judges, and especially not at the inferences from them drawn by Coke. Where there are no statutes, the Philosopher is sometimes prepared to provide what are claimed to be rational distinctions, as for example between different types of homicide.[84] The Philosopher is particularly scathing about some of Coke's claims about the common law, for example, that attempted arson is not a crime or that one cannot steal things growing on land, such as standing wheat or apples from a tree. He sneers at Coke's justification for the punishment of treason – Coke found a passage in the Bible for each part of the punishment inflicted. Hobbes is insistent that Coke is wrong about the law of heresy, which Hobbes regards as repealed. He is especially critical of Coke's opinion that accidental killing and killing in self-defense are crimes, arguing that they are not crimes by statute and cannot be crimes by the common law, an unwritten law, and so a law of reason.[85]

Perhaps Hobbes's strongest abhorrence for a common-law position is expressed in his discussions of Coke's assertion that there is an irrebuttable presumption in English law that someone who is accused of a felony and flees, but is subsequently tried and found not guilty, shall nonetheless forfeit all goods and chattels as a felon. Hobbes calls this abominable and unchristian. Not only does this punish the innocent, but it violates the general rule that presumptions are rebuttable – only statutes can make exceptions to general rules. Moreover, refusal to hear evidence is a refusal to do justice. Hobbes's objection is fully expressed in *Leviathan*, where it is clear that a written law might forbid accused persons fleeing justice and impose penalties on that act. His objection is that there is no such statute; it is not grounded upon a presumption of law, but of the judges. Such a judge-made rule, not in accordance with reason, can provide no valid precedent: it is no law.[86]

Hobbes's hostility to Coke and the common law is a direct result of his adherence to the primacy of legislation. From Hobbes's point of view, Coke's view attributes sovereignty to the judges. Hobbes's own conception of English law allowed him to draw a parallel between it and Roman law, in which each of the seven sorts of Civil Law has an English counterpart: edicts, decrees; and rescripts of the emperor, royal proclamations; decrees of the whole people (*leges*), acts of parliament; decrees of the people (*plebs*), orders of the Commons; decrees of the senate (*Senatus consulta*), acts of council; edicts of the praetors, decisions of the chief justices in court; opinions of jurists (*responsa prudentum*), reports of law cases that are binding for other judges; customs.[87] But all these are law because the sovereign authorizes them as such, the former authority of the people under the Roman republic having passed to the sovereign emperor, just as the king is sovereign in England.

VI. LEGAL TERMS IN HOBBES'S PHILOSOPHY

Just as legality is central to Hobbes's conception of the state, both in the sense that the sovereign establishes a legal system and acts mainly through law, so too certain legal terms are central to Hobbes's formulation of his political philosophy.

Unlike much previous and contemporary usage, Hobbes insists on a sharp distinction between law and right. Whereas others could use *ius* both for law and for (objective) right, Hobbes rejected this usage. For Hobbes, law imposes obligation and right indicates a liberty (the absence of obligation) or a charter or privilege granted by law.[88] So, *ius* for Hobbes must be distinguished from *lex* as obligation is distinct from liberty. Yet, although Hobbes generally emphasizes right as the absence of obligation and so as the contrary of law, he occasionally uses it in the sense of something authorized by law. For example in the *Dialogue*, he speaks of the liberties granted by the kings of England.[89] In *Leviathan* the penultimate paragraph of Chapter 26 sets out rights as liberties in the first sense, while the final paragraph explains the second, legal privilege or charter sense as an exemption from law.[90]

Hobbes's contractual language is even more peculiar. Roughly (and briefly), in English common law in the seventeenth century, a contract is an agreement that creates a debt, that is, it transfers a property right to the other party. That party may sue for that thing as a debt. In other words, the thing had been transferred, and its detention or withholding was a damage to the other party. A covenant, on the other hand, is a sealed instrument creating an obligation on the part of the covenanting party to act (or not to act) in some way in the future.

What Hobbes does is to systematize these terms in an idiosyncratic way. For him "all contract is mutuall transfer or exchange of right." The words of transfer must be of the present or past tense, not of the future. They may be accompanied or substituted by actions that signify the same intention to engage in giving or receiving a right. The transfer must be made "in consideration of some Right reciprocally transferred to himselfe; or for some good he hopeth for thereby." This may occur in several ways. Either party may deliver the thing itself with the right – "as in buying or selling with ready mony; or exchange of goods, or lands." Alternatively, one or both of the parties may covenant (or 'pact') to perform in the future. Hobbes thus turns contract into a general term for an agreement in which rights are exchanged.[91]

Hobbes is especially concerned with contracts in which individuals in a state of nature exchange mutual covenants to obey a sovereign that they are setting up. Within society, the person who is to perform first is clearly obligated to do so. But it seems that such covenants are void, or at least voidable, upon any reasonable suspicion that the other party (or parties) will not perform. Thus, sovereignty by institution seems a difficult, but perhaps not an impossible, way to set up a society.[92]

In sovereignty by acquisition, the sovereign accepts the covenants to obey of the conquered (or the mother the implicit covenant of the infant), but does not covenant in return. Instead of promising, the sovereign performs by providing a good to the subject – allowing the subject or the infant to live by preserving or not killing it.[93] Thus, Hobbes contends, the sovereign is not bound by contractual promises given in the course of setting up society, but the subjects are always so bound.

NOTES

1 Written in 1640; originally published as two separate tracts in 1650: *Humane Nature: or, the Fundamental Elements of Policie* and *De Corpore Politico, or the Elements of Law, Moral and Politick*, and so reproduced in further editions and in various editions of Hobbes's works until the work was edited from a number of surviving manuscripts by Ferdinand Tönnies in 1889. The principal discussion of law occurs in *Elements of Law*, Part II, chap. x (hereafter cited giving part, chapter and section: II, x, 5).

2 First edition 1642; revised second edition 1647; English translation 1651 as *Philosophical Rudiments Concerning Government and Society*. The main discussion of law in *De cive* is in Chapter xiv (hereafter cited giving chapter and section: xiv, 8).

3 First published 1651; Latin translation first published in *Opera Philosophica* in 1668. The main discussion of law is Chapter 26. *Leviathan* – hereafter *Lev.* – is cited with chapter and page number of the first English edition. (Page numbers of the first edition are given in the editions of C. B. Macpherson [Harmondsworth: Penguin, 1968], W. G. Pogson Smith [Oxford: Clarendon, 1909], and Richard Tuck [Cambridge: Cambridge University Press, 1991]. Tuck's edition also provides a concordance of page numbers with the editions of Molesworth, *English Works*, Volume III [London, 1839] and Michael Oakeshott [Oxford: Blackwell, 1946].)

4 Originally published posthumously in 1681 and issued (separately pagi-

nated) in *The Art of Rhetoric, with A Discourse of the Laws of England* (London: William Crooke, 1681) and in *Tracts of Thomas Hobbs* (London: William Crooke, 1681); in *English Works*, ed. Molesworth, Vol. VI; ed. Joseph Cropsey (Chicago: University of Chicago Press, 1971), cited as *Dialogue* with page numbers from the Cropsey edition.

The *Dialogue* was published posthumously by Hobbes's publisher, William Crooke. The preface to the original printing claims that the work had been finished "many years" (Macdonald and Hargreaves, *Hobbes*, p. 9). John Aubrey identifies the *Dialogue* with the "treatise *De Legibus*" which he had encouraged Hobbes to write, lending him a copy of Bacon's "Elements of the Law" to stimulate him (*Aub.*, I, 341). The contention that the *Dialogue* had been finished for some time is supported by a catalogue of Hobbes's works that Crooke printed in 1675 with Hobbes's poem, *De mirabilis pecci*. In the catalogue, Crooke claimed that Hobbes had delivered to him six works, the second of which is the *Dialogue*. The catalogue, along with the poem, also appears in a collection of works, otherwise already separately published, which Crooke called *A Supplement to Mr. Hobbes His Works* (1675). (See Macdonald and Hargreaves, *Hobbes*, items 13, 106, addendum to 9.)

However finished the *Dialogue* might have been, it has certainly not been corrected for publication. It ends, and perhaps even begins, fairly abruptly. Moreover, there are some repeated passages (e.g. on p. 55) as well as a number of speeches that seem to have been assigned to the wrong speaker.

5 *Lev.*, ch. 26, 137. See *De cive*, ch. vi, 9; xiv, 1; *EL*, Pt II, ch. x, 1.

6 *Dial.*, 71.

7 *De cive*, ch. vi, 9.

8 Hart, *Concept of Law*, pp. 26–48.

9 See *Lev.*, ch. 26, 141. For Dworkin's pedigree test, see "The model of rules I," p. 17. See below, section 4, for a discussion of Hobbes's conception of the relation of natural and positive law.

10 *De cive*, ch. xiv, 4, 13; also see ch. xiv, 19, where Hobbes insists that atheists do not commit the sin of injustice, but rather of imprudence: having denied God's existence, they violate no prior obligation to obey God and God's laws.

11 John Austin, *The Province of Jurisprudence Determined*, pp. 10–15, 193–5.

12 Hart, *Concept of Law*, pp. 6–7, 18–19.

13 Austin, pp. 18–24.

14 Ibid., pp. 15–18.

15 *Lev.*, ch. 26, 148. In *Dial.*, when the Lawyer suggests that there is a fault in the Philosopher's definition of law as command because some laws

prescribe penalties, the Philosopher responds that such a law is a command to the judge (p. 72).

16 *De cive*, ch. xiv, 6–8.

17 *EL*, Pt II, ch. x, 6. Hobbes used the same biblical example to illustrate the same distinction at *Dialogue*, p. 72.

18 Hart, *Concept of Law*, pp. 112–3; and Hans Kelsen, *General Theory*, pp. 29–49.

19 *De cive*, ch. xiv, 23. Note that the discussion is specifically directed against the distinction between active and passive obedience.

20 *Lev.*, ch. 26, 137.

21 See *Lev.*, ch. 18, 91: sovereignty includes the whole power of prescribing the rules about what actions the subjects may do and what goods they may enjoy, that is, property or propriety, the rules of *meum* and *tuum*, right and wrong, good and evil, just and unjust, lawful and unlawful. See M. M. Goldsmith, "Hobbes's 'Mortal' God.' "

22 See *Corpus iuris civilis* Digest I.4.iv: *princeps legibus solutus est*.

23 See Ivor Wilks, "A Note on Sovereignty," pp. 197–205.

24 Kelsen, *General Theory*, pp. 110–18; Hart, *Concept of Law*, pp. 102–3.

25 Hart, *Concept of Law*, p. 103.

26 *Lev.*, ch. 18, 91.

27 For further discussion of Hobbes's terminology, see section vi below. Note that the English version of *De cive* is inconsistent and misleading in its translation of Hobbes's terminology in this matter; see P. Milton, "Did Hobbes translate *De Cive*?," pp. 631–7.

28 Promises by papal candidates no longer bind after they become pope. Nevertheless, the contention that the contract of authorization overrides previous agreements is apparently contrary to the principle that an earlier covenant has precedence over a later one: *Lev.*, ch. 14, 69.

29 Nevertheless, Hobbes does mention the problem that individuals to obtain sovereignty have unwisely agreed to limits: *Lev.*, ch. 29, 167–8.

30 *Lev.*, ch. 18, 89; see also ch. 17, 87; ch. 18, 89–90.

31 Subsequent restriction of sovereign powers by royal grants, acts, or consents that vested rights in the subjects or institutions, thereby limiting the absolute powers of the king, were sometimes relied on by seventeenth-century English royalists to account for constitutional limitations on the monarch. See John Sanderson, *'But the People's Creatures'*, pp. 59–62 (citing esp. Bramhall and Ferne). The possibility of subsequent contractual restriction is also canvassed by Grotius, *Of the Laws of War and Peace*, Bk. I, ch. 3, 16.

32 Jean Hampton, *Hobbes and the Social Contract Tradition*, pp. 189–207, 220–39.

33 *Lev.*, ch 19, 98–9.

34 Ibid., ch. 29, 170, 171–3.
35 Ibid., ch. 29, pp. 167–8.
36 *Dial.*, 69–70; *Lev.*, ch. 30, 181–2.
37 *Lev.*, ch. 26, 137, 140; *De cive*, ch. xiv, 13.
38 See Hart's account of legal continuity in *Concept of Law*, pp. 50–60.
39 Ibid., ch. 26, 140.
40 Ibid., ch. 26, 140.
41 Ibid., ch. 26, 141–2.
42 Ibid., ch. 27, 152.
43 Ibid., ch. 27, 153. See also 51; *De cive*, ch. vi, 9 where civil laws are defined as directed at future actions of the citizens.
44 *Lev.*, ch. 13, 77. See also *B.*, 37, where one of Hobbes's interlocutors asks whether Ship Money was alleged to be illegal because it was against statute, against previous judgments, recorded in reports, or against equity (equivalent to the law of nature). The other speaker, responding, asserts that common-law judgments have force only by virtue of the king's authority: "Besides it were unreasonable that a corrupt or foolish judge's unjust sentence should by any time, how long soever, obtain the authority and force of a law."
45 *Dial.*, 59–61, 63–64. See *Lev.*, ch. 21, 113.
46 *Dial.*, 64, 71.
47 *Lev.*, ch. 21, 113.
48 *B.*, 51.
49 *De cive*, ch. xiv, 4, 14; see also *Lev.*, ch. 26, 138–41, 143.
50 *Dial.*, 55–6.
51 *Lev.*, ch. 26, 138. See *De cive*, ch. xiv, 10.
52 *Dial.*, 58.
53 *Lev.*, ch. 26, 138; *Dial.*, pp. 58–9: "It is also a Dictate of the Law of Reason, that Statute Laws are a necessary means of the safety and well being of Man in the present World, and are to be obeyed by all Subjects, as the Law of Reason ought to be obeyed, both by King and Subjects, because it is the Law of God."
54 *Lev.*, ch. 21, 111–2.
55 Thomas Aquinas, *Summa Theologiae* I–II, qu. 90, art. 4, p. 17. For a similar definition, see John Finnis, *Natural Law and Natural Rights* (Oxford: Clarendon Press, 1980), pp. 276–7: "law" refers to "rules made, in accordance with regulative legal rules, by a determinate and effective authority (itself identified, and, standardly, constituted as an institution by legal rules) for a complete community, and buttressed by sanctions in accordance with the rule-guided stipulations of adjudicative institutions, this ensemble of rules and institutions is directed to reasonably resolving any of the community's coordination problems (and to

ratifying, tolerating, regulating, or overriding coordination solutions from any other institutions or sources of norms) for the common good of that community, according to a manner and form itself adapted to that common good by features of specificity, minimization of arbitrariness, and maintenance of a quality of reciprocity between the subjects of the law both amongst themselves and in their relations with the lawful authorities."

56 Aquinas, *Summa Theologiae* I–II, qu. 95, art. 2, 4, pp. 58–60, 70–71.

57 *De cive*, ch. vi, 16.

58 The first dialogue of *Doctor and Student* appeared in Latin in 1523; two versions appeared in English in 1531 and 1531–2. The second dialogue (in English) was first published in 1530; a second version appeared in 1532. The English versions of the first dialogue were not direct translations of the Latin. Subsequent versions of the dialogues contained additions.

   Doctor and Student was a standard work on English law, frequently republished in the sixteenth and seventeenth centuries; there were editions in 1638, 1660, 1668, and 1673, as well as an abridged edition in 1658. It was certainly known to Hobbes, who cites it in *Dial.*, 86.

   As far as I know there is only one serious consideration of the relation between *Doctor and Student* and Hobbes's thought. Robinson A. Grover, "The Legal Origins of Thomas Hobbes's Doctrine of Contract," argues Hobbes knew and used *Doctor and Student* in formulating his natural law and contract theories in *The Elements of Law* as well as turning to it later when composing the *Dialogue*.

59 Holdsworth, *History of English Law*, vol. 5, p. 267.

60 See Grover, "Hobbes's Doctrine of Contract," p. 180. It is curious that Joseph Cropsey's "Introduction" to *Dial.* does not mention *Doctor and Student*.

61 *Doctor and Student*, pp. 13–19.

62 *Dial.*, 58–9, 61.

63 Ibid., 58.

64 Ibid., 60–1.

65 Ibid., 54.

66 See ibid., pp. 102–3, 111–2. Cp. Hart's account of the minimum content of natural law, *Concept of Law*, pp. 189–95.

67 *Dial.*, 58.

68 See ibid., 116.

69 Ibid., 55.

70 *Lev.*, ch. 26, pp. 139–40; *Dial.*, 54–5.

71 On Coke's views, see Charles Gray, "Reason, Authority, and Imagina-

tion: The Jurisprudence of Sir Edward Coke," pp. 25–66, and "Parliament, Liberty, and the Law," pp. 155–200. See also J. G. A. Pocock, *The Ancient Constitution and the Feudal Law,* pp. 35–70.

72 *Dial.,* 142.

73 As is suggested by Gray, "Reason, Authority, and Imagination," pp. 33–4, 42. For a contemporary coherence theory, see Ronald Dworkin, *Law's Empire,* pp. 176–254.

74 Gray, "Reason, Authority, and Imagination," pp. 41–2.

75 See *Lev.,* ch. 26, 139–40; *Dial.,* 55.

76 *Dial.,* 16–17.

77 Ibid., 79–101.

78 Hale, *Reflections,* pp. 500–3.

79 Hale, *Reflections,* pp. 503–4.

80 Both Holdsworth, *History of English Law,* vol. 5, p. 504 n, and Pocock, *The Ancient Constitution,* pp. 170–81, point to the Burkean parallel. See also Gray, "Reason, Authority, and Imagination," pp. 49 n9, 52 n17.

81 *Dial.,* 133–9.

82 Ibid., 140.

83 Ibid., 142.

84 Ibid., 112–5.

85 Ibid., 145–51.

86 *Lev.,* ch. 26, 144–5; *Dial.,* 150–1. It is sometimes mistakenly thought that legal positivists are precluded from criticizing existing law; the position requires only that the validity of legal rules be distinguished from their content. Hobbes makes the criterion of validity the sovereign's will and presumes that, where the sovereign has not legislated, the law must be in accordance with reason. He is therefore able to deny that unreasonable common law isn't actually law, but in any case he was not debarred from criticizing it as iniquitous or bad. For a contrary view, see Martin Kriele, "Hobbes and the English Jurists."

87 *Lev.,* ch. 26, 147.

88 Ibid., ch. 26, 150. The same distinction is made in *Dial.,* 73. See also *De cive,* xiv, 3; *EL,* Pt II, ch. x, 5, 186–7. Hobbes frequently uses and emphasizes right as the absence of law, but also occasionally uses the other meaning: the penultimate paragraph of Chapter 26 of *Leviathan* cited above states the first meaning, the final paragraph the second.

89 *Dial.,* 63. For a discussion of Hobbes and the development of natural rights theories, see Richard Tuck, *Natural Rights Theories;* see also M. M. Goldsmith, "Hobbes: Ancient and Modern," esp. pp. 326–30.

90 For a late use of the notion of a right as a privilege or charter, see the document published by Quentin Skinner in "Hobbes on Sovereignty."

91 *Lev.*, ch. 14, 65–70; *De cive*, ch. ii, 4–23; *EL*, II, xv, 3–18, pp. 75–81. See
    A. W. B. Simpson, *A History of the Common Law of Contract.* For a
    discussion of Hobbes's views, see P. Milton, "Did Hobbes Translate *De
    Cive*."

92 *Lev.*, ch. 18, 88.

93 Ibid., ch. 20, 101–5.

12 History in Hobbes's thought

Hobbes was very close to important figures in the history of politics and science as well as philosophy. His long life was marked by the disturbances that England underwent in the middle of the seventeenth century. The temptation is therefore strong to explain away as a mere consequence of the political upheavals of the 1640s his setting aside of the project of a complete philosophical system and his turning to a series of works of political philosophy. The main purpose of this essay will be to emphasize the inner consistency of Hobbes's philosophical and scientific system, to identify the place and function of history in his system, and only then to study his performance as historian.[1]

Instead of a description – that is, a history – of Hobbes's views on history, I will adopt three successive perspectives upon this subject. The first perspective is provided by the taxonomy of sciences in *Leviathan* and its theory of science. The functions and modes of history as defined in the early preface to the translation of Thucydides and in later historical works is the second perspective, with particular emphasis on the *Leviathan–Behemoth* diptych. The final part examines Hobbes's performance as a historian in the light of the criteria identified in the first two parts.

Hobbes produced texts on history throughout his career. From his introduction to Thucydides to the *Dialogue of the Common Laws of England*, *Behemoth*, or the *Historical Narration Concerning Heresy and the Punishment Thereof*, he kept in touch with history as a means of political education and as a literary genre. The shift from his first humanist concerns to his philosophical grand design has been studied and debated often, but the consequences for his conception and practice of history of this change of emphasis from history as a didactic and critical narrative to logic and geometry as the demonstrative framework of philosophy and science have been overlooked.[2]

Hobbes seems to have undergone an epistemological crisis on one of his journeys to the Continent with one of his Cavendish pupils about 1630. In a library, he saw a book of Euclid's *Elements* and started to read the demonstrations backward and forward, until he was convinced by the inner logic of the reasoning.[3] His previous work as Bacon's secretary and as tutor to the Cavendish heirs had oriented his enquiries in a typically humanist direction, with the publication in 1629 of his translation of Thucydides's *History of the Peloponnesian Wars* and his translation and epitomes of Aristotle's Rhetoric (1637). After the Long Parliament was called in England, Hobbes chose exile in France.

When the *Elements of Law* circulated in manuscript, after 1640, Hobbes was already known in scientific and philosophical circles as a follower of the New Science. His *Short Tract on First Principles* had been written in 1630–1, and between 1638 and 1642 Lord Edward Herbert of Cherbury had taken notes (*De Principiis*)[4] for what was to become *De Corpore*, the first part of the intended trilogy of the *Elements of Philosophy* that should have been followed by *De Homine* and *De Cive*. The inversion of the intended order of the trilogy has often been taken to show that Hobbes was primarily a political thinker who had conceived his philosophy of motion and his criticism of metaphysics as an afterthought. Recent scholarship in the history of science has cast doubt on that hypothesis. The *First Draught of the Optics* was completed in 1646, between the last two versions of the political philosophy, and Hobbes's answer to Davenant's dedication of *Gondibert* borrows terms and images from *De Principiis*, at the time of the conception of *Leviathan*.[5]

Thus, Hobbes already had a theory of science when he produced the *Elements of Law* and *De Cive*, and he kept refining his method and approach until he produced his masterpiece, *Leviathan*. As he penetrated deeper into the elaboration of his system, he drifted away from writing history, and as his table of knowledge in *Leviathan*, chapter 9, shows, he also gave history less value as a field of knowledge. But as he drew away from history, the demonstrative strength of his philosophy increased. He had to get rid of whatever sounded like a narrative style to achieve the effect of demonstrative science, as the analysis of the evolution of his style in his state-of-nature chapters between the *Elements of Law* and *Leviathan* will show.

His objections to history as a likely foundation for a science of politics are linked to his theory of science, and also to his conceptions of time and memory.[6] In Part I of *Leviathan,* the dynamic theory of man's psychology and ethics is intimately linked to the theory of scientific knowledge. As history is a knowledge of the past, it has some relation for Hobbes to the nature of memory. A science of politics, on the other hand, has to be based on strong deductive grounds, on undebatable premises. Can history, as knowledge of the past, provide such a foundation? *Leviathan* suggests that the answer is no.

THE UNCERTAINTY OF HISTORY

Chapter IX of *Leviathan* mostly consists of a table of the hierarchy of sciences, based on the degree of certainty each science is likely to afford. It is preceded by a definition of knowledge:

There are of KNOWLEDGE two kinds; whereof one is *Knowledge of Fact:* the other *Knowledge of the Consequence of one Affirmation to another.* The former is nothing else, but Sense and Memory, and is *Absolute Knowledge* [. . .] and this is the Knowledge required in a Witness. The later is called *Science;* and is *Conditionall;* as when we know, that, *If the figure shown be a circle, then any straight line through the Center shall divide it into two equall parts.* And this is the Knowledge required in a Philosopher; that is to say, of him that pretends to Reasoning.

The Register of *Knowledge of Fact* is called *History.* Whereof there be two sorts: one called *Naturall History;* which is the History of such Facts, or Effects of Nature, as have no dependence on mans *Will;* such as are the Histories of *Metals, Plants, Animals, Regions,* and the like. The other, is *Civill History;* which is the History of the Voluntary Actions of Men in Common-wealths.

The Registers of Science, are such *Books* as contain the *Demonstrations* of Consequences of one Affirmation, to another; and are commonly called *Books of Philosophy.*[7]

To distinguish the two branches of knowledge, Hobbes uses the adjectives "absolute" and "conditional": memory and sense relate to facts and to absolute knowledge, the knowledge of a witness in court. Science is related to conditional mental operations, to deduction from definitions. The most scientific philosophy of the workings of commonwealths might therefore be that which started from the absolute knowledge of the witness and proceeded by deduction to certain conclusions, or backward by induction to safe and secure foundations of political, legal, or ecclesiastical knowledge. The ideal civil history would be as close as possible to the registers of fact of natural history, and would consist in narratives and descriptions of actions and events, certified annals of men's actions.

But, on reflection, does the subject matter of civil history lend itself to scientific treatment? Consider Hobbes's definition of civil history as the history of the *voluntary* actions of men in commonwealths. "Civil" does not concern man as a natural being, but as a social and political animal, as if Hobbes thought of a social or political anthropology; "voluntary" refers to the driving force of man's psychology: desire, appetite, or endeavor. Whether in the state of nature or in the state of civil society, men act according to a combination of their wills and appetites; the covenant is the operation through which the wills of men act together for the first time according to reason rather than appetite. Men's reason can be depraved by their appetites and aversions, and this depravity can pervert their wills; hence the absurd and suicidal individual behaviors in the state of nature and the collective ones in the state of society. Evidence of rational or irrational acts of the will may not then be reasonable and might even lead to unphilosophical conclusions.

Hobbes's earlier definition of memory in the first part of *Leviathan* may justify even deeper doubt concerning the possibility of a scientific civil history.

The decay of Sense in men waking, is not the decay of the motion made in sense; but an obscuring of it . . . And any object being removed from our eyes, though the impression it made in us remain; yet other objects more present succeeding, and working on us, the imagination of the past is obscured, and make weak. . . . From whence it followeth, that the longer the time is, after the sight or Sense of any object, the weaker is the imagination. For the continual change of man's body destroys in time the parts which in sense were moved . . . This decaying sense, when we would express the thing it self, (I mean fancy it self,) we call imagination, as I said before: but when we would express the decay, and signify that the Sense is fading, old, and past, it is called Memory. So that *Imagination* and *Memory* are but one thing, which for divers considerations hath divers names.[8]

The knowledge ideally required of the witness must rely on memory, therefore on decaying sense, "fading, old and past"; what is remembered is mere decayed imagination. One may therefore conclude that, whereas the geometrician can reckon with quantities and shapes, although he does not have them before his eyes, the political thinker or the historian must use the register of the evidence of dead men, based on their memory or decayed sense, whose import is the more remote as their language or time is distant in time or space. The motions and changes in man's body and mind alter his perception and understanding of events, and the pen of the recorder is influenced by the same accidents. Although the witness is required to be accurate, can he be relied upon to be so? Can documentary, material evidence be treated as conveying absolute knowledge?

Another use of remembered sense lies in experience. "Much memory, or memory of many things, is called *Experience*," Hobbes writes in Chapter 2 of *Leviathan*;[9] whether this knowledge is always valuable for an individual or a community is unclear. On the quality and dependability of historical knowledge will depend the scientific quality of the political prudence and practice that will be grounded on it, and ultimately the efficiency of its use by the sovereign and subjects for the furtherance of common peace.

The debate on prudence and experience is a topos of moral and political philosophy. In his endeavors to break from the Aristotelian tradition, Hobbes also wanted to take issue with what he perceived as a bulwark of the parliamentarian and republican doctrines.[10] As J. G. A. Pocock has repeatedly shown, the upholders of the representative system in early modern England were constantly in search of an historical vocabulary to ground their political designs in a tradition. The myths of the Norman yoke and of the ancient constitution were sometimes blended with the vocabulary of apocalyptic Christianity (the Elect Nation), thus relating political intellects to a backward-looking time-scheme and to a prospective one.[11] The use of history to produce ideological myths in order to found a political rebellion may have been one of Hobbes's objections to history as a foundation for a science of politics, but he also had an epistemological argument to raise against it.

Sometime a man desires to know the event of an action; and then he thinketh of some like action past, and the events thereof one after another;

supposing like events will follow like actions. . . . Which kind of thoughts, is called *Foresight*, and *Prudence*, or *Providence*; and sometimes *Wisdome*; though such conjecture, through the difficulty of observing all circumstances, be very fallacious.[12]

Foresight, prudence, providence, and even wisdom are but fallacious and conjectural. As for its epistemological status, the past is as reliable as memory: "The *Present* onely has a being in Nature; things *Past* have a being in the Memory onely, but things *to come* have no being at all; the *Future* being but a fiction of the mind, applying the sequels of actions Past, to the actions that are Present."[13]

If the Epicurean definition of time stated above governs the object of historiography, then the likelihood of developing a certain knowledge of politics from the study of the past is very weak. Memory as a mode of cognition can have its use in private life, for "him that has most experience . . . but not with certainty enough."

And though it be called Prudence, when the Event answereth our Expectation; yet in its own nature, it is but Presumption. For the foresight of things to come, which is Providence, belongs only to him by whose will they are to come. From him only, and supernaturally, proceeds Prophecy. The best Prophet naturally is the best guesser; and the best guesser, he that is most versed and studied in the matters he guesses at: for he hath most *Signes* to guess by.[14]

God has the most foresight, for it is on His will that the whole course of nature depends. Everyone else's foresight is guesswork. Apart from the God-inspired prophet, the best guesser is the best student of the matter he guesses about. This could be read as an argument for the study of history, but it comes after such a negative definition of the past that it has already been made invalid. The Puritan saint, the millenarist preacher or soldier, can pretend to inspiration, but the definition of inspiration in Chapter 34 of *Leviathan* ruins their pretense to prophetic knowledge. Prophetic knowledge died out – like miracles – at the end of apostolic times.[15]

There can be a knowledge of the past, but the nature and the modalities of this knowledge make history a precarious kind of knowledge.[16] The nature of science, on the other hand, lies in the certainty of its deduction, which in turn depends on the certainty of its premises. The definition of science is in total opposition to the nature of the knowledge a man can have of the past. Science implies the use of reason, which is not gained by the meditation of the past experience of a man or community; it has to do with the very matter of ratiocination, well-defined signs and words.

It appears that Reason is not as Sense, and Memory, borne with us; nor gotten by Experience onely, as Prudence is; but attayned by Industry; first in apt imposing of Names; and secondly by getting a good and orderly Method in proceeding from the Elements, which are Names, to Assertions made by Connexion of one of them to another; and so to Syllogismes, which are the Connexions of one Assertion to another, till we come to a knowledge of all the Consequences of names appertaining to the subject in hand; and that is it, men call SCIENCE. And whereas Sense and Memory are but knowledge of Fact, which is a thing past, and irrevocable; *Science* is the knowledge of Consequences, and dependence of one fact upon another.[17]

The difference between prudence and experience, on the one hand, and science, on the other, does not lie in the behavior they permit, like the ability to behave aptly and opportunely in varying circumstances. Here, as in the definitions of science and history, the difference is between fact and causality. The past is irrevocable as fact; the knowledge deduced by the scientific intellect relies on logical and causal reasoning, which teaches more knowledge of fact. The correct definition of words is the primary instrument of science. Understanding the proper meanings of terms matters more than the knowledge of some alleged factuality of what they refer to. As the phantasm of a thing is different from the thing represented, the word denoting a thing is not the thing itself. Instead it defines the thing and enables the intellect to include the thing in its reckoning operations.

Words are like counters, Hobbes says in the chapter on speech of *Leviathan;* and their relationship to truth changes when they are used by wise men or by fools.[18] The trouble with history is that a good historian will always try to verify the "truth" of the facts he reports, but the reader will not do likewise. If a bad historian improves on the facts to embellish his discourse, it becomes impossible to make good use of historiography, and it becomes a tool for the fools who worship the Goddess of Rhetoric. In the introduction to his translation of Thucydides's *History of the Peloponnesian War,* Hobbes debated with the ideas of Dionysius of Halicarnassus on the best historiographic skills and purposes. The ideas of Hobbes's maturity, outlined above, eventually contradicted some of the ideas of his youth, but he was nevertheless already writing in 1628 with the strong conviction that history must fit the facts, whether or not it is able to account for them.

THE FUNCTIONS OF HISTORY

From his presentation of Thucydides to *Leviathan* and *Behemoth*, Hobbes claims that history must teach its readers, and that it never teaches as well as when it shows how a destructive crisis was caused by inaccurate understanding and correspondingly inappropriate be- havior on the part of the men in power. The appropriateness of political behavior comes from the right understanding of the princi- ples on which sovereignty rests, which depends in its turn on the accuracy of the language used to teach these principles to the men who rule and to those who are ruled. The dissolution of common- wealths is the fault of the men who misunderstand the foundations of authority.[19] Good history will rest on good philosophy, as good policy must rest on the good procreation of the commonwealth.

This will be explained first with the definitions of good historiogra- phy outlined in the presentation of Thucydides, then by defining historical change and the causes of the dissolution of states from *Leviathan* 29, then by studying the didactic remedies Hobbes pro- poses to cure these ills in *Leviathan* and in historical texts.

Hobbes's first published work is a translation of Thucydides. It was published in 1629, the year when Charles I, who had been ruling for four years, began eleven years of personal rule without calling parliaments. The dedication and the introduction attempt to define the genres of historiography, the purposes it must achieve, and the audiences for whom it is written.[20]

The historical modes contrasted in Hobbes's presentation of Thu- cydides tell us a lot about his own approach as a practicing historian. He opposes the views of Thucydides to those of the rhetorician Dionysius of Halicarnassus and contrasts the two writers in respect of truth and style. Dionysius objects to Thucydides's choices as regards the matter and the manner of his history: such a crisis, such defeats, such ill-advised actions as those of the Peloponnesian War are not to the credit of the Athenians; Dionysius thought that Thu- cydides should have begun much earlier in time, and he should have embellished actions that were not praiseworthy, concealing defeats and rash decisions.[21] To Hobbes, such changes are "most manifest vices." Dionysius was a rhetorician, and he preferred what could be embellished, not what was true and useful.

For his part, Hobbes praises Thucydides for the two dominant qualities of his work, "*truth* and *elocution*. For in truth consisteth the soul, and in elocution the body of history. The latter without the former, is but a picture of history; and the former without the latter, unapt to instruct."[22] Thucydides wrote of recent times and endeavored to gather as much information as he could from direct witnesses and actors in the events: "He used as much diligence in search of the truth, (noting every thing whilst it was fresh in memory, and laying out his wealth upon intelligence), as was possible for a man to use."[23] In the humanist phase of his career, Hobbes does not underrate memory as a source of knowledge, but he considers a historian, not a philosopher.

Truth in history means, among other things, accuracy, which implies the search for authoritative information. Truth also bears a relation to the sequel and train of events, their causes and effects, and the reality of the results reported. Dionysius is therefore wrong to blame Thucydides for his lack of respect toward his country. The picture Thucydides paints of the Greek peoples is realistic and unpleasant; should we read in it the opinions of Hobbes at forty on his contemporaries before the war, as foreshadowing the first pages of *Behemoth* written forty years later?

In those days it was impossible for any man to give good and profitable counsel for the commonwealth, and not incur the displeasure of the people. For their opinion was such of their own power, and of the facility of achieving whatsoever action they undertook, that such men only swayed the assemblies, and were esteemed good commonwealth's men, as did put them upon the most dangerous and desperate enterprises.[24]

The *dispositio* of Thucydides's work is praised for its linear qualities. A history must follow the chronological order of events and avoid digressions; digressions should be reserved for extrapolations, and tentative analyses should be avoided by proper historians. "Digressions for instruction's cause, and other such open conveyances of precepts, (which is the philosopher's part), he never useth; as having so clearly set before men's eyes the ways and events of good and evil counsels, that the narration itself doth secretly instruct the reader, and more effectually than can possibly be done by precept."[25] *Behemoth* might thus be read as a Thucydidean history with philosophical digressions to instruct and reform a people who were not less guilty of the sin of pride than the Athenians of Thucydides's century.

Truth and accuracy in the narrative also involve the exposition of the open and concealed causes and motivations of the individual and collective agents of history, and the mark of the good historian is to distinguish between these categories and provide his reader with an enlightening hierarchy of those. Hobbes praises Thucydides for the order and relevance of his presentation, which we shall find in *Behemoth* later. An *exordium* "derives the state of Greece from the cradle to [its] vigorous stature", proceeds then to explain the causes "both real and pretended" of the war, the rest being dedicated to the chronological narrative, year by year, divided between winter and summer. The motivations are presented before the narrative of each action, or he "contriveth them into the form of *deliberative orations* in the persons of such as from time to time bare sway in the commonwealth. After the actions, when there is just occasion, he giveth his judgment of them."[26] The older Hobbes would not have approved of the use of fictive "deliberative orations," which he refrains from using in *Behemoth*, although the use of dialogues to convey at once the story, the explanations, the commentary, and the philosophical interpretation can be perceived as a form of fictional setting to the historical narrative.[27] The order of the presentation of open and concealed motives is commended in the criticism of Dionysius; Thucydides chose to present the open causes before the more putative hidden ones:

For it is plain that a cause of war divulged and avowed, how slight soever it be, comes within the task of the historiographer, no less than the war itself. . . . This pretext is always an injury received, or pretended to be received. Whereas the inward motive to hostility is but conjectural; and not of that evidence, that a historiographer should be always bound to take notice of it.[28]

The translation of Thucydides aims at two kinds of readers. In general they are literate men, men of substance, men who are likely to be involved in community politics at a local level at least, but men who are so involved that although they might have studied classical

languages in their youth, they would rather read an English translation for their self-improvement. These are the people addressed by the
advertisement to the reader. The men aimed at by the dedication,
beyond the still too young William Earl of Devonshire, the son of
Hobbes's recently deceased master and contemporary, are the men
who are likely to come close to the throne and can be sure of a seat in
Parliament or Council. Kings could also consider the text worthy of
their attention, as Thucydides belonged to a family of kings.

In his *Behemoth*, Hobbes addressed all men from the king to the
subjects of the lowest rank, reminding them of the foundations of
their political and social relationship. The dialogue between a older
and a younger man replaced the invention of speeches, reduced the
role of fiction, and allowed philosophical and didactic digressions to
develop more naturally, though always under control.

HOBBES ON POLITICAL CHANGE

From Hobbes's pronouncements on history and historiography in
two phases of his intellectual career, we can now turn to his understanding of change and, in particular, political change.

For Hobbes, men are both the matter and the makers of the commonwealth. As each man gives up his right to govern himself on the
condition that every other man does so also, so every covenanter
makes himself subject to the man or assembly of men that becomes
sovereign as representative of them all. The covenanters are the
matter of the commonwealth, and each of them is, with the others, a
maker of the commonwealth, an author of the acts of the sovereign
representative. From every man's double participation in the generation of the commonwealth, Hobbes builds up the theory of men's
double responsibility in the dissolution of the commonwealth. As
makers of the commonwealth, men are responsible for a possible
imperfect generation of the commonwealth, for example, if they
have introduced constitutional principles that contradict the ends
for which the commonwealth was erected. As they are all the matter
of the commonwealth, they are the sovereign's subjects, and they
may hold false – viz. misinformed – opinions about the ends for
which the sovereign was erected. Worse, they may act on the false
opinions, and may therefore destroy their own peace and security.
Their only insurance against this is the use of reason.

if men had the use of reason they pretend to, their Commonwealths might be secured, at least, from perishing by internall diseases. Therefore when they come to be dissolved, not by externall violence, but intestine disorder, the fault is not in men, as they are the *Matter*; but as they are the *Makers*, and orderers of them. . . . so for want, both of the art of making fit Lawes, to square their actions by, and also of humility, and patience, to suffer the rude and cumbersome points of their present greatness to be taken off, they cannot without the help of a very able Architect, be compiled, into any other than a crazy building.[29]

This passage raises a question that pertains to the realm of the historian: How do commonwealths fall? History analyzes the apparent causes (internal or external dissolution), but it also suggests philosophical explanations. Human weakness has to do with the practical use of reason in action; men are not able to find out clearly enough the laws they must make "to square their actions by." Mere practical reason is weak and can but be weak, since the law must exist before men can behave morally. In the final philosophical formulation of Hobbes's politics, we find historical questions and philosophical answers. This helps one to understand the difference between Hobbes's practice as a writer of history and the views on the writing of history that he formed at the beginning of his career.

Chapters 29 and 30 of *Leviathan* offer both a practical and a philosophical set of principles to govern a state and prevent internal dissolution. Machiavelli offered rules to govern oneself, but Hobbes suggests that whoever wants to preserve his sovereignty must first bear in mind that his business is to rule. Chapter 30 begins with a useful reminder.

The Office of the Soveraign, (be it a monarch, or an assembly), consisteth in the end, for which he was trusted with the Soveraign Power, namely the procuration of *the safety of the people*; to which he is obliged by the Law of Nature, and to render an account thereof to God, the Author of that Law, and to none but him.[30]

Hobbes's prince is absolute indeed, the sole ruler under God, but he is reminded of the end for which sovereignty is established: *salus populi*. Chapter 29 of *Leviathan* is the chapter in which Hobbes uses the organicist metaphorical register of the body politic most consistently. He does hold a philosophy of body, but his "bodies" are those of physics, not of the Tudor or early-Stuart organicist ideology. As the body of the commonwealth can die of imperfect procreation, likewise it can suffer from diseases and even be poisoned.

> I observe the *Diseases* of a Common-wealth, that proceed from the poyson of seditious doctrines, whereof one is, *That every private man is Judge of Good and Evill actions.* This is true in the condition of meer Nature, where there are no Civill Lawes; and also under Civill Government, in such cases as are not determined by the Law. But otherwise, it is manifest, that the measure of Good and Evill actions, is the Civill Law; and the Judge the Legislator, who is always Representative of the Common-wealth. From this false doctrine, men are disposed to debate with themselves, and dispute the commands of the Common-wealth; and afterwards to obey, or disobey them, as in their private judgements they shall think fit.[31]

Hobbes then enumerates six poisons that ruin the bodies politic: "*whatsoever a man does against his Conscience, is Sinne,*" "*Faith and Sanctity, are not to be attained by Study and Reason, but by supernaturall Inspiration . . .* , which granted, I see not . . . why any man should take the Law of his Country, rather than his own Inspiration, for the rule of his action," which will lead to power men who pretend to divine inspiration;[32] "*he that hath the Soveraign Power, is subject to the Civill Lawes*"; "*every private man has an absolute Propriety in his Goods; such, as excludeth the Right of the Soveraign*";[33] "*the Soveraign Power may be divided.*" The others are the desire to imitate the neighboring nations and the excessive admiration of the culture of the ancient Greeks and Romans.[34]

The diptych constituted by Chapters 29 and 30 redirects the intellects of the readers toward the practical dimensions of politics and toward their recent collective and individual history. Each reader is faced with opinions that he may have held or read in the preceding ten years.[35]

Restoring the true definitions of words and notions used by men to denote their moral and political relations to one another and to the state is the first antidote that Hobbes prescribes for the poisons he identifies. Taking this antidote makes his readers realize that the sovereign is the source of all civil laws, which they are obliged to follow. Again, by the definition of the notion of sovereignty, ecclesiastical and religious laws are equally the laws of the sovereign representative. So are the articles of faith, which, whether they are believed or not, must be professed without any doubt in one's salvation. As the sovereign is not party to the covenanting process and so does not give up his right to govern himself, *he* is above the civil laws, which enables him both to make and change them as circumstances require. The same argument explains why sovereignty cannot be divided: If spiritual and political authorities are separate, they may enter into conflict and command different loyalties, contrary to the covenant that erects the sovereign as the unitary representative of everyone else and the source of law for everyone else. It is true that for the civil laws to have their effect, the sovereign must see to it that they are put into force properly: they must be made explicit to all subjects, and it is better for there to be few rather than many laws and for them to be expressed in few rather than many words. This implies a simplification of the common law. But because the civil magistrate is also supposed to have authority over religion, it implies the clarification through law of the scope of divinity.

CIVIL LAW AND CIVIL INSTRUCTION IN *BEHEMOTH* AND THE *DIALOGUE*

Behemoth, Hobbes's history of the civil war, takes further the philosophical case for treating the sovereign as the only author of law and as the only real legal authority. A character in *Behemoth* wonders why Christians are so often preached to about their religion even though they are already believers, when what they really need to have preached to them is obedience and justice. Hobbes's point is partly humorous, but he is also alluding to the sovereign's duty as defined in Chapter 30 of *Leviathan*. As men are not yet used to the notion that all types of legislation and rules are effectively and ultimately civil legislation issuing from the sovereign, Hobbes sets out to enumerate sensitive areas in which special care must be taken to educate and warn subjects. He repeatedly touches upon this point in *Behemoth*, where all the consequences of inaccurate civil education are proven by reference to history, and in the *Dialogue between a Philosopher and a Student of the Common Laws of England*, in which Hobbes openly debates with an imaginary Cokean lawyer on the preconceptions and mistakes of the common-law mind.

The general program of reformation in *Behemoth* should be quoted before the theoretical discussion of the theme.

The core of rebellion, as you have seen by this, and read of other rebellions, are the Universities; which nevertheless are not to be cast away, but to be better disciplined: . . . that the politics there taught *be made to be*, as true politics should be, such as are *fit to make men know*, that it is their duty to obey all laws whatsoever that shall by the authority of the King be enacted, till by the same authority they shall be repealed; such as are *fit to make men understand*, that the civil laws are God's laws, as they that make them are by God appointed to make them; and *to make men know*, that the people and the Church are one thing, and have but one head, the King; and that no man has title to govern under him, that has it not from him; that the King owes his crown to God only, and to no man, ecclesiastic or other.[36]

This program is remote from Bacon's instauration. Inquiry into the workings of nature is not the most important task of reformation; Hobbes thought it could do no harm and could therefore be left free and uncontrolled. Other intellectual pursuits, by contrast, were more open to disputation and likely to cause rebellion. Because the universities trained mostly future preachers and churchmen, one of his targets was clear enough, but he knew that men of substance and ambition also went to university for a few years before they completed their studies at the Inns of Court, a regular course of training for young gentlemen aiming for a seat in parliament or an important county position. Rather than imbuing them with the principles of the old republics, the universities needed to teach them the grounds of their obedience.

In the passage just quoted, I italicized a few typical phrases that insist on pressure on the universities in order to get the universities to act on the rest of society. Men must be *made* to think correctly and know their duty, in their own interest and in the interest of their own individual salvation. Men of substance and authority must be properly trained in universities, and people of more modest rank must be properly taught by their preachers in church.

The first mover of this reformation is the sovereign, "by a general Providence, contained in publique Instruction, both of Doctrine, and Example; and in the making, and executing of good Lawes, to which individual persons may apply their own cases."[37] If the sovereign fails to do so, he will encounter the same dangers as Charles I, whose subjects were very dangerously biased.

Lastly, the people in general were so ignorant of their duty, as that not one perhaps of ten thousand knew what right any man had to command him, or what necessity there was of King or Commonwealth, for which he was to part with his money against his will; but thought himself to be so much master of whatsoever he possessed, that it could not be taken from him upon any pretence of common safety without his own consent. King, they thought, was but a title of the highest honour, which gentleman, knight, baron, earl, duke, were but steps to ascend to, with the help of riches; they had no rule of equity, but precedents and custom; and he was thought wisest and fittest to be chosen for a Parliament, that was most averse to the granting of subsidies or other public payments.[38]

The elements of the program for good legislation and teaching are inspired by this list of misconceptions. The poison of the seditious doctrines is there: the source of sovereignty, the right of the sovereign on the subjects' goods, the nature of the sovereign's function, the misapprehension of common interest. Better teaching would eradicate these evils; the misconceptions were at the root of disobedience.

The Dialogue of the Common Laws is also very strict on the issue of informing the subjects of the source of the law. The philosopher constantly attacks the lawyer for exaggerating the importance of legal knowledge, which is taken by judges to be the source and life of the law. For the philosopher, the most important laws must be the Statutes of the Realm, made by Rex in Parlamento, which can be read and examined by any man, not framed by the caste of lawyers in the practice of their courts and in the idiom of their profession, which prevents men from learning their duty.[39] The self-centeredness of lawyers is then as serious a danger as that of the clerics.

Religion was not omitted in Hobbes's program of reform for educational institutions, and the terms in which Hobbes chooses to describe and define civic Christianity are consistent with the minimalist creed he had proposed in Leviathan.

... and that the religion they teach there, be a quiet waiting for the coming again of our blessed Saviour, and in the mean time a resolution to obey the King's laws, which also are God's laws; to injure no man, to be in charity with all men ... without mingling our religion with points of natural philosophy, as freedom of will, incorporeal substance, everlasting nows, ubiquities, hypostases, which the people understand not, nor will ever care for.[40]

The fundamental antimillenarism of Hobbes's exegesis is here again, to smother the serpent of the chiliastic expectations that prompt men of misdirected faith and energy to rebel against the lawful authority of their kings – who yet are kings by God's laws – led to it by the preachers' use of incomprehensible words.[41]

Hobbes had gone so far as to write that the only points necessary for salvation were to profess that "Jesus is the Christ," as Saint Paul says, and to obey the laws of one's sovereign, although one may profess a form of faith one rejects.[42] Reading disobedience in any passage from Scripture is sinful and will mislead. An incorrect interpretation of history can be derived from a misinterpretation of sacred history: as the Bible presents history as mankind's march toward its cataclysmic ending, so, producing a correct and receivable reading of these paradoxically apocalyptic (viz. revealing) texts belongs to the office of the obedient divines of the Church which is the Commonwealth at prayer.

The sovereign must be better taught as well, and this may be the business of treatises like *Leviathan*. A sovereign who would deny himself the means to rule would be guilty to God and his people. The unity of all legislation is shown by the list of appointments to be made: soldiers, ministers, teachers; defense of the commonwealth, counsel and policy-making and religion are in his province. Seduction must be forestalled by education and good laws. The king must set the example, but also enforce discipline and see to it that correct doctrine be taught; the correctness of the doctrine is very clearly defined and oriented: "the defence, peace, and good of the people."[43]

As men are activated by their internal motions, whatever misdirects these motions also misleads men in their collective behavior. The frontispiece of *Leviathan* shows the river of men flowing up the regulated channels of the body politic; without these channels, the water would be spilled, or, in other terms, the flock scattered – and the shepherd's head, toward which all the flock is gazing, would not be there. The sovereigns must be taught by good philosophy and good histories, which should not necessarily be polished encomia of their ancestors, as Hobbes already knew when he wrote his presentation of Thucydides.

HOBBES AS HISTORIAN

In his advertisement to the readers of his translation of Thucydides, Hobbes said that "the principal and proper work of history, [is] to instruct and enable men, by the knowledge of actions past, to bear themselves prudently in the present and providently towards the future."[44] As we have seen above, these views are to be read with caution after the epistemological break of the 1630s, but after such a catastrophe as the English Revolution, Hobbes felt the urge to expose to the world the *true* causes of the cataclysmic decades. The medium for this instruction was a history.

The originality of Hobbes's history-writing lies in the use of dialogues. The narrative is shared between two characters in *Behemoth*, the *Dialogue of the Common Laws* and the appendix on heresy of the Latin *Leviathan*. Whereas *Behemoth* brings together two men of similar opinions, the *Dialogue* involves two conflicting lines of thought. When the lawyer begins to define heresy in professionally centered terms (who is judge of heresy?), the philosopher retorts with a definition of the words and ideas that are judged to be heretical.[45] As the previous pages have shown, the question of heresy is central to Hobbes's reflection on what may be publicly professed in relation to religion, and as the determination of what may and may not be taught is an essential means of securing *salus populi* by the sovereign, history, too, will be essential for the sovereign's purposes: it will help to explain the sense of words and the beginnings of phenomena. The preoccupation with heresy in so many works of Hobbes may also come from his awareness of the originality of some of the theological views he professed.[46]

Chronology and the definition of the continuities and discontinuities in events are essential to Hobbes's histories, but he often resorts to *analepsis* as well to explain contemporary events.[47] Thus the structure of *Behemoth* is often difficult to follow when the abuses of the Stuart clergy are explained by repeated references to Ethiopia or Egypt as seen by Diodorus Siculus.[48] These narratives often include a reminder of the conditions in which Constantine called and sanctioned the Nicene Council, sometimes with a commentary of its Creed in its Latin and Greek versions.[49]

Truth and accuracy are measured not only in terms of narration, but in corrections to the historical record by criticism of documentary evidence. The philological methods applied in the narratives of heresy belong to a methodology that the historians of the antiquarian school had promoted: collecting and editing sources to restore the truth of past documents. Lorenzo Valla with Constantine's Donation and the Reformers and humanists of the sixteenth century had opened the way. Myths were difficult to uphold when the fallacies of forged documents were exposed or new documents unearthed. When Hobbes redefines the word "heresy," when he compares Latin and Greek texts of the Creed on notions like *consubstantialis* or *homoousios*,[50] or when he exposes the misreadings of the Bible by Papal theologians,[51] he belongs to an already venerable school of historiography, and he is more scientific for the modern historian than when he blends his anthropology with the social and economic causes of the English Revolution.[52]

Hobbes seldom gives precise references in his philosophical works, but in historical texts he tends to be more careful, as when he mentions Heath's chronicle of the revolution as his source for *Behemoth*,[53] or when he quotes common-law treatises, or statutes. A statute he quotes frequently is 1 Eliz. I c.1 (36), on the definition of heresy.[54] When he studies legal texts and polemical works of the revolutionary period, the quality of his syntheses indicates a direct knowledge of the sources (*Nineteen Propositions* of 1642, the Cromwellian *Instruments of Government* of 1653 and 1658).[55]

Explaining causes and motivations is one of the tasks of the historian, Hobbes says in the introduction to Thucydides. He spends most of the first two dialogues of *Behemoth* enumerating the causes of the revolution. He produces political and economic causes (the importance of market towns and corporate towns, ruined gentlemen, reluctance to pay taxes) and ideological causes (the power of the Presbyterians, the alleged strength of Catholics, and the influence of classical education).

In *Behemoth*, he retains the narrative approach of his first work on history, as he follows the same sequence as Thucydides, but ideology plays a prominent part.

The first [dialogue] contains the seed of it, certain opinions in divinity and politics. The second hath the growth of it in declarations, remonstrances, and other writings between the King and Parliament published. The two last are a very short epitome of the war itself, drawn out of Mr Heath's chronicle.[56]

Two dialogues analyze the growth of the war. They are the most philosophical part of the book, as they are mostly concerned with the remote historical and ideological causes and with the contemporary evolutions of men's thinking.

Hobbes's philosophy contributes to the historiography of its period mainly by its use of psychological explanation in terms of the appetites and aversions of agents.[57] The manipulation of minds by the trouble-makers is consistently explained. The power of men often consists of their reputation of power. Using reputation gives power, and slander gives power. When the Presbyterians accuse Bishop Laud of "Romish" sympathies, they are readily believed because free will was branded as "popery" and Laud had forbidden the preaching of predestination.[58] The faction that manipulates the minds of the people will turn their affections away from the legitimate power and toward subversive notions. The king's assent to the division of sovereignty in his answer to parliament's *Nineteen Propositions* of 1642 was therefore a serious mistake, and it becomes clearer why *Behemoth*'s publication was prohibited by Charles II.[59] Charles I was economically and politically weak because his opponents had enough control of the people's ideological representations to deprive him of the support of the middle-classes and market towns, which provided the sinews of war to the parliamentary side. Had he been better aware of his rights and obligations, he would have enforced a better control over minds. Yet, the freedom allowed to the clerical Arminian William Laud is criticized when the crisis of the Scottish Prayer Book of 1637 is discussed.[60] To Hobbes, Arminian bishops and Presbyterian ministers were equally convinced of their divine right. Although the Presbyterians' belief caused the war, the bishops' belief precluded resistance on the part of the followers of the established church.[61] Hobbes's anticlericalism was an English tradition from before the Reformation, continued by the popular anti-prelatical polemics of the *Martin Marprelate* tracts of the Elizabethan era, which were very fashionable in his youth. Yet the tone is totally different: no abuses, no slander, no coarse language, but hostility all the same.

Hobbes used history to take the "Goddess of rhetoric" off her pedestal and restore the true use of political language; he had already praised Thucydides for his part in this struggle.[62] He produced an epitome of Aristotle's *Rhetoric, The Art of Rhetoric*.[63] He used rhetoric against rhetoric, history against rhetoric, but also history against history. The ideological allegiances were fixed early, as the Thucydides texts show; the desire to restore stable and secure language and notions in politics was also present; the novelty resides in the way Hobbes arranges for an interaction between history and political philosophy as fields of knowledge.

History is the laboratory of the hobbist philosopher; *Behemoth* is the practical face of *Leviathan*, the field of experimentation of the science of justice and injustice. The anthropology of Hobbes rests on the inner motions conducing to action, and the record of men's voluntary actions is called history; therefore the verification *par excellence* of a political and philosophical theory is the kind of history it can produce, because it shows the results of the mental ratiocinations, the outcome of the trajectories of all the endeavors of men in a given place during a given period; *then only* can a piece of historical writing be safely used for instruction. The resolutive-compositive method has then run its course. If the science of politics cannot be founded on history, on the past, on what there can be no science of, history can be a verification or application of scientific truth and can thus become a necessary auxiliary of the science of sovereignty and obedience.

NOTES

1 See Borot, "Science et histoire," pp. 119–26, introduction to *Béhémoth*, pp. 10–32.
2 See Goldsmith, *Science of Politics*; Zarka, *Décision*. For two differing views: Leo Strauss, *Political Philosophy*, and Tom Sorell, *Hobbes*. About *Behemoth* and history, see bibliography in Borot, *Béhémoth*, pp. 27–32.
3 Aubrey, *Brief Lives*, p. 230.
4 Jacquot, Jones, '*De Mundo*,' appendix II, pp. 449–60.
5 *Gondibert*,' p. 49; *Gondibert* was published in 1651.
6 Zarka, "Histoire," p. 167.
7 *Lev.*, ch. 9 (Macpherson, ed.) 147–8.
8 Ibid., ch. 2, 88–9.
9 Ibid., ch. 2, 89.
10 See Aristotle, *Nicomachean Ethics*, VI, 3–6; Hobbes, *B*, I, p. 3; Pocock, *Moment*, ch. XI, pp. 371, 372.
11 Pocock, *Ancient Constitution*, chs. II, III, pp. 30–69; *Moment*, chs. X, XI, pp. 333–400.
12 *Lev.*, ch. 3, 97.

13 Ibid.

14 Ibid.

15 Hobbes, ch. 34, pp. 428–42; Pocock, *Moment*, ch. XI, p. 370, and "Time," pp. 148–201.

16 Polybius and his *anakuklosis*, Machiavelli and his rotation of the location of *virtù*, Bodin and his spiral of time, Bacon and his restoration of knowledge and development of the human mind, the millenarists and their lineal and catastrophic vision of historical time as eschatology, have no positive echo in Hobbes, as Pocock and Zarka have shown. When eschatology is debated in Part III of *Leviathan*, it is in a materialist perspective; this led Hobbes's seventeenth-century readers to brand him an atheist. There is no teleology in Hobbes's conception of historical time. The reverence owed to the past is to be understood and taught in the light of political purposes that some may regard as ideological options (Zarka, "Histoire," pp. 166, 170; Pocock, *Moment* and "Time," *loc. cit.*).

17 *Lev.*, ch. 5, 115.

18 *Lev.*, ch. 4, 106.

19 The best study of dissolution in Hobbes is Nicastro, "Dissolution" with its bibliography. For relation between *Leviathan* 29 and *Behemoth*, see Zarka, "Histoire," p. 176.

20 See Franck Lessay's excellent presentation of the preliminary texts of the Thucydides translation, in *Hérésie*, p. 119–29.

21 *EW* VIII 1, p. xxvi.

22 Ibid., p. xx.

23 Ibid., p. xxi.

24 Ibid., p. xvi. See *B.*, I, p. 4, quoted below, and *B.*, II, pp. 68–9.

25 Ibid., p. xxii.

26 Ibid., p. xxi–xxii.

27 *B.* (Borot ed.) pp. 13, 14, and p. 90, note 2.

28 *EW*, VIII 1, pp. xxvii–xxviii.

29 *Lev.*, ch. 29, 363.

30 Ibid., ch. 30, 376.

31 Ibid., ch. 29, 365.

32 Ibid., ch. 29, 366. Even the royalists would allow mental restrictions of this kind: *B.*, I, p. 47–52, on Richard Allestree's *Whole Duty of Man, Laid down in a Plain and Familiar Way* (1658).

33 *Lev.*, ch. 29, 367.

34 Ibid., 368–9.

35 Quentin Skinner studies the immediate context of *Leviathan* in his articles "Hobbes's *Leviathan*," "History and Ideology in the English Revolu-

tion," "The Ideological Context of Hobbes's Political Thought," "Conquest and Consent: Thomas Hobbes and the Engagement Controversy."

36 *B.*, I, p. 58; italics mine. Also see *B.*, I, pp. 16–17.

37 *Lev.*, 30, p. 376.

38 *B.*, I, p. 4; see intro. to Thucydides, *EW*, VIII / 1, p. xvi quoted above.

39 *Dial* (Cropsey, ed.) 55–6, 69, 71.

40 *B.*, I, p. 58; italics mine.

41 Hobbes explains terms related to Second Coming, Judgment, and Redemption in *Lev.*, 38, pp. 478–96.

42 *Lev.*, ch. 43, 615.

43 Ibid., ch. 30, 377.

44 *EW*, VIII 1, p. vii.

45 *Dial* 122.

46 This seems to have obsessed Hobbes very early, as he seems to sympathize with Thucydides who was accused of atheism, like him twenty years later, *EW*, VIII 1, p. xv. The history of the meanings of the word "heresy" is taken up in several texts; it includes a narrative of philosophical schools from Plato to the primitive Church, but it also implies a history of the semantic charge of the word used by conflicting schools of thought. From a neutral to a passionate meaning, the stages are always: the development of rhetorical training by inferior disciples of minor philosophers; the development of the primitive church, which recruited its first teachers among men who had been trained in the schools; and the passage of the semantical charge of the term from difference of opinion to sin is always located around the calling of the Nicene council by Constantine the Great, the first Christian Emperor, who made the religious canons into civil laws.

47 In narratological parlance, *analepsis* is what film directors would call a "flashback." I use the term as most appropriate to history-writing, as it is also a form of narrative and can be analyzed with the same stylistical instruments as a novel.

48 *B.*, I, pp. 9–22 for the political history of the Christian doctrine from Nice to the Reformation; II, 91–4 for Diodorus.

49 Latin *Lev.*, appendices I and II; *OL*, III, pp. 511–69; *Historical Narration Concerning Heresy and the Punishment Thereof*, *EW* IV, 391–6. See Lessay on this text and the other *Narration* on heresy, *Heresy*, pp. 18–27, 59–63. *DCL*, 126 and *B.*, I, p. 9–11, do not include a theological commentary but lay stress on imperial power.

50 *HN*, *EW* IV, 392; Latin *Leviathan*, all of appendix I, and appendix II; *OL*, III, p. 544.

51 *B.*, I, 19.

52 Pocock, *Ancient Constitution*, IV–V, pp. 70–123; Fussner, *Historical Revolution*, pp. 92–3.

53 *B.*, dedication, p. v; James Health, *A Brief Chronicle of all the Chief Actions of the Late Intestine Wars* (1662) and *A Brief Chronicle of the Late Intestine Wars* (1663).

54 *B.*, I, p. 9; *Dial.*, p. 131, the text also examines the Lollard cases of the reigns of Richard II, Henry IV, and Henry V, pp. 128–9. Latin *Leviathan*, appendix II; *OL*, III, p. 546; *Historical Narration, EW*, IV, 405, also mentions an act of the fifth year of her reign.

55 *B.*, II, p. 104–8 and IV, 183, 89–90. *Nineteen Propositions*, Kenyon (ed.); *Stuart Constitution*, pp. 21–3; their constitutional implications are studied by Pocock, *Moment*, ch. XI, p. 361–66.

56 *B.*, dedication, p. v.

57 *B.*, I, p. 2–4. Borot, "Science et histoire", p. 125; *Béhémoth*, p. 16–17.

58 *B.*, II, p. 61–2.

59 See *B.*, II, p. 104–8. On this crisis of obedience, see also *DCL*, p. 63–4.

60 *B.*, I, p. 28.

61 *B.*, I, p. 19 for the bishops' allegation since the time of the Henrician Reformation; pp. 22–6 for the presbyterians' methods.

62 *EW*, VIII 1, xvi–xvii.

63 The *Whole Art of Rhetoric, The Art of Rhetoric* and *The Art of Sophistry* are in *EW*, VI, p. 419–510, 511–28, 529–36. Compare with Henry Peachman, *The Garden of Eloquence* (1593), facs., W. G. Crane (ed.) (Delmar, NY: Scholars' Facsimiles, 1977); George Puttenham, *The Arte of English Poesie* (1589), Baxter Hattaway, ed., (Kent State University Press, 1970).

13   Hobbes on rhetoric

It is sometimes possible to catch philosophy "doing rhetoric" – which is to say seducing us with mere play of words – where it professes not to, thereby compromising its own claims to truth. Doing rhetoric means orchestrating a subtle slippage of meanings where philosophy has imposed distinctions, surreptitiously evading if not subverting philosophical categories and constraints, and asserting one sort of order but pursuing another. Hobbes offers a particularly tempting target for such criticism, inasmuch as he makes his science linguistic and formal rather than experimental and material. That is to say, he makes science a matter of how we use words. But there is also a considerable, indeed ancient history to this pastime of partitioning off philosophy from rhetoric, perhaps inaugurated by Plato, who depicts Socrates as opposing his sort of speech to the speech of the great Sophists Gorgias and Protagoras, as well as to such virtuoso orators as Lysias.[1]

I

One does dialectic or philosophy to teach, said Socrates; one does rhetoric to please. Although rhetoric had the upper hand at the time, philosophy has long since eclipsed its erstwhile rival. For philosophy aspires to truth, and rhetoric aims only at persuasion. Philosophy disinterestedly seeks the good and the just, but rhetoric seeks to gain power by giving pleasure. To put the distinction in terms of speech, the philosopher says what is or is not the case, but the rhetorician speaks only for personal advantage on either side of a question – regardless of the truth – in order to capture belief. So complete and intransigently moral a separation was not left uncontested by rhetoricians: Cicero and, following him, Quintilian sought to break down the barrier Plato had erected, not least by enlisting the Plato of the *Phaedrus,* where Socrates in a manner unites philosophy to rhetoric, knowledge to pleasure, by arguing that the best speaker is the one who knows of what he speaks.[2] In other words, knowing the truth and knowing what persuades are not incompatible but complementary arts. This is also in some measure the position of Aristotle in his lectures on rhetoric, in which he makes both dialectic and rhetoric modes of probable argument, differing only in that rhetoric proves its contentions in public, and logic in private or by technique.[3] Neither attains to the status of *apodeixis,* which is the certain demonstration of science in Aristotle's canon of speeches. While Aristotle's discrimination would thus seem to replace dialectic with science in opposing rhetoric, and to that extent, familiarly to distinguish mere knowledge of words from knowledge of things, the case is not that simple. For Aristotle's distinction presupposes a world informed by *logos,* which is at once the faculty of understanding and speech, order and articulation.[4] So to the Greek mind, at least, the progenitor equally of science and rhetoric in western culture, there is no knowledge that escapes language, only different purposes and ways of speaking – about natural or human affairs, to savants or to lay auditors or to persons in authority, in the academy or in political assemblies or in the courts of justice.

Socrates himself also employed a kind of speech that, by implication, conveyed the stuff of *arete* or civic-minded excellence, which is to say, knowledge of the public good and how to serve it.[5] The Sophists, whom Socrates opposed, claimed knowledge of the subjects they spoke about. The difference, observes Cicero on the authority of the *Phaedrus,* was merely one of occasion and discursive mode, not of motive or substance. Both the philosopher and the rhetorician conceived this speech as having an extraordinary cognitive and moral power not only to shape the mind to virtue but, in doing so, to foster political order and the common good. In the opening of his great dialogue on such efficacious speech, *De Oratore,*[6] Cicero writes:

For the one point in which we have our very greatest advantage over the brute creation is that we hold converse one with another, and can reproduce our thought in word. Who therefore would not rightly admire this faculty and deem it his duty to exert himself to the utmost in this field, that by so doing he may surpass men themselves in that particular respect wherein chiefly men are superior to animals? To come, however, at length to the highest achievements of eloquence, what other power could have been strong enough either to gather scattered humanity into one place, or to lead it out of its brutish existence in the wilderness up to our present condition of civilization as men and as citizens, or, after the establishment of social communities, to give shape to laws, tribunals, and civic rights? And not to pursue any further instances – wellnigh countless as they are – I will conclude the whole matter in a few words, for my assertion is this: that the wise control of the complete orator is that which chiefly upholds not only his own dignity, but the safety of countless individuals and of the entire state. (*De Oratore* I.34)

The argument made here for the power of speech embodies the assumption, as ancient as Heraclitus, that the faculty of language is what organizes humanity, placing each person in community by placing him in communication with all others and with the universal order of things. Speech endows us with a sense of self and provides the means to order our lives relative to the world and to others. Thus speech also creates a public realm, a society out of brute individuals. Implicit in this picture of how humanity moves out of the state of nature is the idea that there is no thought apart from speech, that is, no reasonable thought, for the condition of reason is language insofar as reason represents the value of meaningfulness. If meaningfulness may be said to assume some degree of reciprocity between our ideas and the world beyond the mind, speech is the palpable token, even guarantor, of that exchange, however partial or limited. That is why *logos* was intially a religious concept for the Greeks and, to varying extents, the singular manifestation of truth for those intellectual cultures, like the Roman, the scholastic, or the humanist, which absorbed Greek texts and with them Greek assumptions about the nature and means of human knowledge. We should try to imagine, as the Greeks evidently did, the marvel of clarity and mastery that speech must have brought to human experience. To say, with the gospel of John, that in the beginning was the word is to express this idea of the efflorescence of a distinctively human being with the inception not so much of speech per se, as its considered, instrumental use.

Of course, as Plato makes clear, some speeches are better because more effective than others, but this efficacy takes two disparate forms. There is speech that we like to hear and want to believe, and there is speech that allows us to understand the consequences of our actions and to anticipate events. Originally or mythically, there was no such separation, because the mind and the world were each dimensions of the same order or *logos*; to know the logos of the one was to know the other. With the separation of the world with speech from the world without it, there arose the value of truth, which is nothing less than the recognition that what we say may not automatically be the case, and that our ideas require some sort of demonstration to gain assent and efficacy. And so we return to the struggle of rhetoric with philosophy.

II

Hobbes was patently engaged with this issue, since he associates science with an order of speech that masters not only objects but persons. That is, he wanted to compose a discourse that would express the truth about things as well as incline humanity to observe the truth, the latter proviso admitting our singular status, as beings with the capacity to intrude the possible and fantastic upon the evident or actual through the agency of speech. For central to Hobbes's politics is the idea that the creation of a stable society depends on people being brought to see their duty – to see the advantage, to the point of necessity, of instituting and obeying sovereign authority. This entails something more than the simple possession of right knowledge, namely the willingness to implement it, which is why Euclidean geometry took Hobbes by storm.

Geometry impressed Hobbes not because its truth was self-evident, for he began by rejecting what the theorem before him asserted; rather, he was moved by the experience of being compelled to admit the very thing he had denied in first glancing at the text. Here was a speech that could inexorably oblige us to see things a given way, in the face of no little resistance; and it was a revelation to him. One might therefore speculate that his putting himself to the task of mastering geometry was also to figure out how he himself might produce a similar effect elsewhere. Yet another facet to Hobbes's attachment to geometry has often been remarked: his recognition that Euclidean geometry persuaded him as it did because it constituted its own artificial truth. That is, once one enters the system of proof, its sheer internal coherence fashions the sense of a proposition's demonstrativeness. So the criterion of knowledge in Hobbes arguably comes down to a particular idea of verbal persuasion that has to do less with the sensation of belief than with a certain force and clarity of understanding that enables us to see for ourselves that something must be the case.

Hobbes's idea of how speech acts upon the mind for the common good is a rhetorical one, very like Cicero's. From the time of its formal inception by the Sophists, the art of rhetoric assumed a psychology, a theory of how the subject is moved to act in the world, and especially how the individual person is induced to create and sustain community with others. For example, are we moved wholly by impressions of pleasure and pain and thus engage in and condone society out of motives of self-interest? Or must these "natural" or primitive motives be displaced or modified by social sanction and education so that we are led conscientiously to uphold the benefits of community over the immediate gratification of our desires? Coinciding with these views of human motive and value were two ideas about the way speech operates to influence our actions. On the one hand was the Gorgianic argument that since we can know nothing certainly, speech moves us by an irresistible sensuous appeal, manipulating our bodily faculties so that we are made to embrace a given end or behavior out of desire alone (the argument of Gorgias's oration the *Helena*).[7] This is speech as an impassioned, voluptuous, and demagogic power, speech, as it were, without a rationale and without accountability, either to the matter addressed or to the community, for which Plato takes Gorgias to task in the dialogue of that name. On the other hand, there was the Protagorean approach in which speech has the cognitive and moral capacity, even responsibility, to change an audience's perception for the better, to form or constitute a new idea of something by virtue of its verisimilitude, or, in other words, language's capacity to project possible worlds.[8] This is speech as *therapeia*, if not in Plato's precise sense, then with a comparable intent, except that the therapy of Platonic dialectic assumes our potential access to the reality of things. The fact remains that speech, Sophistic or Socratic, can have such pivotal impact only if neither it nor the ideas speech conveys have a necessary or evident relationship to the world of things, so that we cannot presume rightly to order subjective or communal life – to ascertain the truth – by these fallible means. As Hobbes himself attests in *Leviathan* and *Behemoth*, this emphasis on the singular power of speech tends to accompany the event of political conflict: whether intellectual – as in debate, institutional – as in a democracy or the courts, or internecine – as in war.

Even before Hobbes knew civil conflict at first hand, he had read about it in Thucydides's history of the Peloponnesian War, whose discourse approaches the cogency of Euclid. Quoting the judgment of Cicero in the *De Oratore*, Hobbes contends "that it is hard to say whether [Thucydides's] words do more illustrate his sentences, or his sentences his words."[9] For Thucydides's history taught Hobbes about the public uses and implications of speech. Accordingly, in the preface to his translation of the history, where he introduces and examines the merits of Thucydides, Hobbes puts forward what are effective rhetorical assumptions about the relations between mind, speech, and truth in civic life. He begins by dedicating his book to the father of the man he properly addresses, the then earl of Devonshire, representing the senior Cavendish as the epitome of Cicero's public man, who happily made a son in his exact image. The image presented the son with a model of one whose interests, knowledge, and practice were political, having to do with "the government of his life and the public good," and whose abilities were "for soundness of advice and clear expression of himself, in matters of difficulty and consequence, both in public and private: so also was he one whom no man was able either to draw or justle out of the straight path of justice" (*T*, 3). Hobbes's Thucydides offered William Cavendish just such an idea of civic virtue and wisdom as his father personified: "For in history, actions of *honour* and *dishonour* do appear plainly and distinctly, which are which; but in the present age they are so disguised, that few there be, and those very careful, that be not grossly mistaken in them" (*T*, 4).

While this is a conventional way to recommend the study of history, as offering its readers vivid examples of human virtue and vice, the context in which Hobbes gives his commendation is not. When he says that Thucydides makes a distinction in his writing that appears less clearly in contemporary experience, and from which the younger Cavendish can learn "when you come to the years to frame your life by your own observation" (*T*, 4), Hobbes means that it is the historian's *method* that is exemplary, not his material. In other words, Hobbes's point is not so much that there is a single, stable human nature that obtains in his day as well as in Thucydides's day, which the historian accurately reproduces. Or that political conditions under the Stuarts verge on those that led to civil war among the Greeks, although this is certainly on his mind. Rather, it is Thucydides's sort of understanding – a model of intellectual order – that Cavendish can bring to his own experience and conduct. For the history supplies a method for distinguishing among human motives and actions that, Hobbes implies, is comparable in its practical force to the exemplary presence of the earl's father and Hobbes's late patron.

Moreover, the method of the history has the integrity and the persuasive power of life itself, because it promotes such understanding without imposing speeches or precepts extrinsic to the events as they occurred. Of the way that Thucydides portrays his fellow Athenians, Hobbes remarks that "no word of his, but their own actions do something reproach them" (*T,* 17). Thus we are supplied an argument about cause – how the war came about and what took place – that consists entirely in the ordering and expression of the historical action. So while we may plausibly infer that the event of civil war bears directly on the confusion of value against which he warns the younger Cavendish, what Hobbes admires in Thucydides is the mode of speech that enables us to see the connection between motive and consequence in the historical action, and equally to discriminate the same species of cause in our own experience. As Hobbes comments, "the author himself so carrieth with him his own light throughout, that the reader may continually see his way before him, and by that which goeth before expect what is to follow" (*T,* 8). As well as letting the reader know what to expect, Thucydides injects the immediacy of "politic historiography."

He filleth his narrations with that choice of matter, and ordereth them with that judgment, and with such perspicuity and efficacy expresseth himself, that, as Plutarch saith, he maketh his auditor a spectator. . . . So that look how much a man of understanding might have added to his experience, if he had then lived a beholder of their proceedings, and familiar with the men and business of the time: so much almost may he profit now, by attentive reading of the same here written. He may from the narrations draw out lessons to himself, and of himself be able to trace the drifts and counsels of the actors to their seat. (*T,* 7)

What Hobbes ascribes to Thucydides's narrative here is an understanding almost equal in its palpability and force to reflective experience. It is a kind of efficacy that Hobbes's critics tend to distinguish from logical cogency, associating it with the rhetorical value of *energeia*, which is to make an idea evident or vivid to one's audience.[10] What is more, Hobbes's critics frequently cite this quality in Hobbes's writings as indicating the intrusion of rhetoric upon his philosophy. But Hobbes himself insists on the compatability of the two.

> Now for [Thucydides's] writings, two things are to be considered in them: *truth* and *elocution*. For in *truth* consisteth the *soul*, and in *elocution* the *body* of history. The latter without the former, is but a picture of history; and the former without the latter, unapt to instruct. (*T*, 16)

He is saying that elocution without truth cannot work upon the world, and is therefore little more than a picture or pleasant fiction of things. But truth without elocution is also powerless, since to the extent that truth cannot of itself move the mind to understanding so it cannot bring about its own observance or implementation. Thus what Hobbes attributes to Thucydides is a speech both true and compelling; for "if the truth of a history did ever appear by the manner of relating it, it doth so in this history: so coherent, perspicuous and persuasive is the whole narration" (*T*, 17).

> Of the *disposition* [or *method*] here used by Thucydides, it will be sufficient in this place briefly to observe only this: that in his first book, first he hath, by way of exordium, derived the state of Greece from the cradle to the vigorous stature it then was at when he began to write: and next, declared the causes, both real and pretended, of the war he was to write of. In the rest, in which he handleth the war itself, he followeth distinctly and purely the order of time throughout. . . . The grounds and motives of every action he setteth down before the action itself, either narratively, or else contriveth them into the form of *deliberative orations* in the persons of such as from time to time bare sway in the commonwealth. After the actions, where there is just occasion, he giveth his judgment of them; shewing by what means the success came either to be furthered or hindered. Digressions for instruction's cause, and other such open conveyances of precepts (which is the philosopher's part), he never useth; as having so clearly set before men's eyes the ways and events of good and evil counsels, that the narration itself

doth secretly instruct the reader, and more effectually than can possibly be done by precept. (*T*, 17–18)

I reproduce this extended treatment of *dispositio*, or the rhetorical ordering of one's subject matter, to make the point first that Hobbes expressly identifies "method" with eloquence – how speech is used to express ideas; and second, that by contrast to Thucydides, Hobbes considers the conveyance of precepts by philosophy much less effective than "secret instruction." If philosophy fails by not effectively – by too heavyhandedly – demonstrating what it contends, Thucydides's "politic" mode of historiography simultaneously asserts and proves its argument, even as Euclidean geometry had done in Hobbes's experience. That is to say, it is politic not simply in what it discusses but in the manner with which it conducts this discussion – working on the mind in a way to convince us.

In addition, Hobbes judges the integrity of the history by its author's credibility – that Thucydides was able to write disinterestedly about what he himself experienced or knew, neither flattering a patron nor pandering to popular opinion (*T*, 17). Now this is to make truth tantamount to *ethopoeia* in that Thucydides may be said to project a kind of ethical appeal by his stated or implied procedures, which suggest a certain moral character to Hobbes – a picture of his author's soul, which is also the soul of the text. In short, Thucydides's literate manners and condition are conceived by Hobbes to command our trust, even as a politician's might. Add to this Hobbes's tendency to justify history by its novel method, which he unabashedly terms its elocution, and the result is an idea of historical argument that is rhetorical.

I call it rhetorical insofar as Thucydides makes us understand things his way and leads us to embrace his truth by the way his speech expresses it – in short, the Protagorean and Ciceronian model of persuasion. Such persuasion gives history a status that is different from that usually ascribed to history as a literary genre, since, in the rhetorical scheme observed more or less until Hobbes's day, history was placed along with panegyric under *epideixis*, or speech engaged in praising or blaming virtue and vice, which it accomplishes for the most part by the device of amplification.[11] In other words, *epideixis* doesn't ordinarily invent, examine, or define the nature of the good, but merely uses an accepted understanding of the good, applying it to particular persons and actions. Thus nothing new is advanced by this historiography because it exists largely to affirm by example the ideas already received by the community. So where political or forensic speech must foment in its audience new or different opinions, *epideixis* is devoted to sheer entertainment, not least by exploring the pleasures of unconstrained verbal ingenuity – elocution for its own sake. It was not the working speech of the civic realm, but speech on holiday, although the rhetorician Isocrates tried to make it work after the fashion of Pericles's funeral oration. That is, he wanted to turn eulogy – the activity of exemplifying the good and the bad – to the serious task of political or civic education, which is of course Thucydides's singular achievement, according to Hobbes, and one of the main purposes of Hobbes's moral philosophy.

That the history succeeds in doing these things is the gist of all Hobbes's prefatory material to his translation, including the letter of dedication, where he extends to Thucydides a force of example surprisingly comparable in kind and effect to intimacy with that civic paragon, the late earl of Devonshire. This is character-fashioning in the sense of *psychogogia*, the leading of souls to the good, a power to which both Sophistic and Socratic speech laid claim. Later, in *Leviathan*, Hobbes eulogizes his beloved Sidney Godolphin in much the same manner as he does Cavendish senior, with Godolphin reconciling reason to eloquence in himself even as Thucydides does in his discourse.[12] For these various persons and speeches do not merely illustrate a moral: like the movements in geometrical proof, they both embody and enact meaning, so that what they say and what they do are mutually coherent. Just as Cavendish educates his son by his own civic example, so Thucydides's history does the same in that ideas and their expression are virtually indivisible.

In good history, then, demonstration and eloquence go together. Even in the discursive scheme Hobbes propounds in *Anti-White*, which has precisely the polemical or controversial force that Hobbes deplores, the difference between logic and rhetoric, history and poetry depends not so much on the presence or absence of certain figures of speech as it does on their intent to divide and confuse or to reconcile meanings and audiences.[13] That is, Hobbes is concerned not so much with the technical integrity of an argument as he is with the integrity of its effect, the way speech works upon other minds, and this is a rhetorical concern. Thus equivocation or meta-

phor fragment understanding by exploiting the desires and prejudices of each individual, who will hear in what is said whatever she
or he wants to hear, without regard for its meaningfulness. But definition and example (what Hobbes calls deeds in reference to history)
consolidate understanding by compelling us to think in a given way,
and so create a community of believers. So when Hobbes says that
"philosophy is not concerned with rhetoric" but with logic, he
means that it should entail a speech that brings about this sort of
coherence in our thoughts about a subject, just as Thucydides succeeds in doing. In short, what Hobbes applauds in the narrative and
calls elocution is the same thing he advocates for philosophy here
and calls deduction.

III

So rather than oppose science or logic to rhetoric and history in
Hobbes's humane or political writings, it seems to me more useful
to put aside such distinctions and simply to talk about the speech he
approves of and tries to emulate, and of the speech he dislikes and
distrusts and wishes to have silenced. He likes language that fosters
a community of understanding, and he dislikes the sort of illusory
language that merely reflects back to us our individual desires. It is
the distinction H. W. Jones makes in his translation of *Anti-White*,
the distinction between speech that "shapes" and speech that
"moves" the mind (*AW*, 25), between assent elicited by an achieved
mutuality of ideas and assent given thoughtlessly out of prejudice or
desire that defeats such shared understanding. Hobbes' expresses the
difference in *De Cive*, in speaking of the causes of sedition and the
subversive eloquence of Cataline:

Now eloquence is twofold. The one is an elegant and clear expression of the
conceptions of the mind; and riseth partly from the contemplation of the
things themselves, partly from an understanding of words taken in their
own proper and definite signification. The other is a commotion of the
passions of the mind, such as are *hope, fear, anger, pity;* and derives from a
metaphorical use of words fitted to the passions. That forms a speech from
true principles; this from opinions already received, what nature soever
they are of. The art of that is logic, of this rhetoric; the end of that is truth, of
this victory. . . . this they have from that sort of eloquence, not which explains things as they are, but from that other, which by moving their minds,

makes all things to appear to bee such as they in their minds prepared before, had already conceived them. (*EW* II 161)

I would argue that this capacity of speech to intervene and, to that extent, condition our experience of the world is one reason why Hobbes approves of Aristotle's *Rhetoric*, although he dislikes almost everything else Aristotle wrote. That Hobbes had an early familiarity with the text appears from his selective paraphrase or *Briefe of the Art of Rhetorique*, published in 1636. Leo Strauss has long since shown the substantive correspondence between Aristotle's definitions of characters, passions, and motives and Hobbes's versions of the same in his psychological and political treatises.[14] But beyond this manifest appropriation is another methodological use to which Hobbes may put the *Rhetoric*. Not only does the *Briefe* confirm the cognitive as against aesthetic or formal approach he takes to discourse and its civil uses; it implies a particular understanding of the status and function of Aristotle's categories, which originally had their place in making ethical and pathetic appeals. But, as John T. Harwood shows,[15] Hobbes eliminates these strategies of appeal in his paraphrase, tacitly placing all the *Rhetoric*'s contents under logical appeal, even as he omits figures of equivocation or deception. Moreover, he removes from his treatment Aristotle's account of the relations between logic and rhetoric, which Harwood sees as an implicit deprecation of the latter, reducing it to a digest of persuasive means without regard for the moral purpose Aristotle discusses. I would argue instead that these editorial maneuvers transform the *Rhetoric* into that version of eloquence he approves in *De Cive*: public discourse that constitutes or shapes perception by a variety of tactics so as to promote social consensus and civil order. In effect, Hobbes effaces the very distinction he tries to establish.

What is more, the *Rhetoric* offers him a model for speaking about the subjective dimension of human being, about motives and desires which are finally hidden from us but which have real consequences for the public or civic realm. And the importance of this contribution of Aristotle's cannot be overestimated. For if we see the *Rhetoric*'s account of our passions as political science in Hobbes's sense, as against a simply descriptive order (the medieval approach to the text, as it were), then Aristotle has composed a methodical speech about human nature designed to engage our consent and observance, even though the subjectivity this discourse articulates remains indemonstrable, very like the existence of God. That is, what Hobbes approves of in the *Rhetoric* is not only its argument but its manner of speech or method, which begins with resolving the matter at hand into its elements, out of which are drawn definitions or terms, and inferring from those terms certain consequences, which in turn are extrapolated into propositions about the way speakers should represent themselves or others to an audience. An example:

We have next to speak of the number and quality of the propositions of which those syllogisms are constructed which have for their object accusation and defense. Three things have to be considered; first, the nature and the number of the motives which lead men to act unjustly; secondly, what is the state of mind of those who so act; thirdly, the character and dispositions of those who are exposed to injustice. We will discuss these questions in order, after we have first defined acting unjustly.

Let injustice, then, be defined as voluntarily causing injury contrary to the law. Now, the law is particular or general. By particular, I mean the written law in accordance with which a state is administered; by general, the unwritten regulations which appear to be universally recognized. Men act voluntarily when they know what they do, and do not act under compulsion. . . . The motives which lead men to do injury and commit wrong actions are depravity and incontinence. For if men have one or more vices, it is in that which makes him vicious that he shows himself unjust. . . . This will be perfectly clear, partly from what has already been said about the virtues, and partly from what will be said about the emotions. It remains to state the motives and character of those who do wrong and of those who suffer from it.[16]

This passage constitutes another prototype for the sort of compulsively intelligible speech Hobbes admires in geometry and Thucydides and later calls science. For unlike the *Politics* and *Nichomachean Ethics*, where a comparably deductive procedure is applied to a similar subject matter, Aristotle doesn't offer the *Rhetoric* as an unmotivated or pure discussion of public and private humanity – of human nature per se. Instead, he presents it as a *means* to persuasion, a method of conceiving and expressing that nature in public discourse so as to persuade others. In sum, the *Rhetoric* is speech for civic use in the way that *Leviathan* claims to be, to the extent that both tell us how we should think about something to the benefit of ourselves and our community, in this case by upholding equity and the rule of law.

Thus the account of injustice here is specifically directed to forensic proof, to arguments that accuse or defend in courts of law. And the propositions, categories, and examples Aristotle educes for his reader compose the material of such persuasive public speech. Furthermore, the *Rhetoric* does not introduce this material as *loci* or commonplaces, that is, received ideas or settled beliefs on a given issue. Instead, the arguments composed from it enforce a particular, integral understanding of the issue, by virtue of their coherence and cogency. Such coherence is part and parcel of Aristotle's presentation, since the treatment of each topic derives from a preceding account and prepares the way for the discussion succeeding it – from the virtue of justice to the commission of injustice to the emotions precipitating such an act. And this general logic will be incorporated into individual speeches on individual occasions, insofar as the person speaking abides by Aristotle's terms and inferences.

The *Rhetoric* strikes Hobbes not only as an account of human nature, but as a logic and a pattern of civic speech. Moreover, such speech assumes an epistemology sympathetic to his own, insofar as Aristotle may be said to infer the motive of an action from the effects or consequences attending it. Thus the causes of fear are not emotions or dispositions in themselves, but are certain effects that are construed as *signs* of these things – the peculiar configuration of appearances we choose to call anger, malice, indignation, or indeed their dissembled absence, as well as the various sorts of advantages we speculate might accrue from doing someone an injury (1382a–b).[17] This is probable or circumstantial argument along the lines Hobbes pursues in *Behemoth*, where he assigns to parliament the desire for sovereign power from the fact of its acquisition, despite the ostensible reasons parliament gives for its actions:[18]

In sum, all actions and habits are to be esteemed good or evil by their causes and usefulness in reference to the commonwealth, and not by their mediocrity, nor by their being commended. For several men praise several customs, and that which is virtue with one, is blamed by others; and, contrarily, what one calls vice, another calls virtue, as their present affections lead them. (B, 45)

Hobbes isn't proposing by this inferential maneuver to sift what we can't see from what we can. Rather, he is organizing evidence in Thucydides's manner on the principle that parliament's actions, like the Athenians', accuse it and reveal its ends. And this is what he means when he talks about demonstrating cause: He is not divining the occult or essential nature of things, but is disposing a set of signs or body of evidence so that they make sense, even as Aristotle does in the *Rhetoric* and Thucydides did before him.

NOTES

1 Plato dramatizes this difference in the dialogues *Gorgias, Protagoras,* and *Theaetetus,* and *Phaedrus,* respectively.

2 Thus Cicero in the *De Oratore* explicitly emulates Plato's *Phaedrus,* by having the participants begin their discussion in the shade of a plane-tree even as Socrates did, and to the purpose of recalling the latter's language and argument in that dialogue (I.28–29). The necessary relationship between a full knowledge of one's subject and its persuasive expression is expounded almost immediately by Crassus, who makes the orator the vehicle of rhetoric's reconciliation to philosophy *by virtue of his practical and political role in the governance of the state.* The same argument, again with reference to the *Phaedrus,* is rehearsed in the *Orator* (12–19). So Quintilian opens the *Institutio Oratoria* by echoing Cicero's insistence that the orator "be such as to have a genuine title to the name of philosopher," again by virtue of his moral and political knowledge (I.9–20).

3 *Rhetoric,* 1354b–55b.

4 See especially Randall's *Aristotle* (Columbia, 1960, 6–7), where he writes that "The structure of the Greek language and the structure of the world are ultimately the same, because the Greek language is a natural instrument for knowing and expressing the world's structure"; "The world lends itself to the grasp of language, it has a 'logical' or 'discursive' character, a systematic structure."

5 See Werner Jaeger's discussion of Plato's *Protagoras, Gorgias, Symposium,* and *Phaedrus* in *Paideia: The Ideals of Greek Culture,* trans. Gilbert Highet (Oxford, 1939–45): 2:107–59, 174–97, and 3:182–96.

6 Loeb Library ed., trans. E. W. Sutton and H. Rackham (Harvard, 1942). In addition to Hobbes's early citations of Cicero in the introduction to his translation of Thucydides, one need only compare this passage to his account of speech in *De Homine* as the means both of covenant and civilization. Notwithstanding the liabilities of language that he lists, as a familiar topos this account is the neat inverse of Hobbes's state of nature.

7 Plato in the *Gorgias* and Untersteiner make similar arguments, but from the vantage point of different epistemologies. See Untersteiner, *Sophists,* 102–25.

8 On Protagoras, see Guthrie, *The Sophists*, 164–88; and Untersteiner, *Sophists*, 41–70.

9 *Hobbes's Thucydides*, ed. Richard Schlatter (Rutgers, 1975), 19. All subsequent references are to this edition.

10 Hobbes calls *energeia* "animation," after Aristotle's use of the term, translated "actuality," a value which both writers associate with metaphorical usages, just as Cicero ascribes the same effect to *ornatus*. For Hobbes's pursuit and achievement of *energeia* as an instrument of rational speech, and the purpose of public persuasion to which he puts it, see David Johnston's *The Rhetoric of Leviathan*, especially 3–25 and 114–33. Johnston tends to downplay Hobbes's nominalism and the idea of discourse as constitutive of the truth, preferring instead to see *energeia* and all such polemical strategies as accessory to right knowledge or science, which thus has a validity independent of its expression. While plausible, this is to conceive rhetoric from the standpoint of philosophy, as somehow extrinsic to the idea per se. Hobbes would seem to suggest otherwise in his preface to Thucydides and in the later *Leviathan* and *Behemoth*. On this point, see also Kahn, *Rhetoric*, 158–65.

11 On this taxonomy, see Cicero, *Orator*, where he describes "that class to which the Greeks Give the name *epideictic* because they were produced as show-pieces, as it were, for the pleasure they will give, a class comprising eulogies, descriptions, histories, and exhortations like the *Panegyric* of Isocrates, and similar orations by many of the Sophists, as they are called, and all other speeches unconnected with battles of public life" (Loeb ed., tr. H. M. Hubbell [Cambridge, 1962], 37–41). Cicero goes on to explain this kind of purely formal or ornamental speech, from which he distinguishes the histories of Herodotus and Thucydides, as "far removed from such tricks, or I might better say, from such folly." In the *De Oratore*, Antonius gives a somewhat different account of history, distinguishing it from eulogy as a species of annals more concerned with evidence, both material and conceptual, than with forcible expression. Yet it is at this point that he makes the remarks about Thucydides's language that Hobbes quotes (Loeb. ed., 2:43–56). It is interesting that in his concept of history, Hobbes himself retains the value of eulogy as Antonius represents it – a speech that exemplifies "the good points of human being" (*quae sint in homine laudanda*).

12 The edition is C. B. Macpherson's *Leviathan*, 718. All subsequent references are to this text.

13 *Thomas White's De Mundo Examined*, trans., Harold Whitmore Jones (Bradford, 1976), 24–26. All subsequent references are to this edition.

14 "Aristotelianism," in *The Political Philosophy of Hobbes: Its Basis and Its Genesis*, trans. Elsa M. Sinclair (Chicago, 1952), 30–43.

15 These observations are made in his exceedingly useful introduction to *A Briefe*, in *The Rhetorics of Thomas Hobbes and Bernard Lamy* (Southern Illinois, 1986), 13–19.

16 *"Art" of Rhetoric*, trans. J. H. Freese, Loeb ed. (Cambridge, 1926), 1368b. In the two paraphrases of Aristotle more or less associated with Hobbes, the *Briefe* and the later *Whole Art of Rhetoric*, it is interesting to note that he more or less reproduces the sequence of Aristotle's reasoning but framed in Hobbesian terms, including the concept of the state or polis as a public or politic person. See *Rhetorics of Hobbes and Lamy*, 61–62; *English Works of Thomas Hobbes*, 6:445–6.

17 The emphasis on signs or circumstantial, interpretive evidence in Aristotle – that is to say, verisimilar or probable representation – is reproduced in the *Briefe* (75), and the *Whole Art* (6:457).

18 This analysis begins with parliament promising Charles "they would make him the most glorious King that ever was in England; which were words that passed well enough for well meaning with the common-people." It ends with the assertion that parliament "desired the whole and absolute sovereignty, and to change the monarchical government into an oligarchy," as a consequence of the claim of the Presbyterians to govern the church by divine right (75).

14 Hobbes on religion

Thomas Hobbes's religious doctrines set a puzzle for his commentators. Among those who have addressed these questions, in increasing numbers in recent years,[1] opinion differs widely on the sincerity and consistency of Hobbes's views. By his own admission, as his faithful biographer John Aubrey recounts, "he liked the religion of the church of England best of all other," a confession made in France on "his (as he thought) deathbed" to Dr. John Cosin (Aub. 1.353). But Aubrey reports another witness to the same occasion, Elizabeth, viscountess Purbec, who claimed that Hobbes dispatched the ministering divines, Catholic, Anglican, and Genevan, with the threat "Let me alone, or els I will detect all your cheates from Aaron to yourselves" (Aub. I.357–8). These apparently contradictory reports are symptomatic of the confusion that surrounds Hobbes's religious beliefs. He himself, in the epistle dedicatory to Charles II of 1662 that prefaces his *Seven Philosophical Problems,* called upon the testimony of Cosin, now Bishop of Durham, "when [Hobbes] was at the point of death at St. Germain's," to bear witness that he was no atheist (*EW,* VII.v). If this claim is true, and Cosin was alive to deny it, the accompanying claim that in *Leviathan* "there is nothing . . . against the episcopacy" (*EW,* VII.v) is certainly false if we consider the spirit rather than the letter of the text. Aubrey reports an additional piece of evidence, supplied by Anthony à Wood, that Hobbes "used to take the sacrament, and acknowledge a supreme being" (Aub, I.353, note 'd' on Wood, folio 47).

In fact, Hobbes's somewhat different purported responses to religion in the face of death may both be true. His religious views, which he stated over and over in various places, show a remarkable consistency – which is not to say that they are coherent, as we shall see. Hobbes both professed official conformity to the doctrines of the Anglican Church and a vehement anticlericalism throughout his long life. While some details of his views were later modified, as commentators have noted of the religious chapters of *De Cive* and *Leviathan*,[2] the grand structure of his arguments was not subject to change. There were times when Hobbes suppressed his views, or others suppressed them for him. So the 2,242 line Latin poem *Historia Ecclesiastica*, in which Hobbes carefully records for posterity his history of religion, although reported by Aubrey to have existed in some 500 lines as early as 1659 and probably completed in 1666, was held back from publication and was even feared lost, appearing only in 1688.[3] Concerning suppression by others, Aubrey (I.360–1) relates a frustrating incident:

Mr. Hobbes wrote a letter to . . . (a colonell, as I remember) concerning Dr. Scargill's recantation sermon, preached at Cambridge, about 1670, which he putt into Sir John Birkenhead's hands to be licensed, which he refused (to collogue and flatter the bishops), and would not returne it, nor give a copie. Mr Hobbes kept no copie, for which he was sorry. He told me he liked it well enough himselfe.

This was an incident over which Hobbes continued to fuss, making several attempts to retrieve his letter. Birkenhead was not the only contemporary who feared to be associated with Hobbes's religious views, and for good reason. Henry Hammond declared that *Leviathan* was "a farrago of all the maddest divinity that ever was read."[4] Hammond was close to the Falkland family, the scion of whom, Viscount Lucius Carey, was said by Aubrey to be Hobbes's "great friend and admirer" (Aub, I.365) and a principal member of the Tew Circle, with which Hobbes was associated between 1630 and 1640. As early as 1662, Roger Coke, in *A Survey of the Politicks of Mr. Thomas White, Mr. Thomas Hobbs and Mr. Hugo Grotius*, concluded of *De Cive*: "It is not worth the examining, what he would have under the title of *Religion*, for men say, the man is of none himself, and complains (they say) he cannot walk the streets, but the Boys point at him saying, There goes HOBBS the Atheist!"[5] In the seventeenth and eighteenth centuries Hobbes was typically smeared as an atheist, a charge thrown at those suspected of heresy, misread by twentieth-century commentators to mean denial of the existence of God. In October 1666, for the first time since the Reformation, a bill had been introduced into the Commons to make Christian heresy a crime. The committee considering the bill was specifically empowered to investigate the views of *Leviathan*, which had earlier been reported to a parliamentary committee as "a most poisonous piece of atheism."[6] Although it failed, similar bills were reintroduced in 1674, 1675, and 1680. And in 1683 at Oxford, *Leviathan* and *De Cive* were burned, a fate Hobbes, fearlessly outspoken in his views, feared for himself. Hobbes's reflections on heresy, which he set out in various places, may therefore be read as a form of self-defense, and so may his rather unusual views on excommunication.

Hobbes's doctrinal anticlericalism and his personal experiences at the hands of the clergy were mutually reinforcing, as Aubrey suggests. He records Hobbes's attempt to endow a foundation at Malmesbury, his birthplace, but Queen Katherine's priests halted it (Aub I.343). Aubrey further records the dean of Christ Church's censorship of Anthony à Wood's life of Hobbes in the *History and Antiquities of the University of Oxford*, Hobbes's response in 1674, and his complaints to the king (Aub I.343–5). The king, Charles II, who was at one time displeased with Hobbes because he failed to understand that *Leviathan* was written not for the support of Cromwell, but for Charles's return (Aub 1.335), later came to have a good opinion of him, characterizing him rather aptly as "*the beare*" and declaring "Here comes the beare to be bayted" (Aub 1.340).

Hobbes had good reason to fear the clerics, although he maintained professional relations with, and even affection, for a few.[7] Aubrey gives an account of Hobbes's removal to Paris in late 1640 in these terms: "he told me that Bishop Manwaring (of St David's) preached his [Hobbes'] doctrine; for which, among other things, he was sent prisoner to the Tower". Then Hobbes bethought himself, "tis time now for me to shift for my selfe, and so withdrew into France, and resided at Paris" (Aub I.334). Roger Maynwaring had been impeached in 1628 for his support of the Forced Loan of 1627, which Hobbes had helped to collect.[8] In this case it was the political views of the clerics Sibthorpe and Maynwaring that placed them under continuing threat, views on the royal prerogative with which Hobbes became associated.

It is difficult to believe that someone as outspokenly frank in his unpopular religious views, and who took such care that his position be entirely understood, stating and restating his doctrines, could be convicted of insincerity. There are different reasons for this. In the first place, modern commentators almost exclusively focus on the major political works, *De Cive* and *Leviathan*, with some attention to *Behemoth* and Hobbes's response to Bishop Bramhall. An English paraphrase of the *Historia Ecclesiastica*, published under the title *A True Ecclesiastical History From Moses to the time of Martin Luther*, appeared in 1722. But Hobbes's major statement of his central views on religious and ecclesiastical history has still not been properly translated and rarely appears in the indices of commentaries (see Springborg-Stäblein retranslation, forthcoming 1998). His *Historical Narrative Concerning Heresy and the Punishment Thereof*, probably written in 1668 but first published in 1680, is similarly neglected.

The analytical focus of *Leviathan* and the method by which it proceeds, that of proposition and demonstration, which Hobbes so much admired in Euclid, produce a universalist political theory and minimalist religious doctrine, purported to be true regardless of time and place, which belie the complexity of his thought. Commentators on Hobbes's religious doctrine have focused largely on the internal consistency of Hobbes's views in *Leviathan* and between *Leviathan* and *De Cive*, without consulting his more personal reflections. In this way Hobbes is rendered more congenial to the modern secular mind, but at considerable cost to the facts. Who would believe, for instance, that the Hobbes who so roundly dispatches demonology in all its forms in the fourth part of *Leviathan*, "Of the Kingdom of Darkness," in which he mocks at the kingdom of fairies and goblins conjured up by those who subscribed to "incorporeal substances," could still have reflected on the existence of witches? And yet a remark from *The Life of William Cavendish, Duke of Newcastle*, records Hobbes "admitt[ing] that 'though he could not rationally believe there were witches, yet he could not be fully satisfied to believe there were none, by reason that they would themselves confess it, if strictly examined.' "[9] Given Hobbes's propensity for deep irony, this remark may be on the order of the recantation of Daniel Scargill, his follower, who pointed out to his accusers the difficulty of believing the sincerity of one committed to professing whatever the state commanded of him. Scargill, as outspoken as his master, had problematized Hobbesian religious beliefs for all time by pointing out they could never be found on the wrong side of the law, whatever their content might be, thus raising the specter of Hobbes and Hobbists as Nicodemists believing in systematic deception to avoid persecution on the grounds of freedom of belief, but not of speech.[10] The significance of witches in sixteenth- and seventeenth-century thought and the precise targets of Hobbes's attacks on demonology are not entirely transparent from the texts, therefore. Nor are they unrelated to the question of religion in general. We have a clue in Hobbes's remark in *Leviathan*, Chapter 2, that their trade "was nearer to a new religion than to a craft or science."[11]

There is a deep puzzle in Hobbes's religious doctrines, then, although it is not clear that there is any way to resolve it, given his commitment to publicly professing what the sovereign required of him. This puzzle chiefly concerns the doctrines' specific content in the face of his rationalist, materialist, Epicurean philosophical system. Hobbes claimed to profess the doctrines of the Church of England as adopted by Elizabeth's High Commission on religious doctrine, which subscribed to the decrees of the first four councils of the early church.[12] How do these elements sit together? How do they sit with, on the one hand, the explicit and systematic defense of the items of the Nicene Creed, which Hobbes sets out in his *Historical Narrative Concerning Heresy*, and, on the other, his highly critical account of the proceedings of the first four councils and indictment of Constantine for ever having admitted church doctors to an area of legitimate state power, in his *Historia Ecclesiastica*?

Hobbes's lengthy deliberations in that work on the problem of one Divine substance and multiple persons of God, to which he provided different answers in the English and Latin *Leviathan*s, display a detailed knowledge of the reflections of the early church councils on the nature of the Trinity and the debate over the term *homoousion* (one substance).[13] They display, at the same time, a commitment to resolving a particular problem of religious doctrine that is rendered absurd in the context of his ontology and epistemology. The religious doctrines of the first four councils posed deep problems for Hobbes, whose metaphysics inclined him to materialism and Epicureanism, but whose religious commitments, however minimalist, committed him to the orthodox doctrines of the Church of England.

The *Historia Ecclesiastica* and Hobbes's essay on heresy were written to absolve himself of the charge that his was a heresy to end all heresies. In *De Cive*, Chapter 15, Hobbes defines the principles of religious epistemology in "the three words of God": reason, science, and prophecy. In the *Historia Ecclesiastica*, he locates the origins of heresy in the departure of the early Christians from "the three words of God," seduced as they were by the philosophy of the Greeks. In *Leviathan* (1991 edn, ch. 42, 399) Hobbes's point is somewhat different: "*Haeresie is nothing else, but a private opinion, obstinately maintained, contrary to the opinion which the Publiique Person* (that is to say, the Representant of the Common-wealth) *hath commanded to bee taught.*" This no-nonsense view is targeted at the doctrine of the fourth Lateran Council, summarized by Pope Innocent III in *De Haereticis*, Chapter 3 (for which Hobbes refers us with a folio note to the collection of Decretals made by Pope Gregory IX), and which commands "*That if a King at the Pope's admonition, doe not purge his Kingdome of Haeresies, and being excommunicate for the same, doe not give satisfaction within a year, his Subjects are absolved of the bond of their obedience*" (*Lev.*, 420; Tuck, notes to 1991 ed, lvi, lviii). Hobbes both rejects the definition of heresy that the Roman Church adopts ("Where by Haeresies are understood all opinions which the Church of Rome hath forbidden to be maintained") and the claim that priests can excommunicate kings, which the church simultaneously stakes out. Priests cannot excommunicate at all, he says, but only the body of the church; and the body of the church is inoperative without its head. In effect then, the power to excommunicate (like the power to declare heresy) is arrogated to the sovereign (*Lev.*, ch. 42, 348–53). Hobbes thus more or less endorses the position of Thomas Erastus on excommunication, for which Erastus was appropriately excommunicated, a fate which Hobbes undoubtedly feared for himself.[14]

He begins "An Historical Narration Concerning Heresy and the Punishment Thereof" (*EW* IV, 387–408) by redefining heresy. Heresy is a Greek word meaning the taking of an opinion, and the chief opinionated philosophers were Pythagoras, Plato, Aristotle, Epicurus, Zeno, and their disciples, "in love with great names, though by their impertinent discourse, sordid and rudiculous manners they

were generally dispised" (*EW* IV, 387). Hobbes's choice of an historical narrative that locates heresy squarely in the pagan era is a strategy to diffuse the contemporary debate and take the heat off himself.
(It is the same strategy that he pursues in the *Historia Ecclesiastica*,
where his point was to show heresy to be an essentially historical
problem and the creation of pagan philosophers.)

Hobbes followed the formula of the great theocracies in making
behavior, and not belief, the test of fidelity. His follower Henry
Stubbe correctly intuited that a religion of ritual was better suited to
the state than a religion of belief, pondering whether Islam was not
preferable; and Falkland declared himself "not only an anti-Trinitarian but a Turk, whensoever more reason appears to me for that,
than for the contrary."[15] Christianity, and specifically the post-
Reformation church, by making piety a test of the heart and catching the ear of the Christian by the voice within, created a dangerous
innovation. It left the truth of ultimate things with the individual
and the community of believers. The English Commonwealth, in
endorsing such a view of the essential nature of the Anglican community, had vacated terrain essential to undivided sovereignty,
which Hobbes strongly advised it to reoccupy. The strategy was to
abandon emphasis on conscience, to withdraw from the individual
the right to interpret Scriptures, to disempower priests, and to make
conformity of morals and manners the test of Christian faith. As a
corollary, Hobbes subscribed to a form of religious toleration that
left citizens free in all but the most central beliefs of the state
church. The "power of the Law," he says, "is the Rule of Actions
onely" and should not be extended "to the very Thoughts and Consciences of men, by Examination, and *Inquisition* of what they
Hold, notwithstanding the Conformity of their Speech and Actions"
(*Lev.*, ch. 46, 471).

Free speech and the right to preach are a different matter, for they
are the ground of public control. The Word is a weapon of such
power that the sovereign relinquishes power over it at his peril;
Hobbes, echoing Lucian, perhaps, in Chapter 5 of *De Cive* (*EW* II, 88)
on Imperium, warns, "The tongue of man is a trumpet of warre, and
sedition; and it is reported of *Pericles*, that he sometimes by his
elegant speeches thundered and lightend, and confounded whole
Greece t'selfe." In the same vein of grand classical allusion, this
time drawn from Lucian's *Heracles*, Hobbes describes in *Leviathan*

the commonwealth's vulnerability to freedom of speech and how to deal with it.

> But as men, for the atteyning of peace, and conservation of themselves thereby, have made an Artificiall Man, which we call a Common-wealth; so also have they made Artificiall Chains, called *Civill Lawes*, which they themselves, by mutual covenants, have fastned at one end, to the lips of that Man, or Assembly, to whom they have given the Soveraigne Power; and at the other end to their own Ears. (*Lev.*, ch. 21, 147)

There is a sense in which Hobbes is an advocate of civic religion in the tradition of Machiavelli and Rousseau,[16] except that Hobbes's position is more complicated. In Chapter 6 of *Leviathan* (42) Hobbes defines religion: "*Feare* of power invisible, feigned by the mind, or imagined from tales publiquely allowed, RELIGION; not allowed, SUPERSTITION. And when the power imagined, is truly such as we imagine, TRUE RELIGION." Willing to profess what is commanded of him because he defines religious belief as lying entirely within the realm of "faith," ambit of the sovereign as commander of the faithful, Hobbes nevertheless takes it upon himself to advise the sovereign what the content of these beliefs should be. He acknowledges an obligation to profess what is commanded, but a desire to believe what he thinks. He subscribes to the Epicurean view that scientific explanation will eventually replace the "Ignorance of naturall causes [which] disposeth a man to Credulity," well-spring of religion (*Lev.*, ch. 11, 74). While the Scriptures have divine approval, falling under the rubric of publicly allowable tales that are independently sanctioned, they do not represent the immediate word of God. Nor were they necessarily written by the authors to whom they are ascribed. His views, sophisticated in his day, on Moses' authorship of the Pentateuch, which he denies, and the circumstances of the composition of the Septuagint – at the command of Ptolemy (*Lev.*, ch. 33, 261) – both affirm the independence of his belief and create the space for a sovereign interpreter.

In many respects Hobbes's doctrine of the union of civil and ecclesiastical power does not depart much from Marsilius's, or from Luther and Hooker's formulations of "the Godly Prince," more or less canonical on the post-Reformation role of the sovereign as God's deputy in the kingdom of this world. Hobbes differed from earlier advocates of "the reunion of the two heads of the eagle"[17] only in his relentless desire for consistency and his capacity to apply philosophic subtlety to each problematic religious doctrine in turn, driven by a greater commitment to Roman publicist theories of state.[18] His play on human fear and timorousness as motives to peace and the godlike qualities of Leviathan, the great governor, thundering his commands to the faithful, and his depiction of the sovereign in the imperial language of the Roman emperor, Roman law, and Bodin's King of France all serve to emphasize the awesome nature of state power. What provoked outrage was his disposition to accommodate the demands of state power as a first principle, thus submitting to the very Leviathan that Job demanded by faith we resist.[19] Insult was added to injury when Hobbes claimed this principle to be deduced by reason and supported by Scripture as a *religious* precept. It did not matter then, if his readers even took the trouble to discover it, that the central doctrines Hobbes recommended them to believe hardly differed from such respected thinkers as Marsilius, Hooker, Grotius, and Pufendorf. Or that he arrived at these beliefs by a similar route.

III. *LEVIATHAN* AND ECCLESIASTICAL POWER

Hobbes's doctrine of ecclesiastical power follows from one central assertion: that the church is not the Kingdom of God. "The greatest and main abuse of Scripture . . . is the wresting of it, to prove that Kingdome of God, mentioned so often in the Scripture, is the present church" (*Lev.*, Ch. 44, 419). The church constitutes the organizational structure of neither the natural nor the prophetic spheres of God's twofold Kingdom.[20] The prophetic sphere has been in suspension since the Jews rejected the rule of God and elected Saul, and it will not be resumed until the Second Coming of Christ as God's lieutenant. The church, if it has any claims as a continuous organization at all, has no claim to being a covenanted body, a peculiar and holy people in the way Jews were. The Kingdom of God is a literal kingdom, but the church is at best an aspect of a kingdom. The church's mission is persuasive and nongovernmental, a time of preaching called the regeneration by Christ himself, "which is not properly a Kingdome, and thereby a warrant to deny obedience to the Magistrates" (*Lev.*, ch. 41, 335). When the Christian Kingdom of God comes at the Resurrection, it will be superior to the Old Testament Jewish kingdom, which Hobbes describes in *De Cive* (xvii.7), more explicitly than in *Leviathan*, as "a *priestly* kingdom, a government most free, in which [God's people] were to be subject to no human power" – in other words, priest-ridden, like all the ancient theocracies. At least the citizen of *Leviathan* avoids this, although suffering subjection to "a mortall God," Leviathan himself. God's kingdom-to-come will both improve on the Jewish kingdom, by dispensing with priests, and on Leviathan, by dispensing with kings, because, "at the Resurrection . . . they that have lived justly, and beleeved that he was the Christ, shall (though they died *Naturall* bodies) rise *Spiritual* bodies," without desire, without fear, without passion, or the capacity to resist his rule. Whatever difficulties this might pose for Hobbes's wholesale demolition of the credentials of spirits and spiritual bodies in Part 4 of *Leviathan*, he points out that Scripture does say that when "our Saviour" shall come to "judge the world, and conquer his Adversaries," He will "make a Spirituall Common-wealth," but that "In the mean time, seeing there are no men on earth, whose bodies are Spirituall; there can be no Spirituall Common-wealth amongst men that are yet in the flesh" (*Lev.*, ch. 42, 399).[21]

If the church does not belong to the prophetic sphere of the Kingdom of God, it is not the agency of divine government in the natural sphere either. In the natural sphere government is not by positive divine command but by natural law, and the form of government depends on the reasonableness with which men set about to secure themselves. Right reason, Hobbes argues, requires the erection of a sovereign who should be given full scope of operation, and all subjects should be susceptible to his will. God rules by proxy through kings. What then is the role of the church in the natural kingdom? "The time between the Ascension, and the generall Resurrecton, is called not a Reigning, but a Regeneration" (*Lev.*, ch. 42, 341–2). Regeneration "is compared by our Saviour, to Fishing, that is, to winning men to obedience, not by Coercion and Punishing, but by Perswasion" (ibid., 342). Preparation for Christ's resumption of his kingdom requires conversion to faith in Jesus Christ. It is a battle for hearts and minds that can be waged with the king or without him. Where Christianity is propagated despite the king, the converted must outwardly conform in manners and customs to the demands of royal allegiance or expect to be persecuted; because Christ's Kingdom can establish no power structures of its own in this interim period, it must be advanced under established power structures. If government produces the equilibrium that citizens need to live their private Christian lives, it is serving its purpose. If the king promotes Christianity, the service that he does the cause requires that religion serve his cause in return. The king requires a civic religion, but if he is Christian it must be "the one true doctrine." His security is ultimately dependent not on coercion but on consent. Consent is fickle unless sustained by a theory of moral obligation, which the church rather than the state is competent to provide. For this reason, Hobbes argues that teaching and governing are mutually dependent functions of the sovereign power. The sovereign cannot allow the constitutions of a supreme pastor over him because "that were to deprive himself of the Civill Power; which depending on the opinion that men have of their Duty to him, and the fear they have of punishment in another world, would depend also on the skill, and loyalty of Doctors, who are no lesse subject, not only to Ambition, but also to Ignorance" (ibid., 373). Hobbes does not neglect the opportunity to point out that fear, the lever of kings, is also the power base of bishops, who are eager to "sliely slip off the Collar of their Civill Subjection, contrary to the unity and defence of the Commonwealth" (ibid., 374).

Hobbes's theory of the role of the church in the natural kingdom follows from his theory of sovereignty, and this is appropriate or not depending on the truth of his assertion that the erection and defense of a sovereign power is required by the laws of nature. His view of church–state relations is in the Marsilian–Lutheran tradition, according to which political order is artificial, power belongs to the human order, and all institutions are of human origin. Far from being natural, political order was seen to be a precarious feat of human engineering, sustained by the strength of the sovereign power. The Christian body politic had two aspects, then, church and state, the church concerned with redemption and the state concerned with government. "The Church's value lies as an aspect of civil society," Marsilius had declared, echoing the famous formula of the fourth-century bishops Eusebius of Caesarea and Optatus of Milevis, who had maintained that "the state is not in the Church, but the Church is in the State."[22] According to Luther, the two aspects of the *Corpus Christianum* are complementary:

The social corpus of Christendom includes secular government as one of its component functions. This government is spiritual in status although it discharges a secular duty. It should operate freely and unhindered upon all the members of the Christian corpus.[23]

That is to say, clerics as well. Marsilius, Luther, and Hobbes agree that the state has a monopoly of government. According to Marsilius (*Defensor Pacis*, bk 2), the church is no more than "a multitude," a common denomination of a number of men; the common invoking the name of Christ is their signification and not the power of superiors vested with apostolic authority. This raises the whole question of the clergy–laity distinction. All three thinkers maintained that hierarchy had no intrinsic merit and that the distinction was to be justified on functional grounds only. To Marsilius, the function of the clergy was the exercise of the powers conferred by Christ to administer the sacraments. The principle of their selection was an extension of the political principle of the division of labor. The formal cause of the diversification and unity of the city is the asymmetry of aptitudes citizens display, but the efficient cause is the will of the prince who appoints each individual to his function. Correspondingly, the fitness of the priest is the formal cause of his being chosen for ordination, but designation by the prince is the efficient cause (Marsilius, *Defensor Pacis*, bk 2). According to Luther's more democratic theology, the sacerdotal powers conferred by Christ do not require a clerical elite to exercise them; the priesthood of the laity is based upon the equality of all believers: "We all have the same authority in regard to the word and sacraments, although no one has a right to administer them without the consent of the members of his church by the call of the majority."[24]

Hobbes maintains, with Marsilius, that the clergy have a function in the exercise of sacerdotal powers and that their selection depends on fitness confirmed by the prince, if the prince is Christian. And he maintains with Luther that previous to the conversion of kings, pastors were appointed by the majority of the congregation. Whereas Christ appointed the twelve apostles, their colleagues and successors, having been called by the Holy Spirit, were chosen and authorized by the assembly of Christians in each city. Of the ecclesiastical officers elected in this way, some were of magisterial and some of ministerial status. The magisterial, called variously bishops, pastors, elders, or doctors, carry on Christ's commission to the apostles to teach, preach, baptize, forgive, and retain sins. And as an extension of this teaching power, they convened councils "to agree upon what Doctrine should be taught, both for Faith and Manners" (*Lev.*, ch. 42, 362). These, the first four church councils, whose teachings were ratified by Elizabeth's ecclesiastical commission and to whose proceedings Hobbes devoted so much space in the *Historia Ecclesiastica,* were binding only by the power of civil sovereigns. Otherwise the counsels they issued obliged just so far as "the Apostles and Elders of that Councell, were obliged even by their entrance into it, to teach the doctrine therein concluded and decreed to be taught, so far forth as no precedent Law, to which they were obliged to yeeld obedience, was to the contrary; but not that all other Christians should be obliged to observe what they taught" (*Lev.*, ch. 42, ibid., 362). If magisterial power (from *magister,* teacher, rather than magistrate) were restricted to the early church councils, unless the sovereign took it upon himself to preach, ministerial powers were confined to officers, known as deacons, chosen by the congregation to attend to its needs.

Hobbes's emphasis on teaching and governing as distinguishable functions would seem to perpetuate a distinction long recognized in medieval Catholic theory and Reformation practice between *potestas ordinis,* the spiritual powers of the clergy, and *potestas jurisdictionis,* the governmental powers to command and coerce. This separation of function, culled from Marsilius by Henry VIII's apologists, reserves governmental power to the king. Hobbes merely restated a familiar doctrine, then, when he maintained that ecclesiastical power was an attribute not of the church, but of the king. The problem was that Hobbes was not consistent, for he went on to claim for the sovereign sacerdotal powers that violated the very functional demarcation he was concerned to establish. The sovereign takes over the role of supreme pastor as both priest and governor. In his hands ecclesiastical authority is power absolute, and by virtue of his headship the organizational structure of the church is an extension of his sovereign domain. Hobbes's anticlericalism shows: the democratic election of pastors in the apostolic church was deemed to represent no more than the election of a functionary by the members of a secret society. But "when an assembly of Christians choose their Pastor in a Christian-Commonwealth, it is the sovereign that electeth him" because it is done by his authority; "in the same manner, as when a Town choose their Maior, it is the act of him that hath the Soveraign Power" (ibid., 373).

Publicist theory, it seems, drives Hobbes into his peculiar definition of the church (*ecclesia*) in the New Testament era as a quasi-parliamentary institution convened in the person of the king. This is paradoxical given that he has consistently maintained the mission of the church to be nongovernmental. He marshals biblical support for his contention, however, choosing this definition from a number of alternatives offered in the Scriptures: The Church, "(when not taken for a house), signifieth the same that *Ecclesia* signified in the Grecian Commonwealths, that is to say, a Congregation or an Assembly of Citizens, called forth, to hear the magistrate speak unto them" (*Lev.*, ch. 39, 320). Covering classical publicist practice and neo-publicist – and specifically Marsilian – theory, this definition makes the powers of the church proportionate to those of the convening authority. As convened by the apostles and their successors, the teaching church could morally oblige those who recognized its claims. As a lawful congregation constituted by the appropriate political authority, the church can act as a corporation: "And in this last sense only it is that the *Church* can be taken for one Person; that is to say, that it can be said to have power to will, to pronounce, to command, to be obeyed, to make laws" (ibid., 321).

The reemployment by Hobbes of the concept *persona* to produce this notion of an ecclesiastical legislative body, the king–in–church, parallel with the secular king-in-parliament, provides the institution through which the sovereign may exercise his power to make the Scriptures law. The effectiveness of spiritual directives does not depend on their being made law, however. Can the national church, narrowly defined as a legislative institution, be successor to the nongovernmental apostolic church? The synod of the teaching church, which for Hobbes metonymizes the church as a whole, was, it is true, even in the time of the apostles, a rule-making body. Is the Christian commonwealth, besides being a rule-making body, still a church? Since Henry VIII, the teaching church as a legislative assembly, presided over by the king, had been king-in-parliament in another capacity. Presuming this to be Hobbes's model, the business, and not the membership of the sovereign legislative assembly, marked the distinction between church and state. If Hobbes's concept of the apostolic church as an assembly of the citizens for the election of officers and the definition of doctrines, was Presbyterian, this concept of the High Church governed by parliament verged on Erastian.[25]

IV. ESSENTIAL CHRISTIAN DOCTRINE

The chief problems for Hobbes's theory arise in integrating a royal church into the scheme of prophetic history of three worlds – past, present, and to come; of two spheres – natural and prophetic, two literal kingdoms – of the Jews and of Christ yet to come, and the three-phase representation of God in the Trinity. The question at issue is whether the national churches as successors to the apostolic church do, in their multiplicity, constitute the third person of the Trinity. In the Holy Spirit "we have the person of God born now the third time," Hobbes says.

For as Moses, and the High Priests, were Gods Representative in the Old Testament; and our Saviour himselfe, as man, during his abode on earth: So the Holy Ghost, that is to say, the Apostles and their successors, in the Office of Preaching and Teaching, that had received the Holy Spirit, have Represented him ever since. (*Lev.*, Ch. 42, 339)

Hobbes's eccentric doctrine of the Trinity is a further employment of the *persona* fiction. More than that, it is an ingenious solution to the problematic concept *homoousion*, that "God has no parts" (*EW* IV, 302, 392, 398), on which he dwelt at length in the "Answer to Bishop Bramhall," in the "Narration Concerning Heresy," and in the *Historia Ecclesiastica* (lines 670–80), as the central concept around which the doctrinal disputes of the early church councils turned. "Constantine took notice of it for a hard word," Hobbes pointed out (*EW* IV, 392), but it was necessary to cull the Arians from the Catholics. The Nicene Creed put the attributes of God "*metonymically*" as in Scripture, but seventeen or eighteen of the bishops present at the council, including Eusebius, bishop of Caesarea, "refused to subscribe until the doctrine of *homoousion* should be better explained," the problem being, as Hobbes darkly notes, that they now had a canon by which to establish heresy (ibid., 397–8). In saying that "God who has been Represented (that is, Personated) thrice, may properly enough be said to be three persons" (*Lev.*, ch. 42, 339),

Hobbes is able to retain the central doctrine of the Nicene Creed, that the persons of God are consubstantial, "though neither the word *Person*, nor *Trinity* be ascribed to him in the Bible" (ibid.). In fact, Hobbes declares, it is precisely to the fact that the Greeks lacked a word for *persona* that post-Nicene heresies about the nature of Christ and the Holy Ghost are due (*EW* IV, 400). But Hobbes's doctrine of the Trinity is by no means orthodox either, for he takes the *persons* of the Father, the Son, and the Holy Ghost to mean that God is personated by three orders of representatives: Moses and the high priests belong to the first order, Christ defines and is the only member of the second order, and the Apostles and their successors constitute the third.

That God is thereby said to be three persons is true only in Hobbes's peculiar sense of person, as one "*whose words and actions are considered, either as his own, or as representing the words or actions of another man*" (*Lev.*, ch. 16, 111). The principle of accumulation of "personalities" was contained in the original definition of a person. Men own their natural personalities, but may assume the artificial personalities of those they act for. It is a small step from this to the assertion that God may own more than one natural personality, and that each of these may in some way be assumed by a number of people acting for him. In the behavioral sense, personality is recognized by function; ordinarily, to know a person is to know the individual whose actions constitute a natural personality – in this way Christ the second person of the God-head was known. But it is also possible to know a person by his works, even if as an individual he is not accessible, and in this way the Holy Spirit "which is the Deity itself" – like the Father – is known to men by his operations. His presence "is not to be understood for *Infusion* of the substance of God," but is to be inferred from the "accumulation of his gifts, such as . . . the gifts of sanctity of life, of tongues, and the like" (*Lev.*, ch. 34, 279). But how the Nicene doctrine of the consubstantiality of the persons of God could be retained on this understanding of "persons" is difficult to see, and Hobbes later retracted the opinion in the appendix to the Latin *Leviathan* (ch. 3, *OL* III, 563) because John Cosin, "now Bishop of Durham," told him "it was not applicable enough to the doctrine of the Trinity" (Hobbes, "Answer to Bishop Bramhall's *Catching of the Leviathan*," *EW* IV, 317).[26]

Hobbes's Trinitarian problems are not so easily resolved, then.

According to his doctrine, ministers of the national churches could be said to share in the third representation of God as successor to the apostles. But this is not the argument he makes, instead turning arbitrarily to the office of Moses for his model: "whosoever in a Christian Commonwealth holdeth the place of Moses, is the sole messenger of God and interpreter of his Commandements" (*Lev.*, ch. 40, 327). He attempts, paradoxically, to secure the king's ecclesiastical supremacy as God's lieutenant, after Moses and Christ, when he has already established that the peculiar kingdom of God is in suspension. Christian kings are clearly not lieutenants in the sense in which Moses and Christ were as the mouthpiece of God. For kings have no personal pact with God, nor do they have the power to personate him; they are divinely sanctioned only to the extent that they are required by the laws of natural reason. Hobbes bases his case for the analogy on two peripheral arguments. The first is that God's lieutenants in the kingdom of the Jews, although partners to a Divine covenant, derived their civil authority from a social covenant; the second is that moral directives under the Divine covenant were legally binding only when promulgated as positive law on the strength of the sovereign's secular authority (*Lev.*, ch. 40).

Hobbes is well within exegetical tradition in taking as an archetype the relations between church and state as outlined by Scripture. But to turn to the Old Testament rather than the New was inappropriate in view of his scheme of prophetic history. He had no wish to argue literally that Christian kings as supreme pastors succeed Moses and his line as representatives of God the Father. And by arguing analogically he prejudiced the case for kings as successors to the apostles through the powers of the Holy Spirit, which consistency required him to establish. This, it seems, is a symptom of the fundamental incoherence of Hobbes's doctrine of religious authority. To be consistent he had to accommodate kings to that order of representatives constituted by the apostles and their successors, who after Moses and the high priests and Christ "have Represented him ever since" (*Lev.*, ch. 42, 339). In fact, Hobbes takes care not to argue the ecclesiastical authority of the king with reference to the doctrine of the Trinity at all, confining himself to a defense in natural law and an analogical argument from the position of Solomon in the peculiar Kingdom of God. Christian kings, like pagan, have the right of ecclesiastical supremacy necessary to peace and the perpetuation of the national interest, which faith in Christ cannot deprive them of: "and therefore Christian Kings are still the Supreme Pastors of their people and have power to ordain what Pastors they please, to teach the Church" (ibid., 372). Like Solomon, Christian kings have "not only the right of ecclesiastical government but also of exercising ecclesiastical functions" (ibid., 377). The ritual imposition of hands that signified the transfer of apostolic power is not required to authorize the sovereign; his sacerdotal powers are founded in natural law:

every Soveraign, before Christianity, had the power of Teaching and Ordaining Teachers; and therefore Christianity gave them no new Right, but only directed them in the way of teaching Truth and consequently they needed no Imposition of Hands (besides that which is done in Baptism) to authorise them to exercise any part of the Pastoral Function, as namely, to Baptise and Consecrate. (ibid.)

Does this constitute a breach in the derivation of ecclesiastical power? It would seem that it does. At the opening of Chapter 42, the transmission of ecclesiastical power in the apostolic church entails some notion of apostolic succession, signified by the imposition of hands; and the doctrine of the Trinity accounted for this theologically. In the course of the chapter, Hobbes establishes that this ecclesiastical power is not power properly speaking, modifying away the imposition of hands as a power-conferring rite, denaturalizing the apostolic succession and, it seems, bringing about the collapse of his doctrine of the Trinity – or, at least, ensuring its practical irrelevance. Thus, if the apostolic church represented God in the person of the Holy Spirit, the national church represents God in the person of the king. The discrepancy between the apostolic church and the national churches is quite apparent. Hobbes says, "that God who is alwaies One and the same, was the Person Represented by Moses; the Person Represented by his Son Incarnate; and the Person Represented by the Apostles. As represented by the Apostles, the Holy Spirit by which they spake, is God" (ibid., 340). But the national church, he says in another place, is "a company of men professing Christian Religion united in the person of one Soveraign" (Lev., ch. 39, 321).

Not the least problem is in making any sense of what Hobbes means by "representation in the person of the Holy Spirit," and then of conceiving of how it could be transferred. This is a peculiar prob-

lem for the author of *Leviathan*, who devotes the fourth part to showing that ghosts, spirits, and demons are a nonsense: "those Idols of the
brain, which represent Bodies to us, where they are not, as in a
Looking-glasse, in a Dream, or to a Distempered brain waking, they
are (as the Apostle saith generally of all Idols) nothing; Nothing at all"
(ch. 34, 270). But while he can reject angels except as messengers (and
here he shows etymological correctness), or in the form of thin or
aerial bodies, because "there is no text in that part of the Old Testament, which the church of England holdeth for Canonicall; from
which we can conclude, there is, or hath been created, any permanent
thing (understood by the name of *Spirit* or *Angel*,) that hath not quantity" (ibid., 277), the Nicene Creed requires him to believe in the Holy
Ghost. Accordingly, he affirms that the Holy Spirit is the Deity in two
places (ibid., 279; ch. 42, 340); this must be on scriptural evidence,
since men have had no knowledge of the Holy Ghost in person – as
they have of Christ – nor directly by his works, because the Holy
Spirit always operates through the church (*Lev.*, ch. 44, 435). Hobbes
does maintain, quite consistently, that the imposition of hands in one
sense signifies the transfer of the person, that is to say the function, of
the Holy Spirit. Early in Chapter 42 it seems that the relation is causal
and that the Holy Ghost is by this ritual act transmitted: "this was
done by the Imposition of hands upon such as were ordained; by
which was signified the giving of the Holy Spirit, or Spirit of God"
(*Lev.*, ch. 42, 339).

Later in the chapter this assertion is modified by the distinction
that the imposition of hands did not give the candidates the Holy
Ghost, "for they were full of the Holy Ghost before they were
chosen", but merely designated them to the office of Christ's ministry (ibid., 376). In another place it is suggested that their ordination
not only did not cause them to receive the Holy Ghost, but did not
even cause them to be authorized, and "though, they were called by
the Holy Ghost, their Calling was declared unto them, and their
Mission authorised by the particular Church" of the area (ibid., 364).
These modifications are consistent with Hobbes's purpose in reducing apostolic powers to the vanishing point: the power of ordination
deemed no more than the power to elect suitable candidates to a
functional office. If he can establish this, he can remove the chief
objection to the exercise of sacerdotal powers by the king. To the

extent that he succeeds in insulating his doctrine of the ecclesiastical supremacy of the king he is destroying his doctrine of the Trinity, or at least seriously undermining its relevance. But Hobbes does not completely succeed in doing either, and instead produces a sacramental theology that is fundamentally incoherent.

Hobbes wished to salvage something of his doctrine of the Trinity, even if this is almost theoretically impossible, and, in the Protestant tradition of his time, he saw the Holy Spirit as the guardian of the ministry of the Word. In defining a person by powers to act and the personal identity that accumulated actions create, Hobbes approximated twentieth-century behavioral theory and its understanding of roles. But to define the Trinity in these terms came perilously close to heresy by anybody's reckoning, as he must have realized, since he revised his doctrine in the appendix to the Latin *Leviathan* (*OL* III, 563).[27] Bramhall, in his "Catching of the Leviathan," certainly noted it; and Hobbes, in his "Answer to Bishop Bramhall," published together with "An Historical Narration Concerning Heresy," conceded some ground, although not the charges Bramhall made.

I confess there is a fault in the ratiocination, which nevertheless his Lordship hath not discovered, but no impiety. All that he objecteth is, that it followeth hereupon, that there be as many persons of a king, as there be petty constables in his kingdom. And so there are, or else he cannot be obeyed. But I never said that a king, and every one of his persons, are the same substance. The fault I here made, and saw not, was this; I was to prove that it is no contradiction, as Lucian and heathen scoffers would have it, to say of God, he was one and three. I saw the true definition of the word *person* would serve my turn in this manner; God, in his own person, both created the world, and instituted a church in Israel, using therein the ministry of Moses: the same God, in the person of his Son God and man, redeemed the same world, and the same church; the same God, in the person of the Holy Ghost, sanctified the same church, and all the faithful men in the world. Is this not a clear proof that it is no contradiciton to say that God is three persons and one substance? And doth not the church distinguish the persons in the same manner? . . . His Lordship all this while hath catched nothing. It is I that catched myself, for saying, instead of *by the ministry of Moses*, in the person of Moses. But this error I no sooner saw, than I no less publicly corrected than I had committed it, in my *Leviathan* converted into Latin. (*EW*, IV 4.315–17)

Hobbes has got himself off one hook, only to impale himself on another. He has retracted the claim that "the person of Moses" constituted the model for kings as personifications of the Holy Spirit by substituting the "ministry of Moses." It is certainly difficult to imagine Charles II as a member of the Trinity, which Hobbes strictly might be required to maintain.[28] But has he now given away too much? The meaning of "church" seems to have shifted back to its typical use to refer to "the community of the faithful." Whatever the case, Hobbes refuses to deny the utility of his notion of "personification" in resolving technical problems of Trinitarian doctrine, devoting the bulk of his "Answer to Bramhall," as of its sequel, the "Narration Concerning Heresy," to just these issues.

V. THE KINGDOM OF DARKNESS

The final chapter of *Leviathan*, "On the Kingdom of Darkness," is an elaborate satire on the claims of different churches to divine light. *Historia Ecclesiastica*, line 9 (*OL* V, 350), fulminates against "fanatics, the new lights of our age," a theme echoed by his contemporary John Ferriby, who, in *The Lawfull Preacher: or short discourse: proving that they only ought to preach who are ordained ministers*,[29] declared, "most of our new lights are but old darknesses." In the Dedication of *Leviathan* to Sidney Godolphin's brother Francis, Hobbes speaks of the plight of England as that of a country "beset with those that contend, on the side for too great liberty, and so on the other side for too much authority." Those who claim too much liberty are easily identifiable as the Independents and the Antinomians, further to the Protestant left, who believe they are free but unto the Word of God. Those who claim too much authority are the Papists and the Laudians, who defend *jure divino* powers. Both sides, left and right, are said to share the kingdom of darkness: for though "The Darkest part of the Kingdom of Satan is that which without the Church of God; that is to say, amongst them that beleeve not in Jesus Christ . . . we cannot say, that therefore the Church enjoyeth . . . all the light (*L*, ch. 44, 418).

It was because the Presbyterians and Papists had denied the authority of the prince as God's lieutenant that England had been plunged into civil war, a jostling in the dark (ibid.). Puritans had denied the principle *cuius regio eius religio* with arguments as vitriolic as those of the Papists.[30] It was for this reason that Milton had declared with anticlerical fervor that "New Presbyter is but old Priest writ large,"[31] and that James I had maintained that "Jesuits are nothing but Puritan-Papists."[32] Hobbes mobilizes his heaviest artillery against the Papists. This is because the authority of the church of Rome represented a direct, and in fact established, threat to the system of authority Hobbes advocated in *Leviathan*. The papacy presented the dual challenge of an international sovereign power and a comprehensive religion legitimized by an entrenched philosophical system. Hobbes's indictment of the Roman Catholic church is three-pronged. He accuses Papists of scriptural misinterpretation, of the propagation of Greek philosophy and heathen demonology, and of the perpetuation of profane traditions and practices. Having shown that Bellarmine and papal apologists had misconstrued the Scriptures to support their claim for the supremacy of the bishop of Rome, Hobbes then set about to demonstrate that their misconstruction was due to philosophical misconception. The case the theologians put up, although ostensibly scriptural, was really a product of Aristotelian bewitchment based on the doctrine of essences.

Hobbes exploits the seventeenth-century tradition of referring to the pope as antichrist, although in fact he does not concur with it (*Lev.*, ch. 42, 382). He makes two pointed charges, the first that medieval theology underpinning papal political theories is (in light of Hobbesian science) no more than demonology, the second that the organizational structure of the Roman church constitutes a ghost kingdom headed by the pope, who sits crowned upon the grave of the deceased Roman Empire (*Lev.*, ch. 47, 480). Hobbes considers philosophy to be concerned with things caused. It is not therefore competent to deal with the nature of God, the uncaused Cause, or with mysteries of faith – such as miracles or immortality of the elect – for which no human cause can be postulated. Christians, therefore, can know for certain no more about the nature of God than that He exists, and about the Christian mysteries no more than what they are persuaded in the Scriptures to believe. In his debate with Descartes, Hobbes claims that we know God "not by means of an idea but by reasoning (*AT* VII 185; *CSM* II 130); there is, however, in the *Meditations*, no proof for the existence of a creator (*AT* VII, 187; *CSM* II 132). Such a theistic position was consistent with Hobbes's hostility to Aristotelianism and Neoplatonism, expressed in his refutation of the doctrine of essences in the debate with Descartes and in the fourth book of Leviathan, *The Kingdom of Darkness*, in the chapter entitled "Of Darkness from Vain Philosophy, and Fabulous Traditions."

There were matters on which Hobbes supported the Romish-leaning Laudians over the puritanical Presbyterians, as for instance on the matter of ceremonial (*EW* IV.67).[33] But there are also indications that he opposed the whole Neoplatonist movement popular with a certain cast of Anglicans, some of whom, including his friend Selden, were infatuated with the ancient wisdom of the Egyptians and the oriental religions. It seems that Hobbes's attack on the doctrine of essences and demonology of the dark kingdom may have had other than Romish targets. He himself displays a surprising interest in what he terms the "absurd opinion of Gentilisme," or pagan beliefs (*Lev.*, ch. 12, 79). Establishing that fear is the main ground of religion, like the state, Hobbes paints a picture of primitive religions and their ability to exploit fear. His principal sources are Herodotus, unacknowledged, and Diodorus Siculus, whom, in the opening lines of *De Homine* (*OL* II, 1), he eulogizes as the wisest and most deservingly celebrated ancient historian on the origins of the human race.[34] Drawing most probably on Diodorus, Hobbes (in *Leviathan* chap. 12) gives an account of the Egyptian creation, beginning with the great god of chaos and replete with astral and solar gods, crocodile and bird gods, deified calves, dogs, snakes, onions, and leeks (*Lev.*, ch. 12, 79). Although characteristically mocking, and interspersing counterparts from Greek and Roman mythology – Greek "daemon," Roman "genius," and "lares" – this account, like others in various of his works,[35] displays a detailed knowledge of the sources. Bearing in mind Hobbes's definition of heresy as private opinion based on philosophizing, we note that he presents "gentilism" here as a form of heresy (ibid.).

Chapter 12 of *Leviathan*, "Of Religion," is devoted to "gentilism," a term that we associate more with John Selden, a friend who remained faithful and left Hobbes a small bequest on his death (Aub. I.337, 369), John Toland (1696), to whom Aubrey showed his own work on this subject, and Aubrey himself.[36] Here Hobbes gives quite an accurate account of certain features of the pagan religions, which Catholicism had carried over: statue cults and certain beliefs in the powers of divine embodiment, such that people, "thinking the gods for whose representation they were made, were really included, and as it were housed within them, might so much the more stand in feare of them" (*Lev.*, ch. 12, 80–1). Not only is he interested in primitive religions, but he expresses a preference for the "Independency of the Primitive Christians" as well, precisely because of the freedom of private belief that it permitted. Clerics had assailed this liberty that tied knots in their freedom that had to be systematically untied (*Lev.*, ch. 47, 478–9).

Why would someone concerned with heresy, who defined it as private opinion that flew in the face of doctrine sanctioned by the public person, harbor such a detailed interest in heterodoxy? Hobbes's religious beliefs ultimately remain a mystery, as perhaps they were meant to: the private views of someone concerned to conform outwardly to what his church required of him, and thereby avoid to heresy, while maintaining intellectual autonomy. The hazard of Hobbes's particular catechism is that he and his supporters could never avoid the suspicion of insincerity. His preparedness to believe whatever the prince demanded of him smacked of heresy in the more usual sense, despite elaborate biblical exegesis designed to prove his orthodoxy. Undoubtedly he realized it even as he wrote the last lines of *Leviathan*, expressing the hope that "I cannot think it will be condemned at this time, either by the Publique Judge of Doctrine, or by any that desires the continuance of Publique Peace." Indicating an intention to return to science, he continued, "I hope the Novelty will as much please, as in the Doctrine of this Artificiall Body it useth to offend" (*Lev.*, Rev. and conc., 491).

NOTES

1 Discussions of Hobbes as a Christian thinker include Hood (1964); Glover (1965); Pocock (1973); Schneider (1974); Letwin (1976); Halliday, Kenyon, and Reeve (1983); Lloyd (1992); and Martinich (1992). Among the treatments of his religious views, those I have found most useful include Ryan (1983); Farr (1990); Schwartz (1985); Skinner (1990a and 1990b); Tuck (1990); Sommerville (1992); and Strong (1993). Thanks to Johann Sommerville and Alan Cromartie for advice and to the Folger Institute and the Woodrow Wilson Center, Washington, D.C., for support.
2 Schwartz (1985); Sommerville (1992), pp. 120–1.
3 The early date Aubrey gives for the *Historia Ecclesiastica*, on which he reports at some length (Aub., 1898, I.338–9, 382), is interesting, given

the focus of the work, to establish that Hobbes was not heretical, an issue that became burning, so to speak, only around 1666 when the work is believed to have been completed. But the wealth of detail on ancient religion and primitive Christianity that it contains could well reflect Hobbes's antiquarian religious interests, material that he reshaped under the heat of the heresy charge. Such an explanation might answer Tuck (1990, p. 159), who believes that the *Historia Ecclesiastica* was written later, around 1666, and was directed very specifically to this charge. He notes that according to the *Calendar of State Papers, Domestic* for 1667–8, Hobbes sent Lord Arlington, a cabal minister who defended him when he was summoned before the Lords, and to whom *Behemoth* was dedicated, his "Narration Concerning Heresy" for comment. The probable date of about 1666 for the *Dialogue of the Common Laws*, about half of which concerns the English law of heresy, strongly relates it to this group of works.

4 See Packer (1969), p. 179.

5 Cited in Sommerville (1992), p. 317.

6 Tuck (1989), p. 33; Sommerville (1992), p. xiv.

7 Hobbes seems to have distinguished between personal friendships and professional disagreements. His objections to Catholicism did not stand in the way of his friendship with Mersenne, a Catholic priest, who together with Pierre Gassendi wrote a letter strongly defending *De Cive*, which is published with the 1647 edition. And he seems to have had interests in common with the Laudians.

8 Sommerville (1992), pp. 80–81.

9 Thomas (1971), pp. 518–19, citing Margaret Cavendish, Duchess of Newcastle's, *The Life of William Cavendish, Duke of Newcastle*, ed. C. H. Firth (1886), p. 198.

10 On Hobbes and Nicodemism, see Zagorin 1990; for Hobbes's peculiar doctrine of religious toleration, see Ryan 1983; Tuck 1990.

11 Cited in Thomas (1971), p. 441.

12 Martinich, in a recent book that considers Hobbes a serious religious thinker, observes that Hobbes's definition of religious orthodoxy is that of Elizabeth I's High Commission on Christian Doctrine, which endorsed the religious decrees of the first four councils of the early church (Martinich 1992, 2). He further considers Hobbes's deep pessimism about human nature to be a product of his Calvinist education at Magdelan Hall in Oxford, and his rejection of Platonic Augustinianism and Aristotelian Thomism in favor of the new science to be a secular account of human nature and theism (ibid., pp. 4, 7). But whatever residues of a Calvinist education remained in Hobbes's general orientation to human nature did not carry over sufficiently in his religious doctrines to impress

the Calvinist synods of the Low Countries, as Johann Sommerville has pointed out to me. G. Cocquius, an Hebraist and one of Hobbes's most percipient critics, who systematically examines Hobbes's biblical exegesis (Cocquius 1680, chs. 3–7), fundamental articles of faith, and his doctrine of the Trinity (ibid., chs. 8–15), notes in his dedication that *Leviathan* was banned by the Synod of Utrecht (ibid., iv).

13 The term *homoousion* (one substance) was used by the Council of Nicaea, A.D. 325, to define the doctrine of the Trinity, as opposed to the term *homoiousion* (like substance) favored by the Arians. It is interesting that the *OED*, overlooking Hobbes's contribution to the debate, gives the first English users of the term as Ralph Cudworth (1678), *Intell. Syst.* I.iv. para 36, 597: "the Genuine Platonists would doubtless acknowledge also, all the Three Hypostases of their Trinity to be Homoousian, Co-Essential or Con-Substantial"; and Gibbon (1781), *Decline and Fall*, II.xxi, 251, 252: "Their [sc. the Arians'] patron, Eusebius of Nicodemia, . . . confessed, that the admission of the *Homoousion*, or Consubstantial . . . was incompatible with the principles of their theological system"; "The mysterious *Homoousion*, which either party was free to interpret according to their peculiar tenets."

14 Hobbes's views on excommunication did not differ much from the fourteenth-century Marsilius of Padua or the sixteenth-century Thomas Cranmer, as Sommerville in his excellent discussion (1992, pp. 127–34) and Marshall (1985, p. 414) point out.

15 Tuck (1989), p. 89; Sommerville (1992), p. 142.

16 Tuck (1989, p. 79) maintains this, going on to endorse the opinion of one of Hobbes's critics who, in 1669, charged "if once it be taken for granted that the Scriptures have no Authority but what the Civil Power gave them, they will soon come, upon a divine account, to have none at all" (cited in Tuck 1989, p. 89).

17 J.-J. Rousseau (*The Social Contract*, bk 4, ch. 8, 1978 ed, 96), characterizes *Leviathan*'s union of ecclesiastical and civil power thus.

18 By "publicist" I mean in the Roman Law tradition, a more accurate characterization of the provenance of Hobbes's particular type of sovereignty than the term "absolutism." I note with interest that the *OED* (1989, 12.782) list of usages for the term *publicist*, which it defines more narrowly as "one who is learned in 'public' or international law . . . a writer on the law of nations," includes Hobbes in the nicely illustrative quotation from the *New British Review* of May 1861, p. 173: "Plato was a publicist when he wrote the Laws and the Republic; Aristotle was a publicist when he wrote the Politics; . . . Machiavel was a publicist in the *Prince*, Hobbes in the *Leviathan*, Montesquieu in the 'Esprit des Lois'."

19 Hobbes's use of the term "Leviathan" involves a strange set of inversions.

To begin with, as the beast of Isaiah 1.27, and the Book of Job, clearly personifying the state, generally ancient Egypt (as opposed to Behemoth, which personifies ancient Assyria) in the Old Testament, and Satan incarnate on some interpretations (see Calvin 1609, p. 260b), Leviathan is a strange choice to name a Christian commonwealth. Not much light is shed on the matter by Hobbes's curt challenge to Bramhall to entitle his critique "*Behemoth against Leviathan.*" Hobbes's challenge is issued in his "Animadversons upon the Bishop's Epistle to the Reader" (*E.W.* 5.25–6), prefacing *The Questions concerning Liberty, Necessity and Chance, clearly stated and debated between Dr. Bramhall, Bishop of Derby and Thomas Hobbes of Malmesbury* (1654). It is interesting to speculate at what point Hobbes decided to use the title *Behemoth* himself, the work that was completed in 1668 and not published until 1679. Hobbes is mute on the significance of its title, at which we can only guess. Did the Long Parliament in any way resemble Behemoth as a figure for the Assyrians, land of Nebuchadnezzar and the Tower of Babel? Once Hobbes used Leviathan to mean the state in its early modern sense, the term was forever transformed, as the *OED* suggests, which blunts the provocation that this innovation must have offered to his contemporaries. After all, it is the papacy, characterized for a millennium as the dragon, or Antichrist (Hill, 1971), that most closely resembled the Old Testament Leviathan, about which the Reformation commentators were willing to say very little (see Oecolompadius 1562; Calvin 1584; Beza 1589?; Broughton 1610; and Abbott 1640). The Christian commonwealth of Hobbes should, by rights, have been an *anti*leviathan. (For further discussion of Hobbes's biblical beasts, Leviathan and Behemoth, see Springborg 1995.)

20 Compare H. Warrender (1957, 224ff.), who thinks that Hobbes believed Christian monarchies to be prophetic kingdoms like the Jewish one. But this interpretation runs counter to many unequivocal statements by Hobbes. In *Review and Conclusion* he declared: "in the Commonwealth of the Jewes, God himself was made the sovereign by pact with the people, who were therefore called his *Peculiar People* to distinguish them from the rest of the world' (*Leviathan*, 1991 ed., 487).

21 See Schwartz's (1985) discussion of Hobbes's views of the superiority of the Christian to the Jewish kingdom of God, in the context of Hobbes's criticisms of "Gentilism" due to the contamination of Judaism by false Greek and Latin notions of God. In the famous passage of *Leviathan* (1991 ed., 149–50), in which Hobbes levies this charge, he is able to deal a deadly blow both to the ancient ideal of liberty, its Israelite, Greek, and Roman advocates, and to contemporary classical republican theorists, declaring perversely that there is no more liberty in Lucca, where it is inscribed on the rooftops, than in Constantinople.

And by reading of these Greek, and Latine Authors, men from their childhood have gotten a habit (under a false shew of Liberty,) of favouring tumults, and of licentious controlling the actions of their Soveraigns; and again of controlling those controllers, with the effusion of so much blood; as I think I may truly say, there was never any thing so deerly bought, as these Western parts have bought the learning of the Greek and Latine tongues.

22 Lagarde (1956), 2.241.

23 Luther (1956 ed.), I.117.

24 Luther (1956 ed.), I.114.

25 Although the efforts of Erastus in the sixteenth century had been specifically aimed at the draconian powers of excommunication claimed by the Calvinist churches, as we have noted, his name became synonymous with the subordination of ecclesiastical to secular power.

26 John Cosin (1594–1672) did not become bishop of Durham until December 1660, and Hobbes's wording suggests that he made his criticism before that, perhaps in Paris, where Cosins acted as chaplain for the Anglicans at the court of Henrietta Maria between 1644 and the Restoration and ministered to Hobbes on, as he thought, his deathbed. Cosin's influence with Hobbes would seem to put paid to Martinich's (1992) general view of Hobbes as a closet Calvinist. A high church Anglican and Arminian, friend of Archbishop Laud, and like his mentor fond of elaborate ritual, Cosin was (unfairly) convicted of being a Romanist. Hobbes seems to have followed Laud and Cosins in his high regard for religious ceremonial, as we know from *Elements of the Law*, where he claims that "to adorn [God's] worship with magnificence and cost" is a natural sign of our honoring him, and "to adorn the place of his worship worse than our own houses [is a manifest sign of] contempt of the Divine Majesty" (*E.W.* 4.67).

27 It is worth noting that the extensive appendix to the Latin *Leviathan* (*L.W.* 3.511–69) is almost wholly devoted to the Nicene Creed (Chap. 1); to rebuttal of claims of heresy and atheism made against Hobbes by (mostly) unnamed sources, to points of biblical exegesis, and to corrections to his doctrine of the Trinity (Chaps. 2 and 3).

28 In fact, of course, the third person of the Trinity had always been problematic, because the Holy Ghost hardly seems to be a person by any stretch of the imagination, and because the debate over the term *homoousion* more strictly concerned the first two persons of the Trinity than the third. Hobbes takes his escape with the model of Moses.

29 1653, sig. B3b, cited in Sommerville (1992), p. 199.

30 One of the most colorful attacks on the principle *cuius regio eius religio*, in the name of which Henry VIII's royal supremacy in matters

ecclesiastical had been declared, was that made by Anthony Gilby, a Calvinist. He expostulated on the revolution that made Henry the godly prince:

> Thus there was no reformation, but a deformation, in the tyme of that tyrant and lecherous monster. The bore I grant was busy rooting and dragging up the earth, and all his pigges that followed him ... This monstrous bore for all this must need be called the head of the Church in paine of treason, displacing Christ our onlie Head, who ought alone to have the title. Wherefore in this point, O England, ye be no better than the Popish antichrist. (quoted by C. McIlwain [1918], pp. xvii–xviii).

31 Milton, *On the New Forces of Conscience under the Long Parliament.*

32 Quoted by McIlwain (1918), p. xxvii.

33 As Johann Sommerville has suggested to me, however, perhaps too much should not be read into Hobbes remarks in the *Elements* (1640), a work dedicated to Newcastle and intended "to insinuate itself with those whom the matter it containeth most nearly concerneth" (*E.W.* 4.ii), namely Charles I, a High Churchman who also loved ceremonial. In Chapter 31 of *Leviathan*, for instance, where the same distinctions are made between internal and external signs of worship, reference to elaborate ceremonial other than well-composed verse and music is absent.

34 Praise that he repeats elsewhere, for instance in *Behemoth*, (*E.W.* 6.278–81), *Decameron Physiologicum* (*E.W.* 7.73–4), and the *Examinatio et Emendatio Mathematicae Hodiernae I. Wallisius* (*L.W.* 4.3–4).

35 Further accounts of the religions of the ancient Egyptians, Chaldeans, Assyrians, Iranians, and Indians are to be found in the *Historia Ecclesiastica*, lines 50–350, and in *Behemoth* (*E.W.* 4.277–82).

36 The "gentilism" that Hobbes discusses here and in the "Narration on Heresy" as the ancient legacy with which the Greek philosophers infected Christianity, is spelled out in 500 lines of Latin verse in the *Ecclesiastical History*. Referring in *Leviathan* (1991 ed., p. 79) to the "absurd opinion of Gentilisme," or pagan beliefs, precisely in the context of his discussion of the primitive religions of ancient Egypt and Mesopotamia, Hobbes is not the first to address this question. The *OED* (1989 ed., 6.449) gives early sources for the term, meaning "Heathenism, paganism, a heathen belief or practice" and occasionally "in opposition to *Judaism*." John Selden (1617 ed.), Gerard Vossius (1668 ed.) and Edward Herbert (1663) all wrote works on gentilism, and even Aubrey's shopping list of pagan religious practices, "old customes, and old wives-

fables," published under the title *Remaines of Gentilisme and Judaisme* (Aub., 1972 ed., Preface, p. 132 and pp. 133–304), qualifies.

REFERENCES

Abbott, George. 1640. *The Whole Booke of Iob Paraphrased, or Made easie for any to understand.* London: Printed by Edward Griffin for Henry Overton. (STC 41)

Aubrey, John. 1898. *'Brief Lives', chiefly of Contemporaries, set down by John Aubrey between the Years 1669 & 1696.* Edited from the Authors Mss. by Andrew Clark. 2 vols. Oxford: The Clarendon Press.

Aubrey, John. 1972 ed. *Remaines of Gentilisme and Judaisme.* In John Buchanan-Brown, ed. *John Aubrey, Three Prose Works.* Fontwell, Sussex: Centaur Press.

Beza, Theodore. 1589(?) *Job Expovnded by Theodore Beza, partly in manner of a Commentary, partly in manner of a Paraphrase.* Faithfully translated out of Latine into English. Printed by Iohn Legatt, Printer to the Uniuersity of Cambridge. (STC 2020)

Bible. 1611, 1911 ed.. Authorized Version 1911, facsimile of 1611 ed. Oxford: Oxford University Press.

Bramhall, John. 1658. *Castigations of Mr. Hobbes his last animadversions, in the case concerning liberty and universal necessity. With an apprendix concerning the catching of LEVIATHAN, or the great whale.* London: Printed by E.T. for John Crook, at the sign of the Ship in Pauls Church-yard. (STC B4215)

Broughton, Hugh. 1606. *The Lamentations of Ieremy, translated with great care of his Hebrew Elegancie, and oratiovs speaches: wherin his sixfold Alphabet Stirreth all to attention of God's Ordered Providence in Kingdomes confusion.* (n.p., bound together with Broughton 1610)

1610. *Iob. To the King. A Colon-Agrippina studie of one moneth, for the metricall translation. But of Many Yeres, for Ebrew Difficulties. Part 2 is Iob. Brought on to familiar dialogue and paraphrase for easier entendement.* (n.p.) (STC 3868)

Brown, Keith C. 1962. "Hobbes' Grounds for Belief in a Deity." *Philosophy* 37: 336–44.

Calvin, John. 1584. *Sermons of Maister Iohn Calvin, vpon the Booke of Iob.* Trans. Arthur Golding. London: George Bishop. (STC 4447)

1609. *A Commentary vpon the Prophecie of Isaiah.* Translated ovt of French . . . by C. C. London: Printed by Felix Kyngston for William Cotton. (STC 4396)

Clive, Megan. 1978. "Hobbes parmi les mouvements religieux de son temps." *Revue des Sciences Philosophiques et Théologiques* 62: 41–59.

Clüver, Johann (Cluverius, Johannis). 1645. *Historiam Totius Mundi. Epitome a prima rerum Origine usque ad annorum Christi MDCXXX.* Leiden.

Clüver, Ph. (Cluverius, Philip). 1657. *An Introduction to Geography both Ancient and Modern, comprised in Sixe Books.* Oxford: Leonard Lichfield.

Coady, C.A.J. 1986. "The Socinian Connection – Further Thoughts on the Religion of Hobbes." *Religious Studies* 22: 277–80.

Cocquius, Gisbertus. 1680. *Hobbesianismi Anatome, Oua innumeris Assertionibus ex Tractatibus de Homine, Cive, Leviathan Juxta seriem locorum Theologiae Christiane Philosophi illius a Religione Christiana Apostasia demonstratur, & refutatur.* Utrecht: Franciscum Halma.

Damrosch, Leopold, Jr. 1979. "Hobbes as Reformation Theologian: Implications of the Freewill Controversy." *Journal of the History of Ideas* 40: 339–52.

Descartes, René. 1934 ed. *The Philosophical Works of Descartes.* Ed. Elizabeth S. Haldane and G.R.T. Ross. 2 vols. Cambridge: Cambridge University Press.

Eisenach, Eldon J. 1982. "Hobbes on Church, State and Religion." *History of Political Thought* 3: 215–43.

Farr, James. 1990. "Atomes of Scripture: Hobbes and the Politics of Biblical Interpretation." In Mary Dietz, ed., *Thomas Hobbes and Political Theory.* Lawrence: University of Kansas Press.

Geach, Peter T. 1981. "The Religion of Thomas Hobbes." *Religious Studies* 17: 549–58.

Glover, Willis B. 1965. "God and Thomas Hobbes." In Keith C. Brown, ed., *Hobbes Studies.* Cambridge: Cambridge University Press.

Halliday, R.J., Timothy Kenyon, and Andrew Reeve. 1983. "Hobbes's Belief in God." *Political Studies* 31: 418–33.

Hepburn, R.W. 1972. "Hobbes on the Knowledge of God." In M. Cranston and R.S. Peters, eds., *Hobbes and Rousseau: A Collection of Critical Essays.* Garden City, N.Y.: Anchor Books.

Herbert, Edward. 1705 ed. *The Ancient Religion of the Gentiles and Causes of Errors Considered.* London: for John Nutt. (English translation of *De religione gentilis, errorumque apud eos causis.* Amstelaedami: Typus Blaeviorum, 1663.)

Hill, Christopher. 1971. *Antichrist in Seventeenth Century England.* Oxford: Oxford University Press.

Hobbes, Thomas. 1688 ed. *Historia ecclesiastica carmine elegiaco concinnata.* Ed. with a preface by Thomas Rymer. London.

1722. *A True Ecclesiastical History From Moses to the time of Martin Luther, in Verse* (English paraphrase of the *Historia Ecclesiastica*). London: E. Curll.

1839–45 ed. *The English Works of Thomas Hobbes*, ed. Sir William Molesworth (11 vols, referred to as *E.W.*); *Thomae Hobbes . . . Opera Philosophica quae Latine scrisit omnia*, ed. Sir William Molesworth. (5 vols, referred to as *L.W.*). London: J. Bohn.

1969 ed. *The Elements of Law Natural and Politic*. Ed. Ferdinand Tönnies (1889); reissued with a new introduction by M. M. Goldsmith.

1976 ed. *Thomas White's 'De Mundo' Examined*. Trans. Harold Whitmore Jones. Bradford: Bradford University Press.

1983 ed. *De Cive: The Latin Version; De Cive: The English Version*. Ed. Howard Warrender. Oxford: The Clarendon Press.

1990. *Behemoth or the Long Parliament*. Ed. Ferdinand Tönnies; reissued with an introduction by Stephen Holmes. Chicago: Chicago University Press.

Hood, F.C. 1964. *The Divine Politics of Thomas Hobbes*. Oxford: The Clarendon Press.

Johnson, Paul J. 1974. "Hobbes's Anglican Doctrine of Salvation." In Ralph Ross, Herbert W. Schneider, and Theodore Waldman, eds., *Thomas Hobbes in His Time*. Minneapolis: University of Minnesota Press.

Johnston, David. 1989. "Hobbes' Mortalism." *History of Political Thought* 10, 4: 647–63.

Lagarde, Georges de. 1956. *La Naissance de l'Esprit Laique au Declin du Moyen Age*. 5 vols. Louvain.

Letwin, Shirley Robin. 1976. "Hobbes and Christianity." *Daedalus* 105: 1–21.

Lloyd, S.A. 1992. *Ideals as Interests in Hobbes's Leviathan*. Cambridge: Cambridge University Press.

Luther, Martin. 1956 ed. *The Reformation Writings of Martin Luther*. Trans. from the definitive Weimar edition by Bertram Lee Wolf. 2 vols. London: Lutterworth Press.

McIlwain, C.H. 1918. *The Political Works of James I*. Cambridge: Cambridge University Press.

Marshall, John. 1985. "The Ecclesiology of the Latitude-men, 1660–1689: Stillingfleet, Tillotson and 'Hobbism'." *Journal of Ecclesiastical History* 36, 3: 407–27.

Marsilius of Padua. 1956 ed. *The Defender of the Peace (Defensor Pacis)*. Trans. Alan Gewirth. New York: Columbia University Press.

Martinich, A. P. 1992. *The Two Gods of Leviathan*. Cambridge: Cambridge University Press.

Milner, Benjamin. 1988. "Hobbes on Religion." *Political Theory* 16: 400–25.

Minz, Samuel I. 1962. *The Hunting of Leviathan: Seventeenth Century Reactions to the Materialism and the Moral Philosophy of Thomas Hobbes.* Cambridge: Cambridge University Press.

Oakley, Francis. 1983. "Legitimation by Consent: the Question of the Meedieval Roots." *Viator* 14: 303–35.

1984. *Omnipotence, Covenants and Order.* Ithaca, N.Y.: Cornell University Press.

Oecolampadius, Jean. 1562. *Exposition de M. Iean Oecolompade svr le Livre de Iob.* Traduit de Latin en François. Edition premiere. A Geneve, par Vincent Bres. (Wing 218–628q)

Pacchi, Arrigo. 1988. "Hobbes and the Problem of God." In G.A.J. Rogers and Alan Ryan, eds., *Perspectives on Thomas Hobbes.* Oxford: The Clarendon Press.

1989. "*Leviathan* and Spinoza's *Tractatus* on Revelation." *History of European Ideas* 4: 577–93.

Packer, John W. 1969. *The Transformation of Anglicanism 1643–1660 with Special Reference to Henry Hammond.* Manchester: Manchester University Press.

Pocock, J.G.A. 1973. "Time, History and Eschatology in the Thought of Thomas Hobbes." In Pocock, *Politics, Language and Time.* London: Methuen.

Rogow, Arnold A. 1986. *Thomas Hobbes: Radical in the Service of Reaction.* New York: W. W. Norton.

Rousseau, J.-J. 1978 ed. *Of the Social Contract.* Trans. Richard W. Crosby. Brunswick, Ohio: King's Court Communications.

Ryan, Alan. 1983. "Hobbes, Toleration and the Inner Life." In David Miller and Larry Siedentop, eds., *The Nature of Political Theory.* Oxford: The Clarendon Press.

Sarasohn, Lisa. 1985. "Motion and Morality: Pierre Gassendi, Thomas Hobbes and the Mechanical World View." *Journal of the History of Ideas* 46: 363–80.

Scargill, Daniel. 1669. "The Recantation of Daniel Scargill Publickly made before the University of Cambridge in Great St. Maries, July 25. 1669." London: A. Maxwel.

Schaffer, Simon. 1988. "Wallification: Thomas Hobbes on School Divinity and Experimental Pneumatics." *Studies in History and Philosophy of Science* 19: 275–98.

Schneider, Herbert W. 1974. "The Piety of Hobbes." In Ralph Ross, Herbert W. Schneider, and Theodore Waldman, eds., *Thomas Hobbes in His Time.* Minneapolis: University of Minnesota Press.

Schwartz, Joel. 1985. "Hobbes and the Two Kingdoms of God." *Polity* 18, 1: 7–24.

Selden, John. 1617. *De dis syriis*. Revised and enlarged ed. 1629.

Shulman, George. 1988. "Hobbes, Puritans and Promethean Politics." *Political Theory* 16: 426–43.

Skinner, Quentin. 1966. "Thomas Hobbes and His Disciples in France and England." *Comparative Studies in Society and History* 8: 153–67.

1990a. "Thomas Hobbes on the Proper Signification of Liberty." *Transactions of the Royal Historical Society* 40: 121–51.

1990b. "Thomas Hobbes: Rhetoric and the Construction of Morality." *Proceedings of the British Academy* 76: 1–61.

Sommerville, Johann P. 1982. "From Suarez to Filmer: a Reappraisal" *Historical Journal* 25: 525–40.

1986. *Politics and Ideology in England,* 11603–40. London: Longman.

1992. *Thomas Hobbes: Political Ideas in Context.* London: Macmillan.

Spenser, Edmund. 1932 ed. *The Faerie Qveene.* 5 vols. In Edwin Greenlaw et al., eds., *Works,* Variorum ed. Baltimore: Johns Hopkins University Press.

Springborg, Patricia. 1975. "*Leviathan* and the Problem of Ecclesiastical Authority." *Political Theory* 3, 3: 289–303.

1976. "*Leviathan,* the Christian Commonwealth Incorporated." *Political Studies* 24, 2: 171–83.

1994. "Hobbes, Heresy and the *Historia Ecclesiastica.*" *Journal of the History of Ideas* 55, 4: 553–71.

1995. "Hobbes' Biblical Beasts: *Leviathan* and *Behemoth.*" *Political Theory* 23, 2: 353–75.

Forthcoming. "Thomas Hobbes and Cardinal Bell armene: *Leviathan* and "The Ghost of the Roman Empire." *History of Political Thought.* 16, 4, Winter 1995.

Forthcoming. "Writing to Redundancy: Hobbes and Cluvecius". *Historical Journal* June 1996.

Springborg, Patricia and Patricia Harris Stäblein. 1998 forthcoming. *Hobbes's Historia Ecclelenasteen: A Critical Edition.* Paris: Voltaire Society.

Forthcoming. "Leviathan. Mythic History and National Historiography." In Donald Kelley and David Harris Sachs, ed., *Philosophy, Rhetoric and the Historical Imagination in Early Modern Britain.* Washington, D.C.: Woodrow Wilson Center.

Strong, Tracy B. 1993. "How to Write Scripture: Words, Writing and Authority in Thomas Hobbes."

Sutherland, Stewart. 1974. "God and Religion in *Leviathan.*" *Journal of Theological Studies* 25: 373–80.

Thomas, Keith. 1971. *Religion and the Decline of Magic: Studies in Popular*

Beliefs in Sixteenth and Seventeenth Century England. London: Weidenfeld and Nicolson.

Toland, John. 1696. *Christianity not Mysterious: or a Treatise shewing, that there is nothing in the Gospel contrary to Reason, nor above it; and that no Christian Doctrine can be properly call'd a Mystery.* London (n.p.).

Tuck, Richard. 1989. *Hobbes.* Oxford: Oxford University Press.

1990. "Hobbes and Locke on Toleration." In Mary Dietz, ed., *Thomas Hobbes and Political Theory.* Lawrence: University of Kansas Press.

Vossius, Gerardus Joannes. 1668 ed. *De theologia gentili, et physiologia christiana; sive de origine ac progressu idolatries, deque naturae mirandis, quibus homo adducitur ad Deum.* Amsterdam.

Willman, Robert. 1970. "Hobbes on the Law of Heresy." *Journal of the History of Ideas* 31.

Zagorin, Perez. 1990. *Ways of Lying: Dissimulation, Persecution and Conformity in Early Modern Europe.* Cambridge: Harvard University Press.

BIBLIOGRAPHY

The literature on Hobbes has been accumulating for hundreds of years in many languages and is vast. Works listed below are confined to those referred to by contributors to the present volume. Two full-scale Hobbes bibliographies are included. Professor Edwin Curley has produced an article comprehensively reviewing recent philosophical literature, mainly in English, on Hobbes's morals and politics. See his "Reflections on Hobbes: Recent Work on His Moral and Political Philosophy," *Journal of Philosophical Research* 15 (1990): 169–250. A counterpart of this survey – on epistemology and metaphysics–is in preparation. Since the late 1980s, annual surveys of books and articles on Hobbes from around the world have been compiled by an international team under the direction of a Hobbes Research Group in the Paris-based Centre National de la Recherche Scientifique. These surveys appear regularly in *Archives de Philosophie*. The journal *Hobbes Studies* has been established recently, and there is a newsletter issued by the International Hobbes Association from its North American base in Colorado.

HOBBES'S WORKS

EDITIONS

Thomae Hobbes Malmesburiensis opera philosophica quae latine scripsit, omnia. Ante quidem per partes, nunc autem, post cognitas omnium objectiones, conjunctim & accuratius edita. Amsterdam, 1668.

The Moral and Political Works of Thomas Hobbes of Malmesbury never before collected together. London, 1750.

The English Works of Thomas Hobbes of Malmesbury. Ed. W. Molesworth. 11 vols. London, 1839–45.

Thomas Hobbes Malmesburiensis opera philosophica quae latine scripsit omina. Ed. W. Molesworth, 5 vols. London, 1845.

381

The Clarendon Edition of the Works of Thomas Hobbes. Ed. H. Warrender et al. Oxford, 1983– .

INDIVIDUAL WORKS

De mirabilibus pecci, carmen. London, 1636?

A Briefe of the Art of Rhetorique. London, 1637?

Elementorum philosophiae sectio tertia de cive (Paris, 1642). 2nd and 3rd editions, Amsterdam, 1647.

"Opticae liber septimus" in M. Mersenne, *Universae geometriae mixtaeque mathematicae synopis, et bini refactionum demonstratarum tractatus.* Paris, 1644. Pp. 567–89.

Elements philosophiques du citoyen Traicté politique, où les fondemens de la société civile sont decouverts. Trans. S. Sorbiere. Amsterdam, 1649.

"The Answer of Mr. Hobs to Sr. William D'Avenant's Preface before Gondibert'." In W. Davenant, *A Discourse upon Gondibert, an Heroick Poem.* Paris, 1650.

De corpore politico; or, The Elements of Law, Moral & Politick. London, 1650.

Humane Nature; or, The Fundamental Elements of Policie. London, 1650.

Leviathan; or, The Matter, Forme, & Power of a Common-wealth Ecclesiasticall and Civill. London, 1651.

Of Libertie and Necessitie a Treatise Wherein all Controversie Concerning Predestination, Election, Free-will, Grace, Merits, Reprobation, &c Is Fully Decided and Cleared. London, 1654.

Elementorum philosophiae sectio prima de corpore. London, 1655.

Elements of Philosophy, the First Section, Concerning Body, with Six Lessons to the Professors of Mathematicks of the Institution of Sr Henry Savile, in the University of Oxford. London, 1656.

The Questions concerning Liberty, Necessity, and Chance Clearly Stated and Debated between Dr Bramhall Bishop of Derry, and Thomas Hobbes of Malmesbury. London, 1656.

. . . Markes of the Absurd Geometry, Rural Language, Scottish Church-Politicks, and Barbarismes of John Wallis Professor of Geometry and Doctor of Divinity. London, 1657.

Elementorum philosophiae sectio secunda de homine. London, 1658.

Examinatio et emendatio mathematicae hodiernae. Qualis explicatur in libris Johannis Wallisii geometriae professoris Saviliani in academia Oxioniensi. Distributa in sex dialogos. London, 1660.

Dialogus physicus, sive de natura aeris conjectura sumpta ab experiments nuper Londini habitis in collegio Greshamensi. Item de duplicatione cubi. London, 1661.

Mr Hobbes Considered in his Loyalty, Religion, Reputation, and Manners. By way of a Letter to Dr Wallis. London, 1662.

Problemata physica [. . .] *adjunctae sunt etiam propositiones duae de duplicatione cubi, e) dimensione circuli.* London, 1662.

De principiis et ratiocinatione geometrarum Ubi ostenditur incertitudinem falsitatemque non minorem inesse scriptis eorum, quam scriptis physicorum e) ethicorum. London, 1666.

Leviathan, Trans. A.T.A.B., Amsterdam, 1667.

Quadratura circuli, cubatio sphaerae, duplicatio cubi, breviter demonstrata. London, 1669.

Quadratura circuli, cubatio sphaerae, duplicatio cubi, una cum respensione ad objectiones geometriae profesoris saviliani Oxoniae editas anno 1669. London, 1669.

Leviathan sive de materia, forma e) potestate civitatis ecclesiasticae et civilis. Amsterdam, 1670.

Rosetum geometricum, sive propositiones aliquot frustra antehace tentatae Cum censura brevi doctrinae Wallisianae de motu. London, 1671.

Lux mathematica Excussa collisionibus Johannis Wallisi [. . .] *et Thomae Hobbesi malmesburiensis.* London, 1672.

Epistola Thomae Hobbes malmesburiensis ad dominum Atonium à Wood authorem Historiae e) antiquitatum universitatis oxoniensis. London, 1674.

Principia et problemata aliquot geometrica antè desparata, nunc breviter explicata e) demonstrata. London, 1674.

Decameron physiologicum; or, Ten Dialogues of Natural Philosophy. London, 1678.

The History of the Civil Wars of England From the Year 1640 to 1660. London, 1679.

Thomae Hobbesii malmesburiensis vita. London, 1679.

Considerations upon the Reputation, Loyalty, Manners, e) Religion of Thomas Hobbes of Malmesbury. London, 1680.

An Historical Narration concerning Heresie, and the Punishment thereof. London, 1680.

An Answer to a Book Published by Dr Bramhall [. . .] *Together with an Historical Narration concerning Heresie, and the Punishment thereof.* London, 1682.

Tracts of Thomas Hobb's containing . . . V. Ten *Dialogues of Natural Philosophy qc.* London, 1681.

Tracts of Mr Thomas Hobbs of Malmesbury, containing [. . .] *iv.* Philosophical Problems, dedicated to the King in 1662 but never printed before. London, 1682.

Historia ecclesiastica carmine elegiaco concinnata. London, 1688.

The Elements of Law: Natural and Politic. Ed. F Tönnies. London, 1889.
"Tractatus opticus: prima edizione integrale." Ed. F. Alessio, *Revista critica di storia dela filosofia 18* (1963): 147–88.
Critique du De mundo de Thomas White. Ed. J Jacquot and H W Jones. Paris, 1973.

OTHER EDITIONS

Behemoth or the Long Parliament. Ed. F. Tönnies. London, 1889.
Dialogue Between a Philosopher and a Student of the Common Laws of England. Ed. J. Cropsey. Chicago, 1971.
Hobbes's Thucydides. Ed. Ruichard Schlatter. New Brunswick, New Jersey, 1975.
Behemoth ou Le Long Parliament. Ed. and trans. Luc Borot. *Oeuvres de Hobbes en Français.* vol. 9. Paris, 1990.
Hérésie et Histoire. Ed. and trans. F. Lessay. *Oeuvres de Hobbes en Français,* vol. 12. Paris, 1993.
Leviathan. Ed. R. Tuck. Cambridge, 1991.

BIBLIOGRAPHIES

Macdonald, H., and Hargreaves, M. *Thomas Hobbes: A Bibliography.* London, 1952.
Sacksteder, W. *Hobbes Studies.* Bowling Green, Kentucky, 1982.

OTHER WORKS

Abbott, G. *The Whole Booke of Job Paraphrased, or Made Easier to Understand.* London, 1640.
Ames, W. *Conscience with the Power and Cases Thereof.* Leyden and London, 1639.
A Fresh Suit against Human Ceremonies. Amsterdam, 1633.
Aquinas, Thomas. *On Law, Morality, and Politics.* Eds. W. Baumgarth and R. Regan. Indianapolis, 1988.
Aristotle. *Complete Works.* Ed. J Barnes. 2 vols. Princeton, New Jersey, 1984.
Aubrey, J. *Wiltshire: The Topographical Collections.* Ed. J. E. Jackson. Devizes, 1862.
Brief Lives, Chiefly of Contemporaries, Set Down by John Aubrey, Between the Years 1669 & 1696. Ed. A. Clark. 2 vols. Oxford, 1898.
Aubrey on Education: A Hitherto Unpublished Manuscript by the Author of Brief Lives. Ed. J. E. Stephens. London, 1972.
Remains of Gentilisme and Judaisme in *John Aubrey, Three Prose Works.* Ed. J Buchanan-Brown. Fontwell, Sussex, 1972.
Auger, L. *Gilles Personne de Roberval* (1602–1675): *son activité intellectuelle, dans les domaines mathématique, physique, méchanique et philosophique.* Paris, 1962.
Austin, John. *The Province of Jurisdiction Determined.* New York, 1954.

Bacon, F. *The Essayes or Counsels, Civill and Morall.* London, 1625.

Works. Eds. J. Spedding and R. Ellis. London: Longman, 1858.

Bacon, R. *Opus Maius.* vol. 2. Ed. Bridges (1897). Reprint Frankfurt, 1964.

Barnouw, J. "Prudence et science chez Hobbes." In *Thomas Hobbes: philosophie première, théorie de la science et politique,* eds. Y. C. Zarka and J. Bernhardt. Paris, 1990.

Barry, B. "Warrender and His Critics." In *Hobbes and Rousseau,* ed. M. Cranston and R. S. Peters. New York, 1972.

Baumgold, D. *Hobbes's Political Theory.* Cambridge, 1988.

Beckmann, P. *A History of π.* New York, 1971.

Bernhardt, J. "Hobbes et le mouvement de la lumiere." *Revue d'histoire des Sciences* 30 (1977): 4–24.

"La polémique de Hobbes contre la Dioptrique de Descartes dans le Tractatus Opticus II (1664)." *Revue Internationale de Philosophie* 129 (1979): 432–42.

"Le rôle des conceptions d'Isaac Beeckman dans la formation de Thomas Hobbes et dans l'élaboration de son *Short Tract.*" *Revue d'histoire des sciences* 40 (1987): 203–15.

Bernstein, Howard R. "*Conatus,* Hobbes and the Young Leibniz." *Studies in the History and Philosophy of Science* 11 (1980): 25–37.

Beza, T. *Job Expounded by Theodore Beza, partly in manner of a Commentary, partly in manner of a Paraphrase.* Cambridge, 1589?

Bible. 1611. Authorized Version Oxford, 1911.

Blay, M. "Genese des couleurs et modeles méchaniques dans l'oeuvre de Thomas Hobbes." In *Thomas Hobbes: Philosophie première, théorie de la science et politique,* ed. Y. C. Zarka and J. Bernhardt. Paris, 1990.

Bloch, O. *La philosophie de Gassendi. Nominalisme, matérialisme et métaphysique.* The Hague, 1971.

Bodington, E.J. "The Church Survey of Wiltshire, 1649–50." *Wiltshire Archaeological and Natural History Magazine* 41 (1920): 1–39.

Borot, L. "Science et histoire chez Hobbes: Le problème de la methode." In *Thomas Hobbes: Philosophie première, théorie de la science et politique,* eds. Y. C. Zarka and J. Bernhardt. Paris, 1990.

Boss, G. "Système et rupture chez Hobbes." *Dialogue* 27 (1988): 215–23.

Boyer, C. "Early Rectifications of Curves." In *Mélanges Alexandre Koyre.* Paris, 1964. I: 30–39.

Bradshaw, W. *Twelve General Arguments, proving that Ceremonies imposed upon the Ministers of our Gospel in England, by our Prelates, are unlawful.* Middleburg, 1605.

Bramhall, J. *Castigations of Mr Hobbes in his last Animadversions, in the case concerning liberty and universal necessity.* London, 1658.

Brandt, F. *Hobbes's Mechanical Conception of Nature.* Copenhagen, 1928.

Brennan, M. G., ed. *The Travel Diary (1611–12) of an English Catholic, Sir*

Charles Somerset. Proceedings of the Leeds Philosophical and Literary Society 23 (1993).

Briedert, W. "Les mathématiques et la méthode mathématique chez Hobbes." *Revue internationale de Philosophie* 129 (1979): 415–32.

Broughton, H. *Job. To the King. A Colon-Agrippina study of one moneth, for the metrical translation. But of Many Yeres, for Ebrew Difficulties. Part 2 is Job. Brought on to familiar dialogue and paraphrase for easier entendement*. N.p. 1610.

Brown, K. C. "Hobbes's Grounds for Belief in a Deity." *Philosophy* 37 (1962): 336–44.

Brown, K.C., ed. *Hobbes Studies*. Oxford, 1965.

Burton, H. *An Apology of an Appeal*. London, 1636.

For God and the King. London, 1636.

Englands Bondage. London, 1641.

Bush, D. "Hobbes, William Cavendish, and 'Essays'." *Notes and Queries*, n.s. 20 (1973): 162–4.

Calvin, John. *Sermons of Master John Calvin, upon the Booke of Job*. Trans. A. Golding. London, 1584.

A Commentary upon the Prophecie of Isaiah. London, 1609.

Cavendish, W. *A Discourse against Flatterie*. London, 1611.

Horae subsecivae. London, 1620.

Cicero, Marcus Tullius. *De Inventione*. Trans. H.M. Hubbel. London, 1949.

De Oratore. Trans. E. W. Sutton and H. Rackham. London, 1942.

De Partitione Oratoria. Ed. H. Rackham. London, 1942.

Clive, M. "Hobbes parmi les mouvements réligieux de son temps." *Revue des Sciences Philosophiques et Théologiques* 62 (1978): 41–59.

Cluver, J. *Historiam Totius Mundi. Epitome a prima rerum Origine usque ad annorum Christi MDCXXX*. Leiden, 1645.

Cluver, Ph. *An Introduction to Geography both Antient and Modern, comprised in six books*. Oxford, 1657.

Coady, C. A. J. "The Socinian Connection: Further Thoughts on the Religion of Hobbes." *Religious Studies* 22 (1986): 277–80.

Cocquius, G. *Hobbesianismi Anatome, Qua innumeris Assertionibus ex Tractatibus de Homine, Cive, Leviathan Juxta seriem locorum Theologiae Christiane Philosophi illius a Religione Christiana Apostasia demonstratur, & refutatur*. Utrecht, 1680.

Consett, H. *The Practice of the Spiritual or Ecclesiastical Courts*. London, 1847.

Cope, E., and Coates, W. H., eds. *Proceedings of the Short Parliament of 1640*. Camden Society, fourth series, vol. 19. London, 1977.

Cosins, R. *An Apologie for Sundrie Proceedings by Iurisdiction Ecclesiasticall*. London, 1593.

Curtius, M. H. *Oxford and Cambridge in Transition, 1558–1642*. Oxford, 1959.

Damrosch, L. "Hobbes as Reformation Theologian: Implications of the Freewill Controversy." *Journal of the History of Ideas* 40 (1979): 339–52.

Davenant, Sir William. *Gondibert: An Heroick Poem*, ed. D. Gladish. Oxford, 1971.

De Dominis, M. A. *De republica ecclesiastica*. 3 vols. London-Hanover, 1617–22.

De Morgan, A. *A Budget of Paradoxes*. London, 1872.

Descartes, R. *Dicours de la methode* [. . .] *plus la dioptrique, les météores et la géometrie* (Leiden, 1637).

Oeuvres. Eds. C. Adam and P. Tannery. 12 vols. Paris: Vrin 1964–76.

Dietz, M., ed. *Thomas Hobbes and Political Theory*. Lawrence, Kansas, 1990.

Dupleix, S. *La métaphysique*. Paris, 1992.

Dworkin, R. "The Model of rules I." In Dworkin, *Taking Rights Seriously*. London, 1977.

Law's Empire. London, 1986.

Dzelzainis, M. "Edward Hyde and Thomas Hobbes's *Elements of Law, Natural and Politic*." *Historical Journal* 32 (1989): 303–17.

Eachard, J. *Mr. Hobbs's State of Nature considered in a Dialogue between Philautus and Timothy*. Ed. P. Ure. English Reprints Series no. 14. Liverpool, 1958.

Eisenach, E. "Hobbes on Church, State and Religion." *History of Political Thought* 3 (1982): 215–43.

Farr, J. "Atomes of Scripture: Hobbes and the Politics of Biblical Interpretation." In *Thomas Hobbes and Political Theory*, ed. M. Dietz. Lawrence, Kansas, 1990.

Feingold, M. *The Mathematicians' Apprenticeship: Science, Universities and Society in England, 1560–1640*. Cambridge, 1984.

Fitzherbert, N. *Oxoniensis in Anglia academiae descriptio*. Rome, 1602.

Foster, J. *Alumni oxonienses: The members of the University of Oxford, 1500–1714*. 4 vols. Oxford, 1891–2.

Francescon, C. M. *Chiesa et stato nei consulti di fra Paolo Sarpi*. Vicenza, 1942.

Fussner, F. *The Historical Revolution: English Historical Writing and Thought, 1580–1640*. London, 1962.

Gabrieli, V. "Bacone, la riforma e Rome nella versione hobbesiana d'un carteggio di Flugenzio Micanzio." *The English Miscellany* 8 (1957): 195–250.

Galilei, Galileo. *Le Opere VI*, ed. G. Barbera. Florence, 1968.

Two New Sciences, Including Centers of Gravity & Force of Percussion. Ed. and trans. Stillman Drake. Madison, Wisconsin, 1974.

Gardiner, S.R. *History of England from the Accession of James I to the outbreak of the Civil War, 1603–1642.* 10 vols. London, 1883.

The Constitutional Documents of the Puritan Revolution 1625–1660. 3rd ed. Oxford, 1906.

Gargani, A. *Hobbes e la scienza.* Turin, 1971.

Gauthier, D. *The Logic of Leviathan.* Oxford, 1969.

Geach, P. "The Religion of Thomas Hobbes." *Religious Studies* 17 (1981): 549–58.

Gibson, S., ed. *Statuta antiqua universitatis oxoniensis.* Oxford, 1931.

Glover, W. "God and Thomas Hobbes." In *Hobbes Studies,* ed. K.C. Brown. Oxford, 1965.

Goldsmith, M.M., *Hobbes's Science of Politics.* New York, 1966.

"Hobbes: Ancient and modern." In *The Rise of Modern Philosophy: The Tension between the New and Traditional Philosophies from Machiavelli to Leibniz,* ed. Tom Sorell. Oxford, 1993.

"Hobbes's 'Mortal God': It There a Fallacy in Hobbes's Theory of Sovereignty?" *History of Political Thought* 1 (1980): 33–50.

Gooch, G.P. *Political Thought in England from Bacon to Halifax.* London, 1923.

Gray, C. "Reason, Authority, and Imagination: The Jurisprudence of Sir Edward Coke." In *Culture and Politics from Puritanism to the Enlightenment.* Berkeley, Ca., 1980.

"Parliament, Liberty, and Law." In *Parliament and Liberty: From the Reign of Elizabeth to the English Civil War,* ed. J. H. Hexter. Stanford, California, 1992.

Grotius, Hugo. *Epistolae, Quotquot reperiri potuerunt.* Amsterdam, 1687.

Grover, R. "The Legal Origins of Thomas Hobbes's Doctrine of Contract." *Journal of the History of Philosophy* 18 (1980): 177–94.

"The Legal Origins of Hobbes's Doctrine of Contract." *Hobbes Studies* 3 (1990).

Guthrie, W. K. C. *A History of Greek Philosophy.* Cambridge, 1962.

The Sophists. Cambridge, 1971.

Hale, M. *Reflections by the Lrd Chiefe Justice Hale on Mr Hobbes His Dialogue of the Lawe.* In Sir W. Holdsworth, *A History of English Law.* Vol. 5. 499–513.

Halliday, R.J., T. Kenyon, and A. Reeve. "Hobbes's Belief in God." *Political Studies* 31 (1983): 418–33.

Halliwell, J., ed. *A Collection of Letters Illustrative of the Progress of Science in England from the Reign of Queen Elizabeth to that of Charles the Second.* London, 1841.

Hamilton, S. G. *Hertford College.* London, 1903.

Hampton, J. *Hobbes and the Social Contract Tradition.* Cambridge, 1986.

Hanson, D. W. "The Meaning of 'Demonstration' in Hobbes's Philosophy of Science.' " *History of Political Thought* 11 (1990): 639–74.

Hart, H. L. A. *The Concept of Law.* Oxford, 1961.

Harwood, J. T., ed. *The Rhetorics of Thomas Hobbes and Bernard Lamy.* Carbondale, Illinois, 1986.

Hayward, J. C. "The *Mores* of Great Tew: Literary, Philosophical, and Political Idealism in Falkland's Circle." Cambridge University Ph.D. thesis, 1983.

Heath, Thomas L. *Mathematics in Aristotle.* Oxford, 1949.

Hepburn, R. "Hobbes on the Knowledge of God." In *Hobbes and Rousseau: A Collection of Critical Essays,* ed. M. Cranston and R. Peters. New York, 1972.

Herbert, E. *The Ancient Religion of the Gentiles and Causes of Errors Considered.* London, 1705.

Herbert, G. *Thomas Hobbes: The Unity of Scientific and Moral Wisdom.* Vancouver, 1989.

Herzog, D. *Happy Slaves.* 1989.

Hill, C. *Antichrist in Seventeenth Century England.* Oxford, 1971.

Hill, N. *Philosophia epicurea, democritian. Theophrastica propositia simpliciter, non edocta.* Geneva, 1619.

Hinnant, C. *Thomas Hobbes.* New York, 1977.

Hintikka, J., and U. Remes. *The Method of Analysis: Its Geometrical Origin and General Significance.* Dordrecht, 1974.

Historical Manuscripts Commission. *Thirteenth Report. The Manuscripts of His Grace the Duke of Portland.* Vol. 2. London, 1893.

Hofmann, J. *Leibniz in Paris, 1672–1676.* Trans. A. Prag and D.T. Whiteside. Cambridge, 1974.

Holdsworth, W. *A History of English Law.* 3rd ed. 16 vols. London, 1945.

Hood, F.C. *The Divine Politics of Thomas Hobbes.* Oxford, 1964.

Hunt, W. *The Puritan Moment: The Coming of Revolution in an English County.* Cambridge, Mass., 1983.

Hutton, C., G. Shaw, and R. Pearson. *The Philosophical Transactions of the Royal Society of London.* London, 1809.

Huygens, C. *Oeuvres complètes.* The Hague, 1888–1950.

Hyde, E. (Earl of Clarendon). *A Brief View and Survey of the Dangerous Errors of Church and State in Mr Hobbes's Book, entitled Leviathan.* Oxford, 1676.

Isham, Sir Gyles, ed. "The Correspondence of Bishop Brian Duppa and Sir Justinian Isham, 1650–1660." *Publications of the Northamptonshire Record Society* 17 (1951).

Jacoby, E. G. "Thomas Hobbes in Europe." *Journal of European Studies* 4 (1974): 57–65.

Jacquot, J. "Sir Charles Cavendish and His Learned Friends." *Annals of Science* 8 (1952): 13–27, 175–91.

"Harriot, Hill, Warner and the New Philosophy." In *Thomas Harriot Renaissance Scientist*, ed. J. W. Shirley. Oxford, 1974. 107–28.

Jaeger, W. *Paideia: The Ideals of Great Culture*. Trans. G. Highet. 3 vols. Oxford, 1939–45.

Jansson, M., ed. "Proceedings in Parliament, 1614 (House of Commons)." *Memoirs of the American Philosophical Society* 172 (1988).

Johnson, Paul. "Hobbes's Anglican Doctrine of Salvation." In *Thomas Hobbes in His Time*, eds. R. Ross, H. Schneider, and T. Waldman. Minneapolis, 1974.

Johnston, D. *The Rhetoric of* Leviathan. Princeton, 1986.

"Hobbes's Mortalism." *History of Political Thought* 10 (1989): 647–63.

Kahn, V. *Rhetoric, Prudence and Skepticism in the Renaissance*. Ithaca, New York, 1985.

Kargon, R. H. *Atomism in England from Hariot to Newton*. Oxford, 1966.

Kavka, G. *Hobbesian Moral and Political Theory*. Princeton, New Jersey, 1986.

Kearney, H. *Scholars and Gentlemen: Universities and Society in Pre-industrial Britain, 1500–1700*. London, 1970.

Kelsen, H. *General Theory of Law and State*. Trans. A Wedberg. Cambridge, Massachusetts, 1945.

Kennedy, G. *The Art of Persuasion in Greece*. London, 1963.

Kenyon, J.P. *The Stuart Constitution: Documents and Commentary*. Cambridge, 1969.

Kepler, J. *Gesammelte Werke. Band II: Astronomiae Pars Optica*. Ed. F. Hammer. Munich, 1939.

Knudsen, O., and M. Pedersen. "The Link between 'Determination' and Conservation of Motion in Descartes' Dynamics." *Centaurus* 13 (1968): 183–6.

Kraynak, R. *History and Modernity in the Thought of Thomas Hobbes*. Ithaca, New York, 1990.

Kriele, M. "Notes on the Controversy betwen Hobbes and the English Jurists. In *Hobbes-Forschungen*, ed. R. Koselleck and R. Schnur. Berlin, 1969, 211–22.

Lagarde, G. *La Naissance de l'Esprit Laïque au Declin du Moyen Age*. 5 vols. Louvain, 1956.

Lessay, F. *Souveraineté et légitimité chez Hobbes*. Paris, 1988.

Letwin, S. "Hobbes and Christianity." *Daedelus* 105 (1976): 1–21.

Lindberg, D. *Theories of Vision from Al-Kindi to Kepler.* Chicago, 1976.

Lloyd, S.A. *Ideas as Interests in Hobbes's* Leviathan. Cambridge, 1991.

Luce, Sir Richard. "An Old Malmesbury Minute Book." *Wiltshire Archaeological and Natural History Magazine* 47 (1935–7): 321–6.

Luther, Martin. *The Reformation Writings of Martin Luther,* ed. B. Wolf. 2 vols. 1956.

Macpherson, C. B. *The Political Theory of Possessive Individualism.* Oxford, 1964.

"Hobbes's Bourgeois Man." In *Hobbes Studies,* ed. K. C. Brown. Oxford, 1965.

"Introduction to *Leviathan.*" Harmondsworth, 1968.

Malcolm, N. R. "Hobbes, Sandys, and the Virginia Company." *The Historical Journal* 24 (1981): 297–321.

De Dominis (1560–1624): Venetian, Anglican, Ecumenist and Relapsed Heretic. London, 1984.

"Hobbes and the Royal Society." In *Perspectives on Thomas Hobbes,* ed. G.A. J. Rogers and A. Ryan, Oxford, 1988, 43–66.

"Hobbes's Science of Politics and His Theory of Science." In *Hobbes Oggi,* ed. A. Napoli and G. Canzoni. Milan, 1990.

Malherbe, M. *Thomas Hobbes ou l'oeuvre et sa raison.* Paris, 1984.

Mandley, V. *Mellficium Mensionis.* 4th ed. London, 1727.

Marshall, J. "The Ecclesiology of the Latitude-men, 1660–1689: Stillingfleet, Tillotson and 'Hobbism.' " *Journal of Ecclesiastical History* 36 (1985): 407–27.

Marsilius of Padua. *The Defender of the Peace.* Ed. A. Gewirth. 2 vols. New York, 1956.

Martinich, A.P. *The Two Gods of Leviathan.* Cambridge, 1992.

McColley, G. "Nicholas Hill and the Philosophia Epicure." *Annals of Science* 4 (1939): 390–405.

McIlwain, C. H., ed. *The Political Works of James I.* Cambridge, 1918.

McNeilly, F.S. *The Anatomy of Leviathan.* London, 1968.

Mendle, M. *Dangerous Positions: Mixed Government, the Estates of the Realm, and the Answer to the xix Propositions.* Alabama, 1985.

Mersenne, M. *Cogitata physico-mathematica, in quibus tam naturae quam artis effectis admirandi certissimis demonstrationibus explicantur.* Paris, 1644.

Corréspondance du P. Marin Mersenne. Ed. de Waard. Paris, 1967.

Universae geometriae mixtaque mathematicae synopsis, et bini refactionum demonstratarum tractatus. Paris, 1644.

Metzger, H-D. *Thomas Hobbes und die Englische Revolution 1640–1660.* Stuttgart/Bad Constance, 1991.

Milner, B. "Hobbes on Religion." *Political Theory* 16 (1988): 400–25.

Milton, P. "Did Hobbes translate *De Cive?*" *History of Political Thought* 11 (1990): 627–38.

Mintz, S. I. *The Hunting of Leviathan: Seventeenth-Century Reactions to the Materialism and Moral Philosophy of Thomas Hobbes.* Cambridge, 1962.

"Hobbes on the Law of Heresy: A New Manuscript." *Journal of the History of Ideas* 29 (1968): 409–14.

Moller Pedersen, K. "Roberval's Comparison of the Arclength of a Spiral and a Parabola." *Centaurus* 15 (1970): 26–43.

Napoli, A. "Hobbes e lo *Short Tract*' *Revista di storia della filosofia* 3 (1990): 539–69.

Newton, Sir Issac. *Sir Isaac Newton's Mathematical Principles of Natural Philosophy and His System of the World.* Trans. Andrew Motte; ed. and rev. Florian Cajori. 2 vols. Berkeley, Ca. 1934.

Nicastro, O. "Le vocabulaire de la dissolution de l'Etat." In *Hobbes et son vocabulaire,* Ed. Y.-C. Zarka. Paris, 1992.

Nightingale, J. E. *The Church Plate of the County of Wiltshire.* Salisbury, 1891.

Notestein, W., F. H. Relft, and H. Simpson, eds. *Commons Debates, 1621.* 7 vols. New Haven, 1935.

Oakeshott, M. *Hobbes on Civil Association.* Oxford, 1975.

Oecolampadius, J. *Exposition de MJ. Oecolompade sur le Livre de Job.* Geneva, 1562.

Ollard, R. *Clarendon and His Friends.* London, 1987.

Pacchi, A. *Convenzione e ipotesi nella formazione della filosofia naturale di Thomas Hobbes.* Florence, 1965.

"Rugero Bacone e Roberto Grossatesta in un inedito Hobbesiano del 1634." *Revista critica di storia della filosofia* 20 (1965): 499–502.

"Una 'biblioteka ideale' di Thomas Hobbes: il MS E2 dell' archivo di Chatsworth." *Acme* 21 (1968): 3–40.

"Hobbes e l'Epicureismo." *Revista critica di storia della filosofia* 33 (1978): 54–71.

"Hobbes and the Problem of God." In *Perspectives on Thomas Hobbes,* eds. G.A.J. Rogers and A. Ryan. Oxford, 1988.

"*Leviathan* and Spinoza's *Tractatus* on Revelation." *History of European Ideas* 4 (1989): 577–93.

Packer, J. *The Transformation of Anglicanism 1643–1660 with special reference to Henry Hammond.* Manchester, 1969.

Pappus of Alexandria. *Book 7 of the "Collection".* Ed. and trans. Alexander Jones. *Sources in the History of Mathematics and Physical Sciences,* 8. 2 vols. New York, 1986.

Parker, R. *A Scholasticall Discourse against Symbolizing with Antichrist in Ceremonies.* Middleburg, 1607.

Pécharman, M. "Philosophie première et théorie de l'action selon Hobbes." In *Thomas Hobbes: Philosophie prèmiére, théorie de la science et politique,* ed. Y-C. Zarka and J. Bernhardt. Paris, 1990, 47–66.

"La vocabulaire de l'être dans la philosophie première: *ens, esse, essentia.*" In *Hobbes et son vocabulaire,* ed. Y. C. Zarka, Paris, 1992, 31–60.

Peters, R.S. *Hobbes.* London, 1956.

Plamenatz, J. "Introduction" to Thomas Hobbes, *Leviathan.*" London, 1962.

Man and Society. London, 1963.

"Mr Warrender's Hobbes." In *Hobbes Studies,* ed. K. C. Brown. Oxford, 1965.

Pocock, J.G. A. *The Ancient Constitution and the Feudal Law.* Cambridge, 1957.

"Time, History and Eschatology in the Thought of Thomas Hobbes." In Pocock, *Politics, Language and Time.* London, 1972.

The Machiavellian Moment. Princeton, New Jersey, 1975.

Prins, J. "Kepler, Hobbes and Medieval Optics." *Philosophia naturalis* 24 (1987).

"Hobbes and the School of Padua: Two Incompatible Approaches to Science." *Archiv für Geschichte der Philosophie* 22 (1990): 26–46.

Walter Warner and His Notes on Animal Organisms. Utrecht, 1992.

Pritchard, A. "The Last Days of Hobbes: Evidence of the Wood Manuscripts." *The Bodleian Library Record* 10 (1980): 178–87.

Pycior, H. "Mathematics and Philosophy: Wallis, Hobbes, Barrow, and Berkeley." *Journal of the History of Ideas* 55 (1987): 265–86.

Quintilian. *Institutio Oratoria.* Ed. and trans. H.E. Butler. London, 1922.

Ramsay, G. D., ed. *Two Sixteenth Century Taxation Lists: 1545 and 1576. Wiltshire Archaeological and Natural History Society, Records Branch* 10 (1954).

Randall, J. H. *Aristotle.* New York, 1960.

Raphael, D. D. *Hobbes: Morals and Politics.* London, 1977.

Reik, M. *The Golden Lands of Thomas Hobbes.* Detroit, 1977.

Rigaud, S. J. *Correspondence of Scientific Men of the Seventeenth Century.* Hildesheim, 1965.

Rismer, F. *Opticae Thesaurus-Alhazeni arabis libri septem, nuc primum editi; ejusdem liber de crepusculis et nubium ascensionibus, item Vitellionis Thuringopoloni libri X . . . A Frederico Risnero.* Ed. D.C. Lindberg. New York, 1972.

Robertson, G.C. *Hobbes.* London, 1910.

Robinet, A. "Pensée et langage chez Hobbes. Physique de parole et *translatio.*" *Revue internationale de philosophie* 129 (1979): 452–83.

Rogow, A. A. *Thomas Hobbes: Radical in the Service of Reaction.* New York, 1986.

Rossi, P. *Alle fonti del deismo e del materialismo moderno.* Florence, 1942.

Rousseau, J-J. *Of the Social Contract.* Trans. R. Crosby. Brunswick, Ohio, 1978.

Russell, C. *The Fall of the British Monarchies, 1637–1642.* Oxford, 1991.

Ryan, A. "Hobbes, Toleration and the Inner Life." In *The Nature of Political Theory,* ed. D. Miller and L. Siedentrop. Oxford, 1983.

"Hobbes and Individualism." In *Perspectives on Thomas Hobbes,* ed. G.A.J. Rogers and A. Ryan. Oxford, 1988.

Sabra, A.I. *Theories of Light from Descartes to Newton.* Cambridge, 1981.

Sacksteder, W. "Three Diverse Sciences in Hobbes: First Philosophy, Geometry and Physics." *Review of Metaphysics* 45 (1992): 739–72.

St. German, C. *Doctor and Student.* Eds. T. Plucknett and J. Barton. London, 1974.

Sanderson, J. "But the People's Creatures." *The Philosophical Basis of the English Civil War.* Manchester, 1989.

Sarasohn, L. "Motion and Morality: Pierre Gassendi, Thomas Hobbes and the Mechanical World View." *Journal of the History of Ideas* 46 (1985): 363–80.

Sarpi, P. *Historia del concilio tridentino.* London, 1619.

Scaliger, J. C. *Exercitationes exotericae ad Cardani libros XV De Subtilitate.* Basil, 1557.

Scargill, D. *The Recantation of Daniel Scargill Publickly made before the University of Cambridge.* London, 1669.

Schaffer, S. "Wallification: Thomas Hobbes on School Divinity and Experimental Pneumatics." *Studies in History and Philosophy of Science* 19 (1988): 275–98.

Schino, A. L. "Tre lettere inedite di Gabriel Naudé." *Rivista di storia della filosofia* 4 (1987): 697–708.

Schmitt, C.B. "Philosophy and Science in Sixteenth-Century Universities: Some Preliminary Comments." In *The Cultural Context of Medieval Learning,* ed. E. Murdoch and D. Sylla. Doredrecht, 1975, 485–530.

John Case and Aristotelianism in Renaissance England. Montreal, 1983.

Schneider, H. W. "The Piety of Hobbes." In *Thomas Hobbes in His Time,* ed. R. Ross, H. Schneider, and T. Waldman. Minneapolis, 1974.

Schuhmann, K. "Le vocabulaire de l'espace." In *Hobbes et son vocabulaire,* ed. Y-C. Zarka. Paris, 1992, 61–82.

Schwartz, J. "Hobbes and the Two Kingdoms of God." *Polity* 18 (1985): 7–24.

Scott, J. F. *The Mathematical Work of John Wallis, D.D., F.R.S. (1616–1703)*. London, 1938.

Selden, J. *De dis syriis*. London, 1617.

Seneca, *Controversiae*. Ed. M. Winterbottom. London, 1974.

Sextus Empiricus. *Against the Logicians*. Trans. R.G. Bury. London, 1936.

Shapin, S., and S. Schaffer. *Leviathan and the Air Pump*. Princeton, 1985.

Shapiro, A. *Rays and Waves: A Study of Seventeenth Century Optics*. New Haven, 1970.

Shapiro, B. *John Wilkins, 1614–72: An Intellectual Biography*. Berkeley, 1969.

Sharpe, K. *The Personal Rule of Charles I*. New Haven, 1992.

Shulman, G. "Hobbes, Puritans and Promethean Politics." *Political Theory* 16 (1988): 426–43.

Simpson, A. W. B. *A History of the Common Law of Contract*. Oxford, 1975.

Skinner, Q. R. D. "Hobbes on Sovereignty: An Unknown Discussion." *Political Studies* 13 (1965): 213–18.

"The Ideological Context of Hobbes's Political Thought." *Historical Journal* 9 (1966).

"Thomas Hobbes and His Disciples in France and England." *Comparative Studies in Society and History* 8 (1966): 153–67.

"Thomas Hobbes and the Nature of the Early Royal Society." *The Historical Journal* 12 (1969): 217–39.

"The Context of Hobbes's Theory of Political Obligation." In *Hobbes and Rousseau*, ed. M. Cranston and R. Peters. New York, 1972.

"Conquest and Consent: Thomas Hobbes and the Engagement Controversy." In *The Interregnum: The Quest for Settlement, 1646–1660*, ed. G.E. Aylmer. London, 1973.

"Thomas Hobbes on the Proper Signification of Liberty." *Transactions of the Royal Historical Society* 40 (1990): 121–51.

"Thomas Hobbes: Rhetoric and the Construction of Morality." *Proceedings of the British Academy* 76 (1991): 1–61.

" 'Scientia civilis' in Classical Rhetoric and in the Early Hobbes." In *Political Discourse in Early Modern Britain*, ed. N. Phillipson and Q. Skinner. Cambridge, 1993, 67–93.

Sommerville, J. *Thomas Hobbes: Political Ideas in Historical Context*. London, 1992.

Sorell, T. *Hobbes*. London: Routledge, 1986.

"The Science in Hobbes's Politics." In *Perspectives on Thomas Hobbes*, ed. G.A.J. Rogers and A. Ryan. Oxford, 67–80.

"Seventeenth Century Materialism: Gassendi and Hobbes." In *Routledge History of Philosophy*, ed. G.H.R. Parkinson. vol. 4. London, 1993, 235–72.

Sorell, T., ed. *The Rise of Modern Philosophy: The Tension between the New and Traditional Philosophies from Machiavelli to Leibniz.* Oxford, 1993.

Spragens, T. *The Politics of Motion.* London, 1973.

Springborg, P. "*Leviathan* and the Problem of Ecclesiastical Authority." *Political Theory* 3 (1975): 289–303.

"*Leviathan*, the Christian Commonwealth Incorporated." *Political Studies* 24 (1976): 171–83.

"Hobbes's Biblical Beasts: *Leviathan and Behemoth.*" *Political Theory* 23, 2 (1995): 353–75.

"Hobbes, Heresy and the *Historia Ecclesiastica.*" *Journal of the History of Ideas,* 55, 4 (194) 553–71.

"Thomas Hobbes and Cardinal Bellarmine: *Leviathan* and the Ghost of the Roman Empire". *History of Political Thought* 16, 4, Winter 1995, forthcoming.

"Writing to Redundancy: Hobbes and Cluverius." *Historical Journal* June 1996, forthcoming.

"Leviathan, Mythic History and National Historiography". In *Philosophy, Rhetoric and the Historical Imagination in Early Modern Britain,* ed. D H. Sachs. Forthcoming.

Stephen, L. *Hobbes.* London, 1904.

Strauss, L. *The Political Philosophy of Hobbes: Its Basis and Genesis.* Trans. E. M. Sinclair. Oxford, 1936.

Natural Right and History. Chicago, 1953.

Stroud, E. *Thomas Hobbes' A minute or first draught of the optiques. A critical edition.* PhD dissertation. University of Wisconsin, Madison, 1983.

Suarez, F. *Opera Omnia.* 28 vols. Paris, 1856–78.

Sutherland, S. "God and Religion in *Leviathan.*" *Journal of Theological Studies* 25 (1974): 373–80.

Talaska, R. "Analytic and Synthetic according to Hobbes." *Journal of the History of Philosophy* 26 (1988): 207–37.

Thomas, K. "The Social Origins of Hobbes's Political Thought." In *Hobbes Studies,* ed. K.C. Brown. Oxford. 1965.

Religion and the Decline of Magic: Studies in Popular Beliefs in Sixteenth and Seventeenth Century England. London, 1971.

Toland, J. *Christianity not Mysterious: or a Treatise shewing, that there is nothing in the Gospel contrary to Reason, nor above it: and that no Christian Doctrine can be properly call'd a Mystery.* London, 1696.

Tönnies, F. "Hobbes-Annalekten." *Archiv für Geschichte der Philosophie* 17 (1903): 294–96.

Studien zür Philosophie und Gesellschaftslehre im 17. Jährhundert. Stuttgart, 1975.

Trevor-Roper, H. R. *Catholics, Anglicans and Puritans: Seventeenth Century Essays.* London, 1987.

Tuck, R. *Natural Rights Theories.* Cambridge, 1979.

"Hobbes and Descartes." In *Perspectives on Thomas Hobbes,* ed. G.A.J. Rogers and A. Ryan. Oxford, 1988, 11–41.

Hobbes. Oxford, 1989.

"Hobbes and Locke on Toleration." In *Thomas Hobbes and Political Theory,* ed. M. Dietz. Lawrence, Kansas, 1990.

"Introduction" to Thomas Hobbes, *Leviathan.* Cambridge, 1991.

Philosophy and Government 1572–1651. Cambridge, 1993.

Tully, J. *An Approach to Political Philosophy: Locke in Contexts.* Cambridge, 1993.

Ulianich, B. "Considerazione e documenti per una ecclesiologia di Paolo Sarpi." In F. Iseloh and P. Manns, *Festgabe Joseph Lortz.* 2 vols. Baden-Baden, 1968. Vol. 2, 363–444.

Untersteiner, M. *The Sophists.* Trans. K. Freeman. Oxford, 1954.

Vaughan, R. *The Protectorate of Oliver Cromwell.* London, 1838.

Vescovini, G. F. *Studia sulla prospettiva medievale.* Turin, 1965.

Viete, F. *The Analytic Art: Nine Studies in Algebra, Geometry, and Trigonometry from the "Opus Restitutae Mathematicae Analyseos, seu Algebra Nova,"* Ed. and trans., T. Richard Witmer. Kent, Ohio, 1983.

Vossius, Gerardus. *De theologia gentili, et physiologia, deque naturae mirandis, quibus homo adducitur ad Deum.* Amsterdam, 1668.

Wallace, K. *Francis Bacon on Communication and Rhetoric.* Chapel Hill, North Carolina, 1943.

Wallis, J. "Animadversions of Dr Wallis, upon Mr Hobbes's late Book, De Principiis et Ratiocinatione Geometrarum. Written to a Friend." *Philosophical Transactions* 16 (1666). In C. Hutton et al., 107–11.

"An Answer to Four Papers of Mr Hobbes, lately published in the Months of August and this Present September, 1671." In C. Hutton et al., 623–31.

Ward, S. *In Thomae Hobbii philosophiam exercitatio epistolica.* Oxford, 1656.

Warner, G. F. ed. *The Nicholas Papers. Correspondence of Sir Edward Nicholas.* 4 vols. London, 1888–1920.

Warrender, H. *The Political Philosophy of Thomas Hobbes: His Theory of Obligation.* Oxford, 1957.

Watkins, J. W. N. *Hobbes's System of Ideas.* London, 1965.

Westfall, R. *Never at Rest: A Biography of Isaac Newton.* Cambridge, 1980.

Weston, C.C. "The Theory of Mixed Monarchy under Charles I and After." *English Historical Review* 75 (1966): 426–33.

Weston, C.C., and Greenberg, J. *Subjects and Sovereigns: The Grand Controversy over Legal Sovereignty in Stuart England.* Cambridge, 1981.

Wheldon, J. Letter to Adam Barker. *Gentleman's Magazine* 54 (1784): 729.

Willman, R. "Hobbes on the Law of Heresy." *Journal of the History of Ideas* 31 (1970).

Wilkins, J., and S. Ward. *Vindiciae academarium: Containing some briefe Animadversions upon Mr Webster's Book, stiled The Examination of Academies.* Oxford, 1654.

Wilks, I. "A Note on Sovereignty." In *In Defense of Sovereignty*, ed. W. J. Stankiewicz. New York, 1969, 197–205.

Williams, N. J., ed. *Tradesmen in Early-Stuart Wiltshire: A Miscellany.* Wiltshire Archaeological and Natural History Society, Records Branch, 15 (1959).

Willman, R. "Hobbes on the Law of Heresy." *Journal of the History of Ideas* 31 (1970): 607–13.

Wolfe, F. *Die neue Wissenschaft des Thomas Hobbes.* Stuttgart, 1969.

Wolin, S. *Politics and Vision.* Boston, 1961.

Hobbes and the Epic Tradition. Los Angeles, 1970.

Woolhouse, R. *The Empiricists.* Oxford, 1988.

Wormald, B. H. G. *Clarendon: Politics, History and Religion, 1640–1660.* Chicago, 1951, 1976.

Zagorin, P. "Clarendon and Hobbes." *Journal of Modern History.* 1985.

Ways of Lying: Dissimulation, Persecution and Conformity in Early Modern Europe. Cambridge, Mass. 1990.

Zarka, Y-C. *La décision métaphysique de Hobbes – conditions de la politique.* Paris, 1987.

"Histoire et developpement chez Hobbes." In *Entre Forme et Histoire*, ed. O. Bloch, B. Balan, and P. Carrive. Paris, 1988.

Zarka, Y.-C., and J. Bernhardt, eds. *Thomas Hobbes: philosophie première, théorie de la science et politique.* Paris, 1990.

"Le vocabulaire de l'apparaître: le champ sémantique de la notion de phantasma." In *Hobbes et son vocabulaire. Etudes de lexicographie philosophique.* Paris, 1992, 13–29.

"Leibniz lecteur de Hobbes: toute puissance divine et perfection du monde." *Studia Leibnitiana* 21 (1992).

"Identité et ipseité chez Hobbes et Locke." *Philosophie* 37 (1993): 5–19.

INDEX

absolutism, 9, 210–11, 256, 259, 264, 283, 290, 294
accidents, 129, 131, 149n5
acephalous societies, 218
agents, 130, 131, 149n6
Alford, Edward, 252
algebra, 5, 108, 112, 113, 114, 115–17, 119
altruism, 168, 169, 173n4
Ames, William, 250
analepsis, 322, 327n47
analysis, 55, 64–65, 74, 92–96, 101, 105n16, 114–16
Anglicanism, 22, 34, 35, 347, 352, 368
animal spirits, 131, 132, 141, 142, 153n46
annihilation hypothesis, 30, 65–66, 77, 82n17
apodeictic, 176, 330
Apollonius, 112
apostles, 361, 362, 363
appetites and aversions, 54, 130, 159–64
Aquinas, Thomas, 286, 288, 289, 301–2n55
Archimedes, 109, 112, 118
arc-length, 123–26
Aristophanes, 118
Aristotle, 46, 49, 81n6, 103n1, 123, 170, 351
  color theory, 137
  disagreement with, 59, 216, 217
  doctrine of causation, 4
  and first philosophy, 62, 63, 64, 67
  in Hobbes's education, 16, 17
  Posterior Analytics, 86
  Rhetoric, 21, 176, 178, 195–96, 306, 324, 330, 340, 341, 342, 343
assemblies, 9, 32, 215, 262
astrology, 46, 47, 50, 51
astronomy, 3, 12, 16, 21, 47, 58
atheism, 35, 261, 299n10, 326n16, 327n46, 346, 347–48
Aubrey, John, 36, 37, 87, 103n5, 110, 111, 346, 368
Austin, John, 275–76
Aylesbury, Sir Thomas, 23

Bacon, Francis, 2, 3, 13, 18, 49, 51–52, 60, 177, 197–201, 204n29, 206–7n36
Bacon, Roger, 146, 155n96
Baillie, Robert, 254–55
Barclay, William, 256

Barebones Parliament, 34
Barrow, Isaac, 113, 147
Bathurst, Ralph, 109
Baynes, Paul, 264
Beale, William, 255, 270n49
Beckmann, Peter, 108
Beeckman, Isaac, 26, 147
Bellarmine, Roberto, 367
Bennet, Henry, 31, 262
biblical interpretation, 1, 222, 258–59, 295, 321, 352–55, 359–60, 362, 364
Birkenhead, Sir John, 347
bodies, 57–58, 83n27
Bodin, Jean, 256
body/accident, 65, 67–70
Bombelli, Rafael, 113
Borot, Luc, vii, 9–10, 12, 305–28
Bosc, Charles du, 28
Boyle, Robert, 90, 102, 105n12, 109, 242n12
Bramhall, John, 30, 36, 77, 82n13, 84n40, 236, 273n66, 349, 360, 361, 365, 366
Buchanan, George, 253
Burroughs, Jeremiah, 254
Burton, Henry, 253

Calvinism, 16, 253, 373n25, 26
canon law, 288, 289
Cartesian metaphysics/science, 4, 26, 60, 66, 116, 148, 247
Cary, Lucius. *See* Falkland, Viscount
cause/effect, 65, 70–71, 92–93, 219
causes, knowledge of, 4, 29, 50, 86, 96, 100, 101, 102
Cavendish, Sir Charles, 2, 22, 23, 24, 30, 32, 33, 42n70, 43n77, 81n4, 131, 152n40
Cavendish, Sir Charles, 261, 271n56
Cavendish, William, 2, 13, 17–20, 28, 199–200, 204–5n30, 205n31, 248, 306, 334
Charles I (king of England), 8, 27, 32, 33, 110, 227, 240, 247–56, 263, 264, 312, 324
Charles II (king of England), 33, 36–37, 109, 261, 262, 263, 264, 265, 324, 348, 366
Charles, Prince of Wales, 31, 109, 248, 260
Christian doctrine, 11, 29, 109, 318, 360–66, 370n12. *See also* religion

Index

churches. *See* religion; *specific denominations*

Cicero, 186, 197, 202n2, 286, 330, 333, 334, 343n2

circle-squaring, 5, 87, 88, 108, 109, 110, 111, 118–20

civil law, 285–87, 318–21

civil science/philosophy, 12, 47–57, 87, 88, 104n6, 105n16

civil war, 19, 48, 168, 120, 335, 366

Clarendon, earl of, 110, 260

Clavius, Christoph, 110, 126n8

Clifton, Sir Gervase, 20–21

Coke, Roger, 347

Coke, Sir Edward, 9, 211, 252, 287, 290–96

color, 136–37, 138, 144–45

colours, 196, 197

command theorist, 275, 276

common law, 9, 19, 211, 251, 282, 285, 288, 291–96, 318

commonwealths, 8–9, 57–58, 88, 104n6, 198, 315–17, 326n19

dissolution of, 8–9, 312, 315–17, 326n19

competition, 161, 162, 220, 221

condensation, 90, 91, 104n9

cone-model, 135–36

Constantine, 322, 327n46, 350, 360

Continental science, 102, 103, 107n24

Continental travels, 2, 17–18, 21, 23–24, 131, 199

contracts and covenants, 168, 225–31, 244n52, 245n53, 279–80, 288, 297–98

Coolidge, Julian Lovell, 108

corpuscular theory of light, 146, 147

Cosin, John, 31, 346, 361, 373n26

Cowley, Abraham, 260, 261

Cromwell, Oliver, 33, 227, 230, 240, 261, 263, 348

Cudworth, Ralph, 13

Davenant, Sir William, 31, 260, 306

Davies, John, 33

Davisson, William, 24

De Dominis, Marc'Antonio, 20, 256

De Morgan, Augustus, 108

De mundo, 3

death, 170, 188, 217, 236, 240, 246, 346

deductive method, 3, 18, 21, 74, 99, 307–8, 341

definitions, 29, 65, 88, 163

democracy, 20, 209, 120, 214, 235, 236

demonology, 349, 350, 364, 367

demonstrations, 88, 94, 100, 102

Descartes, René, 3, 24, 25, 26, 28, 37, 64, 77, 81n4, 81n7, 102, 115, 122, 123

on *De Cive*, 247

Discourse, 60, 132, 191

Essais, 132

and light, 138–41, 145, 148, 149n9, 155n86, 155n88

Meditations, 49, 53, 63

Principles of Philosophy, 52–53

and religion, 367, 368

scheme of science, 52–54

and sensible qualities, 152–53n46

determinism, 6, 70–71, 78, 171–72

Devonshire, first earl of, 17, 18

Devonshire, second earl of, 2, 17, 20, 204n30, 248

Devonshire, third earl of, 2, 20, 21, 23, 31, 32, 33, 36, 199, 205n30, 246, 315

Diderot, Denis, 108

Digby, Sir Kenelm, 14, 24, 25, 26, 42n70, 62, 80n3, 132

Digges, Sir Dudley, 251

Dionysius, 311, 312, 313

division of philosophy. *See* scheme of the sciences

Du Verdus, François, 37

Dupleix, Scipion, 63

duplication of a cube, 118, 120–23

Duppa, Brian, 34, 247

Dworkin, Ronald, 275, 299n9

Eachard, John, 247

ecclesiastical power, 354–60

economic theory, 213, 214

education, 166, 170, 209, 236

egoism, 6, 165–69, 173n2, 173n4

emotions. *See* passions

emphythemes, 196

energeia, 336, 344n10

English Civil War, 8–9, 210, 218, 249, 254, 259–67, 323–24

English law, 287–96

Epicurus, 176, 350, 351, 353

epideixis, 337–38, 344n11

Erastus, Thomas, 351, 360, 373n25

essences, 30, 69

ethics, 50, 175, 17–80

Euclid, 16, 18, 21, 58, 61n14, 87, 103n5, 111, 112, 115, 119, 306, 334, 349

Euler, Leonhard, 147

Eusebius of Caesarea, 356, 360

excommunication, 258, 348, 351, 371n14, 373n25

experience, 9, 10, 55, 99, 161, 214–15, 309, 311

experimental methodology, British, 102, 103

eye, 132–34, 142–44, 150n23, 154n69, 154n72, 155n92

Fabri, Honoratus, 1145

Falkland, Viscount (Lucius Cary), 2, 22, 23, 253, 254, 265, 347, 352

fear, 161, 162, 209, 220, 221, 225, 228, 356

Fell, John, 36

Fermat, Pierre de, 115

Ferriby, John, 366

Filmer, Sir Robert, 8, 217, 222, 255, 258

first philosophy, 3–4, 5, 11, 48, 49, 50, 51, 59, 62–80

first principles, 94, 95, 102, 129, 246, 354

Forced Loan, 251, 256, 348

Fortescue, Sir John, 251–52

Francesca, Piero della, 108

freedom, 211, 233, 235, 236

Freud, Sigmund, 172

future, 171, 219, 220

Galileo, 26, 46, 58, 95, 96, 106n19, 106n20, 153n46, 148

Gassendi, Pierre, 3, 29, 32, 37, 54, 84n49, 199, 370n7
Gauthier, D., 185, 193
gentilism, 368, 372n21, 374n36
geometry, 4–5, 11, 34, 102, 108–26
    discovery of, 21, 103n5, 332
    and natural philosophy, 87–92
    and physics, 147
    and politics, 214
    proofs in, 34
    in scheme of sciences, 47–50, 58
    teaching of, 16
Gerson, Jean, 288, 289
Gert, Bernard, vii, 6, 157–74
glory, 161, 162, 184, 201, 221–22
God, 46, 47, 64, 85n62, 117
    and Bacon, 52
    Descartes on, 52–54, 63
    entire cause, 4, 78–80
    kingdom of, 230
    knowledge of, 216, 242n26, 367
    Locke on, 223
    reasonableness of, 22
    and sovereignty, 232, 237, 259
    and Trinity, 350, 352, 360–66, 371n13
Godolphin, Francis, 267, 366
Godolphin, Sidney, 338, 366
Goldsmith, Maurice, vii, 9, 274–304
good and evil, 79, 164–65, 169–71, 180, 192, 274–75, 317
Gorgias, 329, 333
Grand Remonstrance, 140, 262
Grant, Hardy, vii, 5, 108–28
Great Tew circle, 2, 22, 23, 347
Greeks, 12, 118, 176, 209, 237, 282, 290, 313, 317, 330, 331, 351
Gregory IX, Pope, 351
Gregory of St. Vincent, 124
Grotius, Hugo, 188, 247, 354

Hale, Sir Matthew, 9, 293–94
Hall, John, 33
Hammond, Henry, 347
Hampton, Jean, 185, 193, 281
Hariot, Thomas, 22, 147
Harrington, Sir James, 8, 214
Hart, H.L.A., 275, 278
Harvey, William, 33, 52, 106n19
Harwood, John T., 340
Heath, Thomas L., 323
Henrietta Maria (queen mother), 33, 260, 373n26
Henry II (king of England), 282
Henry VIII (king of England), 358, 359, 373n30
Heraclitus, 331
Herbert, Lord Edward, 306
heresy, 35–36, 234, 295, 322–23, 327n46, 347–48, 351–54, 360, 368–69, 370n3
Herodotus, 368
Heylin, Peter, 253, 255, 256, 259
Hill, Nicholas, 147
history, 9–12, 247, 305–325
    and Bacon, 52
    civil and natural, 46
    functions of, 312–15
    and prudence, 212, 214

and rhetoric, 10
and science, 9–10, 11, 47, 49
uncertainty of, 307–12
Hobbes, Edmund, 14, 15
Hobbes, Francis, 14, 15
Hobbes, Robert, 15
Hobbes, Thomas, 1–3, 11–45, 59, 208–12, 205n30, 306, 321–25
    Anti-White, 4, 29, 80–81n4, 81n5, 82n13, 82n24, 62, 68, 77, 142, 338
    Behemoth, 9, 210, 214, 262, 264–65, 285, 305, 314, 318–19, 322, 325, 372n19
    De cive, 1, 3, 9, 25, 28–29, 32, 37, 41n52, 42n70, 45, 50, 55, 57–59, 274
    De corpore, 3, 25, 29–31, 34–35, 45, 62–64, 66–69, 71, 74, 76–78, 93, 125, 146
    De homine, 3, 5, 6, 25, 30, 35, 45, 53, 58–59, 146, 155n92, 173n2
    De Principiis et Ratiocinatione Geometrarum, 88
    Decameron physiologicum, 35, 89
    Dialogue . . . Common Law, 210, 274, 299n4, 318, 320, 322
    Dialogus physicus de natura aeris, 102
    Elementorum philosophiae, 8, 25, 29, 55, 62, 175
    Elements of Law, 9, 21, 27, 28, 29, 32, 41n52, 136, 142, 274, 306
    Historia ecclesiastica, 36
    "Latin Optical MS", 25, 26, 41n52
    Leviathan, 1, 31–37, 49–51, 56, 99, 111, 145, 178, 259–67, 305–7, 348, 366–69
    Minute or First Draft of the Optiques, A, 129, 145, 146
    Mr. Hobbes Considered, 36
    Of Libertie and Necessitie, 30, 33
    Problemata physica, 35, 36
    Short Tract, 6, 25, 84n40, 130, 131, 132, 137, 138, 146–47, 306
    Six Lessons to the Professors of Geometry, 45, 125–26
    Third Objections, 63
    Tractacus Opticus I, 129, 132, 134, 136, 137, 138, 141, 142
    Tractacus Opticus II, 129, 141, 142, 144
Hobbes, William, 14, 15
Hobbes's system. See scheme of the sciences
Hofmann, Joseph, 126
Holdsworth, W.A., 289
Holy Spirit/Ghost, 360–66, 373n28
homoousion, 323, 350, 360, 371n13, 373n28
Hooker, Richard, 353, 354
Hudson, Michael, 271n53
human behavior, 157–73
human nature, 6, 12, 165–68, 173n2, 216, 247, 342, 370n12
human philosophy, 51–52
human rights, 233, 235. See also subjects' rights
humanism, 17, 175
Hume, David, 171, 172, 174n5, 187
Huygens, Christian, 109, 110, 126, 147
Hyde, Sir Edward, 22, 23, 31, 32, 43n84, 110, 254, 260, 261, 262, 264, 265, 266, 272n65
hypotheses, 4–5, 89, 93–94, 101–2, 142, 107n26, 213

identity and difference, 65, 71–73
illumination. *See* light
imaginary space, 83n24, 83n26, 83n27
imagination, 6, 66, 131, 147, 157–59, 308
individuation, 71–73
inductive method, 18, 308
Innocent III, Pope, 351
instruction, 10, 12, 94, 358
introspection, 160–61, 164

James I, king of England, 367
Jeane, Richard, 15
Jermyn, Henry, 260, 261
Jesseph, Douglas, viii, 4–5, 86–107
Jesus Christ, 354, 355, 357, 360, 362, 366
Jews, 354, 355, 360, 362, 372n20, 21
Johnston, D., 185
Jones, H.W., 339
just and unjust, 50, 79, 274, 280
justice, 55, 169, 180

Kant, Immanuel, 238
Kelsen, H., 278
Kepler, Johann, 142, 146, 149n9, 154n83
kinematic, 124–25, 134, 138, 148
kingdom of darkness, 366–69
knowledge, foundation of, 62–80
Kynaston, Sir Francis, 255, 258

language, 96–100, 106n17, 158, 163, 172–73,
   176, 180–84, 339, 343n4
Latimer, Robert, 15–16
Laud, William, 255, 324
Laudians, 22, 266, 366, 368
law, 1, 7, 9, 19, 12, 55, 210–11, 274–98
laws of nature, 7, 171, 189–93, 208, 222–23,
   225, 230, 239, 285–87
legal positivism, 275, 303n86
legal system, characteristics of, 283–85
legal terms, 296–98
Leibniz, Gottfried Wilhelm, 5, 37, 110, 117
liberty, 162, 172, 208, 235–36, 286, 297
light, 6, 94, 129–48, 150n17, 153n61
line segments, 112, 113
Lloyd, S.A., 185
Locke, John, 13, 84n46, 202–3n14, 217, 223,
   229, 232, 234, 237, 238, 245n62
logic, 30, 50, 176
Long Parliament, 28, 249, 254, 255, 260, 263,
   306
Lucian, 352, 365
lumen, 130, 149n9, 150n25, 153n60
Lupus, Rutilius, 203n25
Luther, Martin, 353, 356, 357
lux, 130, 149n9, 150n25, 153n60
Lysias, 329

Machiavelli, Niccolò, 232, 236, 237, 316
Magna Carta, 252, 290
Maignan, Emanuel, 147
Malcolm, Noel, viii, 2, 6, 13–44, 206n36
Marsilius of Padua, 289, 353, 354, 356, 357,
   358, 359, 371n14
Martel, Thomas de, 29, 37
materialism, 59, 80, 109, 157–58, 160, 171–
   72, 350
mathematics, 3, 5, 16, 21, 35, 93, 94, 108–26

Maynwaring, Roger, 250, 251, 255, 256, 259,
   348
mechanical philosophy, 4–5, 34, 48, 53, 57–
   58, 86, 129, 131, 134
medicine, 52, 53, 54, 60
medieval optics, 146, 147
memory, 6, 10, 99, 307–9, 311, 313
mental disorders, 164–65, 166
Mersenne, Marin, 2–3, 24, 26, 28, 29, 32, 37,
   107n24, 123–24, 132, 199, 370n7
metaphysics, 1, 3, 25, 26, 29, 52, 60, 63, 81n10
method of natural science, 86–103
methodological unity, 57–58
Micanzio, Fulgenzio, 19, 20, 206–7n36
Milton, John, 367
Mintz, Samuel, 109
monarchies, 211, 236, 247, 252, 254, 255, 265,
   266
Montaigne, Michel de, 187, 192–93, 198
Montucla, Jean-Etienne, 108
moral agreement, 186–89
moral philosophy, 6, 7, 12, 48, 51, 53, 54–55,
   84n53, 175–201
More, Henry, 13
Morley, George, 22
Moses, 34, 353, 361, 362, 363, 365, 366
motion, 24–26, 54, 84n51, 89–91, 105n8, 112
   and civil philosophy, 56–57
   knowledge of, 4, 5
   light and vision, 129, 131, 138, 145, 146,
      150n17
   and mind, 157
   projectile, 106n20
   science of, 3, 49
   as unifying element, 11
   universal cause, 106n18
   vital and voluntary, 159
motivation, 6, 7
Mydorge, Claude, 3, 24
myths, 309, 368

names, 5, 69, 82n14, 87, 96–102, 181, 311
natural condition. *See* state of nature
natural science/philosophy, 4–5, 24, 47–51,
   54, 57, 86–103, 105n16
Neil, William, 126
Neoplatonism, 367, 368
new science, 3, 11–12, 34, 306
Newcastle, earl of, 22, 23, 24, 27, 131, 248,
   259, 261, 265
Newcastle, marquess of, 30, 31
Newton, Sir Isaac, 102, 107n26, 113, 116, 147
Nicene Council/Creed, 322, 327n46, 350, 360,
   361, 364, 373n27
Nicholas, Sir Edward, 261, 272n65
non-science, 11, 45–47
North American Indians, 218, 243n35
Northumberland, earl of, 22
number, 112–14

occult powers, 146, 149n8
Oldenburg, Henry, 109
omnipotence, 77–80
Optatus of Milevis, 356
optics, 3, 5–6, 12, 25–26, 30, 35, 58, 129–48
oratio, 180–84

organization of science. *See* scheme of the sciences
Ormonde, marquis of, 261, 272n65

Pacchi, Arrigo, 111
Paduan school, 95, 96, 106n19, 289
pain. *See* pleasure and pain
Palmer, Geoffrey, 262
Papists, 366–67
parabolas, 124–26
paradiastole, 196–97, 203–4n25
Paraeus, David, 253
Parker, Henry, 262
parliaments, 251–52, 255, 312, 342, 345n18
Pascal, Blaise, 113
passions, 48, 53–56, 159–64, 167, 171, 179, 184–86
patients, 130, 149n6
patriarchalist theory of government, 217, 222
Payne, Robert, 2, 6, 22, 23, 25, 31, 271n62
peace, 7, 48, 161–62, 169, 189, 217, 221–25, 241, 287
Pecham, John, 146
Pell, John, 30
Percy, Henry, 260, 261, 265
Pericles, 209–10, 338
persuasion. *See* rhetoric
Petition of Right, 251, 252
phantasms, 65–67, 89, 93, 97, 105n17, 131, 134, 141, 145–46, 157–58
Phelips, Sir Robert, 252
philosophy, 10, 13–14, 58–60
physics, 48, 50–53, 147, 176
Plato, 92, 113, 114, 176, 329, 330, 331, 333, 343n1, 351
pleasure and pain, 157, 159–64, 170, 188
plenism, 90, 102
Plutarch, 335
Pocock, G.A., 309
political change, 315–18
political philosophy, 3, 7, 21, 29, 208–41
politics, 27, 175, 177–80, 246–67
power, 55, 168, 170, 219
power/act, 65, 70–71
Prat, Abraham du, 29, 37
Presbyterians, 16, 34–35, 261, 265, 266, 323, 324, 328n61, 345n18, 366, 368
pride. *See* glory
Prins, Jan, viii, 5, 6, 129–56
Prisoners' Dilemma, 193, 195, 214, 224–25, 244n46
property, 9, 27, 235, 239, 246, 252–53, 256–58, 270n49, 274
Protagoras, 329, 333
Protestants, 22, 251, 365, 366
prudence, 10, 96, 106n22, 186, 120, 212–16, 309, 311
Prynne, William, 253–54
psychology, 11, 51, 53, 54, 57, 130, 157–73
Ptolemy, 353
publicist, 354, 371n18
punishment, 8, 208, 233, 238–40, 245n71, 276–77, 281, 295
Puritanism, 16, 150, 253–54, 366, 267
Pycior, Helena, 113
Pym, John, 28, 253
Pythagoras, 113, 351

Quintilian, 176, 197, 202n2, 330, 343n2

rarefaction, 90, 91, 104n9
ratiocination, 93, 102, 105n17, 223
rationality, 163–64, 165, 169–71
ray of light, 134–35, 151n31, 152n36
reason, 6, 2, 10, 27, 96, 171, 174n5
rechstaat, 283
rectification of arc, 123–26
rectilinear propagation of light, 130, 148
reflection, 138–41, 145, 148
refraction, 132, 134–38, 138, 140–41, 145–48, 152n36
religion, 10–11, 16, 29, 30, 33–36, 46–47, 63–64, 109, 346–69
anti-clericalism, 258–59, 266, 348
and Bacon, 52
Descartes on, 52–54
and fear, 209
and first philosophy, 4, 77–79, 85n62
and the law, 211–12, 320–21
in political systems, 208, 241n1
rational, 22
shaping human behavior, 166
and sovereignty, 234, 265
Renaissance, 175, 176, 195, 201
resistance to sovereignty, 237–41
rhetoric, 7, 10, 12, 50, 176, 186–87, 195–201, 246, 329–43
Rizzetti, Giovanni, 147
Roberval, Gilles Personne de, 3, 39, 124
Roman Catholicism, 22, 33, 34, 251, 265, 323, 351, 358, 367, 368, 370n7
Romans, 12, 176, 182, 188, 196, 197, 212, 222, 237, 282, 289, 290, 296, 317, 331, 354, 367
Root and Branch Petition, 120
Rous, Francis, 251
Rousseau, Jean Jacque, 8, 217, 219, 236, 238, 239
Royal Society, 5, 35, 90, 102, 109, 242n12
royalists, 9, 20, 27, 32, 247–49, 254, 259, 264, 266, 326n32
Rufus, William, 282
Rump Parliament, 260, 263, 264, 266
Ryan, Alan, viii, 7, 208–45

safety, 8, 32, 232, 241
St. German, Christopher, *Doctor and Student*, 287–88, 289, 302n58
St. John, Oliver, 253
Sandys, Sir Edwin, 20
sapience, 10, 106n22, 212
Sarpi, Paolo, 19, 20, 206n36
Scarborough, Charles, 33
Scargill, Daniel, 349
scheme of the sciences, 3, 24, 45–61, 175–80
scholasticism, 17, 18, 26, 86–87, 89, 103n3, 146–47, 154n83
science, 9–11, 46–48, 58–60, 106n22, 246–67, 310–11
Scottish Covenanters, 253
seditious doctrines, 249–50, 263, 320
Selden, John, 20, 33, 368
self-interest, 6, 32, 168, 219
self-preservation, 7, 163, 185, 188–91, 213, 240, 266, 281
Seneca, 197, 198

senses, 4, 6–7, 73, 99, 129, 130–31, 138, 144, 146, 147, 157–59
Seymour, Sir Francis, 251
Sheldon, Gilbert, 22, 271n62
Sherland, Christopher, 251
Ship Money, 27, 252, 256, 265, 301n44
Short Parliament, 27, 248–49, 251, 252, 255
Sibthorpe, Robert, 255, 348
Siculus, Diodorus, 322, 368
Silver, Victoria, viii, 10, 329–45
Socrates, 176, 329, 330, 333, 338
Solomon, 362–63
Sommerville, Johann, viii–ix, 8–9, 246–73
Sophists, 329, 333, 338
Sorbière, Samuel, 29, 31, 37
Sorell, Tom, ix, 1–12, 45–61
Sorites paradox, 186
sovereignty, 32, 54, 194, 208, 250
  absoluteness of, 27, 28, 164, 168, 230, 300n31, 316, 345n18
  and contracts, 227, 228
  divisibility of, 1, 251–52, 256
  and law, 7–8, 9, 274–75, 277–85, 290, 298, 300n214, 317–18, 319
  power of, 27, 56
  and religion, 11, 321, 353, 356, 358, 359, 362, 364–65
  resistance to, 237–41
  rights and duties of, 9, 170, 231–37
space/time, 65, 66–67
species theory, 130, 146, 147, 149n6, 155n86, 155n96
Spinoza, Baruch, 37
spirals, 124–26
Springborg, Patricia, ix, 10–11, 346–80
squaring of the circle. See circle-squaring
state of nature, 208, 209, 214, 216–25, 227–29, 231, 239, 257, 290
statute law, 9, 291–93, 296, 301n53
Stevin, Simon, 113
Strauss, Leo, 340
Stroud, E., 143
Stubbe, Henry, 33–34, 352
subjective and objective, 65–67
subjects' rights, 208, 230, 235, 237, 250–51, 253. See also human rights
substances, 130–31, 149n5
syllogisms, 94, 95, 99
synthesis, 55, 56, 59, 61n9, 74, 87, 92–96, 101, 105n16, 114–16

table of the sciences. See scheme of the sciences

Tacitus, 199, 205n30
taxes, 230, 234, 239, 252–53, 265, 323
Taylor-Warrender thesis, 187
theology. See religion
theorems, 114–15
threshold hypothesis, 143, 144
Thucydides, 10, 20, 205n30, 209, 210, 212, 248, 305, 306, 311, 313, 321–22, 323, 324–25, 327n46
Thucydides, 334–368
Toland, John, 368
Tönnies, Ferdinand, 129, 149n4, 205n31
Torricelli, Evangelista, 117, 124
Trinity, 350, 352, 360–66, 371n13
trisection of an arbitrary angle, 118
truth, 10, 97, 100, 55, 313, 329, 330, 332, 336
Tuck, Richard, ix, 6–7, 175–207, 265, 271n62, 272n65
tyrannicide, 237, 150, 253–54

understanding, 130, 147, 158
universal definitions, 48, 94, 95
universities, 16, 34, 109, 111, 249, 319

Valla, Lorenzo, 322
values, 7, 79
Vaughan, John, 33, 37
Viète, François, 92, 115, 116
vision, 6, 26, 129–48
voluntarism, theological, 4, 79, 80

Waller, Edmund, 22, 23, 31, 260, 261
Wallis, John, 5, 34–35, 103n4, 109–10, 113, 116, 119, 120, 121, 122, 126
war, 7, 55, 161, 162, 169, 185, 189, 234
Ward, Seth, 34, 43n90
Warner, Walter, 22, 23, 131, 147
Warrender, Howard, 190–92, 256
Welbeck academy, 22, 23, 24, 248
welfare state, 235
White, Thomas, 29, 62, 77
  De mundo, 3, 33, 141
Wilkinson, John, 16, 17
will, 30, 171–72, 236, 324
William the Conqueror, 282
Williers, George, 261
witches, 349, 350
Wood, Anthony, 37, 346, 348

Young, Thomas, 147

Zabarella, Jacopo, 95, 106n19
Zarka, Yves-Charles, ix, 4, 6, 62–85